Organic Gardening For Dummies®

Reasons to Be an Organic Gardener

Here are just a few of the many reasons to garden organically:

- **Human health:** Many pesticides harm people, causing illness when consumed or when they make contact with exposed skin. Some pesticides can accumulate in the environment and contribute to illness long after application.

- **Water pollution:** Excess fertilizer washes into groundwater, streams, lakes, rivers, and coastal waters where it contributes to the death and disruption of natural ecosystems. According to the U.S. Environmental Protection Agency, pesticides already contaminate the groundwater in more than three-quarters of the U.S. states.

- **Soil erosion and depletion:** The urgency to protect the world's remaining agricultural land from erosion, development, pollution, and diminishing water resources has reached a global crisis. The collective efforts of many organic gardeners do have an impact.

- **Ecological balance and diversity:** Insect predators and prey keep each other in check, and plants grow best when in a balanced environment. Organic gardeners respect all parts of the interconnected web of life and use practices that support it.

- **Future generations:** Sustainable gardening, agriculture, and landscaping means thinking about the future, using renewable resources wisely and efficiently, and taking only as much as nature can replace.

- **Cost savings:** Prevention costs less than the cure. Provide habitat for the beneficial insects, and they will reduce the populations of bad bugs. Feed the soil organisms that make nutrients available, and your plants will flourish.

Average Annual Minimum Temperature by Zone

Use the following chart and Chapter 3 to find your USDA Hardiness Zone.

Temperature F	USDA Zone	Temperature C
−50° to −40°	2	−45.5° to −40.1°
−40° to −30°	3	−40.0° to −34.5°
−30° to −20°	4	−34.3° to −28.9°
−20° to −10°	5	−28.8° to −23.4°
−10° to 0°	6	−23.3° to −17.8°
0° to 10°	7	−17.7° to −12.3°
10° to 20°	8	−12.2° to −6.7°
20° to 30°	9	−6.6° to −1.2°
30° to 40°	10	−1.1° to 4.4°
40° and above	11	4.5° and above

For Dummies: Bestselling Book Series for Beginners

Organic Gardening For Dummies®

Assessing Your Site

Match plants to your site by first taking an inventory of what your site has to offer. Choose only those plants that can grow to their full potential where you plan to put them. See Chapter 3 for further details:

- **Sun and shade:** Duration and time of day and year that sun shines directly on the site.
- **Soil:** Structure, texture, pH, drainage, and moisture.
- **Views:** Unsightly views to screen; pleasant views to enhance or preserve.
- **Slope:** Steep, flat, valley floors.
- **Wind:** Speed and direction at different times of year.
- **Hardiness zone:** Average winter low temperatures.
- **Obstacles:** Locations of buildings, overhead and buried utilities, roads, and property boundaries.

Principles of Integrated Pest Management (IPM)

IPM is a practice that uses crop, environmental, and pest information to find the least toxic and least invasive insect-, disease-, and weed-control strategies. The key practices include the following:

- **Using cultural techniques to promote plant health:** Rotating crops, sanitizing gardens, using traps and barriers, mulching, promoting air circulation and water drainage, conserving soil moisture, planting companion and disease-resistant varieties, composting, and building soil health.

- **Identifying and monitoring pests:** Identifying the pests and diseases that affect your crops, predicting when they will appear, and using observation and traps to determine the extent of the problem.

- **Using control methods:** First using the least toxic methods (beneficial insects and microbes and insecticidal soaps and oils), and then resorting to more toxic organic pesticides only when the value of the crop or landscape plant justifies their use.

Conversions

Use the following chart to convert U.S. and metric measurements. In each case, the conversions are approximately equal.

1 centimeter ≈ 0.4 inch	
1 meter ≈ 39 inches ≈ 1.1 yards	
1 kilometer ≈ 0.6 mile	
1 liter ≈ 1.1 quarts	
1 kilogram ≈ 2.2 pounds	
1 gram ≈ 0.04 ounce	
1 inch ≈ 2.5 centimeters	
1 yard ≈ 0.9 meter	
1 mile ≈ 1.6 kilometers	
1 quart ≈ 0.9 liter	
1 pound ≈ 0.4 kilogram	
1 ounce ≈ 31 grams	

For Dummies: Bestselling Book Series for Beginners

Praise for Organic Gardening For Dummies

"Organic gardening methods help the planet and yield healthier plants and people. Now, this book makes it easy for anyone to grow organically."

— Bill Wolf, Past-President, Organic Trade Association

"*Organic Gardening For Dummies* is a well-organized instruction book of the what, when, where, why, how, and who of not only growing plants but also protecting our environment and living in harmony with nature."

— Malcolm Beck, Organic Farmer, Author, Lecturer

Praise for Roses For Dummies, 2nd Edition

"As an all-organic gardener, I've always dreamed of having a rose expert/enthusiast come to my gardens for tea and spend the afternoon sharing and teaching me all about roses. *Roses For Dummies* is written as a friend, answering all my puzzling questions and providing easy solutions that are budget friendly."

— Jan Weverka, Editor of *The Rose Garden*, a monthly organic newsletter

"This book is fun to read and loaded with information — just what I'd expect from Lance Walheim, who really knows gardening from the ground up. It takes the mystery, but not the magic, out of growing roses. Beginners as well as advanced rose growers will find advice that's abundant and extremely helpful."

— Bill Marken, Editor-in-Chief of eHow.com and former Editor-in-Chief of *Rebecca's Garden*

Praise for Gardening For Dummies, 2nd Edition

"Creating a successful garden just got easier with the 2nd Edition of *Gardening For Dummies*. It's packed with down-to-earth gardening advice that both novice and experienced gardeners will find useful."

— Doug Jimerson, VP, Editor-in-Chief, garden.com

"Despite the humorous title, *Gardening For Dummies* is a valuable book, full of down-to-earth garden advice. I've been gardening most of my life, and I still found something new to learn in this well-organized book."

— Larry Sombke, public radio's *Natural Gardener*

"*Gardening For Dummies* offers the perfect map for a new generation of gardeners . . . with this book and a little time for practicing in the garden, you won't be a gardening dummy for long!"

— William Raap, President, Gardener's Supply Co.

Praise for Vegetable Gardening For Dummies

"This book contains all the basic requirements for the average American to plan and maintain a healthy and hardy vegetable garden. The chapters are comprehensive, witty, and easy to read. Planting and culture descriptions of individual vegetables are excellent with colorful descriptions and scrumptious recipes."

— Michael D. Orzolek, Professor of Vegetable Crops, Penn State University

Praise for Annuals For Dummies

"The subject of annuals was just waiting for the straightforward, quiet-humor delivery of Californian Bill Marken. (The *Californian* tag is part of Bill's mastery: In growing annuals year 'round, mild-climate gardeners accumulate twice the lifetime experience available to cold-winter people.) In small takes, the book gives you the full range of instructions for growing and displaying these charming, one-act plants."

— Joseph F. Williamson, Former Garden Editor and Managing Editor of *Sunset Magazine*

"*Annuals For Dummies* is a masterful blend of tips, tricks, and techniques that even an experienced gardener can use to create a successful and spectacular flower garden. It's like having a garden designer at your fingertips."

— Doug Jimerson, VP, Editor-in-Chief, garden.com

Organic Gardening

FOR

DUMMIES®

Organic Gardening FOR DUMMIES®

by Ann Whitman and the
Editors of the National
Gardening Association

Hungry Minds™

Best-Selling Books • Digital Downloads • e-Books • Answer Networks • e-Newsletters • Branded Web Sites • e-Learning

New York, NY ◆ Cleveland, OH ◆ Indianapolis, IN

Organic Gardening For Dummies®

Published by
Hungry Minds, Inc.
909 Third Avenue
New York, NY 10022
www.hungryminds.com
www.dummies.com

Library of Congress Control Number: 00-110904

ISBN: 0-7645-5320-8

Printed in the United States of America

10 9 8 7 6 5 4 3 2

1O/ST/RQ/QR/IN

Distributed in the United States by Hungry Minds, Inc.

Distributed by CDG Books Canada Inc. for Canada; by Transworld Publishers Limited in the United Kingdom; by IDG Norge Books for Norway; by IDG Sweden Books for Sweden; by IDG Books Australia Publishing Corporation Pty. Ltd. for Australia and New Zealand; by TransQuest Publishers Pte Ltd. for Singapore, Malaysia, Thailand, Indonesia, and Hong Kong; by Gotop Information Inc. for Taiwan; by ICG Muse, Inc. for Japan; by Intersoft for South Africa; by Eyrolles for France; by International Thomson Publishing for Germany, Austria and Switzerland; by Distribuidora Cuspide for Argentina; by LR International for Brazil; by Galileo Libros for Chile; by Ediciones ZETA S.C.R. Ltda. for Peru; by WS Computer Publishing Corporation, Inc., for the Philippines; by Contemporanea de Ediciones for Venezuela; by Express Computer Distributors for the Caribbean and West Indies; by Micronesia Media Distributor, Inc. for Micronesia; by Chips Computadoras S.A. de C.V. for Mexico; by Editorial Norma de Panama S.A. for Panama; by American Bookshops for Finland.

For general information on Hungry Minds' products and services please contact our Customer Care Department within the U.S. at 800-762-2974, outside the U.S. at 317-572-3993 or fax 317-572-4002.

For sales inquiries and reseller information, including discounts, premium and bulk quantity sales, and foreign-language translations, please contact our Customer Care Department at 800-434-3422, fax 317-572-4002, or write to Hungry Minds, Inc., Attn: Customer Care Department, 10475 Crosspoint Boulevard, Indianapolis, IN 46256.

For information on licensing foreign or domestic rights, please contact our Sub-Rights Customer Care Department at 212-884-5000.

For information on using Hungry Minds' products and services in the classroom or for ordering examination copies, please contact our Educational Sales Department at 800-434-2086 or fax 317-572-4005.

Please contact our Public Relations Department at 212-884-5163 for press review copies or 212-884-5000 for author interviews and other publicity information or fax 212-884-5400.

For authorization to photocopy items for corporate, personal, or educational use, please contact Copyright Clearance Center, 222 Rosewood Drive, Danvers, MA 01923, or fax 978-750-4470.

Hungry Minds™ is a trademark of Hungry Minds, Inc.

About the Author

Ann Whitman was fortunate enough to grow up around parents, grandparents, aunts, and uncles who kept compost piles out back and had keen interest in growing food and flowers. She's been tending her own patches of soil for over 25 years. Her current garden projects include hardy perennial flowers and bulbs; blueberries, raspberries, and strawberries; fruit and nut trees; and a vegetable garden big enough to feed a family of four with leftovers. A flock of hens recycles the scraps and keeps vigilant eyes open for careless bugs.

Ann earned a Bachelor of Science degree in Plant and Soil Science at the University of Vermont and thought studying soil was the most boring subject she ever had to take. After she got out into the real world, though, she wished that she had paid more attention in class. A strong believer in life-long learning, she also completed a Master of Arts in Landscape Design from the Conway School of Landscape Design in Massachusetts. There, she learned to look for and appreciate connections and relationships among all parts of the environment and to hone her speaking and writing skills.

Ann is the author of *Trees and Shrubs For Dummies* (Hungry Minds, Inc.), as well as *How-To Landscaping Basics* and *Water Gardens: Simple Steps to Adding the Beauty of Water to Your Garden,* both published by Time Life. She also contributes to gardening magazines and Web sites. When she's not writing, Ann gardens on fertile river-bottom soil in Vermont where the winters are long and the summers short, but worth it.

The National Gardening Association (NGA) is committed to sustaining and renewing the fundamental links between people, plants, and the earth. Founded in 1972 as "Gardens For All" to spearhead the community garden movement, today's NGA promotes environmental responsibility, advances multidisciplinary learning and scientific literacy, and creates partnerships that restore and enhance communities.

NGA is best known for its garden-based curricula, educational journals, international initiatives, and several youth garden grant programs. Together, these reach more than 300,000 children nationwide each year. NGA's Web sites, one for home gardeners and another for those who garden with kids, build community and offer a wealth of custom content.

To find out more about the National Gardening Association, write to 1100 Dorset St., South Burlington, VT 05403, or visit its Web sites at www.nationalgardening.com or www.kidsgardening.com.

Dedication

I dedicate this book to gardeners everywhere who believe that we can make this a better world — now and for our children — one garden at a time. Our choices do make a difference.

Authors' Acknowledgments

It takes a whole lot of people to bring a book to life and I'd like to thank a few of them for their help.

On this book, it's been my great fortune to work with Tere Drenth, the project editor who fit all the pieces together and kept everybody on track. Her keen eyes, tireless energy, and insightful editing skills made this book something we can all be proud of. And thank you, Linda Ingroia, for having faith.

I owe a debt of gratitude to Pat Patterson, an organic Master Gardener and teacher with many years of hands-on organic gardening experience. She reviewed this manuscript and offered many valuable suggestions that made this a more useful book. Happy trails, Pat!

Big thanks go to DD Dowden who turned my words into pictures and drew all of the illustrations. (I especially like the bugs in Chapters 7 and 8.) Great job!

Contributors who shared their time and expertise include Charlie Nardozzi, Mr. Compost himself and an all-around good vegetable gardener who helped with the vegetable, soil building, and fertilizer chapters. Warren Schultz lent his considerable experience to the lawn chapter. Kathy Bond Borie contributed valuable advice and writing skills to the chapter on beneficial insects and other physical pest controls. Michael MacCaskey generously gave his time and knowledge to the subject of growing roses organically. Thanks, all — this book is much richer for your contributions.

My family deserves big thanks, too, for giving me the time and space to write. Don, David, and Kate — you're the best!

Ann Whitman, Author

NGA is proud of this book and thanks its core team: Linda Ingroia and Tere Drenth at Hungry Minds, Inc., and Michael MacCaskey and Ann Whitman, our executive editor and principal author, respectively. Thanks to our online media team at NationalGardening.com and mySeasons.com for their support, and thanks finally to the many National Gardening contributors over the years whose wisdom and experience found their way into these pages.

Valerie Kelsey, President and CEO
National Gardening Association

Publisher's Acknowledgments

We're proud of this book; please send us your comments through our Online Registration Form located at www.dummies.com.

Some of the people who helped bring this book to market include the following:

Acquisitions, Editorial, and Media Development

Project Editor: Tere Drenth

Senior Acquisitions Editor: Linda Ingroia

Acquisitions Coordinator: Erin Connell

General Reviewer: Patricia Patterson, Master Gardener

Editorial Manager: Pamela Mourouzis

Editorial Administrator: Michelle Hacker

Cover Photo: ©ImageBank/Werner Bodelberg

Production

Project Coordinator: Nancee Reeves

Layout and Graphics: Amy Adrian, LeAndra Johnson, Heather Pope, Jacque Schneider, Brian Torwelle, Julie Trippetti, Jeremey Unger

Special Art: DD Dowden

Proofreaders: Andy Hollandbeck, Angel Perez, Marianne Santy, Charles Spencer, York Production Services, Inc.

Indexer: York Production Services, Inc.

General and Administrative

Hungry Minds, Inc.: John Kilcullen, CEO; Bill Barry, President and COO; John Ball, Executive VP, Operations & Administration; John Harris, Executive VP and CFO

Hungry Minds Consumer Reference Group

Business: Kathleen A. Welton, Vice President and Publisher; Kevin Thornton, Acquisitions Manager

Cooking/Gardening: Jennifer Feldman, Associate Vice President and Publisher

Education/Reference: Diane Graves Steele, Vice President and Publisher

Lifestyles/Pets: Kathleen Nebenhaus, Vice President and Publisher; Tracy Boggier, Managing Editor

Travel: Michael Spring, Vice President and Publisher; Suzanne Jannetta, Editorial Director; Brice Gosnell, Publishing Director

Hungry Minds Consumer Editorial Services: Kathleen Nebenhaus, Vice President and Publisher; Kristin A. Cocks, Editorial Director; Cindy Kitchel, Editorial Director

Hungry Minds Consumer Production: Debbie Stailey, Production Director

Contents at a Glance

Introduction *1*

Part 1: Understanding the Basics of Organic Gardening ...*5*

Chapter 1: Defining Organic Gardening 7

Chapter 2: Organic Gardening 101 17

Chapter 3: Designing for Diversity 27

Part 11: Working with Your Soil *41*

Chapter 4: Building Healthy Soil 43

Chapter 5: Using Organic Fertilizers 61

Part 111: Keeping Plants Healthy *73*

Chapter 6: Weed It and Reap! 75

Chapter 7: Sleuthing Out the Suspects 85

Chapter 8: Getting Physical with Pests 103

Chapter 9: Controlling Pests Safely 123

Chapter 10: Battling Plant Diseases 135

Part 1V: Growing Organically in Your Yard and Garden *149*

Chapter 11: Raising Organic Vegetables 151

Chapter 12: Herbs for Home and Garden 179

Chapter 13: Picking from the Berry Patch 193

Chapter 14: Fruits and Nuts for Your Organic Orchard 207

Chapter 15: Say It with Flowers 229

Chapter 16: Run for the Roses 249

Chapter 17: Managing Landscape Trees and Shrubs 265

Chapter 18: Caring for Your Organic Lawn 285

Part V: The Part of Tens *309*

Chapter 19: Ten Best Organic Gardening Practices 311

Chapter 20: Ten Ways to Be an Eco-Smart Gardener 315

Index *321*

Cartoons at a Glance

By Rich Tennant

"So? How's the soil, Al? Too much acid? What? Come on, Al – don't spoil your lunch."

page 41

"I used an all natural method of pest control, but we're still getting an occasional vacuum cleaner salesman in the garden."

page 73

I don't think they actually believe it, but they wouldn't be as inspired to work in the garden if they knew it was rutabaga and turnips.

page 309

"I'll be right in! I'm just sprinkling the garden with salty bar snacks to attract the slugs to the beer traps."

page 149

"I just think it's ironic that someone with a face lift, an eye job, implants, and a hair weave should all of a sudden become Miss Natural-Organic-Gardener."

page 5

Cartoon Information:
Fax: 978-546-7747
E-Mail: richtennant@the5thwave.com
World Wide Web: www.the5thwave.com

Table of Contents

Introduction 1

About This Book 1
Conventions Used in This Book 1
Foolish Assumptions 2
How This Book Is Organized 2
Part I: Understanding the Basics of Organic Gardening 3
Part II: Working with Your Soil 3
Part III: Keeping Plants Healthy 3
Part IV: Growing Organically in Your Yard and Garden 3
Part V: The Part of Tens 3
Color photo section 4
Icons Used in This Book 4
Where to Go from Here 4

Part 1: Understanding the Basics of Organic Gardening ...5

Chapter 1: Defining Organic Gardening 7

Naturally Speaking 7
All together now 8
Gardening for the future 9
Organic versus non-toxic 9
For Land's Sake 9
Erosion 10
Wildlife and habitat 10
Pollution 11
Disease 12
Organized Organics 12
Biodynamic agriculture 12
Biodynamic/French-intensive method 13
Biointensive mini-farming 13
Polyculture 14
Permaculture 14
Forest gardening 15
Rodale Institute 15
Federal and state involvement 15

Chapter 2: Organic Gardening 101 17

Simplifying Soil and Fertility 17
Getting down to the nitty-gritty 18
Breathing space 19

Structurally sound 20
Fertile ground 21
Pondering Pests and Diseases 21
Using integrated pest management (IPM) 22
Cleaning up your act 23
And in this corner — the good guys 24
Putting poisons in their place 24
Beating the Weeds 25

Chapter 3: Designing for Diversity **27**
Putting the Right Plants in the Right Place 27
Sun and shade 28
Water 29
Soil 30
Considering Climate 30
Microclimates 31
Plant hardiness 32
Zoning out 33
Resisting Diseases and Pests Naturally 36
Culturing Community 36
Designing Low-Maintenance Landscapes 37
Planning for low maintenance 37
Making a map 38
Putting it all together 40

Part II: Working with Your Soil *41*

Chapter 4: Building Healthy Soil **43**
Knowing Your Soil 44
Let it drain 46
The soil test 46
Organic Matter: The Soul of the Soil 48
Dung ho! 49
Green manure 50
Compost: The prince of organic matter 52
To Till or Not to Till 59

Chapter 5: Using Organic Fertilizers **61**
Knowing the Nutrients 61
The big three 62
Secondary nutrients 64
Micronutrients 65
Fertilizer forms 65
Considering the Sources of Organic Fertilizers 66
Plant-based fertilizers 67
Animal-based fertilizers 68
Rock on with mineral-based fertilizers 70

Part III: Keeping Plants Healthy 73

Chapter 6: Weed It and Reap! **75**
Winning the Weed Wars 75
    Mulch 76
    Solarization 78
    Cover cropping 79
    Flaming 80
    Cultivating 81
    Organic herbicides 82
Home Sweet Home 83

Chapter 7: Sleuthing Out the Suspects **85**
Understanding Insects 85
Managing Pests 86
Rounding Up the Suspects 88

Chapter 8: Getting Physical with Pests **103**
Making the Garden Less Inviting to Pests 104
    Giving plants the advantage 104
    Confusing insects by mixing plants 104
    Keeping time on your side 104
    Rotating crops 105
    Not overdoing a good thing 105
Benefiting from Beneficial Insects 106
    Identifying the good guys 106
    Attracting beneficial insects 112
Encouraging Other Insect Predators 113
Setting Up Roadblocks For Pests 114
Sticking to the Subject 116
Practicing Good Outdoor Housekeeping 117
Outwitting Critters 119

Chapter 9: Controlling Pests Safely **123**
Sorting Out the Products 123
    Dust to dust 124
    Watching the soaps and other oily characters 125
    Getting small with microbes 126
    Becoming botanically correct 128
Understanding Pesticide Toxicity 129
Using Pesticides Safely 131
    Personal safety 131
    Plant safety 132
    Protecting the environment 132
    Keeping records 133

Chapter 10: Battling Plant Diseases 135

What's Wrong with This Picture? 135
And the Nominees Are 136
Dastardly diseases 136
Environmental diseases 142
Preventing Problems 145
Understanding Disease-Control Methods 146

Part IV: Growing Organically in Your Yard and Garden 149

Chapter 11: Raising Organic Vegetables 151

Planning Your Vegetable Garden 151
A place to grow 152
Preparing the soil 152
Designing your vegetable garden 153
When to start? 156
Growing Veggies 101 157
Sowing seeds 158
Feed me 158
Weeds and water 159
Garden tricks and season extenders 160
Harvest time 162
Vegetables From A to Z 163
Alliums: Onions, shallots, garlic, and leeks 163
Asparagus 165
Cole crops: Broccoli, cauliflower, cabbage, and company 166
Eggplant 167
Leafy greens: Lettuce, Swiss chard, spinach, and friends 167
Legumes: Peas and beans 169
Peppers 170
Potatoes 171
Root crops: Carrots, beets, and radishes 172
Sweet corn 173
Tomatoes 174
Vining crops: Cucumbers, squash, pumpkins, and melons 175

Chapter 12: Herbs for Home and Garden 179

Herban Development 180
Life cycles 180
Parts is parts 180
Go forth and multiply 182
Growing Herbs 182
Using Herbs 184

Encyclopedia of Herbs 185
   Basil (Ocimum basilicum) 185
   Caraway (Carum carvi) 185
   Chamomile (Matricaria recutita, Chamaemelum nobile) 186
   Chives (Allium schoenoprasum) 186
   Coriander and cilantro
      (Coriandrum sativum) 187
   Dill (Anethum graveolens) 188
   Fennel (Foeniculum vulgare) 188
   Horseradish (Armoracia rusticana) 188
   Lavender (Lavandula) 189
   Mints (Mentha) 189
   Oregano (Origanum vulgare) 190
   Parsley (Petroselinum crispum) 190
   Rosemary (Rosemarinus officinalis) 191
   Sage (Salvia officinalis) 191
   Sweet marjoram (Origanum majorana) 192
   Thymes (Thymus) 192

Chapter 13: Picking from the Berry Patch **193**

Berry Patch Basics 193
   Weed control 194
   Buying plants 195
Small Fruits Guide 196
   Beautiful blueberry 196
   Ramblin' brambles 197
   Keeping current with currants and gooseberries 200
   Elegant elderberry 201
   Going ape for grapes 201
   Have a hardy kiwi, mate? 203
   Sublime strawberries 204

Chapter 14: Fruits and Nuts for Your Organic Orchard **207**

Anatomy of a Fruit Tree 207
   Size does matter 208
   Sex and the single tree 210
   Chill out 210
   Budding genius 211
Cultural Exchange 212
   Planting for success 212
   Pruning fruit trees 213
   Preventing pests and diseases 216
Temperate-Climate Trees and Shrubs 216
   Apples (Malus sylvestris) 217
   European and Asian pears (Pyrus) 218
   Sweet and sour cherries (Prunus) 219
   Peaches and nectarines (Prunus persica) 220
   European and Asian apricots (Prunus) 221
   Plums and prunes (Prunus) 221

Warm-Climate Fruit Trees 223
   Citrus (Citrus) 223
   Figs (Ficus carica) 224
   Persimmon (Diospyros kaki, D. virginiana) 225
Oh, Nuts! 226
   Filberts (Corylus avellana, C. americana) 226
   Almonds (Prunus amygdalus) 226
   Pecans (Carya illinoensis) 227
   Walnuts (Juglans) 227

Chapter 15: Say It with Flowers **229**
Mixing It Up 229
   Strength through diversity 230
   Designing for year-round beauty 230
Buying and Planting 232
   Buying the best 233
   Breaking ground 234
   Caring for your flower garden 236
Annual Events 238
Perennial Favorites 240
   Making more perennials 241
   Popular perennials 243
Blooming Bulbs 244
   Finding the best source 244
   This side up — putting down roots 245
   Protecting your assets 246

Chapter 16: Run for the Roses **249**
Making the Right Choice 250
   Choosing disease-resistant roses 250
   Picking a winter survivor 251
Buying Roses 251
Planting Roses 253
   Picking an ideal time and place 253
   Preparing the planting site 254
   Planting a bareroot rose 255
   Planting a container-grown rose 256
Cultivating Roses 257
   Fertilizing 258
   Watering 258
Pruning 259
   Making the cut 260
   Pruning climbing roses 262
Preparing Roses for Winter 262
Solving Common Rose Troubles 263
   Rose diseases 264
   Insect pests of roses 264

Chapter 17: Managing Landscape Trees and Shrubs 265

   Planning for Low-Maintenance 265
      A place for everything and everything in its place 266
      Avoiding troublemakers 266
   Planting for Success 267
      There is a season 267
      Picking out a healthy plant 268
      Digging the ten-dollar hole 270
   Long-Term Care for Landscape Trees and Shrubs 272
      Fertilizing follies 272
      Runs with scissors 272
   Choosing the Perfect Trees and Shrubs 274
      Shade trees 274
      Flowering and ornamental trees 277
      Flowering and ornamental shrubs 279
      Conifers 281

Chapter 18: Caring for Your Organic Lawn .285

   Getting Down to Grassroots 285
   Choosing the Right Grass 286
      Too cool, man 287
      Some like it hot 288
      Regional preferences 289
   Preparing the Soil 291
   Planting the Lawn 292
      Choosing seed versus sod 292
      Installing sod 293
      Seed-sowing basics 294
   Maintaining an Organic Lawn 295
      There's more to mowing 295
      Watering 297
      Feeding the lawn 298
      Knowing when to feed 299
      Thinking about thatch 300
      Loosening up the soil 301
      Topdressing 301
      Weeding 302
      Managing pests 303
      Getting rid of diseases 304
   Lawn Alternatives 305
      Using low-maintenance grass 305
      Uncovering ground covers 306
      Making a meadow 307

Part V: The Part of Tens **309**

Chapter 19: Ten Best Organic Gardening Practices 311

Enrich Your Soil 311
Let Nature Do the Weeding 312
Choose Healthy and Disease-Resistant Plants 312
Put Plants in the Right Place 313
Encourage Beneficial Insects 313
Practice Integrated Pest Management 313
Use Companion Planting 314
Add Traps and Barriers to Your Arsenal 314
Promote Diversity 314

Chapter 20: Ten Ways to Be an Eco-Smart Gardener 315

Don't Be a Perfectionist 316
Compost Your Kitchen Scraps and Yard Debris 316
Make Friends with Your Garden's Bugs 316
Encourage Wildlife (Within Limits) 317
Don't Spray or Spread Toxic Stuff 317
Choose Plants to Suit Your Site 317
Reduce (Or Eliminate) Your Lawn 318
Plant a Tree 318
Teach Your Children Well 319
Support Organic Farmers 319

Index **321**

Introduction

This book is for people who want to grow food and maintain their landscape without using synthetic chemical pesticides and fertilizers. But, organic gardening is more than just safe food and it's bigger than non-toxic lawns. Organic gardening is also about making conscious decisions and taking responsibility for actions that affect the world outside your backdoor, beyond the end of your driveway, and outside the boundaries of your hometown.

When pollsters ask the question, most people proudly admit to being environmentalists, but not everyone knows how to be a good steward of his or her own yard, let alone the entire planet. This book gets you started on the path toward healthier choices for your own garden and landscape.

Each person is a drop of water that flows into small tributaries, joining others that run together in rivers into the sea of humanity. The size, direction, and force of the river depend on the number of waterdrops within it. Grab this book and go with the flow.

About This Book

Organic gardening covers a lot of ground, so to speak — from maintaining a lawn and growing roses to harvesting fresh fruits and vegetables. If you've read this far, you must be curious about how to garden organically in your own yard. This book takes you step by step through building and maintaining healthy soil, encouraging helpful insects and other organisms, choosing problem-free plants, and getting them off to the right start.

I cover the basic concepts of organic gardening in Parts I, II, and III. For specific garden and landscape plant types, turn to Part IV, and you'll find details about growing vegetables, herbs, flowers, trees and shrubs, fruits and nuts, roses, and lawns — without harmful pesticides or synthetic chemical fertilizers.

Conventions Used in This Book

When I refer to plant hardiness — its ability to survive the winter extremes — I use the United States Department of Agriculture Plant Hardiness Zone Map, which you can find in Chapter 3.

All temperatures are given in degrees Fahrenheit and measurements in feet or inches.

When I refer to a "local extension office," I'm referring to government- or university-sponsored services that offer helpful information on gardening. Look under "Extension office" or "Cooperative extension service" in the phone book. The name of the extension office may also be preceded by the name of your local land-grant college, for example, "The Ohio State University."

Look for icons in the page margins to alert you to tips, warnings, and definitions, as well as sources, such as Web sites, books, and organizations, where you can get more information.

Foolish Assumptions

I assume that you don't know anything about gardening, but that you're interested in giving it a try. Whether you come to this book in total gardening ignorance or have some experience under your fingernails, you'll find plenty of hands-on, how-to information to make your organic garden and landscape the best ever.

If you want more detailed information about specific landscape plants, look for my book, *Trees and Shrubs For Dummies,* as well as *Roses For Dummies,* 2nd Edition, and *Lawn Care For Dummies* by Lance Waltheim. Interested in flowers? Seek out *Perennials For Dummies* by Marcia Tatro, *Flowering Bulbs For Dummies* by Judy Glattstein, and *Annuals For Dummies* by Bill Marken. If it's food you're after, check out *Vegetable Gardening For Dummies* by Charlie Nardozzi and *Herb Gardening For Dummies* by Karan Davis Cutler and Kathleen Fisher (all published by IDG Books Worldwide, Inc.).

How This Book Is Organized

To make navigating through this book easier, it's divided into parts. Each part contains chapters with similar themes. Part I, for example, defines organic gardening, its history and most basic concepts. Part II gives you the scoop on soil and fertilizers. Part III focuses on plant health — from weeds to pest and diseases and how to keep them under control.

In Part IV, each chapter is devoted to a particular category of garden or landscape plant. It starts out with edible crops — vegetables, herbs, and fruits — and ends with landscape plants, including trees, shrubs, roses, and lawn care. The last section, Part V, contains the customary short chapters of lists. In the middle of the book, the color photos offer examples of successful organic gardening practices.

Part I: Understanding the Basics of Organic Gardening

If you think you may want to become an organic gardener but aren't sure what that entails, start with Chapter 1. I've provided enough scary statistics there to start you running down the path toward Chapters 2 and 3, which explain the basic concepts of organic gardening, from soil health to planning low-maintenance landscapes.

Part II: Working with Your Soil

Healthy plants and gardens start with the soil. Turn to this part to get started on soil testing; making compost; and buying and using natural, organic fertilizers.

Part III: Keeping Plants Healthy

Weeds! bugs! diseases! — this part has it all. Turn to this part whenever you spot trouble in paradise and need to know what it is and what to do about it. Chapter 7 describes the most pernicious pests, while Chapters 8 and 9 give you plenty of preventative techniques to keep insects and larger pests at bay. Flip to Chapter 10 for leaf spots, root rots, and other maladies and treatments.

Part IV: Growing Organically in Your Yard and Garden

The chapters in this part describe how to grow the most popular vegetables, herbs, fruits and nuts, trees and shrubs, roses, flowers, bulbs, and lawns. In each chapter, I offer advice about the best plants, how to plant and maintain them, and where to obtain more information.

Part V: The Part of Tens

Use the handy lists in this part to impress your friends at parties and win them over to an organic lifestyle. I've listed best organic practices and ten ways to be an environmentally friendly gardener. Go spread the word!

Color photo section

The color photo section near the center of this book shows you some organic gardening techniques you can apply right away. Flip to the photo section for colorful inspiration, examples of organic controls, and details that would be difficult to spot in a black and white photo.

Icons Used in This Book

To help you quickly locate really neat tips as well as common pitfalls and to alert you to new words and concepts more quickly; I've put *icons* on the page margins. An icon is a little picture that tells a bigger story. Here's what they mean:

If I think of something that saves you time, money, or helps you make a better decision, I've got it flagged.

This icon alerts you to actions that may be dangerous to you, your plants, or the environment. Proceed with caution!

Whenever I use a word for the first time that may be unfamiliar to you, I put it *italics* and pop this icon in the margin. Look for it to increase your vocabulary.

If it's good for the environment, I've got it flagged. For earth-friendly methods, look here.

When you want to know where to find particular plants, equipment, or help, look for this symbol.

Where to Go from Here

When you're done reading the cartoons, jump into any chapter that grabs your attention. You don't have to read this book in any particular order — each chapter stands alone, while providing you with references to find related information in the book.

Part I

Understanding the Basics of Organic Gardening

The 5th Wave   By Rich Tennant

"I just think it's ironic that someone with a face lift, an eye job, implants, and a hair weave should all of a sudden become Miss Natural-Organic-Gardener."

In this part . . .

Not sure what organic gardening is all about? Jump right into this part for an overview of what "organic" means. Chapter 2 gently introduces the "big three" gardening concerns — soil, pests, and weeds. When you're ready to start planning a low-maintenance landscape or garden, get yourself over to Chapter 3 where I talk about how to put plants where they will naturally thrive.

And if you need to defend your organic preferences against naysayers, turn to Chapter 1 for some scary statistics and other good reasons why gardening for the future of the earth is a good idea.

Chapter 1

Defining Organic Gardening

In This Chapter
▶ Understanding the philosophy behind organic gardening
▶ Gardening to protect the environment
▶ Finding out who's who in organic gardening

*O*rganic gardening means different things to different people. All agree that it means avoiding synthetic fertilizers and pesticides. But the philosophy and practice of organic gardening often goes far beyond that simple concept. Growing organic food, flowers, and landscapes represents a commitment to a sustainable system of living in harmony with nature. For many people, organic gardening is a way of life.

The way that people use — and misuse — soil, water, and air affects the lives and habitats of plants, insects, birds, fish, and animals, as well as humans. Dedicated organic gardeners adopt methods that improve soil health and fertility, decrease erosion, and reduce pests and diseases through cultural and natural biological processes. They encourage plant and animal diversity in their landscapes.

Naturally Speaking

Observing your natural environment — watching the weather or noting the arrival of migrating birds and emerging insects — helps you choose the most appropriate ways to plant and nurture your vegetables, flowers, and landscape plants. When you see white butterflies fluttering around your garden, you know it's time to protect your cabbages, broccoli, and cauliflower from cabbageworm. Instead of sprinkling on a pesticide after the caterpillars hatch, you can cover the plants with a special fabric (see Chapter 8 for details) to prevent the butterflies from laying eggs in the first place. That's what organic gardening is all about: preventing and treating problems in the least obtrusive, most non-toxic ways.

All together now . . .

Plants and animals live in *ecosystems* — communities in which each part contributes to and affects the lives of the other parts. In a balanced ecosystem, each plant and animal species has enough food, water, and *habitat* (place to live). The predators have enough prey and the prey have enough predators. When one part of an ecosystem dies out or becomes too scarce, the plants and animals that depend on its function in the environment get out of balance, too. If honeybees disappeared, for example, the plants that need bees for flower pollination wouldn't be able to produce seeds. If predators, such as ladybugs, become scarce, the insects they normally prey upon — aphids — could become so numerous that they would seriously injure or even kill the plants upon which they feed.

Some call this the web of life, but ecosystems contain important non-living parts, too. Soil nutrients, sunlight, water, and decaying plants and animals also contribute to the community health. When decayed organic material, called *humus,* becomes scarce, the soil microorganisms that feed on it die. Many of these microorganisms help release soil nutrients that plants need for growth. Without them, plants starve. Humus also holds moisture in the soil and helps soil particles stick together. When humus becomes depleted, the soil dries out too quickly, parching the plants and risking erosion.

Organic gardeners observe and use these natural relationships to grow healthy crops and landscape plants. For example, I shred the leaves that fall from my landscape trees and use them to mulch my perennial flowers. The leaves suppress weeds and, as they decompose, they release plant nutrients and feed earthworms, which loosen and aerate the soil. When plants grow in such a balanced ecosystem, they receive all the nourishment they need from the soil and sun, and they bear plentiful flowers, fruits, and seeds. Insect pests and diseases do little long-term damage.

Taking from the soil without giving anything back breaks that natural cycle. Harvesting crops, bagging the lawn clippings, and raking fallen leaves removes organic material that's ordinarily destined for the soil on which it falls. If the organic material isn't replenished, the soil loses humus and its natural fertility. Substituting synthetic chemical fertilizers for naturally occurring nutrients may feed plants, but it starves the soil.

Pesticides also upset the natural balance. Using pesticides to kill insects deprives the pests' natural predators of food, which causes the predators to decline, necessitating more pesticides to achieve pest control. It's a vicious cycle. In addition, pesticides often kill more that their intended targets. Beneficial insects and spiders that prey on plant pests and pollinate flowers die, too. And if pesticides drift on the wind or water away from their target, fish and birds may become poisoned, as well.

Gardening for the future

Depleting soil fertility, damaging and polluting ecosystems, and consuming excess water threatens the future of earth's safe and abundant food supply. The way that farmers and individual gardeners and homeowners choose to farm, garden, and maintain their landscapes makes a difference in whether our land can continue to house, feed, and clothe us.

Organic gardeners grow plants using sustainable methods. According to Webster's dictionary, *sustain* means "to keep in existence, to provide sustenance or nourishment." Sustainable gardening practices, such as composting, conserving resources, and using non-toxic pest controls, ensure safe and plentiful food for future generations.

Organic versus non-toxic

Many people assume that "organic" means "non-toxic," but that's not really correct. Some commonly accepted organic pesticides are just as toxic, if not more so, than some synthetic chemical pesticides. *Organic pesticides* are derived from plant, animal, and mineral sources. *Synthetic chemical pesticides* come from petroleum and other chemical sources, and that's the main difference between the two types.

Traditional farmers worldwide have used some plant, animal, and mineral-based pesticides for centuries. Indeed, home gardeners continue to use concoctions of garlic, hot peppers, onions, and other plants and substances to discourage pests. Although organic pesticides generally have far fewer health side effects than synthetic pesticides, that's not always the case. Nicotine, for example, although derived from a plant and used as an organic pesticide, is highly toxic to humans and many other species.

Pesticides pose another problem. Some hang around in the environment long after their job is done. Chemists measure this persistence of chemicals by their *half-life,* or number of days it takes for half of the original quantity to break down into its components. Sunlight, water, soil microorganisms, and composition of the pesticide influence the half-life of these chemicals. Organic pesticides, and some synthetic ones, have half-lives of only a few days. Others, however, remain toxic in the environment for months or even years after the farmer or homeowner sprays or sprinkles them on a pest.

For Land's Sake

The earth's population continues to grow, but the amount of land available for growing food is rapidly disappearing. Erosion, development, pollution, dwindling water supplies, and other human-induced and natural disruptions threaten safe food and water supplies. Plant and animal species continue to disappear at alarming rates as humans damage and encroach upon their habitats.

Many gardeners work to improve this grim picture by making personal choices that, at the very least, do no harm to the environment. The way you choose to grow flowers and food and maintain the landscape can actually improve the quality of the soil, air, water, and lives of the organisms that depend on it. Organic gardening is based on the principle of working with nature instead of against it.

Erosion

It takes 500 years to produce one inch of natural *topsoil,* the rich matrix of humus, minerals, and microorganisms that plants depend on for growth. Plants, in turn, hold the topsoil in place with their roots and shelter it with their leaves. Soil without plants *erodes* easily — washing away with runoff from rain and snow or blowing away in the wind.

When soil washes into streams, rivers, and lakes, it significantly disrupts those ecosystems and pollutes the water. In fact, sediment accounts for nearly half of all lake pollution and 22 percent of river pollution, according a 1991 United States government report. Erosion devastates farmland, too. The U.S. loses 2 million acres of *arable land* (land that's suitable for growing crops) each year due to soil erosion. The Iowa Department of Agriculture reported that half of that state's topsoil had eroded by the early 1980s. Experts report that 30 percent of arable land was lost worldwide in the last 40 years of the 20th century due, in part, to erosion.

What happens in your own small garden plot may seem insignificant compared to these mind-numbing statistics, but how you garden does play a role in the bigger picture. Gardeners can help reduce erosion by keeping plants growing on or covering the soil throughout the year, preserving and encouraging humus formation, and avoiding excessive tilling, disruption, or compacting of the soil.

Wildlife and habitat

Pesticides kill pests, but unfortunately they harm innocent bystanders, as well. Some pesticides are very highly toxic to fish and aquatic organisms, birds and beneficial insects, such as bees. Poisons harm innocent animals in two ways — either immediately or slowly over a period of time. A fast-acting pesticide, such as pyrethrum, kills bees and fish, as well as pests, on contact, but it breaks down rapidly in the environment. Within a few days, it's harmless.

Other pesticides, such as the infamous DDT, accumulate in the bodies of animals, harming them over a long period of time. In the case of DDT, which was banned in the U.S. in 1972, the chemical accumulated in fish, rodents, and other animals. When predators, such as hawks and eagles, ate the animals they accumulated increasingly larger quantities of DDT, too. As a result, they laid eggs with thin shells that broke before they hatched, destroying generations of birds and sending many species to the brink of extinction.

Pesticide contamination of wildlife has serious implications for humans, too. In its report, *Chemicals in Sportfish and Game Health Advisories 2000-2001,* the New York State Department of Health lists 73 bodies of water within the state from which fish shouldn't be eaten at all by women of childbearing age and children under the age of 15. At most, the department recommends eating no more than ½ pound of fish per month from the least contaminated of these waters. Find the full report at www.health.state.ny.us/nysdoh/environ/fish.htm or call 800-458-1158, extension 27815.

Sadly, advisories such as this exist throughout the United States.

Pollution

The U.S. Environmental Protection Agency reports pesticide contamination of groundwater in 39 states. *Groundwater* flows below ground in the cracks in bedrock and between soil particles where it collects in large, saturated areas called *aquifers.* The EPA estimated that, as of 1994, one percent of the country's groundwater was already contaminated, and that the percentage was increasing rapidly. Half of the U.S. population uses groundwater sources for their drinking water — the other half gets their drinking water from *surface water,* such as rivers, lakes, and reservoirs. Surface waters become polluted from *runoff* — water that runs over the ground, carrying pesticides, fertilizers, and soil with it.

Surface waters are even more vulnerable to pollution than groundwater. Traces of triazine herbicides, for example, which farmers use on corn and other crops, have been found in about 98 percent of Midwestern surface waters. Researchers also found triazines in raindrops in 23 states.

Excess nitrogen and phosphorus fertilizers from lawns, farms, and gardens wash into streams, lakes, and oceans where they contribute to excess algae growth. Densely growing algae depletes the oxygen in the water, which can kill fish and suffocate the native plant species. Nitrogen, the main element in most fertilizers, also moves easily through the soil, especially when mixed with water from rain, snowmelt, or irrigation. Depending on soil conditions, nitrogen percolates down through the soil and enters the groundwater, contaminating wells and other sources of drinking water. High concentrations of nitrate — a common nitrogen compound — can be toxic to children under the age of 6 months and to other mammals, including horses.

Disease

One of the main reasons that I garden organically is to provide my family with safe, wholesome food and a toxic-free environment. It seems that every time I turn around, another pesticide is making headline news and hastily being pulled off the market. *Chlorpyrifos,* the active ingredient in Dursban and Lorsban, for example, is the sixth most commonly used pesticide in the U.S. Although used extensively in homes, yards, and farms to kill fleas, roaches, ants, termites, lice, and agricultural pests, the chemical is now banned for home use due to its effects on humans. Agricultural use of chlorpyrifos also is being curtailed. As it turns out, chlorpyrifos harms the central nervous system, cardiovascular system, and respiratory system. Children are particularly vulnerable because they crawl around and play on the floor and soil where the chemical is sprinkled and sprayed.

Despite extensive testing by chemical companies in controlled trials, it's hard to know exactly what pesticides will do in the real world. Ponder this: The EPA now considers 60 percent of all herbicides, 90 percent of all fungicides, and 30 percent of all insecticides to be potentially *carcinogenic,* or able to cause cancer. A study conducted by the National Cancer Institute found that farmers exposed to chemical herbicides had six times greater risks of developing cancer than farmers who were not exposed. Scary stuff.

Organized Organics

Agricultural practices changed dramatically in the 1930s and 1940s when synthetic chemical fertilizers and pesticides became widely available. The new fertilizers replaced many traditional plant and animal manures, while pesticides and herbicides wiped out insects, diseases, and weeds, allowing farmers to grow larger areas of single crops, with less labor, than ever before. The small, labor-intensive, traditionally diversified farms began disappearing. Specialized, single-crop farms took their places.

The farming revolution came with hidden costs, however. Synthetic pesticides and fertilizers and changing farming practices disrupted the natural ecological order, creating an escalating cycle of dependency on stronger and newer chemicals.

Biodynamic agriculture

As agricultural practices changed, some people, such as Rudolf Steiner, raised the alarm. Steiner, an Austrian philosopher, observed the effects of newly introduced chemical fertilizers and pesticides on soil and crops in Europe in the early 1920s. He initiated studies and experiments into the relationships between plants and their environment and developed a holistic growing system, called *biodynamic agriculture,* which made use of plants' rates of growth, favored environments, and relationships with other plants. He found, for example, that some plants grow better — or worse — when grown next to other specific plant species.

Steiner also devoted much attention to perfecting and using compost and plant extracts to increase plant health and yields. Recycling organic materials and conserving resources are key components of biodynamic agriculture, which is widely practiced and taught throughout the world. For more information, contact The Biodynamic Farming and Gardening Association, Inc., Building 1002B, Thoreau Center, The Presidio, PO Box 29135, San Francisco, CA 94129 or visit their Web site at www.biodynamics.com.

Biodynamic/French-intensive method

Although ridiculed by many of his contemporaries, Rudolf Steiner found a follower in Alan Chadwick who used his mentor's ideas of the relationships among plants and the elements in their environment to form his own gardening system. He combined biodynamics and with the productive *French intensive* agricultural practices he learned in France, in which plants grow in wide rows of deeply loosened compost-fed soil. Chadwick, an accomplished British actor and artist, as well as gardener, eventually brought his techniques to the U.S. in the 1960s when he accepted a teaching position at the University of California at Santa Cruz. Chadwick introduced his biodynamic/French intensive methods to many eager students, including John Jeavons.

Biointensive mini-farming

In the 1970s, using the methods he learned from Chadwick and combining them with other sustainable agricultural practices from ancient world cultures, John Jeavons created a new organic method he called *biointensive mini-farming.* He wanted to find the smallest area needed to derive all of his own food, clothing, income, and building materials.

Jeavons techniques include thorough soil preparation, adding compost, and digging planting beds 2 feet deep. His biointensively-managed gardens use less water, fertilizer, and space, while producing far more food per square foot than conventional farming methods. Jeavons mini-farming techniques — explained in his popular book, *How to Grow More Food* — allow anyone, anywhere with 100 square feet and a four to six month long growing season to produce all the vegetables one person needs for a year. For more information, contact Ecology Action Sustainable Biointensive Mini-Farming at 5798 Ridgewood Road, Willits, CA 95490.

Polyculture

In contrast to Jeavons' intensive gardening, Masanoba Fukuoka, a Japanese farmer, developed a system of agriculture that uses no compost or soil turning. Instead the Fukuoka method makes use of specific mixes of plants and animals to feed and protect the soil while growing grain, fruit, and vegetables. He noted that weeds became less problematic when he stopped tilling the soil and instead kept it covered with crops and mulch. Fukuoka grows clover, which adds nitrogen to the soil, instead of adding fertilizer or compost, and mulches with straw from the grain crops. He starts new crops before harvesting the old crops on the same land. *Polyculture,* the practice of growing multiple crops together so that each benefits the others, is part of his natural farming system.

Wes Jackson, at the Land Institute in Kansas, also promotes polyculture as opposed to *monoculture,* in which only a single crop occupies the land at any given time. He observed the mixed grasses of the prairie and developed a system of growing perennial grain crops together to create a permanent ground cover that protects the soil while increasing crop yields.

For more information about Fukuoka's techniques, refer to his book, *The One-Straw Revolution,* and others.

Permaculture

Bill Mollison, an Australian ecologist, and his student, David Holmgren, founded permaculture in the 1970s. Meaning *permanent culture,* permaculture focuses on sustainable agricultural practices that cooperate with nature. Mollison considers the entire landscape in his agricultural designs. He observes that, as in natural ecosystems, all aspects of the garden are interconnected — changing one condition affects other parts of the whole. Design and long-range planning are key to permaculture gardens and landscapes.

In a permaculture system, the gardener designs the garden and landscape to mimic nature's diversity, stability, and resilience, in which everything remains within the system — collected rainwater irrigates the crops, and plant and animal waste returns to the soil. Plants and animals mutually benefit one another and serve more than one purpose, such as food, mulch, fertilizer, windbreak, shade, and compost. Mollison's system minimizes outside inputs, such as water and nutrients, and instead depends on the strategic use and placement of existing elements.

Many books, magazines, Web sites, regional organizations, and schools exist worldwide to help you learn more about permaculture. Good places to start are at www.permaculture.org, www.permaculture-hawaii.com/links.html, and www.permaculture.com, where you can find basic information and lots of links to other Web sites and resources.

Forest gardening

Another gardening pioneer, Robert Hart, spent time observing the food-growing practices of indigenous peoples who live in and near forests worldwide. He noted that rather than grow food in a single layer on the ground, as is done in most "civilized" gardens, traditional forest gardeners obtained their food from many layers of the forest and surrounding areas. Trees provide fruit, nuts, fuel, and building materials, as well as shelter for the fruiting vines and shrubs that grow beneath them. Perennial and annual vegetables, grains, bulbs, and herbs form the lowest layer. Similar in many ways to permaculture, forest gardening depends on careful and creative design and observation of natural relationships to create a garden ecosystem that benefits plants and animals, as well as humans. Find out more from Hart's book, *Forest Gardening.*

Rodale Institute

At the same time that European gardeners were developing and promoting organic gardening techniques in the 1940s and '50s, an American publisher, J. I. Rodale, established an organic farm in Pennsylvania. Drawing upon the research and writings of British agronomist Sir Albert Howard, Rodale connected soil health with human health and began promoting composting and other natural farming techniques as alternatives to burgeoning use of synthetic chemicals in agriculture.

Rodale began publishing *Organic Gardening and Farming* magazine in 1942 and founded the Soil and Health Foundation, now called the Rodale Institute, in 1947. His son, Robert Rodale, took over the reins in the 1970s, buying more farmland and establishing the Rodale Institute Experimental Farm. He called his vision of sustainable food culture *regenerative agriculture,* and worked to spread his techniques and philosophy worldwide. The Rodale Institute has made a major impact on organic gardening in the U.S. and countries around the world through a variety of initiatives, teaching programs, and publications.

To contact the Rodale Institute for more information about their many activities, visit their Web site at www.rodaleinstitute.org.

Federal and state involvement

Federal, state, and provincial governments now play increasingly important roles in educating farmers and gardeners and supporting sustainable agricultural practices. Many colleges and most state universities offer alternative agriculture programs, too.

Congress addressed sustainable agriculture in the 1990 "Farm Bill." Under that law, "the term *sustainable agriculture* means an integrated system of plant and animal production practices having a site-specific application that will, over the long term:

- Satisfy human food and fiber needs
- Enhance environmental quality and the natural resource base upon which the agricultural economy depends
- Make the most efficient use of nonrenewable resources and on-farm resources
- Biological cycles and controls
- Sustain the economic viability of farm operations
- Enhance the quality of life for farmers and society as a whole

The Federal Alternative Farming Systems Information Center publishes a wealth of information, both in print and on the Internet. Start your search at their Web site, www.nal.usda.gov/afsic/agnic/agnic.htm.

Another great source of down-to-earth information, and one of my favorites, is the Appropriate Technology Transfer for Rural Areas program, known as ATTRA for short. Also federally funded, ATTRA publishes tons of helpful material on everything from growing individual crops to raising livestock to marketing and more. Find their amazing database of articles and links to worldwide resources at www.attra.org.

Chapter 2

Organic Gardening 101

- -

In This Chapter

▶ Sorting out soil texture and structure

▶ Understanding soil fertility

▶ Controlling pests naturally

▶ Winning against weeds

- -

Soil, weeds, pests, and diseases occupy the minds of most gardeners. To keep food and landscapes safe from toxic chemicals and synthetic fertilizers, however, organic gardeners work with nature to overcome problems and build success. In this chapter, I introduce you to some of organic gardening's most important concepts and practices. You can find more details about each topic in Parts II and III of this book.

Simplifying Soil and Fertility

Soil is made up of small mineral pieces that come from underlying rocks. If you dig down deeply into the soil, you can see that it is composed of layers, as shown in Figure 2-1. The *subsurface soils* are the deep layers that remain undisturbed by cultivation and weather. Subsurface soils contain little organic matter and few microorganisms. Sometimes a hard, impervious layer called *caliche* or *hardpan* forms in the subsoil, and it prevents water from penetrating. *Surface soils* lie above the subsoil where plows, gardeners, and weather can alter them. Most plant roots and soil microorganisms live in the surface soil.

Two basic kinds of surface soil exist — mineral and organic. *Organic* soils occur mostly in swamps and marshes and consist of 80 to 95 percent organic matter or decayed plants. *Mineral* soils — the kind that most people garden with — typically contain mostly weathered minerals and only one to ten percent organic matter, depending on the climate in which it was formed, as well as its location and the plants and animals it supports.

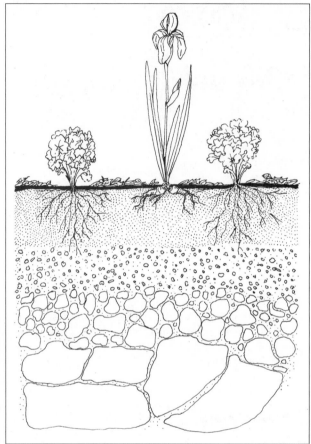

Figure 2-1:
Soil is
composed
of layers
called the
subsoil and
surface soil.

Getting down to the nitty-gritty

Soil particles vary in size from microscopic to large and coarse. Three basic soil particles exist and they differ mostly in their size and shape, as shown in Figure 2-2.

- ✔ *Clay* consists of the smallest, flattest particles, which pack tightly together.

- ✔ *Silt* particles are more angular and larger than clay, but still microscopic.

- ✔ *Sand* is the largest and most angular of the three.

The relative amounts of these particles determine your *soil texture*. The ideal mixture of all three soil particles is called *loam*, which consists of approximately 40 percent sand, 40 percent silt, and 20 percent clay. You can find out more about soil texture in Chapter 4.

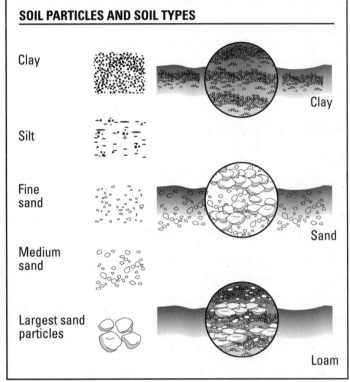

SOIL PARTICLES AND SOIL TYPES

Clay

Silt

Fine
sand

Medium
sand

Largest sand
particles

Clay

Sand

Loam

Figure 2-2:
Soil consists
of clay, silt,
and sand
particles,
which differ
in size and
shape. Loam
is a mixture
of silt, sand,
and clay.

Breathing space

Organic matter and minerals are only two of the important ingredients in soil.
The other two are air and water. Air and water lie in the spaces, called *pores,*
between the solid soil particles. The ideal ratio is about 50 percent pore
space and 50 percent solid particles, but the proportions of minerals, organic
matter, air, and water in soil varies greatly depending on many factors, including the following:

- ✔ **Weather and lay of the land:** Flooded soil holds little air because the
  pore spaces fill with water.

- ✔ **Soil disturbance:** Driving, walking, digging, and other activities com-
  press the soil particles together, squeezing out air.

- ✔ **Organic matter content:** Decomposing plant and animal material
  increases the amount of water and air that soil can hold.

- ✔ **Size and shape of soil particles:** Very small, flat particles pack together
  more tightly than larger, angular ones, which means less space for air
  and water. Large particles generally have large, air-filled pore spaces
  between them.

Water, which carries soil nutrients used by plants, moves through pore spaces in the soil. When the soil contains very little pore space, the plants can't get enough water and dissolved nutrients. Air also occupies the spaces between soil particles. Roots and soil microorganisms, which decompose organic material and make nutrients available to plants, depend on air in the soil to do their work.

Structurally sound

The way that the soil particles align themselves or clump together is called *soil structure*. The best garden soils have a loose, crumb-like structure that water, air, and plant roots can easily penetrate. *Unstructured soils,* such as beach sand, don't clump together, which allows water to flow through them too rapidly for most plant growth. *Poorly structured soils,* such as heavy clay, clump together so tightly that little water and air can pass through.

Many things affect soil structure, but the most important ones from a gardener's point of view include the following:

- **Organic matter:** Decayed plants and animals become *humus* — a substance that promotes crumbly soil texture. Soils that lack enough humus may clump together too tightly or not at all. Organic matter improves the structure of both sandy and clay soils.

- **Earthworms:** As they tunnel through the soil, earthworms open up spaces between soil particles, which allow air, water, and roots to pass through easily. Earthworm *castings* (excrement) are also rich in organic matter and nutrients.

- **Frequent digging and rotary tilling:** Churning the soil through rotary tiller blades changes the soil structure. Although tilling can initially add more air to the soil, it also damages earthworms and can promote too-rapid breakdown and loss of organic matter.

- **Working with wet soil:** Wet soil, especially clay, packs together tightly when compressed and can stay that way even after it dries, forming hard clods.

Organic gardeners strive to build good soil structure because it contains the right proportions of air, water, organic matter, and mineral particles that plant roots need for good growth. Many organic gardening schools, such as French intensive and biointensive (see Chapter 1), recommend building good soil structure to a depth of 18 to 24 inches to encourage lush and productive plants.

Fertile ground

All this talk of soil texture and structure isn't complete without adding a third critical component — *soil fertility.* Fertility is the capacity of a soil to supply nutrients to plants. The nutrients that plants need in the largest quantities are called *macronutrients* and consist of nitrogen, phosphorus, potassium, calcium, magnesium, and sulfur. In addition, plants need smaller amounts of so-called *micronutrients,* such as iron, manganese, boron, copper, zinc, molybdenum, chlorine, and nickel. Several factors influence soil fertility:

- **Amount of nutrients in the soil:** Soils contain differing levels of each element that plants need for growth. When enough of each element is present, plants grow optimally. But if even one element is in short supply, plants can't grow as well. Think of it as the weakest-link theory, which says that a chain is only as strong as its weakest link.

- **Soil texture:** The kind and relative amounts of soil particles you have in your garden soil also affect its fertility. Clay and silt soils tend to hold more nutrients than sand because they have larger surface areas and smaller pore spaces. Sandy soil drains quickly, which washes nutrients away.

- **Organic matter:** As plant and animal matter decomposes, it releases nutrients into the soil. It also helps hold nutrients in place.

- **Soil pH:** *pH* is the measure of a liquid's acidity or alkalinity. *Acid* is considered 0 to just under 7 and *alkaline* is just over 7 to 14, with pH 7 being neutral. Depending on the pH of water in the soil, nutrients form different compounds, some of which plants can't use. Phosphorus, for example, becomes less available for plants at a pH level below 6 and above 7. No matter how much phosphorus the soil actually contains, the plants can't use it if the pH is too high or low. The ideal soil pH for most plants is between about 6 and 7.

For organic gardeners, feeding plants responsibly isn't just a matter of pouring on the fertilizer. Instead, gardeners build the natural fertility of their soil by adding organic matter, preserving and improving the soil structure, and modifying the soil pH. When, as an organic gardener, you do use fertilizer, you need much less to keep the plants growing strong.

For more on soil pH and organic matter, flip to Chapter 4. Look in Chapter 5 if you want to know about organic fertilizers and how to use them.

Pondering Pests and Diseases

If you've gardened before, you know how frustrating it is to find a rose bush devastated by beetles or a tomato munched by slugs. Maybe you know the heartbreak of finding your flower and vegetable seedlings keeled over from fungus or cutworms. While many gardeners automatically reach for a can or jar of poison in these circumstances, organic gardeners choose a different approach. Instead of fighting pests and disease with chemical warfare, organic gardeners look for the least toxic and least environmentally disruptive solutions first.

Using integrated pest management (IPM)

Farmers always seek the most cost-effective ways to produce their crops, and with pest control, cost is a major factor. Pesticides are expensive to buy and use, plus environmental concerns make many of them increasingly difficult to justify. So it's little wonder that farmers — and home gardeners — embrace a system of pest control that cuts costs and decreases their reliance on pesticides.

Integrated pest management, also known as *IPM,* is a system that combines biological, cultural, physical, and chemical strategies to control pests. In plain English, that means using the easiest, least environmentally harmful, cheapest methods first, and using the more expensive, toxic methods only as a last resort.

Careful observation or *crop monitoring* is the first and most important step in IPM. You have to know exactly what pest you're dealing with, when it appears, how many you have, and on what plants. For example, after you can recognize aphids, you may find them on a few rose buds on a single plant in the front lawn or covering every bush in your prize-winning rose garden. It may be the beginning of your gardening season or near the end. How you choose to control the aphids — or whether you choose to control them at all — depends on all these factors and more.

Integrated pest management strategies are like a series of steps. The first steps are the least toxic and least harmful control methods. The most potentially toxic controls are last resort steps. Here's how the steps stack up.

 ✔ **Cultural control:** Giving plants optimal growing conditions — soil fertility, water, light, and freedom from competing weeds — is the key to this first step. Other good cultural practices include using pest and disease-resistant varieties, and *crop rotation,* which means moving particular crops to new parts of the garden each year.

 ✔ **Crop sanitation:** Keeping pests and diseases out of the garden in the first place is more than half the battle won. Inspecting new plants, cleaning your tools, eliminating weeds, and using best watering practices help prevent the spread of potential problems. Find out more in Part III.

 ✔ **Mechanical control:** Prevent pests from getting on your plants by covering them with special fabrics or using hot water, air, fire, and the heat of the sun to kill them without poisons. Simply knocking pests into a can of soapy water does the trick, too.

- ✔ **Biological control:** Every pest has a natural control, whether it's predator or a disease. You can buy and release many of these control organisms or encourage the ones that already exist around your garden. Find out how to get physical with pests in Chapter 8.

- ✔ **Chemical control:** As a last resort, apply the least toxic pesticides. The best ones target only the pest and don't affect the innocent bystanders, such as bees, spiders, and other beneficial insects. These pesticides also don't hang around in the environment where they can continue to affect other organisms long after their use. For more information about chemical controls, jump to Chapter 9.

Another factor that farmers — and you — must consider is how much pest or disease damage you can tolerate. Perfection comes at a very high price. Even farmers who must make a living or go bust based on the success of their crops have what they call an *economic threshold,* when the cost of the damage exceeds the cost of control. They expect to lose a portion of the crop completely and probably have another portion somewhat blemished. For them, it's an economic reality, but for most home gardeners, it's a matter of accepting less than perfection on 100 percent of your flowers and vegetables.

Some wise gardeners I know make an allowance for their inevitable losses by planting a little more than they actually plan to harvest. If pests take their share, these gardeners still have plenty for themselves. If pests fail to put in an appearance, the gardeners have enough to share with the neighbors. It's a win-win situation.

Cleaning up your act

People say that good hygiene starts at home, but I think that it starts in the garden. Soil-borne diseases, weed seeds, and other little pests gladly hitch a ride on dirty shoes, tools, containers, hoses, and new plants from the nursery or neighbor. Diseases that spread through splashing water love it when you brush through the rows of dew-covered berries, flowers, and vegetables. The best organic pest control technique is simply prevention.

Healthy, thriving plants attract fewer problems than those compromised by poor nutrition, unsuitable growing conditions, or mechanical damage. So, as they say in sports, your best defense is a good offense. Pump up your plants! Build your soil's fertility, add compost, and give plants the climate, sun, and moisture conditions they prefer. Choose particular varieties the resist the diseases or pests that plague your area and avoid the pest-prone ones.

Learn as much as you can about the problems you encounter. Look for pests' vulnerable spots. For example, black spot disease on roses is a fungus that spreads in water droplets and spends part of its life on the ground under its host. The ways to prevent black spot include keeping plant leaves dry, and removing and replacing the mulch under your bushes at least once a year. As another example, consider the small, but voracious flea beetle. When vegetable and flower plants are mere seedlings, these beetles can wipe them out. But, cover the plants with a lightweight fabric cover, and voilá! — beetles can't reach the plants.

And in this corner — the good guys

About 98 percent of the bugs you encounter won't do you or your plants any harm. Luckily, many of that silent majority preys upon the pestilent 2 percent. These beneficial organisms attack their prey in several ways:

- ✔ **Predators:** It's a bug-eat-bug world out there. These insects, such as ladybugs, capture and eat other insects.

- ✔ **Parasites:** Remember the movie *Alien* in which creatures from outer space reproduce by laying eggs in humans? Luckily, that was science fiction, but it's science fact for much of the insect kingdom. Many parasitic wasps and flies lay eggs in or on another host insect, which is consumed by the hatching larvae.

- ✔ **Disease:** Everything gets sick sometime, including insects. You can help that process along by introducing fungi, bacteria, and viruses that hurt specific insect pests.

Many beneficial organisms live on wild plants near your garden. You can encourage them to set up housekeeping by growing or maintaining the right ones. Turn to Chapter 8 for specific predators, parasites, and diseases that can help control insect pests, as well as how to attract and use them. That chapter also tells you where you can purchase beneficial organisms.

Putting poisons in their place

Once in awhile, even organic gardeners have to resort to pesticides or risk losing an entire crop or special plant. Sometimes, using a relatively benign pesticide is actually the most environmentally friendly way to reduce a pest population. The secret is to use materials that only affect your target pest and use them in such a way that harmless and beneficial organisms aren't harmed. Fine oil spray is a good example of a least toxic pesticide. It kills insects by coating their bodies and suffocating them and is very effective against insects, such as aphids and scales, that don't move around much.

Timing is everything, too. When you do choose to use a pesticide that could harm innocent insects, apply it when it will do the least damage. Bees, for example, return to their hives in evening, making them less vulnerable to pesticides applied at that time of day. Go to Chapter 9 for more about safe and smart pesticides.

Beating the Weeds

Weeds are plants that grow where you don't want them to. Yet they rank high on every gardener's hit list, because you probably spend a disproportionate amount of garden time trying to eradicate them.

Weeds spread in a number of ways:

- **Seeds:** A single ragweed plant can produce over 3,000 seeds and pigweed as many as 120,000 seeds per plant. That's a harsh penalty to pay for allowing a few weeds to reproduce in your garden. Seeds also blow in from neighboring wild areas, cling to your clothes and pets, and travel on the bottoms of your shoes. The seeds of many common weeds can live for years in the soil before they sprout.

- **Runners over and under the ground:** Some plants make clones of themselves by sending out special horizontal stems that sprout into a new plant at the end. These weeds tend to live from one year to the next and may eventually form large, tenacious colonies.

- **Plant parts:** When you chop up some plants, the little bits grow roots and start over. What started as one weed turns into ten weeds. A gardener's nightmare!

So what you do you? Getting weeds out of your garden takes perseverance and a variety of strategies. The methods you choose depend on how much time you have before you intend to plant your garden, the size of your garden (or proposed garden), and the kinds of weeds you're dealing with. Weed controlling strategies include the following:

- **Pull 'em out.** Yank by hand or dislodge with a hoe or other weeding tool of your choice. If they don't contain seeds, add them to your compost.

- **Eat them up.** Many weeds are edible and nutritious, especially young plants that haven't flowered. Try boiling up a batch of lamb's quarters, dandelion greens, or stinging nettles, which lose their "sting" when cooked.

- **Smother them and keep them in the dark.** Cover the ground with mulch to prevent the weed seeds from germinating and young plants from growing.

- **Change the environment.** Some weeds prefer certain soil and sun conditions and fail to thrive when deprived of their ideal situation.

- **Give them competition.** Plant more desirable plants that grow faster and stronger than the weeds do.

- **Burn them up.** Use clear plastic to heat up the soil and kill the seeds or use a *weed flamer* (see Chapter 6) to shrivel the young plants.

✔ **Use chemical warfare.** As a last resort, some new, low-toxicity herbicides can control some weeds, especially when they're young or sprouting.

Many weeds are actually symptoms of another underlying problem with your soil or gardening practices. Some weeds show up in poorly drained soil; others in overly acidic or alkaline soil. The presence of others can indicate the depletion of valuable humus. For more on this topic, look for *Weeds and What They Tell* by Ehrenfried E. Pfeiffer, published by the Biodynamic Farming and Gardening Association. Written nearly 50 years ago, some of its information is out of date, but the book remains unique and useful.

Despite most people's preoccupation with ridding their gardens of weeds, some weeds may actually be beneficial. Some ways that weeds can help include the following:

✔ Provide habitat for desirable insects

✔ Bring nutrients from deep in the soil

✔ Add nitrogen to the soil

✔ Break up hard-packed earth

✔ Protect soil from erosion

To find out more about weeds, turn to Chapter 6 for the rest of the story.

Chapter 3

Designing For Diversity

. . . .

In This Chapter

▶ Taking inventory of your site

▶ Choosing plants that resist problems

▶ Understanding climate and microclimate

▶ Designing a low-input landscape

. . . .

Design is fundamental to successful organic gardening. Garden design means planting with a purpose — making decisions based on soil, sun, wind, and climate, as well as plant needs and your own desires and expectations. If you put plants where they can naturally thrive and give them what they need, you won't have many insects or diseases to worry about. Well-placed plants can shelter your house, provide refuge for wildlife, and give you all the fruits and vegetables and flowers you desire.

This chapter may be the most important one in the book because it's about putting plants in the right places and starting them off on the right foot, so to speak.

Putting the Right Plants in the Right Place

Healthy plants suffer from fewer pest and disease problems and tolerate drought, flood, and other adverse situations more easily than do struggling plants, so it makes sense to put plants in the right places to encourage their natural resilience. The natural rhythm of the seasons, including the winter low temperatures and the summer highs, sets the most obvious limits within which you garden. Other, more subtle factors, including moisture, nutrients, soil, and sun, also influence how and where plants grow best.

Choosing trees, shrubs, and perennial landscape plants that match your existing conditions makes growing them less difficult. Vegetables, herbs, and flowers that live for one season grow more vigorously when you modify their site to suit their needs.

Sun and shade

If you've lived in your house for a year or more, you've probably noticed that the amount of sun that falls on your house and garden varies from one season to the next. In the summer, the sun rises higher in the sky, coming up farther to the east and setting more to the west than it does in the winter, reaching its eastern and western-most points and rising highest in the sky on the summer solstice. On the winter solstice, the opposite is true. When the sun is low in the sky, it casts longer shadows, as shown in Figure 3-1.

Figure 3-1:
The angle of the sun and where it rises and sets changes throughout the year. In the southern hemisphere, these dates are reversed.

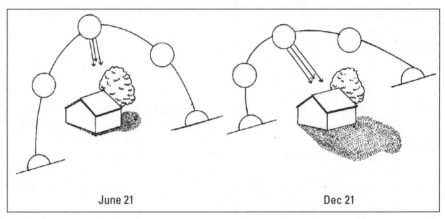

June 21   Dec 21

When you work out your garden and landscape plans, it helps to know where the sun shines and shadows fall at different times of the year. Not only can you put plants where they'll be happiest, but you can use them to help conserve energy and make your own life more comfortable, too.

Block the hot summer rays with leafy trees on the south and west to keep your house and patio cooler, but let the sun shine in to warm the house in the cooler months. Avoid planting trees that keep their leaves all winter on the south side of your house. Plant *deciduous* trees, which drop their leaves, instead.

Where you live also affects the sun's intensity. Gardeners in the southern latitudes and at higher elevations enjoy stronger sunlight than gardeners who live in the north and at lower elevations, and that makes a difference to your plants. Garden books use terms, such as *full sun* or *part shade* to describe where plants grow best, but full sun in San Diego, California is not the same as full sun in Eugene, Oregon or Boulder, Colorado. Plants that grow happily in the sun all day long in Eugene, for example, may prefer a little mid-day shade in sunny southern California or mountain-high Boulder.

Figuring out just what kind of sun and shade that you have can be confusing, too. Plant descriptions in this book and many others use the following terms:

- ✔ **Deep or dense shade** occurs on the north sides of buildings and walls and under trees with low branches and dense leaves. No direct sunlight reaches the ground.
- ✔ **Partial shade** occurs in places that receive direct morning or afternoon sun, but none at midday, from about 10:00 to 2:00.
- ✔ **Light shade** falls under trees with high branches or sparse foliage.
- ✔ **Full sun** means direct sunlight for at least 6 hours or more each day, including some or all of the midday hours.

Use the patterns of sun and shade to your advantage. Plant sun-loving vegetables, flowers, and fruits in the spots that receive full sun and choose shady characters for sites with less sun. I often combine sun- and shade-loving plants, letting one protect the other. In my vegetable garden, for example, I plant leaf lettuce seeds between the broccoli plants because the broccoli shades the sprouting lettuce, which prefers cooler, shadier soil. I use tall, shade-casting corn in the same way, putting crops that like cooler temperatures and less midday sun on the north side of the corn patch.

Water

While the scarcity of water is a limiting factor for some gardeners, others have more than enough. Your climate determines how much water falls on your garden, while the slope of the land and type of soil determine whether it puddles or runs away. But you can also influence what happens to it after it falls from the sky or flows out of the faucet by designing your garden and landscape to take advantage of the natural conditions.

In arid climates, where rain falls infrequently, you can grow a lush, colorful garden and landscape and conserve water, too. Here's how:

- ✔ **Choose plants that naturally thrive** with little rainfall in your climate. Plant water-hungry exotics sparingly — in containers or as accent specimens only. Seek out plant nurseries that specialize in drought-tolerant species.
- ✔ **Protect existing native plants** during construction and landscaping projects on your property. They are naturally adapted to the site and require little maintenance. Use them to guide your design plan.
- ✔ **Install rain barrels or a cistern** to collect and store whatever rain does fall. Use this water for your garden instead of drawing on municipal services or depleting your well water.

✔ **Use drip irrigation** to deliver water efficiently and directly to the plant roots through a pipe or hose. Avoid wasteful overhead sprinklers.

✔ **Alter the slope or make channels** to direct the surface water, if you find that rainfall runs off too quickly. Check local regulations before altering any natural wetland or bodies of water or affecting water flow onto a neighboring property.

✔ **Use ground-covering plants** to preserve soil moisture and cool the surrounding area. Avoid heat-reflecting mulches and surfaces, which can increase plants' need for water.

Gardeners who regularly deal with too much moisture, which results in plant disease, have several options:

✔ **Choose plants that enjoy plenty of water**, including plants native to your area. Many attractive trees, shrubs, and perennial plants grow happily in marshy soil.

✔ **Build raised gardens** from timber, berms of soil, or more permanent materials. The soil in a raised garden may drain more quickly than the surrounding soil, especially if you add plenty of organic material.

✔ **Install buried drainpipe** to carry away excess surface water.

Soil

Gardens begin with the soil — nothing you do in your garden is more important than building healthy, fertile, organically rich soil. Soil does much more than simply hold plants in place — it's the source of nearly all plant nutrition and water. Many of the microorganisms that live in soil benefit plants, too. In fact, some plants have vital relationships with particular soil organisms without which they can't thrive.

Soil is so important, in fact, that I've devoted an entire chapter to the subject. Flip to Chapter 4 for the complete story of soil.

Considering Climate

The predominating weather conditions, including temperature, humidity, precipitation, and wind patterns, of an area, measured over a long period of time, determine a region's *climate*. Proximity to mountains and large bodies of water, distance above sea level, position on the planet relative to the equator, and *prevailing wind* — the direction from which the wind usually blows — have an effect on climate.

Two places near each other, geographically, can have very different climates, if one is high on a mountainside and the other is on the valley floor. On the other hand, widely separated regions often share similar climates, depending on the influencing factors.

When planning and planting an organic landscape, use climate as your first design criteria. Plants have evolved to adapt to particular climates and grow with fewer problems when you give them the conditions they enjoy. When you attempt to grow plants in climates where they do not naturally thrive, they often require more nurturing and intervention. Their new habitat may even contain pests and diseases to which they have no natural resistance. Some researchers have also shown that unhealthy plants emit a chemical signal that attracts damaging insects.

Microclimates

Within larger climates, smaller pockets exist that differ somewhat from the prevailing weather around them. These *microclimates* occur wherever a building, body of water, dense shrubs, or hillside modifies the larger climate, as shown in Figure 3-2.

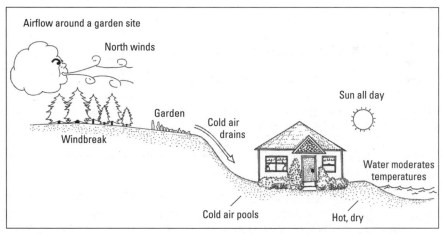

Figure 3-2: Microclimates exist where buildings, slopes, plants, and bodies of water modify the larger climate.

Microclimates may be very small, such as the sunny side of your house or under a shady tree, or as large as a village. A town on the shore of Lake Michigan has a different microclimate than a town 20 miles inland, for example. Common microclimates around your property may include the following:

✔ **North side of house:** Cool and shady year 'round

✔ **South side of house:** Hot and sunny all day; often dry

- **East side of house:** Warm morning sun and cool afternoon shade
- **West side of house:** Morning shade and hot afternoon sun
- **Top of hill:** Exposed to wind and sun; soil dries quickly
- **Bottom of hill:** Collects cold air and may be poorly drained due to precipitation that runs down the slope

No doubt you can find other examples on your site, as you closely observe the patterns of sun, water, wind, and temperature throughout the year.

Many gardeners set out rain gauges to record rainfall amounts so that they can make more informed decisions about when to water. In addition, farmers routinely track daily temperatures on their farms to help them calculate when certain insect will emerge and crops will flower or ripen. Humidity levels and wind also give clues to expected plant growth and development, as well as the prevalence of some diseases and pests.

Plan your landscape and gardens to take advantage of microclimates. Use wind-sheltered areas to protect tender plants from drying winter winds in cold climates and hot, dry winds in arid places. Put leaf-disease prone plants, such as phlox and lilac, in breezy garden spots to naturally prevent infections. Avoid putting frost-tender plants at the bottom of hills where cold-air pockets form.

Plant hardiness

The ability of a plant to survive is called its *hardiness.* Plant catalogs often use the term *hardy* rather loosely to indicate whether or not you can expect a particular plant to live in a cold-winter climate. Many things influence plant hardiness. It helps to think of all the factors as links in a chain — the weakest link determines the strength of the chain or, in this case, the hardiness of the plant. Some of the factors have to do with the plant itself, including the following:

- **Genetics:** Plants inherit the ability to adapt to cold temperatures, among other things. The genetic adaptability of plants to specific climates and soils is called *provenance.* Provenance is a major factor to consider when choosing landscape trees and shrubs and some perennial plants.
- **Stage of growth:** Plants begin adjusting to winter cold by going through a series of physical changes. The timing of *acclimation,* or winter readiness, varies with each species and partly depends on growing conditions, such as soil moisture and fertility. Soft, new shoots, for example, may suffer frost injury in the autumn, whereas woody stems that grew earlier in the summer remain undamaged.

- ✔ **Health:** Environmental stress, such as drought, flooding, storm damage, diseases, and pests weaken plants and can make them more vulnerable to cold damage.

- ✔ **Plant parts:** Flower buds and roots are less cold hardy than the woody stems of trees and shrubs, and they may be damaged or killed before stem damage occurs. That's why some flowering shrubs, such as forsythia, fail to bloom in the spring after a particularly cold winter. A late spring cold snap often kills frost-tender flowers, but does little harm to other plant parts. In perennial plants, the opposite is true. The roots remain alive through the winter, but the leaves and stems die.

The climate itself also affects plant hardiness. Climatic factors that influence plant survival include the following:

- ✔ **Duration of winter:** Genetic programming signals some plants to begin flowering and growing after receiving a particular number of hours of cold temperatures followed by warm temperatures. Even before winter really ends, some plants — especially those growing outside their preferred range — may begin growing (or *break dormancy*) and be damaged by spring frost.

- ✔ **Duration of extreme cold:** Prolonged periods of extreme cold usually cause more damage than a single night of unusually cold temperatures.

- ✔ **Wind:** Wind increases moisture loss from trees and shrubs. Unfortunately, plants can't replace lost moisture while the soil is frozen and plant is dormant. Evergreens, which keep their leaves all year round, are especially vulnerable to the effects of drying winds in winter.

- ✔ **Precipitation:** Snow provides an insulating blanket that protects plant roots and stems from extreme cold. In areas that receive little snow, the soil temperature gets much colder than areas with snow cover.

  Also, plants that receive adequate moisture during the growing season are hardier than those that suffer from drought stress.

- ✔ **Sun exposure:** The sun can also increase moisture loss from winter foliage and stems. Another problem occurs in some trees when the winter sun thaws the bark of a tree. Then, when the temperature suddenly drops at sunset, the bark may freeze and split.

Zoning out

Low winter temperatures limit where most plants will grow. Some plants survive the harshest winters, while others keel right over when the thermometer skirts the freezing mark. After compiling weather data collected over a period of many years, the United States Department of Agriculture (USDA) divided North America, Europe, and China into 11 zones based on each area's expected average annual minimum temperature, and then plotted them on a map. On the USDA Plant Hardiness Zone Map for North America (see Figure 3-3), each of the 11 zones is 10°F warmer or colder in an average winter than the adjacent zone. The warmest zone, Zone 11, — reaches an average low annual temperature of 40°F or higher. In Zone 1, the lowest average annual temperature drops to –50°F or colder. Brrr!

Zones 2 through 10 on some North American maps are further subdivided into *a* and *b* regions. The lowest average annual temperature in Zone 5a, for example, is 5°F warmer than the temperature in Zone 5b. When choosing plants that are just barely hardy in your zone, knowing whether your garden falls into the *a* or *b* category can ease your decision. After a few years of personal weather observation in your own garden, you'll have a pretty clear idea of what to expect for winter low temperatures, too.

Most books, catalogs, magazines, and plant labels use the USDA zone system. For a color version, which may be a bit easier to read, take a look at my book, *Trees & Shrubs For Dummies* (IDG Books Worldwide, Inc.) Or, head to the Internet and visit the National Arboretum Web site, which offers a map of North America and individual regions at www.ars-grin.gov/ars/Beltsville/na/hardzone/ushzmap.html?. For a complete Canadian zone map, visit www.icangarden.com/zone.htm. You can find links to these and other hardiness zone maps for China and Australia (and lots of other useful links, too) at www.ecologycal.com/socsmisc.html#1Climate%20Zones.

Another factor that limits some plants' growth is summer heat. To help gardeners in warm climates, the American Horticultural Society (AHS) developed the *AHS Plant Heat-Zone Map*. The heat-zone map divides the U.S. into 12 zones based on the average number of days each year that may reach temperatures of 86°F or higher. According to the AHS, 86°F is the point where many plants begin to suffer damage from heat.

Although I don't use the heat zones in the plant descriptions in this book, some plant catalogs do refer to them. Order your own color poster of the $15 AHS Plant Heat-Zone Map by calling the AHS at 800-777-7931, extension 10. Visit the American Horticulture Society's Web site for more information and a downloadable map at www.ahs.org/publications/heat_zone_map.htm. The site also offers a zip code search feature to locate your particular Heat Zone.

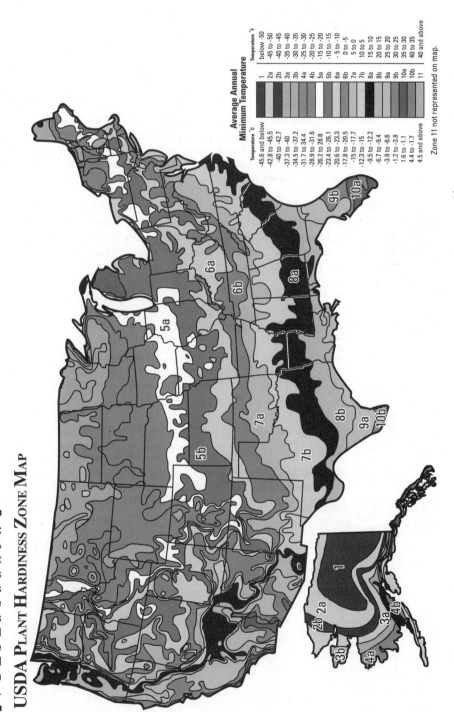

Figure 3-3: The USDA Plant Hardiness Zone Maps indicate each zone's expected average annual minimum temperature.

USDA Plant Hardiness Zone Map

Average Annual Minimum Temperature

Zone	Temperature °C	Temperature °F
1	-45.6 and below	below -50
2a	-42.8 to -45.5	-45 to -50
2b	-40 to -42.7	-40 to -45
3a	-37.3 to -40	-35 to -40
3b	-34.5 to -37.2	-30 to -35
4a	-31.7 to -34.4	-25 to -30
4b	-28.9 to -31.6	-20 to -25
5a	-26.2 to -28.8	-15 to -20
5b	-23.4 to -26.1	-10 to -15
6a	-20.6 to -23.3	- 5 to -10
6b	-17.8 to -20.5	0 to -5
7a	-15 to -17.7	5 to 0
7b	-12.3 to -15	10 to 5
8a	-9.5 to -12.2	15 to 10
8b	-6.7 to -9.4	20 to 15
9a	-3.9 to -6.6	25 to 20
9b	-1.2 to -3.8	30 to 25
10a	1.6 to -1.1	35 to 30
10b	4.4 to -1.7	40 to 35
11	4.5 and above	40 and above

Zone 11 not represented on map.

Resisting Diseases and Pests Naturally

Plant breeders work constantly to introduce more *varieties,* or plant selections, that offer unique characteristics different from that of the original species. One of the most important factors that breeders look for in a variety is *disease resistance* — the ability to remain unaffected or only slightly damaged by a particular disease. Many modern plant varieties resist devastating plant diseases, such as the potato blight that led to the Irish famine and the apple scab fungus that disfigures fruits and foliage. Some plants are completely immune to infection and others suffer only minimal damage compared to other, susceptible varieties.

It helps to know which diseases and pests are most likely to affect the plants that you want to grow. I mention these potential problems in the plant descriptions in Part IV. Whenever they're available, I also recommend disease-resistant varieties. Catalog write-ups often mention disease resistance as well, because it's a good selling point.

Culturing Community

Natural plant communities contain many species of trees, shrubs, and perennial and annual plants. This rich diversity helps each plant species survive in many ways:

- **Scattered populations** avoid insect and disease devastation because all the plants of a particular species aren't located next to each other. While pests damage or kill some plants, they may overlook others.

- **Beneficial insects** and other creatures that prey on plant pests find habitat in neighboring plant species.

- **Deep-rooted plants** often bring soil nutrients to the surface where they are released by decomposition, benefiting more shallow-rooted species.

- **Nitrogen-fixing plants,** which can take nitrogen from the air and deposit it in the soil, benefit other species nearby.

- **Tall, sun-loving species** provide shade, shelter, and support for lower-growing, shade-preferring species.

When plants grow artificially in *monocultures,* which are large colonies of a single species, they lose the benefits of a diverse plant community. Pests and diseases spread easily from one plant to the next and plants rapidly deplete the soil of nutrients.

Many farmers and gardeners recognize and take advantage of the benefits of *polyculture;* that is, growing more than one crop in a field. In fact, whole agricultural systems are based on polyculture, such as those discussed in Chapter 1. Growing plants that mutually benefit one another makes sense, and is simple to do in home gardens and landscapes. Examples include adding clover, which takes nitrogen from the air and adds it to the soil, to your lawn and planting shade-loving, ground-covering plants under leafy trees to protect soil and tree roots from erosion.

Designing Low-Maintenance Landscapes

The best designs conserve energy — both yours and the environment's — and look pleasing to the eye. Good designers observe and discover how the different parts of the landscape — home, gardens, and other functional areas of a site — relate to each other and use those relationships to direct their design. For example, the kitchen, compost bin, and vegetable garden relate to each other, so they should be as close together as possible; gardens that require frequent watering must be located near a water source; and so on.

The idea of saving time and energy is key for busy gardeners — even organic ones. People often think that an organic garden requires more work than a chemically-dependent one, but actually, the opposite is true. Initially, an organic garden and landscape does take work to design and install, but the payoff is in much less work and healthier plants down the road.

Planning for low maintenance

Planning a low-maintenance landscape isn't complicated, if you take it one step at a time. Think through each of the following steps as completely as you can and use plenty of paper to take notes and scribble ideas.

1. **Write down what you want from your landscape — vegetable garden, herb patch, flowers for bouquets, fruit trees or shrubs, a compost bin, tool storage, recycling bins — everything you can think of.**

2. **Look at your list and think about how the different items on it relate to each other.**

   Consider the distance between places that depend on each other. Does it make more sense to put the vegetable garden at the far corner of the backyard or close to the kitchen and tool-storage area in the garage?

3. **Think about how often you will visit each area and jot down that information.**

   Places that you visit daily, like the trash, compost, and vegetable garden, should be located closest to the house. Areas that need infrequent maintenance, such as an orchard, can be situated farther away.

4. **Consider how many functions each element can fulfill.**

   Trees can provide shade, fruit, ornament, and windbreak, among other things. Vegetable gardens can be ornamental and provide food. Flowers attract hummingbirds, color the yard, provide garnish for salads and bouquets for the table, and provide habitat for beneficial insects.

When you're done brainstorming your list, it's time to draw up a plan that makes sense on the ground (see the following section).

Making a map

Before you can put your plan into action, you must assess your site as it currently exists. One of the most important ways that organic gardeners encourage healthy, pest-resistant plants is to plant them where they can naturally thrive. But you have to know something about your site before you can match the plants to their right places.

Grab a buddy, the longest tape measure you own or can borrow, and pencil and paper and head outside. I'm going to lead you through a quick and dirty map-making exercise.

1. **Draw the outlines of major features of your property, including buildings and property lines.**

   Use your tape measure and do your best to draw to scale, with everything in the correct proportion to everything else, but don't agonize over it: Neatness doesn't count. For long distances, measure the length of your stride, and multiply it times the number of strides it takes you to get from one end to the other.

   Sketch in the location of important rooms, windows, and exterior doors of your house. Remember to add permanent features, like the driveway, deck, and shed.

   Make an arrow on your map to indicate the direction of north — you'll need that information as you plan your garden.

2. **Note the following natural features on your map.**

   • **Sun and shade:** Label the sunny and shady spots around your yard, so that you can take advantage of them. If you have lived in the house long enough, note the sun and shade at different times of the day and year.

- **Views:** If you plan to do some landscaping, note the nice and not-so-nice views around your property. Remember to check the views out your windows, too.

- **Soil, slope, and water:** Draw arrows on your map that point down slopes. Circle areas where water pools or runs after a rainstorm. Note places where your soil stays muddy or drains quickly.

- **Wind:** Note the direction and strength of the prevailing winds across your site at different times of the year.

- **Existing plants and natural features:** Use circles to draw existing trees and shrubs that you intend to keep. Record the width of the plant *canopy* by measuring from one edge of the *drip line* — where rain drips from the foliage to the ground — to the other. Note the location and sizes of gardens, large rocks, and other features you want to preserve.

Your map may resemble the one in Figure 3-4 when you're done. Resist the temptation to add "things to do" to this map at this stage. Save that for the following section.

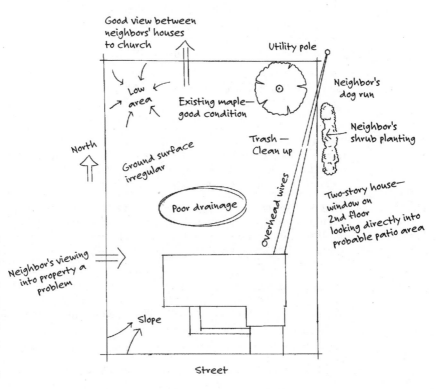

Figure 3-4:
A detailed map of your property notes the location of significant features.

Putting it all together

Here's where your dreams meet reality. The idea is to take your list of projects and match them to the most appropriate places in your yard. For this project, lay tracing paper over your map or make a bunch of photocopies so that you can doodle ideas at will without messing up the original. As you try out different combinations and placements, keep the following tips in mind:

- **Prioritize your list of desires.** Put them into a timeframe or order of steps. For example, you may have to build a deer-excluding fence before planting an orchard or vegetable garden. Preparing soil comes before planting.

- **Think long-term.** Some things take a day to accomplish, while other projects stretch out for months or even years. Break up long projects into shorter, prioritized steps.

- **Concentrate on the areas closest to the house first.** Put your most intensive gardens and use areas near the house and plan to install them before you tackle the outlying areas.

- **Conserve energy.** Use gravity, sun, shade, wind, and precipitation to your advantage. It's easier to move a barrel of water or a cart of compost downhill, for example, than uphill. Note the places where soil warms up first in the spring and plant your early-season vegetables there.

- **Consider maintenance.** Decide how much time you can realistically devote to maintaining your gardens and landscape plants and plan accordingly. Don't sketch in a 400 square foot vegetable garden if you only have time to weed and harvest a garden half that size.

- **Think multi-purpose.** Make plants and built-in features serve more that one function. For example, use a fence or plants to support an ornamental or food-producing vine, screen an unpleasant view, prevent trespassing, enclose a private space, and deflect wind.

- **Play matchmaker.** Make a list of plants that you want to grow. Next to each one, write down whether it needs full sun, part shade, or shade. In another column, note soil and moisture preferences. Group plants with similar needs and look at the places on your map where each group would be happiest.

- **Avoid obstacles.** Put trees, shrubs, and perennial plants where they will have room to mature. If you have overhead utility lines, avoid planting trees under or near them. Choose shrubs that won't cover the windows of your house and plant them so that they won't rub on the siding in 5 or 10 years.

Part II
Working with Your Soil

The 5th Wave   By Rich Tennant

"So? How's the soil, Al? Too much acid?
What? Come on, Al – don't spoil your lunch."

In this part . . .

Ready to get down and dirty? This part is the heart of the book because healthy soil is where organic gardening — and healthy plants — begin.

Chapter 4 gives you the tools to evaluate the soil that you have and good ideas about how to improve it. Compost is king in this chapter, and I get up close and personal with manure, too (whew!). Flip to Chapter 5 for the lowdown on fertilizers that come from plants, animals, and minerals — and find out how to use them.

Chapter 4

Building Healthy Soil

In This Chapter

▶ Understanding the type of soil you have
▶ Adjusting the pH and nutrient levels
▶ Getting in touch with organic matter
▶ Making compost
▶ Working the soil

*O*rganic gardeners know that if you feed the soil, plants will feed themselves. Building healthy soil is the single most important thing you can do to ensure the success of your garden and landscape plants.

Healthy soil is alive with microorganisms that feed upon and decompose organic matter and release nutrients for plants to use. Beneficial microorganisms in the soil prey on harmful ones and protect plant roots from diseases and pests. Earthworms and other soil creatures tunnel through the soil, opening up spaces for oxygen, water, and nutrients to move freely.

New research into soil and plant health is showing just how important the life below ground is to the health and well-being of the life above ground. Many pesticides and synthetic fertilizers destroy that subterranean life, while organic gardening practices intend to promote it.

Soil health is so important that I suggest that before starting a vegetable, perennial, or annual flower garden, you consider spending one growing season just building the fertility of the soil — *before* planting. I know that takes discipline, but one season spent adding organic matter, nutrients, and adjusting the pH may save you years of struggling to produce healthy plants. The soil and the life within it are that important to your garden.

Knowing Your Soil

Soil has several facets to its personality, including pH, organic matter and nutrient levels, and soil type, and it's important to understand a little about each of them. The most basic factor you need to know about is *soil type,* which is the composition of the soil's particles you inherit in your garden. Knowing your soil's type helps you determine what you'll need to do — or not do, — to build healthy soil.

Soil types come in three main categories, called sand, silt, and clay, but many combinations of these exist. Each types has its strengths and weaknesses:

- ✔ **Clay soil:** Clay soil has the most potentially high natural fertility, but it can be difficult to work with. Clay's individual soil particles are so small that they have little room for water and air to squeeze between them. On a practical level, this means that clay soil stays wet longer, contains little oxygen, and dries as hard as concrete. A wet spring may mean a delay in planting, while a dry summer causes the soil to crack and harden.

- ✔ **Sandy soil:** Sand particles are large, leaving lots of room for water and air to move between them, allowing sandy soil dry out quickly. Nutrients leach through sandy soils quickly, too, however, making them naturally less fertile and prone to drought.

- ✔ **Silt soils:** Silt soils have moderate-sized particles that hold some water and air, but also allow the water to drain. They have moderate amounts of fertility, are easy to work with, and make life easy for the gardener.

You may have heard some gardeners singing the praises of loam and wondered what the term meant. *Loam* is soil that consists of about 40 percent sand, 40 percent silt, and 20 percent clay. It holds optimum amounts of water, oxygen, and nutrients for most plant growth.

So how do you know what type of soil you have? You probably have a mixture of sand, silt, and clay, but to find the predominant type of soil in your garden all you need to do is reach out and touch it. Take a small handful of damp soil in your hand, as shown in Figure 4-1. Rub a pinch of it between your thumb and pointing finger. If it feels gritty, it's mostly sand; if it feels slick and slimy, it's mostly clay. If it feels like something between those two, it's mostly silt.

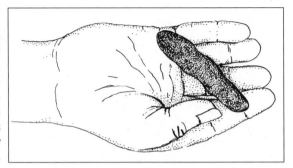

Figure 4-1:
Squeeze a
clump of soil
in your hand
and then
look at the
soil to
determine
whether it's
mostly clay
or sand.

For a more accurate measurement of the amounts of clay, silt, and sand in your soil, you can do the jar test. Here's how to do it:

1. **Collect soil from several places in your garden.**

   Mix the samples thoroughly and measure out 1 cup of it.

2. **Let the soil air dry on a sheet of paper until crumbly. Crush chunks until the soil is very fine. Remove stones and debris.**

3. **Place soil in a narrow glass jar, such as a pint-sized canning jar.**

4. **Add 1 teaspoon of non-sudsy dishwasher detergent.**

5. **Fill jar ⅔ full of water, seal, and shake vigorously to mix the contents.**

6. **Put down the jar and start a timer.**

7. **Measure and mark the level of settled soil after 1 minute.**

   This is sand. Measure again in 2 hours and subtract the sand layer to find the amount of silt. After several days, the clay will settle out. Measure this top layer, subtracting the sand and silt, to find the amount of clay.

8. **Divide the height of each level by the total height of the settled soil and multiply by 100 to find the percentage of each.**

   For example, if the total settled soil is 6 inches high and the sand portion is 3 inches, the percent sand is 50 percent. (3/6 × 100 = 50%)

Let it drain

Knowing your type of soil helps you determine how well water will drain through it. What's the big deal with drainage? Well, certain plants, such as lavender, need soil that drains quickly to thrive, while other plants, such as willows, can survive and flourish in wet soils. Sometimes drainage is obvious. Puddles in your lawn a day or two after heavy rains certainly indicate poor drainage. But, sometimes a layer of clay lurks underneath a loamy or sandy soil, which causes water to linger in otherwise well-drained soil. So, before you plant, especially trees and shrubs, dig a hole to check what lies beneath the surface.

Here's how to check for *percolation* or soil drainage:

1. **Dig a 1-foot diameter hole, 1 foot deep.**

2. **Fill the hole with water.**

3. **Time how long it takes for the water to drain.**

If the water drains out in 10 minutes or less, your soil drains too fast and probably dries out too quickly. In well-drained soils, the water drains within 10 to 30 minutes. If it drains within 4 hours, the drainage is okay for most plants. If it takes more than 4 hours, the soil is poorly drained. Use this information to help choose the most appropriate plants for your soil. Keep in mind that adding organic matter, such as compost, to the soil can improve the drainage of both sandy and clayey soils. See the "Organic Matter: The Soul of the Soil" section in this chapter.

The soil test

After you know the type of soil you have and how well it drains (see the previous section), you need to know its pH and nutrient levels. The *soil pH* measures the alkalinity (sweetness) or acidity (sourness) of the soil. It's important to know whether your soil is acid, which is below pH 7 on a scale from 0 to 14, or alkaline (above pH 7), because some nutrients are available to plants only within a specific pH range. Most plants prefer pH between pH 5.5 and 7.5.

A simple rule is that if your plants are growing, flowering, and fruiting well, the nutrient levels are fine. If you're just starting out or if you aren't satisfied with the growth of your plants, a little testing can help you get to the root of the matter. Too high or too low pH or unbalanced nutrient levels can result in yellow, stunted, and unproductive plants. Unhealthy plants are more prone to insects and disease attacks, which translates into more work for you and less satisfaction from your garden. And that's not what you want!

Ready, set, test!

Testing your soil is like doing home repairs. You can do it yourself or have someone else do it for you. Doing it yourself with a home test kit is simple and gives you a basic pH reading and an estimation of the major nutrients in your soil. You can buy test kits at nurseries and garden centers, and they range from extremely simple to elaborate. The more sophisticated tests cost more, but give you more accurate results.

You can also send a soil sample to a lab for testing. You simply take a representative sample of the soil from your garden, fill out a form, and mail or take it to the lab. The results are more accurate and detailed than if you do the test yourself with a home kit, plus testing labs can look for things that home kits cannot, such as organic matter and micronutrients. Soil-testing labs also can test for heavy metals and other industrial residues. Soils near heavily traveled roads or on old industrial sites can contain lead and other unwanted metals that you may want to know about before planting a vegetable garden.

Lab reports give you the current levels of nutrients and soil pH and also offer specific recommendations about which nutrients to add to your soil and in what quantity for your plants' optimum growth. Lab tests can get costly, however, especially if you have many different types of plantings, such as perennial flowers, vegetables, and lawn, and you do separate tests for each type. Check the phone book under "Soil Testing" for private soil labs in your area or contact your state university's extension service. Many state universities test soil for a small fee or can recommend a private testing lab.

pH test results

Soil tests measure two components: your soil pH and its major nutrients. Most plants grow best in the range between 6.0 and 7.0. Some plants, however, such as blueberries and rhododendrons, like a highly acid soil (pH below 5.0), so you may need to adjust the pH to individual plants.

In general, you add lime or limestone to raise the pH and sulfur to lower it. How much lime or sulfur you need to add depends on the type of soil you have and its current pH. The soil-testing lab will make a specific recommendation based on that information.

When adding lime or sulfur to your soil, remember to wear gloves and a dust mask because this material can be very dusty and irritating if inhaled. You can spread the material by hand or use a drop spreader made to spread grass seed on a lawn. In the garden, work the lime or sulfur into the top few inches of soil with a rake or shovel after spreading.

Don't expect results right away. Most limestone or powdered sulfur products take a few months to react with the soil enough to change the pH to the desired levels — another good reason to prepare your soil a season before you plan to plant.

Nutrient test results

Soil tests also show the quantities of soil nutrients that are available to plants, especially the three nutrients that plants use in the greatest amount — nitrogen, phosphorus, and potassium. Soils also contain many micronutrients, such as magnesium and calcium, that plants need in smaller amounts. If any nutrient is insufficient, plants will not grow to their maximum potential.

More important than the actual levels of the nutrients, however, is the balance of nutrients with each other for the proper functioning of your plants. For example, too much of one nutrient may create a situation where other nutrients, though plentiful in the soil, won't be taken up by the plants. For more on nutrients and fertilizers, turn to Chapter 5.

Organic Matter: The Soul of the Soil

"Organic matter" is the mantra of the organic gardener and farmer. It's the soul of the soil and a universal component of healthy earth.

Organic matter is basically dead plant and animal stuff, including grass clippings, leaves, hay, straw, pine needles, wood chips, sawdust, manure, and anything else that used to be alive. It's a miracle worker that improves soil in several vital ways.

- ✔ **Feeds microorganisms and other soil life.** Beneficial bacteria, protozoa, fungi, beneficial nematodes, and other soil microbes consume the carbon in organic matter (and each other) and excrete nitrogen, which plants use for growth. Earthworms, beetles, and other creatures also eat organic matter and tunnel through the soil, creating beneficial air spaces and excreting nutrients.

- ✔ **Decreases harmful disease organisms.** As beneficial microbes increase in numbers, they prey upon and control harmful, plant-damaging nematodes and fungi.

- ✔ **Improves the soil structure.** As organic matter decomposes, bacteria and fungi form *humus,* which helps improve all soils. It helps sandy soils stick together better and hold water and nutrients. It also helps open up spaces between small, sticky clay particles so that clay soil drains better and contains more oxygen.

- ✔ **Increases reserve of soil nutrients.** Soil microbes store nutrients in their bodies, which they release as they die or are consumed by other microbes. The more microbes the soil contains, the more nutrients it can store.

Add organic matter any time you can to your plantings — whether it's straw mulch between vegetable garden beds, compost around perennial flowers, or bark mulch around trees or shrubs. I like to add a 3- to 4-inch layer of dead leaves to my garden, either in the fall or up to one month before I start my vegetable or annual flower garden, and work it into the soil.

Soil microbes don't work efficiently when the soil is cold and wet, such as in early spring. They also use nutrients in the soil to fuel their eating, so if you give them too much carbon-rich material to work with at once, they tie up the nutrients, creating a deficiency for the plants. If you live in a cold-winter climate, add straw, leaves, and other raw organic matter in the summer or autumn when the soil is still warm to allow them plenty of time to decompose before plants need the nutrients.

Dung ho!

Few things get me as excited as a good pile of aged animal manure, especially if it's free and the owner has a bucket loader. If you're not yet a connoisseur of manure, think of it as processed organic matter, which has already begun decomposing. It does wonders for soil health and plant growth.

You can add the droppings of many different farm (and sometimes wild) animals to your garden, giving the soil all the benefits of organic matter plus a little higher boost of the N-P-K nutrients (see the "Nutrient test results" section, earlier in this chapter and Chapter 5). Like a fine wine, however, manure is best when aged before using. Fresh manure may be too potent for tender plants and can contain bacteria that make people sick. It's a good idea to let manure age for six months to a year before using, or you can compost it (see the "Compost: The prince of organic matter" section, later in this chapter). If you add fresh manure to your garden in the fall and mix it into the soil, it will be ready for planting in the spring. Table 4-1 shows animal manures that you may find locally or bagged at your garden center, along with their relative nutrient values (dry weight) and some additional comments.

Table 4-1	Common Animal Manures	
Animal	*Percent N-P-K*	*Tips*
Chicken	3-1-1	Strong smell, don't use fresh on young plants.
Cow	3-0.5-2	Can be very moist.
Horse	2.5-0.5-1	May contain lots of weed seeds.
Llama, alpaca	4-0.6-2	Compost before using.
Rabbit	5-3-2	Strong smell, compost before using.
Sheep	3.5-0.5-2	Mild smell

If you live near a zoo, you may have access to the manures of wild animals, such as elephants and giraffes You can also use fish water from your freshwater aquarium.

Keep these rules in mind when using manures:

- **Compost fresh manures before using.** Mix into a compost pile and age before using or spread on the garden and work it into the soil at least a month before planting.

- **Select manure from the oldest pile at the farm.** Many farm manure piles contain lots of additional organic matter such as sawdust from horse or chicken bedding. Chances are good that manure from the oldest pile has naturally decomposed this bedding the most and can be used directly on your garden

- **Use bagged manures.** They're usually composted and ready-to-use. If you need lots of manure, however, buying bags can be costly.

- **Avoid cat, dog, pig, and human manures.** They can carry diseases that affect humans.

- **Apply composted manure annually.** In general, add a 2- to 3-inch layer of manure to garden beds and around perennial plants at least once a year.

Green manure

Another great way to get organic matter into your garden is to grow your own. *Green manures* are plants that you grow specifically to cut down and mix into the soil to add organic matter and nutrients. If you don't have access to a good supply of animal manures, don't want to buy bags and bags of manure, have a large garden area, or don't have other forms of organic matter, such as hay, try growing green manures. Broadcast the seed as you would for a lawn and let the green manure crop grow through the gardening season. Turn the plants under the soil before they produce seeds, if you want to prevent the plants from returning next season. In addition to adding organic matter, green manures provide other advantages, including the following:

- **Control erosion:** Hardy crops such as winter rye and wheat cover the soil over the dormant season, preventing wind and rain from eroding precious topsoil.

- **Loosen compacted soils:** Some green manures, such as alfalfa, have aggressive roots, which can grow 3 feet deep into the soil. They break up compacted soils and even "mine" nutrients deep in the soil, bringing them to the surface where other plants can use them.

✔ **Balance nutrients:** Some green manures, such as clover, vetch, peas, and beans, are legumes, which means that they have the unique ability to take nitrogen from the air and make it available to plants — often in the same year. These crops are great to grow right before you grow a heavy nitrogen-feeding crop, such as sweet corn.

✔ **Control weeds:** Some green manures, such as buckwheat, grow so quickly and aggressively that they can shade or crowd out weeds growing in the same ground.

✔ **Maintain high levels of soil microorganisms:** When the plants are incorporated into the soil, they feed the essential microbes that make nutrients available to plants. The plant residues also provide surfaces on which the microbes can live.

✔ **Attract beneficial insects:** Some green manures, such as clover, have flowers that beneficial insects love. These insects help with pollination and insect pest control in your garden.

The following plants are valuable green manures that you can grow in your garden. Farm supply stores and mail-order catalogs usually offer the widest selection, but many garden centers sell the most common ones. Consult the package or catalog description for the amount of seed you need to sow per square foot.

✔ Berseem clover

✔ Crimson clover

✔ Hairy vetch

✔ Fava beans

✔ Cowpeas

✔ Oats

✔ Barley

✔ Winter wheat

✔ Annual ryegrass

✔ Buckwheat

✔ Winter rye

A variation on the green manure theme is to use *cover crops,* plants that grow during the dormant season to add organic matter and prevent erosion. Many of the same plants listed as green manures, such as winter rye and winter wheat, can be grown as cover crops. Plant these before your dormant season (fall in the north or early summer in the deep southern and southwestern U.S.) and let them grow. A few weeks before planting, work the crops into the soil and you'll get the benefits of adding organic matter, plus you protect your soil when normally nothing else would have been growing.

Compost: The prince of organic matter

The best and most refined of organic matters is *compost,* which is organic matter and/or manures that have decomposed until they resemble loamy soil. Thoroughly decomposed compost contains lots of humus — the beneficial, soil-improving material your plants need. Whether the original source was grass clippings, sawdust, animal manure, or vegetable scraps from your kitchen, all organic matter eventually becomes compost.

Whether you make your own compost (see the "Compost happens" section, later in this chapter), or buy it ready-made, you can add finished compost anytime to the garden or around plants. I pile on a 2- to 3-inch layer annually around my plants and on my garden beds.

Why not just add raw organic matter to your garden instead of composting it? By composting the materials first, the final product is uniform in color, nutrients, and texture; is odor free; and contains fewer viable weed seeds and potential disease organisms (depending on how it was composted). Your plants will be happy with you for treating them so well.

Buying compost

As gardeners have become more aware of the value of compost, more sources of it have become available. You can buy compost from a number of sources either in bulk (back the truck right up) or bagged, depending on where you live.

- **Bagged:** Bagged compost is obviously the easiest way to buy it, especially if you have a small yard or container garden. The down side, however, is that you don't really know the quality of the compost until you get it home.

  Often, what you'll find is bagged manure, which is basically compost made from animal manures, and it may be made from a variety of sources. The benefits of bagged compost and bagged manure are similar because they both are primarily organic matter. Look for the word "organic" on the bag or some other indication that the contents don't come from contaminated sources, including sewage sludge.

- **Bulk:** For larger quantities of compost, buy it in bulk. The price is less per quantity and you can check the quality of the compost, as well. Many private companies, municipalities, and community groups make and sell compost. Often they'll even deliver the compost to your yard for a fee.

Use these tips to evaluate bulk compost:

- **Consider the source.** Before buying the compost, ask about the primary organic matter sources that were used to make the compost. Compost made from yard waste (leaves and grass clippings) is usually considered the safest and best. Other compost may contain ingredients that had contaminants, such as herbicides from agricultural crop residues and heavy metals from municipal wastes, which may affect the growth of your plants or accumulate toxins in your soil.

- **Look at the color and texture.** Finished compost should look dark and have a crumbly texture without any large pieces of undecomposed organic matter, such as branches or pieces of wood.

- **Squeeze it.** If water oozes out when you squeeze a handful of the material, it's too wet; if it blows away easily, it's too dry.

- **Give it a whiff.** The smell should be earthy without a strong ammonia or sour smell.

Private and university laboratories can test compost for organic matter content, maturity, and impurities. An organic matter content test indicates whether you're buying compost or soil mixed with compost. (Good quality compost should be made of least 40 percent organic matter). A compost maturity test also tells the rate of decomposition of the compost. If the rate is high, the material may not be finished decomposing. The ideal compost is slightly warm and "approaching maturity" (as defined by the compost maturity test). The laboratories can also test your garden soil for organic matter and make recommendations about how much more you need to add.

Compost happens

Making your own is probably the simplest way to ensure high quality compost and save some money. It's really not as complicated as you may think: The many commercial composting bins and containers on the market make it a mess-free and hassle-free process.

At least two schools of thought exist on building composting piles:

- ✔ The active school makes uniform piles, mixes materials thoroughly at the correct ratios of carbon (brown stuff) and nitrogen (green stuff) (see the "Let's talk ratios" section for more on carbon/nitrogen ratios), and keeps the pile watered just enough to keep it moist, but has enough air to breathe. They enjoy finished compost a month or two from the start.

- ✔ A second school says, pile it in the backyard somewhere and eventually (within six months or so) it'll turn into usable compost. After all, everything rots doesn't it?

While the second school of thought is technically correct, you may find advantages to building a pile by the rules espoused by the first school. A well-constructed pile — built with the proper dimensions and maintained correctly — heats up fast; decomposes uniformly and quickly; kill many diseases, insects, and weed seeds; doesn't smell; and is easy to turn and maintain. Conversely, a pile just thrown together rarely heats up and, therefore, takes longer to decompose. This type of *cold composting* doesn't kill any diseases, insects, or weed seeds; may smell bad; and definitely looks messy.

Containing your compost pile makes it look neater, helps you maintain the correct moisture, and prevents animals from getting into it. You can build your own, as shown in Figure 4-2, or buy a commercial home composting unit. The advantages of a commercial composter include the availability of a wide range of attractive sizes and shapes and ease of use. Choose from box-shaped plastic and wooden bins and barrels or elevated and easy-to-turn tumblers, as shown in Figure 4-3. Store-bought bins are costly, however, and produce only small quantities of compost at a time, especially compared to a homemade bin that's built from scrap lumber or wire.

Figure 4-2:
Build a simple wooden bin to hold your compost pile.

Figure 4-3:
Commercial
composters
help you
make
compost
yourself.

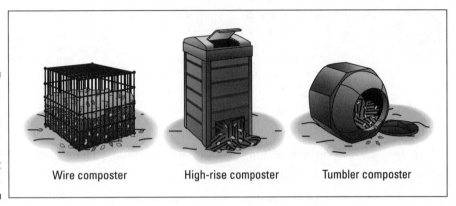

Wire composter   High-rise composter   Tumbler composter

Here's what you need to know to build a good compost pile:

1. **Choose a shady location, out of the way, but still within view so that you don't forget about the pile.**

   The soil under it should be well drained.

2. **Make a bin.**

   Create a wire cylinder that's 3- to 4-feet in diameter or build a three-sided box (similar to the one in Figure 4-2), that's 4- to 5-feet high and wide.

3. **Add brown materials.**

   Add a 6-inch layer of "brown" organic matter, such as hay, straw, old leaves, and sawdust, to the bottom of the container.

4. **Add green materials.**

   Add a 2- to 3-inch layer of "green" organic matter, such as green grass clippings, manure, table scraps, or even high-nitrogen fertilizer, such as cottonseed meal, on top of the brown layer.

5. **Repeat these layers, watering each one as you go, until the pile is 4- to 5-feet tall and fills the bin.**

   A smaller pile won't heat up well and a larger pile can be difficult to manage.

6. **Within two days, mix the layers together thoroughly.**

   Particle size should be varied, smaller particles hasten decomposition.

7. **Cover the pile with a tarp to keep rain away and preserve moisture.**

   If the pile gets too soggy or too dry, it won't heat up.

Use the following tips to figure out what to add to a pile, what not to add, and in what ratios to add it:

- **What to add to the pile or composter:** What you put in the compost pile is up to you — just remember that it needs to be from an organic material. Here's a short list of possibilities:

  - Hay, straw, pine needles

  - Leaves

  - Kitchen scraps (egg shells, old bread, vegetable and fruit scraps)

  - Animal manure, except for dog, cat, pig, or human

  - Old vegetables, flowers, or trimmings from trees and shrubs

  - Sawdust

  - Wood chips

  - Weeds

  - Shredded black and white newspaper. (In the past, color printing used heavy metals in the ink. Most color printing now uses soy-based inks, but I think it's better to avoid them in the garden altogether to be on the safe side.)

- **What not to add:** Some items don't belong in your compost pile. While hot compost piles can kill off many diseases, weed seeds, and insects, it's not a sure thing and some of these unpleasant guests may survive to invade your garden again. Certain materials can also invite unwanted wildlife to the pile or spread human diseases. Avoid adding the following to your compost bin:

  - Kitchen scraps like meats, oils, fish, dairy products, and bones. They attract unwanted animals, such as rats and raccoons, to the pile.

  - Weeds that have gone to seed or that spread by their roots, such as quackgrass.

  - Diseased or insect-infested vegetable or flower plants.

  - Herbicide-treated grass clippings or weeds.

  - Dog, cat, or pig feces.

- **Let's talk ratios:** In composting corners, you often hear about the *C/N ratio* or *carbon to nitrogen ratio*. Basically, all organic matter can be divided into carbon-rich (brown stuff) and nitrogen-rich (green stuff) materials. Using the right mixture of brown to green stuff when building a compost pile encourages the pile to heat up and decompose efficiently. Although nearly any combination of organic materials eventually decomposes, for the fastest and most efficient compost pile in town, strike the correct balance (C/N ratio) between the two types — usually 25 to 1.

Table 4-2 shows which common compost materials are high in carbon and which materials are high in nitrogen. Notice that the softer materials, such as fresh grass clippings, tend to be higher in nitrogen than hard materials, such as sawdust. Mix these together to form a pile with an average C/N ratio of 25:1 to 30:1, and you'll be well on your way to beautiful compost. Use the following ratios as guidelines. Actual ratios vary depending on the sources of the materials and other factors. And speaking of sources — be sure that your compost materials haven't been contaminated with pesticides or other chemicals.

Table 4-2	Carbon/Nitrogen Ratios of Various Materials
Material	*C/N Ratio*
Table scraps	15:1
Grass clippings	19:1
Old manure	20:1
Fresh alfalfa hay	12:1
Fruit waste	25:1
Corn stalks	60:1
Old leaves	80:1
Straw	80:1
Paper	170:1
Sawdust	500:1
Wood	700:1

Quick and easy compost recipes

To make the most compost in the shortest amount of time, try some of these proven recipes. For each recipe, mix the ingredients thoroughly and follow the directions in the next section, "Keeping your pile happy." Depending on weather and compost ingredients, you should have finished compost within one to two months.

✔ **Recipe #1:** Four parts kitchen scraps from fruits and vegetables, 2 parts chicken or cow manure, 1 part shredded newspaper (black ink only), and 1 part shredded dry leaves.

✔ **Recipe #2:** Two parts kitchen scraps, 1 part chicken manure, and 1 part shredded leaves.

✔ **Recipe #3:** Two parts grass clippings, 1 part chicken manure, and 1 part shredded leaves.

Keeping your pile happy

A hot pile is a happy pile. If you follow the method of just throwing every-thing together, the pile will rarely heat up. If you follow the method of build-ing the pile carefully with the recommended C/N ratio, as covered in the "Compost happens (making your own)" section, the pile will start to cook within a week. Now you need to keep it cooking. Here's the procedure:

1. **Keep the pile moist by periodically watering it.**

   Dig into the pile about 1 foot to see if it's moist. If not, water the pile thoroughly, but not so that it's soggy. The pile needs air, too, and adding too much water removes air spaces. If you built the pile with moist ingredients, such as kitchen scraps, it won't need watering at first.

2. **Turn the pile when it cools down.**

   Using a garden fork, remove the outside layers and put them aside. Remove the inside layers into another pile and then switch. Place the outside layers in the center of the new pile and the inside layers along the outside of the new pile.

3. **Let it cook again.**

   How hot it gets and how long it cooks depends on the ratio of C/N mate-rials in the pile and whether you have the correct moisture levels.

4. **When it's cool, turn it again.**

   You should have finished compost after two to three turnings. The fin-ished product should be cool, crumbly, dark colored, and earthy smelling.

Sometimes, a compost pile never heats up, smells bad, or contains pieces of undecomposed materials. Chances are that one of the following conditions occurred:

- The pile was too wet or dry.

- You added too many carbon materials and not enough nitrogen materials.

- The pieces of material were too big or packed together. Shred leaves, branches, and pieces of wood to decompose more quickly.

- The pile was too small.

You can find lots of compost aids on the market. *Bioactivators* — packages of concentrated microbes — are one of the most popular because they can speed the decomposition process. These microbes occur naturally, however, and many are already present in a well-constructed compost pile. I advise you to save your money and use microbe-rich compost materials instead. See the "Quick and easy compost recipes" section for ideas.

To Till or Not to Till

Whether or not to use a rotary tiller is an on-going philosophical debate among gardeners, with promoters and detractors on both sides of the issue. Rotary tillers, often called *tillers* for short, are machines with blades or *tines* that chop into the soil, churning (or *tilling*) it and blending everything in the top 6 to 12 inches of soil. The following are some of the factors to consider and arguments on both sides of the fence.

Till at will:

- Tilling is an easy way to incorporate soil amendments, such as lime, compost, and green manure crops into the soil.
- Tilling turns weeds under, facilitating their decomposition.
- Tilling can kill some insects and diseases that may be lurking around the soil surface.
- Tilling makes for a clean garden bed that's easy to plant.

Just say no to tilling:

- Tilling can damage soil structure, increasing the risk of creating a poorly drained and hard-to-work soil, especially if the area is tilled when the soil is still too wet.
- Tilling can kill earthworms and other beneficial soil creatures.
- Tilling hastens the breakdown of desirable organic matter, so you will have to add it more frequently and in greater quantities.
- Tilling promotes erosion, especially when gardening on a slope or very windy area.
- Tilling brings weed seeds up to the surface of the soil where they can readily germinate.

An alternative to tilling that's easier on the soil and gives you more exercise is to use turning tools such as a garden fork, shovel, or U-bar (shown in Figure 4-4). These tools work especially well on small, raised beds where you don't have a lot of earth to turn. A few weeks before planting, add any compost or amendments and use these tools to turn the soil over. Rake the bed smooth and plant to your heart's content.

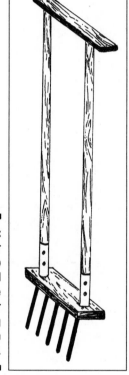

Figure 4-4:
Use a U-bar tool to loosen soil and prepare your planting beds each year.

Chapter 5

Using Organic Fertilizers

In This Chapter

▶ Getting familiar with major and minor nutrients

▶ Knowing when to apply fertilizers

▶ Choosing the right kind of fertilizer

*P*lants need nutrients to grow, flourish, and fend off pests, diseases, and environmental stresses. Giving them the nutrients they need is the real key to successful organic gardening. Healthy soil that contains plenty of compost or organic matter goes a long way toward providing essential nutrients for plant growth, but your plants may still need additional nutrients to grow to their full potential. You need to know which nutrients your plants need for proper growth, what the signs of possible nutrient deficiencies and excesses are, and which sources of organic fertilizers that can supply those nutrients. In this chapter, I give you the lowdown on *organic fertilizers* @those derived from natural plant, animal, and mineral sources — and how to use them.

Why bother with organic fertilizers? Organic fertilizers have many benefits over synthetic chemical fertilizers for both soil and plants. Organic fertilizers release their nutrients more slowly in the soil, when the plants need them, so they last longer. They're also less likely to burn young roots of seedlings, and they enhance the soil health by not harming soil microbes (bacteria, fungi, and company), which help to make many of the soil nutrients available to plants. In general, organic fertilizers are a kinder, gentler way to give plants the nutrients they need.

Knowing the Nutrients

Every organism, including plants, needs certain nutrients to grow and reproduce, fend off diseases and pests, and repair itself. If any nutrients are lacking, plant health is compromised and they can't grow to their full potential. I like to use the example of a leaky bucket. If a bucket has no holes, you can fill it to the top with water and use its full capacity. If it has a hole in its side, though, no matter how small, the bucket's capacity is reduced to the level where the water begins to leak out.

Overall, plants need 16 essential elements or nutrients for proper growth. The nutrients that plants need in the largest quantities are carbon, hydrogen, and oxygen, which provide the fuel for *photosynthesis*. In photosynthesis, green plants take carbon dioxide (carbon and oxygen) from the air (oxygen) and water (hydrogen and oxygen) in the soil to produce the sugars that make plants grow.

The other important plant nutrients come from minerals in the soil, and plants need them in varying quantities. If any of these essential nutrients is deficient in the soil or unavailable due to soil pH (see Chapter 4), plants may show deficiency symptoms. In some cases, an excess amount of a nutrient can cause plant distress or crop failure, too. Excess nitrogen, for example, makes tomatoes produce lots of leaves, but little fruit.

Sometimes soil contains enough nutrients, but environmental conditions, such as soil temperature, nutrient imbalance, and high or low pH, can make some of them unavailable for plants. For example, elements combine with each other in different ways, depending on the soil pH: If the pH is below 5.0, phosphorus combines with iron, aluminum, and manganese to form compounds that plants cannot use. Most nutrients are available in the ideal 6.0 to 7.0 range of soil pH. In cold soil, microorganisms that break down nutrients into plant-usable forms are sluggish and less efficient.

Before adding fertilizer to your soil, take a soil sample to a soil testing lab or farm and garden store or use a home test kit to find out the soil pH and exactly which minerals your plants need and in what quantities. Even if your plants show signs of a nutrient deficiency, your soil may need a pH adjustment, as discussed in Chapter 4, instead of fertilizer. Also note that some plants have special pH and nutrient requirements. Check the plant descriptions in Part IV to find out more.

The big three

No, I'm not talking about the automobile industry, but plant nutrition. Nitrogen, phosphorous, and potassium are often called *macronutrients* or *primary* nutrients because plants need them in the largest quantities. Healthy, fertile soil naturally contains these three elements and plants can easily take them up. But in many cases, you must supplement the soil with fertilizers, especially if you're growing vegetables, fruits, or other demanding crops.

Complete fertilizers contain all three macronutrients — nitrogen (N), phosphorous (P), and potassium (K) — but don't let the term "complete" fool you. It doesn't mean that the fertilizer has all the nutrients that plants need, just that it contains all three of the major ones.

Bags of complete fertilizers contain three numbers, such as 5-3-3, for example. Each number represents a percentage of N-P-K in that bag, as measured by weight. In this case, a bag of 5-3-3 fertilizer contains 5 percent nitrogen, 3 percent phosphorous, and 3 percent potassium. To determine the amount in pounds of each nutrient in the bag, multiply the weight of the bag (say 50 pounds) by the percentage of each nutrient: 50 pounds $\times$ .05 = 2.5 pounds of nitrogen. You need to know the actual amount of nutrients in the bag because a soil test often recommends pounds of *actual* N-P-K to add per square foot to your garden.

Each of these three nutrients plays a critical role in plant growth and development. Here's what they do and their deficiency symptoms to watch for.

- **Nitrogen (N):** This critical element is responsible for the healthy green foliage of plants, as well as protein and chlorophyll development. *Chlorophyll* is the pigment that makes plants green and is a vital component in photosynthesis. Nitrogen moves easily in the soil and leaches out rapidly, especially from sandy soils and in high rainfall areas or irrigated gardens. Plants use lots of nitrogen during the growing season, so it's commonly the most deficient element. If you add too much nitrogen, however, plants will have dark green, leafy growth, but less root development and delayed flowering and fruiting. Symptoms of nitrogen deficiency include slow growth and yellowing leaves, especially on older foliage. Animal manures, soybean meal, and cottonseed meal provide high levels of nitrogen.

- **Phosphorous (P):** Plants need phosphorus for strong root growth; fruit, stem, and seed development; disease resistance; and general plant vigor. Phosphorous doesn't move in the soil as easily as nitrogen does so you don't have to add it as frequently. Depending on where you live in the country, your soil may have plenty of phosphorous, but it may be unavailable to plants. Phosphorus availability depends on warm soil temperatures, pH range, and the levels of other nutrients, such as calcium and potassium, in the soil. Maintain the soil pH between 5 and 7 to keep phosphorous available. Work phosphorous-rich fertilizers into the soil around the root zone at planting time to make them readily accessible by the plant roots. Deficiency symptoms include stunted plants with dark green foliage, reddish-purple stems or leaves, and fruits that drop early. Rock phosphate and bone meal are good sources of phosphorous.

✔ **Potassium (K):** This nutrient, sometimes called *potash,* is essential for vigorous growth, disease resistance, fruit and vegetable flavor and development, and general plant function. Potassium doesn't move around in the soil, so work the fertilizer into the root zone. Potassium also breaks down slowly, so you won't need to add it often. Annual applications of organic matter may supply enough potassium fertilizer, but a soil test is the surest way to determine need. Avoid adding too much potassium fertilizer because it can upset the N-P-K balance in the soil and make other nutrients, such as magnesium, unavailable. Deficiency symptoms include yellow areas along the leaf veins and leaf edges, crinkled and rolled up leaves, and dead twigs. In *conifers* (needle-bearing evergreens), all the needles on the tree become dark blue-green and then turn yellow to reddish-brown. (Note that some conifers, mainly pines, normally shed older, yellow needles.) Florida palms are especially prone to deficiency of this nutrient: Their leaves develop yellow to orange spots on the oldest foliage first and then the leaf edges turn brown and die. Fruit trees may have fruit with poor flavor or not develop properly. Certain animal manures and mineral fertilizers, such as greensand, add potassium to the soil.

Secondary nutrients

Plants need fairly large amounts of three additional essential nutrients, but not in the same quantities as nitrogen, phosphorous, and potassium (see the previous section). Calcium, magnesium, and sulfur are called *secondary* elements. They're essential not only for plant growth, but also for adjusting and maintaining soil pH — the amount of acidity and alkalinity in the soil (see Chapter 4). Calcium and magnesium, found in *dolomitic limestone,* help raise the pH of acid soils toward neutral where most plants grow best. In alkaline soils, sulfur helps lower the pH to the optimum level. These nutrients are also vital to plant functioning and, if excessive or deficient, can upset plants' ability to use other nutrients in the soil.

Although it's rare for home garden soils to be deficient in these nutrients, keep your eye out for these deficiency symptoms.

✔ **Calcium:** Calcium-deficient plants may have twisted, dark green new leaves and leaf tip burn. Flowers may have weak stems, and fruit may develop rotten spots on the bottom (opposite from the stem end).

✔ **Magnesium:** Magnesium-deficient plants have curled leaf edges and discolored older leaves.

✔ **Sulfur:** Sulfur-deficiency results in slow growth and small, spindly plants.

Micronutrients

The essential nutrients that plants need in the smallest quantities are called *micronutrients,* and they include iron, manganese, copper, boron, molybdenum, chlorine, and zinc. Adding too much of any one of these micronutrients can cause more problems than adding none at all. Luckily, organic matter usually supplies adequate amounts of these nutrients. Micronutrient deficiency is often hard to spot because plants vary in their specific needs and symptoms. For example, too little iron can causes blueberry leaves to turn yellow between the veins, while too little boron can cause black spots on beet roots. Maintaining the pH between 6.0 and 7.0 and adding manures and compost often is enough to make micronutrients available for plant use. The microorganisms that feed on organic matter help plants take up these and other nutrients — another good reason to use compost and other organic fertilizers! Other micronutrient sources include kelp/seaweed, bone meal, and blood meal.

Some fertilizers contain additional micronutrients. The most common additives include iron, zinc, molybdenum, and manganese. These elements are usually *chelated,* or chemically attached to other nutrients, so that plants can absorb them more easily. A soil test or tissue analysis is the best way to determine whether these nutrients are deficient.

Fertilizer forms

Garden centers, farm stores, and catalog suppliers offer fertilizers in so many different forms that you may get confused about which ones to choose. Make your decision based on the cost of the actual nutrients, ease of application, and how quickly you want the nutrients to become available to the plants. The application methods simply come down to spraying, spreading, or sprinkling.

- ✔ **Granular:** Among the most common and easily applied forms, granular fertilizers are also among the most economical. Sprinkle by hand or spread them with a lawn spreader around plants or the lawn. Many complete organic fertilizers and specialty fertilizers, such as soybean meal and limestone, come in this form.

  Some granular fertilizers do take time to break down and release their contents to the soil, so apply them a few weeks before planting vegetables and flowers or spread around trees, shrubs, lawns, and perennials for longer-term effect. Generally, the smaller the particle size, the more quickly the fertilizer will become available to plant roots.

If your flowering and vegetable plants need additional nutrients during the growing season, use a complete granular fertilizer as a *side dressing,* sprinkled around the plants. Use liquid or granular fertilizers that dissolve quickly in the soil that will help immediately with the plant's growth. In general, apply a side dressing fertilizer once a month during the active growing season, but always check for signs of over- and under-fertilization before application.

✔ **Liquid:** Although expensive, liquid fertilizers give plants a quick nutrient boost. They are most useful for spraying directly on plant leaves (called *foliar feeding*), and for adding to irrigation systems. For foliar feeding, use water with neutral pH (7.0) and apply only when air temperatures are below 85°. Common liquid fertilizers include fish emulsion, compost or manure tea. You can find a recipe for compost and manure tea in the "Animal-based fertilizers" section in this chapter.

✔ **Bulk:** Organic gardeners use some organic soil amendments, such as manure and compost, in large quantities. More useful as soil conditioners than actual fertilizers (see Chapter 4), you can purchase these products in bags or load the loose product into your pickup truck from local farms and nurseries. They're heavy and harder to handle than granular or liquid fertilizers, but have the added benefit of enhancing the soil structure.

Considering the Sources of Organic Fertilizers

Organic fertilizers generally come from plants, animals, or minerals. Soil organisms break down the material into nutrients that plants can use. Some organic fertilizers contain significant amounts of only one of the major nutrients, such as phosphorus in bone meal, but they often have trace amounts of many other beneficial nutrients. In addition, some gardeners add organic material that improves soil structure and supports soil microorganisms, which helps make nutrients available more quickly, especially in warm weather when they are more active. As a general rule, organic fertilizers release about half their nutrients in the first season and continue to feed the soil over subsequent years.

Commercially formulated fertilizers list specific nutrients levels on the package, but bulk products, such as compost and manure, have widely variable contents. The nutrient levels I mention for each fertilizer in this section are approximate because they vary somewhat depending on the product and supplier.

Plant-based fertilizers

Fertilizers made from plants generally have low to moderate N-P-K values, but their nutrients quickly become available in the soil for your plants to use. Some of them even provide an extra dose of trace minerals and micronutrients. If you don't find all of these at the garden center, check out your local feed store. The most commonly available plant-based fertilizers include the following:

- ✔ **Alfalfa meal:** Derived from alfalfa plants and pressed into a pellet form, alfalfa meal is beneficial for adding nitrogen and potassium (about 2 percent each), as well as trace minerals and growth stimulants. Roses, in particular, seem to like this fertilizer and benefit from up to 5 cups of alfalfa meal per plant every ten weeks, worked into the soil. Add it to your compost pile to speed up the process.

- ✔ **Compost:** As I discussed Chapter 4, compost is mostly beneficial for adding organic matter to the soil. It doesn't add much in the way of fertilizer nutrients itself, but it does enhance and help make available any nutrients in the soil.

- ✔ **Corn gluten meal:** Derived from corn, this powder contains 10 percent nitrogen fertilizer. Apply it only to actively growing plants because it inhibits the growth of seeds. The manufacturer recommends allowing 1 to 4 months after using this product before planting seeds, depending on the soil and weather conditions. Use it on lawns in early spring to green up the grass and prevent annual weed seeds from sprouting.

- ✔ **Cottonseed meal:** Derived from the seed in cotton bolls, this granular fertilizer is particularly good at supplying nitrogen (6 percent) and potassium (1.5 percent). Look for organic cottonseed meal because traditional cotton crops are heavily sprayed with pesticides, some of which can remain in the seed oils. Peaceful Valley Farm Supply carries it (see the "Take-out menu" sidebar in this chapter).

- ✔ **Kelp/seaweed:** Derived from sea plants, you can find this product offered in liquid, powder, or pellet form. Although containing only small amounts of N-P-K fertilizer, kelp meal adds valuable micronutrients, growth hormones, and vitamins that can help increase yields, reduce the plant stress from drought, and increase frost tolerance. Apply it to the soil or as a foliar spray.

- ✔ **Soybean meal:** Derived from soybeans and used in a pellet form, soybean meal is prized for its high nitrogen (7 percent) content and as a source of phosphorous (2 percent). Like alfalfa meal, it is particularly beneficial to nitrogen-loving plants, such as roses.

- **Humus:** When looking at organic fertilizer products, you'll invariably come across those containing humus, humic acid, or humates. Some of these products have almost magical claims as to what they can do for your plants. *Humus, humates,* and *humic acids* are organic compounds often found in compost. Humus is touted to increase soil microbial activity, improve soil structure, and enhance root development of plants. These products have no fertilizer value, but rather are used as stimulants to support soil microbial life that, in turn, support the plants. Use them as supplements, but not to replace proper soil building and nutrition.

Animal-based fertilizers

Whether by land, by air, or by sea, animals, fish, and birds all provide organic fertilizers that can help plants grow. Most animal-based fertilizers provide lots of nitrogen, which plants need for leafy growth. The following are some of the most commonly available ones:

- **Manures:** Animal manures provide lots of organic matter to the soil, but most have low nutrient value. A few, such as chicken manure, do have high available nitrogen content, but should only be used composted because the fresh manure can burn the roots of tender seedlings. You can find much more information on manures and the many available types in Chapter 4.

- **Bat/seabird guano:** Yes, this is what it sounds like — the poop from bats and seabirds. It comes in powdered or pellet form and is actually high in nitrogen (10 to 12 percent). Bat guano only provides about 2 percent phosphorous and no potassium, but seabird guano contains 10 to 12 percent P, plus 2 percent K. The concentrated nitrogen in these products can burn young plants if not used carefully. Use them to make manure tea, as described in this section. They tend to be more expensive than land-animal manures.

- **Blood meal:** It's a bit gruesome, but blood meal is the powdered blood from slaughtered animals. It contains about 14 percent nitrogen and many micronutrients. Leafy, nitrogen-loving plants, such as lettuce, grow well with this fertilizer. It also reportedly repels deer, but may attract dogs and cats.

- **Bone meal:** A popular source of phosphorous (11 percent) and calcium (22 percent), bone meal is derived from animal or fish bones and commonly used in a powdered form on root crops and bulbs. It also contains 2 percent nitrogen and many micronutrients. It may attract rodents.

✔ **Fish products:** Fish by-products make excellent fertilizers. You can buy them in several different forms. *Fish emulsion* is derived from fermented remains of fish. This liquid product can have a fishy smell (even the deodorized version), but it's a great complete fertilizer (5-2-2) and adds trace elements to the soil. When mixed with water, it is gentle, yet effective for stimulating the growth of young seedlings. *Hydrolyzed fish powder* has higher nitrogen content (12 percent) and is mixed with water and sprayed on plants. *Fish meal* is high in nitrogen and phosphorus and is applied to the soil. Some products blend fish with seaweed or kelp for added nutrition and growth stimulation.

You can use animal manures and compost to make liquid fertilizers called *manure tea* or *compost tea*. The nutrients in these teas are readily available for plant use; the teas are gentle enough to use on young plants or spray on the plant foliage to give them a quick boost. Here's how to make manure or compost tea.

1. **Place a shovelful of composted manure in a burlap or other porous cloth bag and secure the top.**

2. **Submerge the bag in about 10 to 15 gallons of water.**

3. **Let the liquid steep for one week or until the water takes on the color of brewed tea.**

   Pour off the manure tea as needed.

4. **Dilute the liquid until it resembles the color of weak brewed tea.**

5. **Use the diluted tea to water around plants.**

Dilute it some more to half-strength tea for young seedlings and as a fertilizer spray.

Using composted human waste to fertilize gardens has been a common practice in countries such as China for generations. In many Western countries, our version of this practice is using composted sewage sludge as fertilizer. Modern sewage treatment plants, however, receive waste from many sources, including industries. Although sludge has fertilizer and soil building value, sewage sludge is *not* generally considered an organic fertilizer because it may contain toxic heavy metals that accumulate in the soil. Although you can buy granular fertilizers made from sludge, organic gardeners generally avoid them.

Rock on with mineral-based fertilizers

Rocks decompose slowly into soil, releasing minerals gradually over a period of years. Organic gardeners use many different minerals to increase the fertility of their soils, but it's a long-term proposition. Some take months or years to fully break down into nutrient forms that plants can use, so one application may last a long time. Rock on!

- **Chilean nitrate of soda:** Mined in the deserts of Chile, this highly soluble, fast-acting granular fertilizer contains 16 percent nitrogen. It's also high in sodium, though, so don't use it on arid soils where salt buildup is likely or on salt-sensitive plants.

- **Epsom salt:** Epsom salt not only helps tired feet; it's a fertilizer too! Containing magnesium (10 percent) and sulfur (13 percent), Epsom salt is a fast-acting fertilizer that you can apply in a granular form or dissolve in water and spray on leaves as a foliar fertilizer. Tomatoes, peppers, and roses love this stuff! Mix 1 tablespoon of Epsom salt in a gallon of water and spray it on when plants start to bloom.

- **Greensand:** Mined in New Jersey from 70 million-year-old marine deposits, greensand contains 3 percent potassium and many micronutrients. It's sold in a powdered form, but breaks down slowly so is used to build the long-term reserves of soil potassium.

- **Gypsum:** This powdered mineral contains calcium (20 percent) and sulfur (15 percent). It's used to add calcium to soils without raising the soil pH.

- **Hard-rock phosphate:** This mineral powder contains 20 percent phosphorous and 48 percent calcium, which can raise soil pH — avoid it if your soil is already alkaline. It breaks down slowly, so use it to build the long-term supply of phosphorous in your soils.

- **Soft-rock phosphate:** Often called colloidal phosphate, soft-rock phosphate contains less phosphorus (16 percent) and calcium (19 percent) than hard-rock phosphate, but the nutrients are in chemical forms that plants can use more easily. This powder breaks down slowly, so one application may last for years in the soil. It also contains many micronutrients.

- **Limestone:** This mined product has various nutrient levels, depending on its source. It's used primarily to raise pH, but *dolomitic* limestone, which is high in calcium (46 percent) and magnesium (38 percent), also adds magnesium to the soil. This powder also comes in an easier to spread granular form. *Calcitic* limestone is high in calcium carbonate (usually above 90 percent). Conduct a soil test (see Chapter 4) for pH and for magnesium to find out which kind of lime and how much to add to your soil.

✔ **Rock dusts:** These powders, which are mined from various rocks, often contain few major nutrients but are loaded with micronutrients and other essentials elements needed in small quantities by plants. One dust, called Azomite, supplies over 50 trace minerals; another, granite dust, breaks down very slowly and contains about 3 to 5 percent potassium plus trace elements. Use them as supplements to regular soil building and fertility programs.

✔ **Sul-Po-Mag:** Also known as K-Mag, this mineral source provides plants with readily accessible potassium (22 percent), magnesium (11 percent), and sulfur (22 percent). Use it to add magnesium to high pH soils without raising the pH.

✔ **Sulfur:** This yellow powder contains 90 percent elemental sulfur, which is used not only as a nutrient for plant growth, but also to lower the pH. Go easy on the application, however, because overuse can decrease soil microbe activity.

Take-out menu

You can find most of the fertilizers discussed in this chapter in your local garden centers and home and garden supply stores. If your local selection is sadly lacking or if you want specialized and hard-to-find products, check out the following list of my favorite mail-order companies. Look for companies in your region, keeping in mind that fertilizers are heavy and cost a lot to ship.

✔ Peaceful Valley Farm Supply, Grass Valley, CA (phone: 888-784-1722; Web site: www.groworganic.com)

✔ Harmony Farm Supply, Graton, CA (phone: 707-823-9125; Web site: www.harmonyfarm.com)

✔ Mellinger's, Inc., Lima, OH (phone: 800-321-7444; Web site: www.mellingers.com)

✔ Worm's Way, Bloomington, IN (phone: 800-274-9676; Web site: www.wormsway.com)

✔ Gardener's Supply Co., Burlington, VT (phone: 800-863-1700; Web site: www.gardeners.com)

✔ Gardens Alive!, 5100 Schenley Place, Lawrenceburg, IN 47025 (phone: 812-537-8650; Web site: www.gardens-alive.com)

✔ Fedco Seeds, P.O. Box 520, Waterville, ME 04903-0520 (phone: 207-873-7333 and leave a message or fax 207-872-8317 to request a catalog)

For a longer list of suppliers plus a wealth of other information, check out the Organic Trade Association's Web site at www.ota.com and click on the member list/links button. This important organization's Web site also lists state organic farming associations and much more.

Part III

Keeping Plants Healthy

The 5th Wave   By Rich Tennant

"I used an all natural method of pest control, but we're still getting an occasional vacuum cleaner salesman in the garden."

In this part . . .

*J*ust like ants at a picnic, you can count on weeds in a garden and bugs on the plants. But they don't have to spoil your fun or your gardening success. Instead of reaching for a pest-killing potion, turn to this part for environmentally safe and effective solutions.

Keep ahead of the weeds with Chapter 6 and get the jump on the baddest bugs in Chapter 7. If you're a control freak, turn to Chapter 8 for the latest in traps and tricks. That's where you can find out how to use good bugs to fight bad bugs, too. If you're ready to "crank it up a notch," as television Chef Emeril Lagasse likes to say, peruse Chapter 9 for organic pesticides. Turn to Chapter 10 for dastardly diseases and what to do about them.

Chapter 6

Weed It and Reap!

- -

In This Chapter

▶ Choosing weeds for beneficial-insect habitat

▶ Eliminating weeds before planting

▶ Controlling weeds safely in the lawn and garden

- -

Weed control — the undoing of many a garden and gardener — is one of the biggest challenges that organic gardeners face. Weeds compete with your lawn and garden plants for food, water, and sun; they harbor injurious pests and diseases; and they run amok, making the yard look unkempt.

By definition, *weeds* are merely plants that are growing where they're not wanted. But because their eradication from lawns, gardens, and agricultural fields has become a national obsession, herbicides have contaminated streams, rivers, lakes, ponds, and groundwater, affecting our drinking water and wildlife habitat.

The organic weed-control methods described in this chapter offer new hope of winning the battle against weeds without poisoning the environment. But *wild plants,* as I prefer to call them, also offer an opportunity. They give observant gardeners clues about the soil in which they grow and provide habitat for helpful insects as well as harmful ones. And some so-called weeds are actually valued garden plants in other regions: One man's trash is another man's treasure.

Winning the Weed Wars

Weeding is not a favorite gardening activity — it's just not glamorous. I don't know about you, but I prefer almost any other chore to crawling around on my knees in the dirt and pulling weeds. And while my tool shed is festooned with quite a number of very effective weeding tools, I've learned by experience that it's preferable to prevent them from sprouting in the first place.

Use the techniques in the following sections to prevent and control weeds in your landscape and garden. Choose the methods that match your needs, whether you're starting a new garden or maintaining an established planting.

Mulch

Just like other plants, weeds and their seeds need air and light to grow, and if you deprive them of these crucial requirements, they will die or fail to sprout. One of the best ways to keep weeds in the dark is to put mulch over them. *Mulch* is anything that covers the soil for the purpose of preventing weeds, conserving moisture, or moderating the soil temperature. Many materials make good mulch: The ones you choose really depend on what's locally available, how much you want to spend, the appearance factor, and where you plan to put it.

The best mulch materials for organic gardens and landscapes also feed the worms and add organic matter to the soil as they decompose. Usually, 2- to 4-inch layers are sufficient to do the job, depending on the density of the material. Take a look at the following popular mulches and their uses:

- ✔ **Tree bark:** The ubiquitous landscape mulch. Available in shreds or various-sized chunks, bark lasts a long time, depending on the particle size, and gives your landscape a finished look. Be sure you're buying real bark, however, by checking the bag label or asking the seller for the content. Wood chips that are dyed to look like bark are becoming prevalent in some areas.

- ✔ **Wood chips, sawdust, and shavings:** Although suitable for mulch, these products break down more quickly than bark and compete with your plants for nitrogen as they decompose. If you use these around food and landscape plants, be sure to add an additional nitrogen source, such as those described in Chapter 5.

Never use materials from chemical- or pressure-treated wood.

- ✔ **Shredded leaves and pine needles:** These are among the best sources of free, attractive, and nutrient-rich mulch for flowerbeds, fruits, and vegetables. Be sure to shred leaves before using to prevent matting in the garden. In fact, I run over fallen leaves with the lawn mower, discharging them into easy-to-rake mounds.

Pine needles and leaves of oak and some other trees will acidify the soil, however. Use these freely around acid-loving plants, but monitor the soil pH around less tolerant plants (see Chapter 4). Some plants are sensitive to the chemicals in certain tree leaves, however. Cabbage-family plants, for example, don't like oak leaves. Many plants are incompatible with walnut leaves.

- ✔ **Seed hulls and crop residue:** These attractive, locally available, lightweight materials include cocoa bean, buckwheat hulls, ground corncobs, and other materials left over from processing an agricultural crop. Use on top of newspaper or other sheet mulch to increase suppression of weeds.

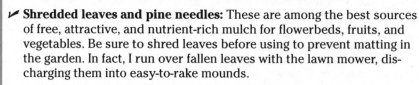

✔ **Straw and hay:** While these are traditional vegetable garden and straw-berry mulches. beware! Hay contains weed seeds that will add to your problems. Straw from grain crops, such as oats and wheat, may contain some crop seeds, but is a better choice as weed-suppressing mulch. Allow the soil to warm up in the spring before putting mulch around tomatoes and other heat-loving crops because straw keeps the soil cool.

✔ **Lawn clippings:** Clippings cost nothing and work best in flower and veg-etable gardens where they decompose quickly. Allow the clippings to dry on the lawn and then rake them up before using. Fresh clippings may mat down and become slimy as they decompose. If you're getting clippings from a well-meaning friend, be sure the clippings don't come from a chemically treated lawn.

✔ **Newspaper and cardboard:** Use cardboard or several layers of whole newspaper sheets in pathways or around landscape plants to smother weeds. (Avoid the colored glossy pages.) Cover with a thick layer of loose mulch, such as bark, shredded leaves, or straw. Depending on rain-fall, you may have to replace newspaper during the growing season.

Some organic mulches can go sour if they get too wet and packed down and begin to decompose without sufficient air. If your mulch smells like vinegar, ammonia, sulfur, or silage, mix and aerate it with a garden fork. Don't apply sour mulch around flowers, vegetables, fruits, or young shrubs and trees — its acidity can damage or even kill the plants. Cover unused mulch piles with a tarp to keep them dry.

No matter what kind of organic mulch you use, keep it away from direct con-tact with plant stems and trunks. Pull it several inches away from the plants to prevent moisture build up around the trunks and to deter insects, slugs, rodents, and diseases. Be sure to loosen the mulch with a rake periodically to allow water to penetrate easily.

Some mulches don't decompose, but have other special uses that make them useful in some situations:

✔ **Gravel and stone** are best for landscapes in fire-prone areas and around buildings where termites and carpenter ants pose problems. They don't add significant nutrients to the soil, however, and usually need land-scape fabric (see the following bullet) under them to prevent weeds. Avoid sand, which attracts cats, ants, and weed seeds.

✔ **Landscape fabrics** allow water to pass through, but shade the ground and prevent weeds from coming up. It also prevents organic material from reaching the soil, however.

While the fabric will last for a long time, it may need to be replaced at some point. I find that shallow-rooted plants, such as blueberries, grow roots into the landscape fabric, making it difficult to remove later. Use it around trees and shrubs or under decks where you don't want weeds, but avoid using landscape fabrics in gardens.

✔ **Plastic sheeting** is useful mainly in rows because clear and colored plastics heat the soil, while white plastic keeps it cool. Don't use plastic sheeting around landscape plants because it prevents water from reaching roots.

  Many specialty kinds now exist in addition to the basic black and clear plastic that you find in the hardware store. *IRT (infrared transmitting) plastic* lets in the warming rays of the sun but blocks the rays that stimulate seed growth. *SRM (selective reflective mulch)* and a special red plastic warm the soil, increase some crop yields, and may repel some pests, but don't prevent weeds as well as other plastics.

Solarization

One of the niftiest ways to beat the weeds is to *solarize* or use the heating power of the sun. The concept is simple: Capture the sun's heat under a sheet of clear plastic and literally bake the weeds and waiting seeds to death. Use solarization to clear existing plants from new gardens (clear plastic works best for this). This technique takes several weeks in warm, sunny climates. If you garden in a cool, cloudy climate, try it during the warmest or sunniest times of year and allow up to eight weeks for the process to work.

Here's how to do it.

1. **Mow closely or till the ground to remove as much of the existing vegetation as you can.**

   Solarization works best on bare ground.

2. **Dampen the soil. Moisture helps speed the process.**

3. **Spread a sheet of heavy-gauge clear plastic over the area.**

   Stretch it tautly to keep it close to the ground, as shown in Figure 6-1.

4. **Anchor with stones.**

   Place a few stones or other weights on the plastic to keep it from blowing around and to hold it near the soil.

5. **Seal the edge of the plastic to hold in the heat by covering it all the way around with soil or boards.**

Avoid tilling the soil after solarization or you may bring new seeds to the surface. If the soil gets hot enough, solarization also eliminates some soil-dwelling pests and diseases.

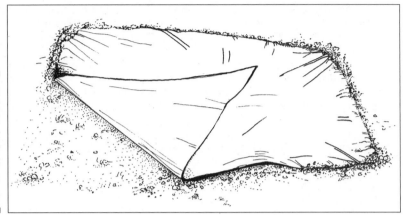

Figure 6-1:
Spread
clear plastic
and anchor
with soil or
boards to
solarize the
soil.

Cover cropping

Open ground is an open invitation for weed seeds to take root and for creeping plants to expand their territory. You can prevent and smother weeds, protect the soil from erosion, and enrich it at the same time by planting crops that you can till into the soil later. Thickly planted cover crops prevent weed seeds from sprouting and crowd out the ones that do. When the cover crop has done its job, you simply rotary till it into the soil, where it decomposes and adds organic matter.

Cover crops fall into two broad categories. Within each group, some live for a single season and others are *perennial,* coming back year after year.

- ✔ **Legumes:** Plants that have the ability to covert nitrogen from the air into nitrogen in the soil are called *legumes.* This group of plants increases the fertility of the soil while they grow and add rich organic matter when rotary tilled under. Some of them, especially alfalfa, have deep roots that bring water and other nutrients to the surface. Legumes provide an excellent source of nectar for bees as well as habitat for numerous beneficial insects. Legumes for cover crops include several types of clover, hairy vetch, soybeans, and alfalfa.

- ✔ **Grasses and buckwheat:** These cover crops grow quickly, allowing you to till under some of them just a few weeks after planting; others can remain in place for months. Either way, they add large amounts of organic matter to the soil. Buckwheat flowers are also valuable for bee nectar. Other cover crops in this group include annual ryegrass, oats, winter rye, and sudangrass.

Cover crops can serve your garden needs in different ways, depending on your goals and time frame, but unlike some other weed-control measures, you do have to plan ahead when using them.

- **New garden preparation:** The year before you intend to plant a vegetable, fruits, or flower garden, turn over the soil and sow a thick cover crop. Depending on the crop used and on whether you have time, turn under the first cover crop and grow another before tilling the garden for food or flowers.

- **Between gardening seasons:** After you harvest the last of your vegetables and remove the crop residue from the garden, sow a cover crop for the winter. If you live in a cold-winter climate, choose a fast-growing grass and plant it at least several weeks before the ground freezes. Turn it under in the spring. In warmer climates, prevent the cover crop from going to seed, otherwise it could become a weed itself.

- **During the garden season:** Some cover crops, especially white clover, are useful as permanent groundcovers in orchards and in the aisles between permanent planting beds. Clover encourages beneficial insects and adds nitrogen to the soil while preventing noxious weeds.

Farm supply stores are usually the least expensive source of cover crop seed. Their knowledgeable staff can help you choose the best crop for your climate and particular need. If you don't have a farm supply store nearby or just need a small amount of seed, buy it from a seed catalog that specializes in organic supplies.

Flaming

One of the latest and most effective weed killers to hit the market, propane-fueled flamers make quick work of weeds. Instead of setting plants on fire, they have special nozzles that work by literally boiling the sap inside the plants and bursting their cells. The least expensive flamers cost little more than a high quality rake and are a worthwhile investment for large gardens, yards, and orchards. Expect to pay from $30 to more than $100 for a flamer hose, fittings, nozzle, and valves. They attach to any standard propane tank, such as the kind used for barbecue grills. The most expensive models allow the fuel tank to be worn as a backpack and include convenient squeeze-control valves.

For the most effective control, use your flamer, shown in Figure 6-2, when weeds are small. Large weeds and tough perennials may need repeat treatments. You can purchase flamers at farm and garden supply stores and mail-order companies, such as Peaceful Valley Farm Supply. See Chapter 5 for contact information.

Avoid using flamers in windy or dry conditions, especially if you live in an arid region. Keep a hose or other water source handy to douse unexpected flames.

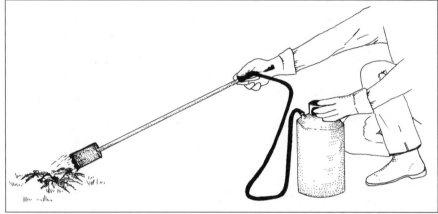

Figure 6-2:
Propane-
powered
flamers are
especially
effective
against
weeds.

Cultivating

Good old-fashioned hand-pulling and hoeing aren't among gardeners' favorite garden chores, but they work — especially if you follow these two basic rules:

- ✔ **Disturb the soil as little as possible.** This first rule is really important because many weed seeds lie dormant in the darkness just under the soil surface. When you churn up the soil, you expose them to the light and air that they need in order to sprout and attain pest status.

- ✔ **Get them while they're small.** Little weeds with fragile roots and stems take little effort to destroy. Large weeds take more work, disrupt more soil, and potentially contribute to the seed population in your soil, if you leave them long enough. Also, the longer the weeds live, the more water and nutrients they rob from your food and landscape plants.

With so many different weeding tools on the market, you may have a difficult time choosing the most effective tools for the job. The kinds of weeds that you're dealing with determine some of your choice. Plants with long taproots, such as dandelions and burdock, for example, need a tool that reaches down into the soil and pulls out the entire root without disturbing your lawn too much. I use a *dandelion weeder,* also called an *asparagus knife,* which consists of a 12-inch-long metal rod with a forked tip and wooden handle.

Most weeds don't require such a specialized tool, however. The most effective and all-around useful weeding tools disturb very little soil as they work. The best hoes for weeding have sharp blades that slice the plants just below the soil surface, as shown in Figure 6-3. All weeding hoes need occasional touching up with a sharpening stone.

- ✔ **Collinear hoe:** The collinear hoe, designed by organic farmer Eliot Coleman, allows you to stand up straight as you weed.

- ✔ **Stirrup hoe:** I use the stirrup hoe frequently because it cuts both on the push and pull action.

- ✔ **Swan neck hoe:** The swan neck hoe gets into tight spots easily.

Smaller hand tools and those with shorter handles exist, too, and let you weed raised beds or weed from a sitting or kneeling position.

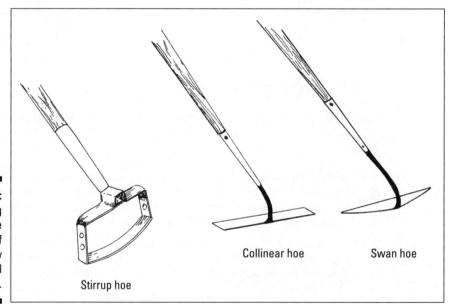

Figure 6-3:
Weeding hoes slice plants off just below the soil surface.

Stirrup hoe

Collinear hoe

Swan hoe

Organic herbicides

When all else fails, gardeners can still turn to herbicides to kill the weeds. Before you accuse me of blaspheme, let me introduce you to some organic weed control chemicals. As with any chemical treatment — organic or synthetic — use the most powerful ones only as a last resort.

Herbicides work in several different ways that depend on a particular plant life stage or characteristic to be effective:

- ✔ **Sprouting seeds send out roots first** and then the stem and first leaves. This vulnerable time is the best and easiest stage to knock them out. *Pre-emergent herbicides* kill these tiny seedlings as they sprout and are especially useful on lawns and other places where mature weeds are difficult to remove. The timing of application is critical, however. If you put them on too early, they may wash away before they have a chance to work. Put them on too late and the seedlings will be too big to be affected.

  The most promising organic pre-emergence herbicide is corn gluten meal, a highly concentrated corn protein extract. It can control weeds for up to 6 weeks, if applied in early spring and again in late summer, and, as a bonus, is high in nitrogen. Trade names of the product include A-maizing Lawn, WOW, and WeedzSTOP. It's available from Gardens Alive!, Gardeners' Supply Company, Peaceful Valley Farm Supply, and other sources in Chapter 5.

- ✔ **Plants have a waxy coating on their leaves,** which prevents moisture loss. Herbicidal soap damages the waxy layer, allowing the plant to dry out and die. This type of herbicide works best on young, tender, actively growing weeds in hot, dry weather. It is less effective on mature plants and perennial weeds. Safer's Superfast Weed Killer is a commonly available product.

- ✔ **Plants are sensitive to changes in pH.** Some products use vinegar, which is acetic acid, or pelargonic acid, which is derived from fruit, as their active ingredient. These acids lower the plant's pH dramatically, killing the sprayed plant parts in a matter of hours. For best results, remove as much of the plant top as you can before treating with the herbicide. Don't use these products where you intend to grow plants again for a few months because they can sterilize the soil. Products that contain pelargonic acid include Weed Eraser and Scythe.

Home Sweet Home

As if weeds themselves aren't bad enough, they contribute to the two other major headaches that gardeners face — pests and diseases. Knowing which insects and diseases that the wild plants around your garden harbor can help you decide whether to encourage their growth or eradicate them.

- ✔ **Insects:** Wild plants provide habitat for a wide range of insects, but not all bugs are bad bugs. Some insects, such as those discussed in Chapter 8, actually help your garden. And many of them depend on wild plants for habitat — places to lay their eggs, forage for food, and spend the winter months.

Wild plants with small flowers — yarrow, goldenrod, pigweed, and wild carrots — attract many beneficial insects. In addition, wasps that prey upon aphids, caterpillars, and other pests also enjoy pollen and nectar-rich flowers, such as dandelions, daisies, clover, nettles, and coneflowers. Leave these plants in the wild places outside your garden, but remove their spent flowers before they go to seed and spread beyond their allotted space.

Wild plants not only provide habitat for beneficial bugs, they also create a haven for damaging insects. Carrot rust flies live on both wild and garden-variety carrots, for example, and wild apple trees harbor curculio, apple maggots, and codling moths that move into your nearby orchard. Consider eliminating these wild plants near your garden if you have trouble with the pests they perpetuate.

Another way that some wild plants benefit your garden is by attracting pests to themselves that would otherwise discover and damage your crops. I'm perfectly happy to encourage the wild grapes and other so-called *trap plants* that Japanese beetles like to munch if they leave my roses alone! In some cases, you may wait to destroy some weeds until they have attracted a load of pests, then you can take care of two problems at once. Flowering mustard, for example, attracts cabbage worms and harlequin bugs. When the wild plants contain plenty of pests, pull them up and destroy them — getting two birds with one stone, so to speak.

✓ **Diseases:** Wild plants often share the same diseases that affect cultivated plants and gladly spread their misery around. Related plants, such as those in the nightshade family, for example, including deadly nightshade, horsenettle, potatoes, tomatoes, and eggplants, can infect one another with Verticillium wilt and other diseases. Wild brambles share viruses with strawberries and cultivated brambles. Insects that feed on these plants often spread diseases as they travel and forage, and soil remains contaminated even after the diseased weeds are gone. Avoid planting vulnerable plants in the same soil where related species grew within the past few years, and control insects that spread diseases. See Chapter 10 for more on diseases and Chapters 7, 8, and 9 for insect identification and control.

Chapter 7

Sleuthing Out the Suspects

· ·

In This Chapter

▶ Understanding integrated pest management

▶ Identifying insect pests and their damage

▶ Finding the best controls for each pest

· ·

*M*ost of the insects in your garden and yard won't harm your plants, but the ones that do cause damage accomplish more than their share to keep gardeners on their toes. As an organic gardener, you've made a commitment to protect the good guys and innocent bystanders from harm while eliminating the bad guys. In order to do that, you have to know a little about insects in general and be able to recognize the beneficial and harmful kinds. After you know what to look for, get as much information as possible about each specific pest — the damage they cause, where they live, and the best organic methods for preventing and eliminating them.

In this chapter, I describe the major pests of vegetables, flowers, fruits, trees, and shrubs and recommend the best control methods. Chapters 8 and 9 have more specific information on how to accomplish each method.

Understanding Insects

Each insect has its preferred foods and methods of feeding. Some mostly eat plants in the carrot family, for example, while others are less fussy. Some pests chew only roots or the youngest new leaves and flower buds of its host, while others tunnel though stems or pierce holes in their host and suck plant sap.

Insects also pass through several life stages on their way to adulthood, and each stage often looks very different from the one that preceded it. At different stages, insects also live in different places — a beetle, for example, may spend parts of its life in the soil, on tree bark, and on leaves. Some life stages are more vulnerable than others to attack by predators, parasites, or control with other methods, such as pesticides and traps. Knowing how to identify all the life stages of a pest gives you more ways to control it. Here's what to look for:

✔ **Eggs:** Each insect species has unique times, places, and methods for laying its eggs. The beneficial lacewing, for example, lays individual eggs and attaches each one to a plant surface with a long stalk. Colorado potato beetles lay clusters of orange eggs underneath plant leaves. Plum curculios and the apple maggot fly lay their eggs inside fruit. Some insects lay eggs that spend the winter in plant debris, the soil, or on host plants, while others lay eggs that hatch in the current growing season.

✔ **Larvae, grubs, nymphs, maggots, and caterpillars:** When the eggs hatch, they become immature insects. The name of this life stage depends on the kind of insect you're describing. Immature moths and butterflies are called caterpillars, for example, while young beetles are called grubs. This immature stage, while it eats and grows rapidly, is often the most plant-destructive period of an insect's life. Plant symptoms include holes or tunnels in leaves, fruits, bark, and stems, as well as stunted and deformed growth.

✔ **Pupae:** Many insects, including beetles, moths, butterflies, and flies, go through a stage between larva and adult when they form a cocoon or hard shell around themselves. They don't eat or cause damage at this stage and don't succumb easily to predators or pesticides. The transformation of a larva into an adult is called *pupating*.

✔ **Adults:** Adult insects are ready to mate and lay eggs. They usually have wings and are at their most mobile life stage. Some adult insects, such as aphids and thrips, feed on plants by piercing or rasping holes and sucking or sponging up the plant juices. Others, such as Japanese beetles, chew on plant parts. Butterflies and moths do no plant damage as adults and actually help pollinate plants.

Many insects spend part of the year, usually winter, in plant debris and fallen fruit. Sometimes the easiest way to control these insects is to rake up debris thoroughly and destroy it. Other insects need access to their hosts only during a very short period of time — using barriers and traps at just the right time may prevent them doing damage or laying their eggs. Get to know your pests and you may find easy ways to control them.

Managing Pests

Sharing your vegetables, flowers, trees, shrubs, and lawn with insects is a balancing act. On the one hand, you want a safe, attractive landscape and bountiful, pesticide-free harvest. On the other hand, armies of marauding insects and other pests may seem intent on destroying your dreams. What's an organic gardener to do?

The answer is *integrated pest management,* called *IPM* for short. Success with IPM depends on careful and regular observation of your plants, the weather, soil conditions, and other factors that influence plant and insect growth. You also have to get very familiar with each important pest. Here's what you need to know.

- ✔ **Pest identification:** You have to know exactly which insect(s) you're dealing with. Capture a few in a jar to get a good look them. Use a magnifying lens for small pests. Ask your local extension office for a color guide to common pests and their symptoms for your particular crop or ornamental plants. Extension *entomologists* (people who study insects) can also identify pests for you.

- ✔ **Understand the pest:** Learn as much as possible about when the pest appears, on which plants, what factors contribute to its abundance, what kind of damage it does, at what life stage it is easiest to control, where it lives when it's not on your plants, and what controls it naturally (beneficial insects or disease, for example).

- ✔ **Population size:** Knowing whether you have just a few aphids or a cast of thousands makes a difference in how you deal with them. After you spot a particular pest or symptoms of its damage, examine as many similar plants in your garden as you can to determine the extent of the population and its distribution. Traps, described in Chapter 8, can help you evaluate the population of some pests.

After you identify and profile a pest, you have a choice about how to control it — and whether to control it at all. Consider the following factors when making your decision:

- ✔ **Crop value:** Are you looking at a small planting of annual zinnias or your family's strawberry patch? Obviously, a valuable fruit crop warrants more intervention than an easily replaced ornamental.

- ✔ **Extent of the damage:** Is the pest confined to a single plant, to the one end of one row, or to the entire crop? Is the damage mostly cosmetic, will you lose a significant percent of the harvest, or will the tree's or shrub's health be significantly reduced?

- ✔ **Your tolerance threshold:** Can your family live with blemished apples, using them for sauce and cider? Or do you plan to sell them for fresh eating at a roadside stand? Are your roses going to be entered in a contest or will they simply grace your own house and garden?

You have many control methods from which to choose. Organic gardeners choose the least invasive and least toxic methods first and only graduate to harsher steps as necessary. See Chapter 2 for more on IPM, Chapter 8 for traps and other physical controls, and Chapter 9 for the lowdown on organic pesticides. Individual plant descriptions in Part IV list the most serious pests for each.

Rounding Up the Suspects

The following list of vegetable, flower, tree, shrub, and fruit pests includes the worst offenders. Many more insects cause damage, of course, and you can get more information about the ones to watch out for in your area from your local extension office.

✔ **Aphids:** These pear-shaped pests, shown in Figure 7-1, pierce holes in plant tissue and suck the juices. Their sizes range up to ⅛ inch, and color varies, depending on the species, from black to green, red, or even translucent. Aphids leave behind sticky sap droppings, called *honeydew,* which attract ants and may turn black if covered with sooty mold. Aphids can proliferate quickly on weakened plants and tend to congregate on the newest leaves and buds. Blast them off with a hose; control with beneficial green lacewings, ladybugs, or sticky yellow traps; or spray with insecticidal soap.

✔ **Apple maggot:** Slightly smaller than houseflies, these pests spend the winter in soil, then appear in June or July, mainly in northern climates, to begin laying eggs in apples, crabapples, plums, and other fruits. Maggots hatch and tunnel through the fruit, ruining it, as shown in Figure 7-2. Rake up and dispose of infested fruit in the fall before the maggots emerge and become established in the soil for the winter. Trap adult flies with red, apple-like spheres coated with sticky goo (see Chapter 8) and baited with a special apple-scented lure. Begin trapping three weeks after the petals begin falling from the blossoms in spring and continue through August, cleaning and refreshing the sticky stuff as needed. Use 1 to 2 traps in young or small, 6- to 8-foot high fruit trees and 6 traps in mature 10- to 25-foot trees.

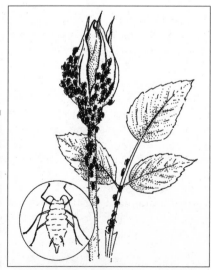

Figure 7-1: Aphids pierce holes in plants and suck out the juice and secrete sticky honeydew.

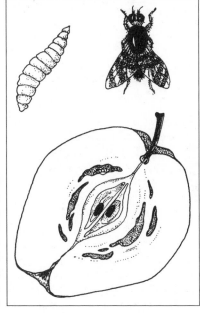

Figure 7-2:
Apple
maggot fly
larvae
tunnel
through
fruit.

✔ **Ataenus spretulus:** These ¼-inch-long black beetles lay eggs in turf grass in the spring. The eggs hatch into small white grubs, which feed on grass roots until mid-summer. After pupating, new adults emerge from the soil and mate, then prepare for winter by burrowing an inch or so deep into the soil. Discourage the pest by reducing lawn thatch and encouraging predatory and parasitic beneficial insects.

✔ **Bagworm:** Adults lay eggs in bags in the fall. After hatching in late spring, bagworm caterpillars use pieces of plant debris to construct 1- to 2-inch-long, dangling, bag-like structures for themselves. The small caterpillars feed on the leaves and twigs of many trees and shrubs, especially arborvitae and juniper. Cut the bags loose, removing silk that wraps around the stem, and destroy. Spray with *Bacillus thuringiensis* (Bt) in early spring or trap adults with sticky *pheromone traps,* which are baited with insect-attracting hormones, in late summer. See Chapter 8 for more on traps and Chapter 9 for more on safe, organic pesticides.

✔ **Bean leaf beetles:** Adult beetles, shown in Figure 7-3, chew large holes in bean leaves and the larvae attack the roots. Control by covering plants with row cover fabric. Spray with the organic pesticide neem, as a last resort. See Chapter 9 for details.

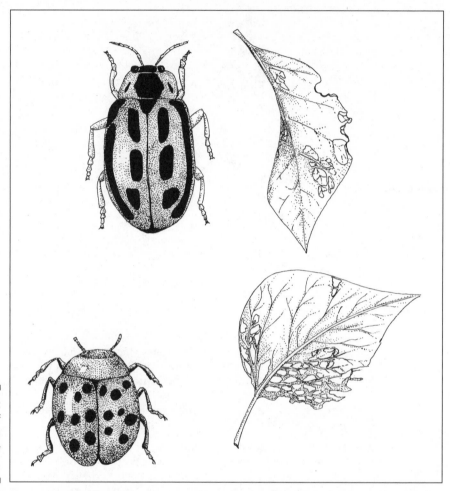

Figure 7-3:
Bean leaf
beetle
adults chew
leaves.

- **Billbugs:** The adult beetles have a long snout and eat turf grass leaves, while the grubs consume the grass roots and lower stems. They're especially fond of zoysia and Bermuda grasses. Control by planting tall fescue and perennial ryegrass varieties that contain *endophytes,* fungi that repel some insect pests. Don't, however, use these grasses where horses, cattle, and sheep will graze, because endophytes produce a toxin that affects animals as well as insect pests.

- **Black vine weevil:** Both adults and larvae of this snout-nosed beetle damage fruit and ornamental plants. The ⅓-inch long black adults emerge from the soil in early summer and lay eggs near the soil on host plants. When the eggs hatch, the larvae burrow into the soil and eat the roots. The adults, meanwhile eat crescent-shaped notches in the leaves. Control by covering crops with floating row cover fabric to screen out adults, or by knocking the adults off the plants into a dropcloth in the evening. Use beneficial nematodes in the soil or spray with Bt.

✓ **Borers:** Some beetle and moth larvae or grubs tunnel into the wood, canes, and stems of raspberries, roses, rhododendrons, squash, fruit trees, and other ornamental trees and shrubs, as shown in Figure 7-4. The tunneling weakens the plant, makes it more disease-prone, and can cut off sap circulation, causing wilting and twig or cane death. Prevent borers by choosing plant species that are less susceptible, wrapping the trunks of young trees to prevent sunburn or other wounds where borers can attack, and covering susceptible vegetable crops with floating row cover fabric. Watch for signs of damage, including dead bark, sawdust piles, dead or wilted canes and limbs, and poor performance. Control by slitting open affected stems and killing the larvae or pruning off and destroying stems. If you find borers or bark beetles, cut off and destroy the severely infested limbs, inject beneficial nematodes into the remaining borer holes, and remove dead or dying trees and plants.

✓ **Cabbage loopers:** The 1-inch-long gray adult moths lay eggs on cabbages, broccoli, cauliflower, and similar types of crops in late spring to early summer. The bright green caterpillars have white stripes down each side of their bodies and move with a looping motion. Control by handpicking the caterpillars, encouraging beneficial wasps, and spraying Bt.

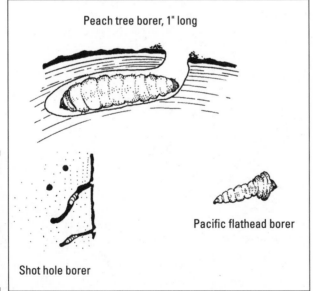

Peach tree borer, 1" long

Pacific flathead borer

Shot hole borer

Figure 7-4:
The larvae of stem-boring insects tunnel into wood and stems.

✓ **Chinch bug:** The immature nymphs and black and white, ⅙-inch long winged adult bugs both cause significant damage to lawns and grain crops by sucking the juice from grasses. Irregular patches of lawn turn brown, and you may detect a foul odor from crushed bugs when you walk over it. Control by planting endophyte-containing grasses (see the bullet for billbugs) and encouraging beneficial predator insects by allowing clover to grow in your lawn. See Chapter 8 for more on attracting beneficial insects.

✓ **Codling moth:** This ½-inch long, brown moth lays its eggs on the leaves and twigs of apples and other fruits, starting when the trees' flower petals begin falling in the spring and continuing through the summer. When the caterpillars hatch, they tunnel through the center of the fruit, as shown in Figure 7-5. Control adult codling moths by trapping, killing, or confusing them with sticky pheromone-baited traps, as described in Chapter 8. Immature larvae spend the winter under the loose bark of fruit trees and in fallen apples. Spray trees with horticultural oil in early spring before the leaves emerge to smother them. You can also trap the larvae by wrapping corrugated cardboard around the tree trunks in summer and then destroying it after the insects crawl inside. Monitor and replace every 1 to 2 weeks.

✓ **Colorado potato beetle:** The yellow and black-striped adults, shown in Figure 7-6, emerge from the soil in early summer, mate, and lay orange eggs on the underside of potato-family leaves, such as potato, eggplant, tomato, and nightshade. The reddish grubs devour the plant leaves, mature, develop into beetles, and lay a second generation of eggs later in the summer. The adults spend the winter in the soil and plant debris. Control by encouraging spiders, lady beetles, predatory stinkbugs, and Tachinid flies. Cover plants by applying a floating row cover or straw mulch, handpicking or flaming adults, crushing egg clusters, and spraying Bt 'San Diego' on very young grubs.

Figure 7-5: Codling moths lay eggs on fruit trees, which hatch into fruit-tunneling caterpillars.

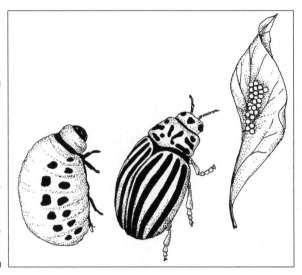

Figure 7-6:
Colorado potato beetle adults and larvae quickly defoliate potato-family crops.

✔ **Corn earworms, tomato fruitworm:** This caterpillar is one and the same critter, but its name changes depending the crop it's damaging. The adult moths emerge in spring and lay their eggs on plant leaves and corn ears. The caterpillars burrow into the fruit or eat the leaves for up to a month before dropping to the soil to pupate. Control in corn by choosing resistant varieties with tight husks on their ears or by applying mineral oil or Bt to the corn silks. Hand pick from other fruits and vegetables, encourage beneficial bugs and wasps, or spray with neem as a last resort.

✔ **Cucumber beetles:** Striped and spotted cucumber beetle species, shown in Figure 7-7, cause significant damage by chewing large holes in leaves and vegetables, and eating their roots. They can also carry viral and bacterial wilt diseases, spreading the diseases throughout your garden. Both adults and larvae feed on plants. Control by covering plants with row covers until flowering to prevent adults from laying eggs. Remove plant residue from the garden to eliminate winter hiding places. Use beneficial nematodes to control grubs in the soil and spray the adults with pyrethrin, a plant-based pesticide. See Chapter 9 for more about pest controls.

✔ **Cutworms and armyworms:** The 1- to 2-inch-long cutworm caterpillars, shown in Figure 7-8, chew through the stems of young plants at night, killing them, then spending the day curled in the soil nearby. Armyworms also feed at night, usually in early summer, stripping the leaves from grasses, grains, and vegetable crops. Control by picking the caterpillars from the soil near decimated seedlings and spraying Bt to kill caterpillars or horticultural oil in mid-summer to kill the eggs on host plants. Remove plant debris from gardens to prevent overwintering by adults. Wrap the stems of young vegetable plants with 2- to 3-inch-wide strips of newspaper so that half of the paper extends below the soil surface.

Figure 7-7:
Striped and spotted cucumber beetles chew the leaves, roots, and fruit of squash, corn, beans, and peas.

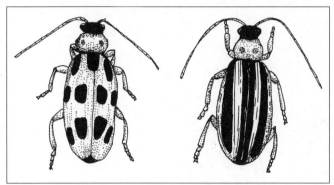

Figure 7-8:
Cutworms feed at night, killing seedlings and stripping leaves from plants.

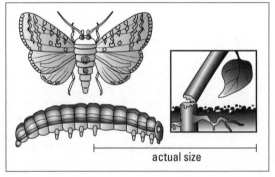

actual size

✓ **Flea beetles:** The highly mobile, shiny blackish beetles are only ¹⁄₁₀-inch long, but they tend to feed in large groups, skeletonizing leaves in a few days time. Adults emerge in spring and do most of their damage by mid-summer. Eggs, laid in the soil, hatch into larvae that eat plant roots until late summer. Control by covering vegetables and susceptible flowering plants with row cover fabric or delaying plantings until the beetles sub-side. Beneficial nematodes attack the grubs. You can also vacuum them up with a small, handheld vacuum cleaner early in the morning while they're still sluggish.

✓ **Gypsy moth:** The adult moths lay masses of eggs under a fuzzy covering on trees and other surfaces in autumn. The caterpillars are 2 inches long and are gray with brown hairs and distinctive red and blue spots — see Figure 7-9. They emerge in spring to eat the foliage on a number of shade trees, including oaks. This pest spreads across the country as caterpillars and egg clusters hitchhike on cars, campers, trains, and trucks. Catch caterpillars as they attempt to crawl up tree trunks by using a sticky pest barrier, as described in Chapter 8, wrapped around the tree. Spray the caterpillars with Bt or neem. If the pests are severely damaging any trees that are too tall for you to treat yourself, call an arborist for help.

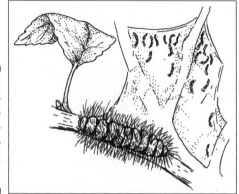

Figure 7-9:
Gypsy
moths lay
eggs under
a fuzzy
covering on
trees.

✔ **Imported cabbage moth:** The white moths have a distinctive black dot
on each wing. They flutter around your garden, laying yellow eggs on the
underside of cabbage, broccoli, and other cole crops in the spring and
early summer. The fuzzy green caterpillars hatch and quickly begin feeding on leaves and developing flower buds, leaving piles of green excrement. Control by covering crops with floating row covers or handpicking
and crushing eggs and caterpillars. Spray with Bt, if necessary. Yellow
sticky traps attract the adults.

✔ **Japanese beetles:** Found mostly east of the Mississippi River, the fat,
white, C-shaped, ¾-inch-long larvae live in the soil under turf, where they
consume grass roots from early spring to early summer. The adults —
½ inch long, metallic blue-green beetles with coppery backs — emerge from
the soil in mid-summer and attack plants with gusto, stripping leaves, buds,
and flowers. Inspect your garden in the evening or early morning for the
beetles, shown in Figure 7-10, knocking them off plants into a can or bucket
of soapy water. To control the larvae, treat your lawn with milky spore
disease, which takes several years to spread through the lawn, or with beneficial nematodes, a quicker-acting helper. Spray with neem, if necessary.

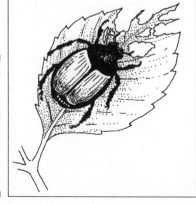

Figure 7-10:
Japanese
beetles can
completely
defoliate
shrubs and
garden
plants.

✔ **Lace bugs:** These ⅛-inch-long insects suck the sap out of the underside of foliage, giving the leaves a whitish or yellow blotchy appearance. Look under the leaves for their brown, sticky droppings. Ornamental plants, including firethorn, mountain laurel, cotoneaster, and rhododendron are vulnerable, as well as vegetables and flowers. Spray with horticultural spray oil to suffocate the pests or use pyrethrin on heavy infestations.

✔ **Leaf miners and sawflies:** The larvae of tiny sawflies, moths, beetles, and flies tunnel through the leaves of trees, shrubs, flowers, and vegetable plants (honeysuckle, tomato, holly, pine, boxwood, birch, and lilac), leaving discolored patches on the foliage. Control by planting vulnerable crops in a new place each year and covering with row-cover fabric in spring. Remove and destroy infested leaves, shown in Figure 7-11, and rake up any that fall. Eliminate host weeds, especially lamb's quarters and dock, but encourage parasitic wasps with carrot family plants. Spray with neem in spring when adults begin to lay eggs.

✔ **Leafhoppers:** These small, wedge-shaped adults jump from plant to plant, especially when disturbed. The adults and immature nymphs suck plant juices, distorting plant growth and spreading plant diseases. Many beneficial insects prey on and parasitize the nymphs. You can also try spraying plants with strong blasts of water to dislodge the immature insects. Spray neem or pyrethrin, if necessary.

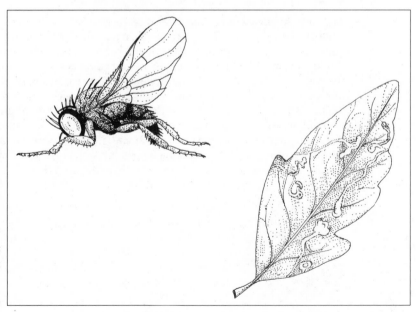

Figure 7-11:
Leafminer
larvae
tunnel
through
leaves,
leaving
discolored
patches.

✔ **Nematodes:** Plant-damaging nematodes are microscopic, worm-like creatures that live in the soil. They usually attack plant roots, causing abnormal growths and decreasing the plant's ability to take up water and nutrients. Some nematodes also attack stems and leaves. Control by rotating vegetable crops and avoid planting susceptible crops in the same place each year. Solarizing the soil with clear plastic (see Chapter 6) and planting some marigolds, which discourage nematodes, also give some control. The marigold *(Tagetes patula)* variety called 'Single Gold', also sold as 'Nema-gone', has proved most effective in Dutch trials. Many nematodes are beneficial, however, and actually attack the harmful kinds. For more information about the good kind, turn to Chapter 8.

✔ **Oriental fruit moth:** These small, slim moths produce several generations of larvae each year in the north and as many as seven generations in the south. In the spring, the first larvae tunnel into the new twigs of fruit trees, causing wilting and twig death. The mid-summer generations burrow into the fruit, leaving sticky residue on the surface. Late-summer larvae tunnel into the stem ends of the fruit, leaving no visible signs but destroying the inside of the fruit. Larvae spend the winter in tiny cocoons on tree bark and surrounding plant debris. To control, work the soil shallowly around infested trees in early spring to kill the larvae and spray trees with horticultural oil spray. Use pheromone traps to catch adult males and disrupt mating. Attract parasitic wasps and flies with flowering plants nearby.

✔ **Plum curculio:** Occurring east of the Rocky Mountains, these ¼-inch-long weevils, shown in Figure 7-12, cause significant damage to apple, pear, and cherry fruit. The female beetles make crescent-shaped cuts in young fruit right after the petals fall from the flowers, and then lay their eggs in the wound. When the grubs hatch, they eat through the fruit, causing it to drop from the tree. The larvae pupate in the soil and emerge as new adults in mid- to late summer. To control the adult beetles, spread out a tarp or old sheet underneath the tree and shake it to knock the beetles off and then step on them. Rake up and destroy fallen fruit, which may contain larvae. Keep plant debris out of small orchards to eliminate hiding places for over-wintering adults. If you happen to have a flock of chickens, as I do, let them forage for insects under the trees.

✔ **Root maggots:** Small flies of several species lay eggs in the soil near host plants or on the base of the plant. When the maggots hatch, they burrow into the roots, killing or stunting the plant. Onions, leeks, vegetables in the cabbage family, radishes, and carrots are common targets. Onion maggots can kill significant numbers of onion seedlings, especially in cool, wet weather. Control by covering susceptible crops with floating row cover fabric or apply beneficial nematodes.

  ✔ **Rose slugs:** The ½-inch long sawfly larvae and adults eat the underside of rose leaves and related plants in spring and early summer, quickly stripping them to skeletons. Handpick small infestations or spray with insecticidal soap or horticultural oil.

Figure 7-12:
Plum
curculio
weevils
make
crescent-
shaped
scars on
apples,
cherries,
and pears.

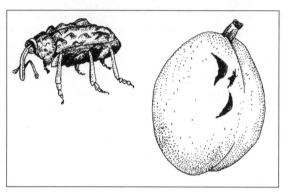

  ✔ **Sawfly:** The caterpillar-like larvae of the sawfly, shown in Figure 7-13, hatch in early spring and devour the foliage of needle-bearing ever-greens, especially pine, hemlock, and spruce. They pupate in the soil, emerging as adults in the fall. Adults lay eggs in cracks in tree bark. Many natural predators eat the larvae and pupae. Control by spreading a drop cloth under infested trees and collecting the larvae as they drop to ground in late summer. Spray trees with horticultural oil in early spring to smother eggs and newly hatched larvae. Avoid using oil on blue spruces, however, because it will permanently discolor the foliage.

Figure 7-13:
Sawfly
larvae strip
the needles
from conifer
trees and
shrubs.

✔ **Scale:** Adult scale insects, shown in Figure 7-14, may have a hard or soft, shell-like exterior that resemble bumps on plant stems and leaves. These pests suck plant sap and can weaken and even kill plants if present in large numbers. Many species secrete sticky honeydew that encourage fungus. Control is difficult on large trees and shrubs — your best bet is to release and encourage predatory beetles and wasps. Remove and destroy badly infested stems and spray with horticultural oil. Indoors or on small plants, clean light infestations off with a cotton ball soaked in soapy water.

Figure 7-14:
Scale
insects
usually
resemble
tiny bumps
on plant
stems and
leaves. They
often
secrete
sticky
honeydew.

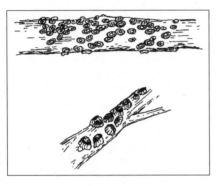

✔ **Snails and slugs:** These pests feed on the tender leaves of many ornamental, fruiting, and vegetable plants during the cool of night or in rainy weather. Sometimes they're hard to spot: All you see is the slime trail they leave behind and holes chewed in leaves and fruit. They proliferate in damp areas, hiding and breeding under rocks, mulch, and other garden debris. Control by placing boards, cabbage leaves, or other hiding places in the garden. In the early morning, lift the traps and destroy the slugs by sprinkling with a 50/50 mix of ammonia and water. Shallow pans of beer also attract and drown these pests. Surround plants and gardens with copper barriers — metal strips that seem to shock slugs if they attempt to crawl across. Diatomaceous earth and wood ash also deter them, but must be refreshed periodically. Look for new, non-toxic baits that contain iron phosphate.

✔ **Spider mites:** These tiny arachnids, shown in Figure 7-15, are almost microscopic, but when they appear in large numbers, you can begin to see the fine webs that they weave. Use a magnifying glass to identify them. They suck plant sap, weakening plants and causing leaf discoloration. They're especially active in arid conditions. Favorite hosts include fruit trees, miniature roses, citrus, pines, and houseplants. To control, wash plants with a strong blast of water, use dormant oil in early spring, or use light horticultural oil or insecticidal soap in summer. Encourage beneficial insects, many of which prey on spider mites.

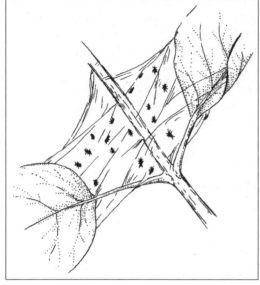

Figure 7-15:
Spider mites spin webs and suck plant juices, leaving weakened and discolored foliage.

✔ **Spruce budworm:** These caterpillars cause significant damage to spruce and fir forests throughout North America and can severely disfigure and kill landscape trees, too. In mid-summer, moths lay eggs, which hatch into small, orange-yellow to brownish caterpillars. The caterpillars hibernate until the following spring when they emerge to eat the mature and newly developing needles. Symptoms include dead shoots and chewed needles and cones. Control the pest by spraying with Bt in late summer as the newly hatched larvae emerge and again in early spring. Release and encourage parasitic trichogramma wasps (see Chapter 8 for more on these and other beneficial insects). Avoid planting spruce and fir trees in areas where the pest is prevalent.

✔ **Squash bugs:** These brown, green, or gray, ½-inch-long bugs and their nymphs attack the leaves of squash and pumpkins, causing the leaves to die. They become a problem when their population swells in late summer. Control by handpicking the bugs, growing vines on trellises, rotating crops, and cleaning up plant debris before winter.

✔ **Squash vine borers:** The adult lays an egg at the base of the stem in spring to early summer. After hatching, the larvae tunnels into the stem, causing the plant to wilt and eventually die. Control by covering plants with floating row covers early in the season, removing at blossom time. Remove larvae from infested stems and cover the stem with soil, allowing it to root. Butternut squash resists this pest.

✔ **Tarnished plant bug:** Among the most destructive pests of strawberries and other crops, plant bugs pierce plant tissues and suck the sap. Their feeding damages the plant, causing swelling, dead spots, bud drop, and distorted growth. The brownish, flattened oval bugs, shown in Figure 7-16, also spread plant diseases. Control by covering crops with floating row covers and encouraging or releasing predatory insects. Knock insects off plants into soapy water in cool morning or evening hours when bugs are sluggish. Spray with pyrethrin, if necessary.

Figure 7-16:
Tarnished
plant bugs
attack
vegetables,
flowers, and
fruits and
move
quickly
when
disturbed.

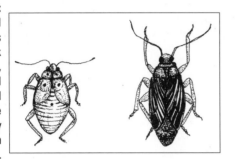

✔ **Tent caterpillars:** Adult moths lay eggs in mid-summer in hard, dark-colored, shiny masses that encircle twigs of deciduous trees. Caterpillars emerge in the spring and form colonies in large tent-like webs on their host trees. Large infestations can defoliate an entire tree. Control by seeking out and destroying the egg masses in late summer, especially on apples, cherries, and aspens. In spring, break up the tents with a long pole and before the caterpillars disperse, spray them with insecticidal soap. Knock caterpillars off severely infested branches with a broom and destroy. Encourage beneficial insects by planting carrot family plants. Spray with Bt in spring.

✔ **Thrips:** These tiny, slender-bodied flying insects damage all soft parts of ornamental and vegetable plants, including leaves, flowers, and roots. Infested flowers and young fruits look distorted. Leaves have silvery or white discolored patches on them, sometimes speckled with black. Use a magnifying lens to identify. Encourage or release lacewings and other predatory beneficial insects. Spray with horticultural oil or hang blue sticky traps.

✔ **Tomato hornworm:** These caterpillars, once seen, are never forgotten. The bright green larvae grow up to 4 inches long and as big around as my little finger, with white diagonal stripes along their sides and a black horn on their tail end. When disturbed, they may rear up and make a clicking sound. Handpick them and drop into soapy water or spray small ones with Bt. The large gray-brown adult moths are 4 to 5 inches across and fly at night.

- **Webworms:** This group includes a number of moth species whose caterpillars spin webs or cocoons around themselves and their host leaf, which they devour. Fall webworms attack trees and shrubs in late summer, garden webworms prefer vegetables and strawberries, and turf webworms go after grass. Control by handpicking, breaking up nests, and spraying with insecticidal soap or Bt. Encourage beneficial insect predators.

- **White grubs:** Many beetle species lay eggs in the soil, which hatch into root-eating grubs. Common grub species include June beetles, Japanese beetles, and rose chafers. Control with beneficial nematodes applied to the soil. See Figure 7-17.

Figure 7-17: White grubs eat plant roots.

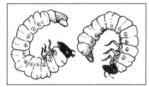

- **Whiteflies:** Resembling small, white moths, shown in Figure 7-18, these insects suck plant sap and spread plant diseases. Infested plants may release clouds of them when disturbed. Control whiteflies with insecticidal soap or light horticultural oil, or by trapping them with yellow sticky traps. Be sure to treat leaf undersides, where whiteflies and their larvae reside. Encourage parasitic wasps and predatory beetles.

Figure 7-18: Whiteflies congregate on the undersides of leaves.

- **Wireworms:** These 1-inch-long, copper-colored worms tunnel through plant roots and tubers, causing significant damage and opening wounds that encourage plant disease. Control the larvae by cultivating frequently and destroying the exposed insects. Chickens do a good cleanup job in my garden before planting time. You can also trap worms with pieces of cut potato placed in the soil. Check the potatoes for worms every few days and discard.

Chapter 8

Getting Physical with Pests

• •

In This Chapter

▶ Making the garden less inviting to pests

▶ Welcoming insect allies

▶ Using barriers and traps

▶ Outwitting hungry critters

• •

Most discussions of garden pests are full of warfare terms, such as "battle," "enemy," and "defeat." You certainly want to arm yourself when you see your rose blossoms ravaged by Japanese beetles or your cabbages full of cabbageworm holes.

But a goal of eliminating the enemy comes at too high a price. If you reach for a pesticide at the first sign of chewed leaves on your plants, you risk harming the beneficial insects that may have taken care of the pest if you'd been more patient. You may inadvertently harm the earthworms and microorganisms that enrich the soil, the bees that plants depend on for pollination, and even birds and other creatures. You also miss the opportunity to discover more about the fascinating interrelationships between plants and the creatures that reside in your garden. Besides, striving for perfection can leave a gardener feeling dispirited. Who needs that — gardening is supposed to be fun!

Organic gardeners embrace a different goal — tolerance. A few aphids on your hibiscus aren't likely to cause any major damage if your garden is a haven for beneficial insects that dine on aphids. As a matter of fact, organic gardeners try *not* to eliminate all insect pests because if they all disappear, so will the insects, birds, and spiders, called *beneficials,* that feed on them. By tolerating a small number of pests, you can keep their predators around in case there's a sudden pest-population explosion. You can benefit from nature's system of checks and balances if you can resist interfering in the natural balance of life in the garden too much.

Making the Garden Less Inviting to Pests

Your garden may be unintentionally rolling out the red carpet for insect pests. Bugs are opportunists that take advantage of weak or stressed plants. They also take up residence where the eating is easy. Keep pests at bay with the prevention strategies covered in the following sections.

Giving plants the advantage

Choose the right location for each plant, taking into account its particular needs for water, sunlight, and nutrients. There's evidence that plants emit a chemical signal when they are weakened, and insects get the message loud and clear. While experts continue to debate on the degree to which stress affects human health, in the plant kingdom, there's no such quibbling. When plants don't get their needs met, they become stressed, and the longer the stressful situation continues, the greater the decline in plant health. Think of insects as opportunists waiting for a weakened plant host to hang out the welcome mat. Of course, even a healthy plant can fall prey to insects and diseases, but it will be better able to survive the attack than will a plant that's already weakened.

 Damaged bark or leaves are ideal entryways for insects and diseases. Even torn leaves caused by a thunderstorm provide an opening for invasion. While you can't lessen the ravages of weather, you can protect plants from mechanical damage from lawn mowers, trimmers, and rotary tillers. Encircling trees and shrubs and perennial beds with a wide band of mulch helps keep the power equipment away from plants.

Confusing insects by mixing plants

Your 50-foot row of squash plants looks like a giant billboard flashing "Squash plants here, come and get 'em" to a squash bug flying around in search of lunch. Insects have chemical receptors that help them zero in on their favorite foods. If you mix different types of plants instead of planting each type in large blocks, insects have a harder time finding all of them. Plant smaller patches of each crop and scatter them throughout the garden or yard.

Keeping time on your side

Young plants, with their tender, succulent stems, are easy prey for pests. As plants grow and become more vigorous, their tissues become more fibrous and less prone to damage. You can take advantage of this tendency by planting a crop so that it's growing strong by the time the predominant pest insect hatches. In some northern regions, for example, early plantings of corn can protect against corn earworm and fall armyworm, which migrate from the south and arrive in the north later in the season. You can also time your plantings for a couple of weeks *after* the pest eggs hatch so that the young larvae will die from lack of food before your plants are up and growing.

You may have noticed that pests emerge earlier in the season if local temperatures have been high and later if temperatures have been cool. Farmers and other agriculture experts use these temperature records to predict the *emergence* of key pests — when they emerge from their winter hiding places. Talk to local growers and your local extension office about pest emergence predictions and recommended planting times.

Rotating crops

Moving each vegetable crop to a new location in the garden every year can help foil pests. At the end of the season, many insects leave eggs or pupae in the soil near their favorite host plants. If the young emerge in the spring looking for food and they don't have far to go because their favorite crop is nearby again, they will have a feeding frenzy. If, on the other hand, their food is on the other side of the garden, they may starve before they find it. Use this technique especially with annual flowers and vegetables that you replant each year.

Not overdoing a good thing

Most discussions of keeping plants healthy emphasize the importance of providing your plants with enough nutrients for good growth. But how much is enough? It's easy to end up applying too much fertilizer in the mistaken belief that if a little is good, more is better. Unfortunately an excess of nutrients is as harmful to plants as is nutrient deficiency. In fact, excess nitrogen causes stems and leaves to grow rapidly and produce juicy growth that's a delicacy for aphids and spider mites because it's easy to puncture and consume. Aphids, as well as other pests, also are attracted to high levels of amino acids in plants, which can be caused by too much nitrogen in the soil. Similarly, an imbalance of phosphorus encourages egg production in spider mites. The easiest way to avoid nutrient imbalances is to provide nutrients in the form of organic matter and organic fertilizers, which make nutrients available gradually.

Benefiting from Beneficial Insects

The average square yard of garden contains over a thousand insects. For the most part, that's a good thing. Some pollinate plants, some help break down organic matter, and some prey on other more damaging pests. Most of the insects in your gardens help — not hurt — your plants. Only a small fraction cause much damage. The following sections help you sort out the predators from the pests and give you tips for keeping the good bugs where you want them — in your garden.

Identifying the good guys

Those insects that prey on or parasitize insect pests are called *beneficial* insects. Whether you know it or not, you rely on these allies to help keep the insect balance from tipping too far in the destructive direction. If you familiarize yourself with these good guys, you can encourage their presence in the garden and avoid killing these innocent bystanders just because they happen to be the insects you spy on your favorite dahlias.

You can also buy many of these beneficial insects from mail-order catalogs to increase your local populations. See the "Sources of beneficial insects" sidebar, later in this chapter, for sources.

The following are some beneficial insects worth befriending:

- **Beneficial nematodes:** If there's one predator that's worth inviting over for dinner (its dinner, that is) it's beneficial nematodes. These tiny, worm-like creatures live in the soil and are effective against the scourge of many gardens — Japanese beetles. The nematodes prey on the grubs, the larval stage of the beetle, as well as on armyworms, cutworms, onion maggots, raspberry cane borers, and sod webworms. The nematodes (available by mail order) should be mixed with water and applied to your lawn and garden soil. According to Ohio State University, beneficial nematodes are most effective in moist soil and at soil temperatures between 60° and 90°. They can be killed by exposure to the sun, so they're best applied in early evening or on cloudy or rainy days when the soil temperature is at least 55°.

- **Big-eyed bug:** These fast-moving, ⅛- to ¼-inch bugs have tiny black spots on their heads and the middle part of their bodies, as shown in Figure 8-1. They resemble the pesky tarnished plant bugs, which are a favorite food of the big-eyes. They also dine on aphids, leafhoppers, spider mites, and some small caterpillars. Because these bugs aren't commercially available, look for them on nearby weeds, such as goldenrod or pigweed, and relocate them to your garden.

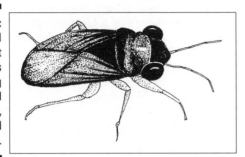

Figure 8-1:
Big-eyed
bugs eat
many pests
including
tarnished
plant bugs,
aphids, and
leafhoppers.

✔ **Braconid wasps:** Several species of braconid wasps, shown in Figure 8-2, parasitize pest insects. Both the slender adults and tiny, cream-colored grubs feed on a range of pests, including aphids, cabbageworms, codling moths, and corn borers. Purchase these ⅒ to ½-inch wasps from suppliers and plant some parsley-family flowers (see Chapter 12) to help keep them around. Adults require carbohydrate food, such as the *honeydew* secreted by aphids, tree sap ooze, or flower nectar.

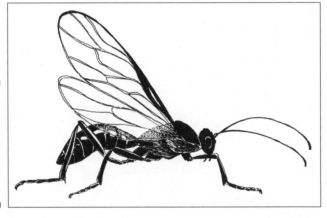

Figure 8-2:
Braconid
wasps and
their larvae
prey on
caterpillars
and aphids.

✔ **Centipedes:** Indoors and out, multi-legged centipedes feed on many insect pests. Most species don't bother humans (unless you count the screech with which they are frequently greeted), and while some south-western species do inflict a temporarily painful bite, none are danger-ous. You can't do much to encourage their presence, but if you can leave them alone to do their job, you'll have fewer insects around.

- **Damsel bugs:** These slender, ⅜- to ½-inch bugs have strong-looking front legs, and they prey upon aphids, caterpillars, leafhoppers, and thrips. They are common in unsprayed alfalfa fields, where you can collect them in a net and relocate them to your yard. Plant flowers in the sunflower family, such as goldenrod and yarrow, to keep them around.

- **Ground beetles:** Many beetle species live in or on the soil where both their larval and adult stages capture and eat harmful insects. They vary in color — black, green, bronze — and in size. While most live close to the ground, feeding on aphids, caterpillars, fruit flies, mites, and slugs, the 1-inch-long caterpillar hunter climbs trees to feed on gypsy moths and other tree-dwelling caterpillars. Because these beetles aren't available commercially, the best thing you can do to encourage their presence is avoid using herbicides and insecticides and learn to distinguish them from other unwanted insects. Ground beetles bear an unfortunate likeness to cockroaches, but the latter have longer antennae and a different overall shape. Most of the helpful ground beetles are large, dark, and fast moving. The often have nasty-looking mandibles and eyes on or near the fronts of their heads.

- **Hover flies:** These insects get their name from the adults' habit of hovering around flowers. The adults, resembling yellow jackets, are important pollinators, while the brownish or greenish caterpillar-like larvae have an appetite for aphids, beetles, caterpillars, sawflies, and thrips. If you grow an abundance of flowers, you're likely to see hover flies.

- **Ichneumonid wasps:** Ichneumonid wasps, introduced into the United States to control the European corn borer during the 1930s, are a valuable ally in controlling many caterpillars and other destructive larvae. The dark-colored adult wasps (see Figure 8-3) vary in size from less than 1 inch to 1½ inches, and they have long antennae and long egg-laying appendages — called *ovipositors* — that are easily mistaken for stingers. The adults need a steady source of nectar-bearing flowers to survive.

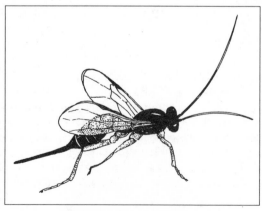

Figure 8-3: Ichneumonid wasps look threatening, but only spell danger for caterpillars and grubs.

✔ **Lacewings:** The delicate, green or brown bodies and transparent wings of these ½- to ¾-inch insects, shown in Figure 8-4, are easily recognized in the garden. Adults live on nectar, while the spindle-shaped, alligator-like, yellowish or brownish larvae feed on a wide variety of soft-bodied pests, such as aphids, scale, thrips, caterpillars, and spider mites. The distinctive, pale green oval eggs each sit at the end of its own long, thin stalk on the undersides of leaves. You can purchase lacewings as eggs, larvae, and adults. To keep the welcome mat out for the adults, allow some weeds to flower nearby.

Figure 8-4:
Lacewings look delicate, but have voracious appetites for soft-bodied insects.

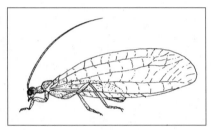

✔ **Lady beetles:** You may be surprised to learn that not all lady beetles (also called ladybugs) are beneficial — the damaging Mexican bean beetle is a type of lady beetle! The convergent lady beetle, however, is what most people think of when they praise lady beetles' appetite for aphids. (This species is distinguished from her pest cousin by two converging white lines on its *thorax* — the segment between the head and the abdomen. The number of spots varies widely.) Both adults and larvae prey on soft-bodied pests, including mealybugs and spider mites. The convergent lady beetle larvae look like small black, segmented pillbugs with rows of knobby or hairy projections and four orange spots on their backs. Although lady beetles are commonly purchased and released into the garden, they often do like the song says and "Fly away home." You can help keep them around by setting out another food source, such as an artificial yeast/sugar or honeydew mixture, which is commercially available from lady beetle suppliers. See the "Sources of beneficial insects" sidebar later in this chapter.

✔ **Minute pirate bug:** These bugs have an appetite for soft-bodied insects, such as thrips, corn earworms, aphids, and spider mites. A single bug can consume 30 or more spider mites a day! The adults are ¼-inch long, somewhat oval-shaped, and black with white wing patches. The fast-moving, immature *nymphs* are yellow-orange to brown in color and teardrop-shaped. You can purchase them for release in your yard.

✔ **Predatory mites:** Similar in appearance to pest mites, such as the two-spotted spider mite, predatory mites are tiny (smaller than ⅟₂₅ inch) and quick. They feed primarily on thrips and pest mites and are widely used to control these insects in commercial orchards and vineyards. They are available to home gardeners, as well, from the places listed in "Sources of beneficial insects" sidebar later in this chapter.

✔ **Praying mantis:** These curious-looking insects eat as many beneficial insects as pest insects. They are available commercially but are not among the most useful of the beneficial insects for helping to control pest populations in the home garden. Other beneficials that target specific pests are usually more effective.

✔ **Rove beetles:** These beetles, which resemble earwigs without pincers, have the distinctive habit of pointing their abdomens upward as they walk. Decaying organic matter is their home, where they feed on soil-dwelling insects, such as root maggot eggs, larvae, and pupae, especially those of the cabbage and onion maggots. In mild, wet climates they also eat slug and snail eggs.

✔ **Soldier beetles:** The favorite diet of both adults and larvae of these common beetles consists of aphids, caterpillars, corn rootworms, cucumber beetles, and grasshopper eggs. The adults, shown in Figure 8-5, are slender, flattened, ⅓- to ½-inch long. The larvae have the same shape and are covered with hairs. They spend much of their life cycle in the soil, so they will be more prevalent in areas where the soil is undisturbed.

Figure 8-5:
Soldier beetles live in the soil where they eat caterpillars and damaging larvae.

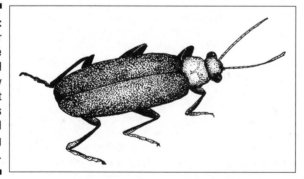

✔ **Spiders:** All spiders are predators, ridding the garden of many common pests. You can provide good habitat for spiders by mulching with hay and straw, which has been found to reduce insect damage by 70 percent due solely to the numbers of resident spiders.

✔ **Spined soldier bugs:** Adult spined soldier bugs dine on the larvae of Colorado potato beetles, Mexican bean beetles, and sawflies, as well as European corn borers, cabbage loopers, and tent caterpillars. The adults, shown in Figure 8-6, resemble tan, shield-shaped stinkbugs with prominent spurs on their shoulders immediately behind the head. They pierce their victims with a harpoon-like mouth. You can purchase them for release in your garden.

Figure 8-6:
Spined soldier bugs resemble stinkbugs with armored shoulders and harpoon-like mouth.

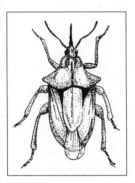

✔ **Tachinid flies:** These large flies feed on tent caterpillars, armyworms, corn borers, cutworms, stinkbugs, and other pests. The adult fly is about the size of a housefly and may hover above squash plants in search of prey. It has a bright orange abdomen, black head and thorax, and a fringe of short black hairs on the hind legs. Coriander, coyote brush, evergreen euonymus, fennel, goldenrod, and white sweet clover attract these flies to your yard.

✔ **Tiger beetles:** A variety of brightly colored and patterned ½- to ¾-inch beetles fall into this group, and they all have distinctively long legs. The tiger beetles in my garden have shiny metallic green bodies and run fast when disturbed. They feed on a wide range of soil-dwelling larvae. If you use an electric bug zapper light, you're inadvertently killing these garden allies.

✔ **Trichogramma wasps:** Tiny as a pencil point, these parasitic wasps inject their eggs inside the eggs of more than 200 species of moths, such as cabbageworms, codling moths, corn earworms, and cutworms. Their developing larvae consume the host. Buy these wasps commercially and release them during their hosts' peak egg-laying times. Suppliers can give you more specific directions on release times.

✔ **Yellow jackets:** I know, I know, it's hard to think of these annoying insects as beneficial, but they do help rid your garden of flies, caterpillars, grasshoppers, and many larvae by taking them home to their young. Yellow jackets are fond of white sweet clover and ivy, so expect to see them near your house if you have either nearby.

Sources of beneficial insects

Buying bugs through the mail may seem like a strange idea, but gardeners need all the natural help they can get! Contact one or more of these suppliers to find the best beneficial insects for your bug-eat-bug garden. Note that some Web sites offer good color photos of beneficial insects and their prey.

✔ Gardens Alive! has been helping home gardeners for years and their Web site offers an excellent reference complete with photographs of pests, diseases, and controls. For a catalog, phone 812-537-8650 or write to 5100 Schenley Place, Lawrenceburg, IN 47025. Visit them on-line at www.gardens-alive.com.

✔ Harmony Farm Supply sells a variety of organic gardening and irrigation supplies. For a catalog, call 707-823-9125 or write to 3244 Hwy.116 North Sebastopol, CA 95472. Visit their Web site at www.harmonyfarm.com.

✔ Gardeners with large acreage or greenhouses may contact IPM Labs at their Web site at www.ipmlabs.com or write to them at Box 300, Locke, NY 13092-0300.

✔ Peaceful Valley Farm Supply offers beneficial insects and far more on their Web site at www.groworganic.com. For more information, phone 916-272-4769 or write to Box 2209 #NG, Grass Valley, CA 95945.

Attracting beneficial insects

You can take important steps to welcome beneficial insects to your yard and encourage those you purchase to stick around. To keep the good guys from flying the coop, try these tips:

✔ **Wait to release beneficials until you've seen their favorite prey in the garden.** If beneficials don't find any food in your garden, they will move elsewhere. You can even purchase food for lady beetles (from the companies that sell the beetles) to encourage them to stay even after aphid populations decline.

✔ **Grow some plants that attract beneficial insects.** With a constant supply of nectar, adult beneficial insects can live much longer than they would without it. Shallow-throated flowers are easier for many of the tiny beneficials to feed from than deep-throated flowers. Goldenrod is a favorite, attracting more than 75 different species of beneficial insects. Include this and other plants from the parsley and sunflower families, such as artemesia, aster, coriander, cumin, daisy, dill, Florence fennel, gazania, goldenrod, marigold, alyssum, sunflower, yarrow, and zinnia.

To make it easier for gardeners to attract beneficial insects, Peaceful Valley Farm Supply and Harmony Farm Supply offer seed mixtures for plants that provide nectar and pollen for beneficial insects. See the "Sources of beneficial insects" sidebar earlier in this chapter for contact information.

- ✔ **Include a diversity of plants in your yard to attract a diversity of insects.** Plant different species, including evergreens, and plants of different sizes and shapes. A mixture of trees, shrubs, perennials, and annuals in the yard provides lots of options for food and hiding places.

- ✔ **Avoid using broad-spectrum insecticides, which kill a wide range of insects, including beneficials.** Even some organic insecticides, such as pyrethrin and rotenone, are toxic to beneficials. Often, beneficials are even more susceptible to the insecticide than pests because, as predators and parasites, they must move quickly over leaf surfaces and thus they come into contact with insecticides more readily. Many insecticides are also toxic to bees. If you must use a chemical as a last resort, spray only in the evening when bees have returned to the hive.

- ✔ **Provide a water source for beneficial insects by filling a shallow birdbath or bowl with stones and water and placing it near the garden.** Change the water frequently to discourage breeding mosquitoes.

Encouraging Other Insect Predators

Many creatures depend on insects for food, and you can enlist them in your pest control efforts. Birds, bats, frogs, toads, lizards, and even small mammals can eat surprisingly large numbers of insects. Offer them the habitat they enjoy and let them get to work.

- ✔ **Bats are beneficial, too:** Let's face it: Bats aren't exactly a welcome sight around most homes, especially if you've ever awakened at night to hear their flapping wings above your head. But bats are often underappreciated. Their steady diet of insects — beetles, moths, and, of course, mosquitoes — makes them worth a gardener's tolerance.

  Some gardeners put up bat houses to help keep bats nearby. Bat houses look like birdhouses with entrance slots in the bottom, and are available at many garden supply outlets, including Gardener's Supply Company (www.gardenerssupply.com) or Peaceful Valley Farm Supply, listed in the "Sources of beneficial insects" sidebar earlier in this chapter. Bat Conservation International also carries houses as well as plans for building your own. Contact them at 512-327-9721, write to P.O. Box 162603, Austin, TX 78716-2603. Their Web site at www.batcon.org offers a wealth of information and further resources.

- ✔ **Welcoming your fine feathered friends:** If you've ever watched a mother bird feeding her young, you know that her nestlings are non-stop feeders. And what's usually on the menu? Insects. Granted, birds do snare valuable, soil-enriching earthworms, but they also consume huge numbers of insects. A house wren, for example, can gobble more than 500 beetles, grubs, and insect eggs in an afternoon. I recently watched a small flock of sparrows pick through my late summer garden and feast on cabbage worms, weeds seeds, and other unwanted creatures.

You can welcome birds to your yard by providing food, such as fruiting trees and shrubs, bird seed, suet, water from bird baths, and shelter that includes a diversity of trees and shrubs, including evergreens. Put up birdhouses to encourage your favorite feathered friends to raise their families nearby.

✔ **Tolerating toads and lizards:** If you're lucky enough to have a resident toad in the garden, consider him an ally. He'll consume up to 100 insects — cutworms, grasshoppers, grubs, slugs — every night during the gardening season. He may even hang around for years if you make your yard hospitable. Toads lay their eggs in water, so a water garden or pond will ensure future generations. You can easily provide drinking water by setting a low dish or birdbath on the ground near some tall plants that offer shelter.

Setting Up Roadblocks For Pests

Sometimes the simplest solution is the most effective. Pests can't damage your plants if they can't get to them. Block their access with simple, but effective barriers around your plants, such as the following:

✔ **Copper bands:** Copper has the unique ability to repel slugs and snails. Their slimy coatings react chemically with copper, generating a toxic reaction — similar to an electric current — that sends them elsewhere. You can use copper sheet metal to fashion permanent edging around your garden beds or staple copper-backed paper (available from garden centers) to the sides of wooden planter beds.

You can also make a tree band out of copper. Cut a 3-inch-wide strip of copper sheet metal long enough to encircle the tree trunk. Punch holes in the ends for string to tie the strip together when you wrap it around the trunk.

✔ **Dust barriers:** You can repel some insects with a barrier of a sharp-particle dust, such as *diatomaceous earth* (DE), or wood ashes. DE consists the fossilized shells of diatoms, a type of algae. (See Chapter 9 for more information.) The particles pierce an insect's exterior cuticle and cause dehydration. A 6-inch circle of wood ashes, talc, DE, or lime spread around a cabbage stem can cause cabbage root maggots to take a detour, and a barrier of DE can also cause slugs to change course. Dusts work best when dry and need to be reapplied after a rain.

✔ **Row covers:** These lightweight air- and water-permeable fabrics were developed to raise the temperature around plants and extend the growing season. They can also keep plants relatively safe from insect pests, such as cabbage maggots, Mexican bean beetles, and squash bugs, as well as birds and even rabbits and groundhogs, if you spread them over your plants early enough in the season. If you wait too long before covering your plants, the insects will have had a chance to set up housekeeping in the garden, and they'll thrive under the protective covering.

As soon as your beds are seeded or planted, cover them loosely with row covers (to allow room for the plants to grow). Secure the edges in the soil or with boards, as shown in Figure 8-7, to keep opportunist insects from slipping in through the sides. If you live in a cool climate, you may be able to keep the covers on all season long without overheating your plants — warm-climate gardeners will need to remove the covers when temperatures rise. Remove the covers from plants, such as squash, that depend on insects for pollination when the plants bloom.

✔ **Cutworm collars:** If you've ever come out to the garden and found transplants flat on the ground with their stems chewed off at the soil level, you've seen the handiwork of cutworms. Their name is quite descriptive of their damage. These caterpillars emerge, hungry, from the soil in the early spring, and your plants will be dinner unless their stems are protected. You can make cutworm collars from empty toilet paper or paper towel rolls, cut into 2-inch cylinders, or from strips of newspaper that encircle the stem completely, but not tightly, and extend 1 inch into the soil. Place the collars around transplants when you put them in the ground.

✔ **Tree protectors:** Trees are a favorite feeding ground for many different creatures. Mice chew on the trunks, and caterpillars and other insects crawl up the trunk en route to the leaves and back down the trunk to rest or pupate in the soil. If mice or rabbits are the problem, use a wire mesh or plastic tree guard, as shown in Figure 8-8, to prevent their feeding.

Figure 8-7:
Row cover
fabric keeps
pests from
getting to
your crops.

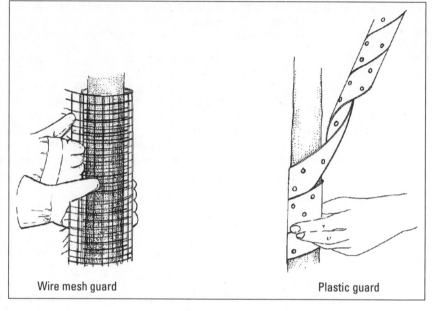

Figure 8-8:
Use wire or
plastic tree
guards to
protect bark
from
gnawing
rodents.

Wire mesh guard   Plastic guard

If you're trying to deter crawling insects, you can make different types of *tree bands,* such as strips of cardboard or fabric that encircle the tree and halt the insects in their travels up and down the trunk. Some insects, such as codling moth, like to hide under corrugated cardboard, especially in the fall as they prepare for the winter. To trap these insect pests, cut old boxes into long strips and wrap them around the tree trunk with the ridges facing the tree. Destroy the infested cardboard strips before spring and replace with fresh ones.

You can also wrap 18-inch-wide burlap strips, folded in half, around the trunk, with string securing the burlap to the tree at the inside of the fold. Insects become trapped under the fold as they head upwards. Even simple, wide, burlap strips wrapped around the trunk collect some caterpillars underneath. These traps are only a temporary detour for most insects, so you need to check the traps frequently and dispose of the insects.

Sticking to the Subject

You can halt insects in their tracks by applying a sticky coating to traps that attract specific insects. You can make your own by mixing equal parts mineral oil or petroleum jelly and liquid dish soap. Or purchase sticky substances, such as Tanglefoot, Stickem, and Sticky Stuff, at local hardware stores or garden centers. To make clean-up easier, cover the lure with plastic wrap before applying the sticky coating. Remove the stickum with Citra-Solv or a petroleum-based product.

Common types of sticky traps include the following:

- **Sticky barriers and traps:** Wrap a piece of fabric around a tree trunk and paint it with a sticky coating to trap crawling insects. The sticky substance can damage bark so always apply it to another material. You can take advantage of insects' color preferences in making traps. If you have some scrap wood, paint it yellow, cover it with a sticky coating, and place it in the garden to lure aphids, imported cabbageworms, fungus gnats, and several types of flies, including whiteflies. Codling moths prefer white-colored traps. Trap thrips with sticky blue cards.

- **Sticky red spheres:** You may have seen these at garden centers or in catalogs, or in your neighbor's orchard. These traps go a step further by mimicking the color and shape of the apple maggot's favorite fruit. They lure adult females searching for apples in which to lay their eggs. You can make your own trap by painting any apple-sized ball red, covering it with sticky coating, and hanging it in an apple tree. The larger the tree, the more traps you'll need. Set out the spheres in early to mid-June, just after the petals have fallen.

- **Sticky pheromone-baited traps:** These traps are baited with a *pheromone* — the scent released by a female moth or butterfly to attract a male of the same species. The artificial pheromone in the trap lures male insects, and a sticky coating prevents them from leaving after they realize they've been hoodwinked. Codling moths, oriental fruit moths, and Japanese beetles are some of the insects easily captured in this type of trap.

There is some evidence that putting up a Japanese beetle trap can attract more trouble than you bargained for. The beetles move so freely from yard to yard that your trap may solve your neighbors' beetle problems and worsen yours. To avoid being the neighborhood lure, place traps at the edge of your property and buy traps for your neighbors, too! Japanese beetle control needs to include large areas, such as whole neighborhoods, to be most effective.

Practicing Good Outdoor Housekeeping

Getting rid of insects can be as simple as handpicking or even vacuuming them. You can incorporate some of these easy techniques into a stroll around your yard.

- **Handpicking insects:** When I go out to tend my plants, I'm never without a can of soapy water — the future final resting-place for any Japanese beetle I encounter. Beetles are as sluggish as I am in the early morning so they can be easily picked or knocked off your plants into a can. You can make this an after-dinner routine as well, when the beetles have slowed down and settled in for the night.

Use this technique on many other insects, as well. Just be careful not to let twigs or leaves fall into the can, where they can form a bridge to freedom. As an alternative to the catch can, spread plastic under plants and shake them to dislodge insects. Then pour the insects from the plastic into a pail of soapy water.

Tiny insects are difficult to pick off, but a little judicious pruning can remove masses of them. Aphids tend to cluster near flower buds and growing tips, so cutting off those portions will help reduce the population and control damage spread. Pick off leaves that have leaf miners and other insects, and remove portions of branches infested with tent caterpillars.

✔ **Vacuuming the leaves:** You can use your Dust Buster to bust more than dust. Pest insects tend to congregate on the upper portions of plants, while beneficials frequently hide on the lower leaves and branches. You can use these tendencies to your advantage by vacuuming the upper leaves with a low-suction vacuum (you don't want to lose the leaves, too) whenever you see pests accumulating. Afterward, dispose of the vacuum bag so that insects can't crawl back out.

✔ **Giving plants a brisk shower:** Many an aphid and spider mite (and other crawling insects) can be deterred from feeding on your plants with a strong blast from the garden hose. Simply knocking the insects off onto the ground can greatly reduce their damage, especially if you spray plants every day or two, before the insects have time to make the journey back up. I use this technique on houseplants, too. Avoid spraying leaves in the evening because wet foliage at night can encourage disease organisms to spread.

✔ **Cleaning up debris:** Fallen leaves, dropped fruit, and other debris can harbor insects, so at season's end, pick up and destroy fallen fruit, and till plant residues into the soil or add them to your compost pile. Burn diseased plants, dispose of them in trash bags, or add to a compost pile that reaches 160°F degrees. Even if you compost your spent plants, cultivate the soil to work in any debris that could shelter insects through the winter. Cultivating also exposes pests to cold temperatures and predators.

An estimated 70 percent of all insect pests spend part of their life cycle in the soil, which is why birds flock to bare soil looking for food. Whenever you cultivate the soil, you help bring larvae and eggs to the surface where they can be picked off by birds and other creatures. Keep in mind that cultivating also warms the soil faster in the spring and encourages insects to emerge from the soil sooner. I let chickens roam free in my gardens after the final harvest and again after turning the soil in the spring. They do an excellent job of cleaning up insects and leftover vegetables.

Outwitting Critters

A discussion of garden pests wouldn't be complete without considering the animals that may plague your gardens — birds, deer, rabbits, ground hogs, gophers, and moles. While insect feeding is subtler and causes incremental damage over time, some of these larger critters can eliminate an entire plant — or row of plants — almost right before your eyes. You can, however, keep damage to a minimum by getting to know their habits.

✔ **Birds:** Birds in the yard are a mixed blessing. You appreciate their appetite for insects, but when they nibble on the tomatoes and devour the ripe blueberries, they cross the line into nuisance territory. You can keep birds away from your plants by draping bird netting or row covers over them, but this isn't always practical. Birds can be startled by noise, fluttering objects, and, of course, anything resembling a predator. Try bordering your garden with string tied to stakes and fastening aluminum pie plates or unwanted CD disks to the string. The noise and flashing of the sun on the shiny surfaces can scare birds away. Or instead of string use only a thin nylon line, which will vibrate and hum in the breeze. You can use the modern version of the scarecrow — balloons and kites with images of predators, such as owls and hawks. Place them in the garden to convince birds that their enemy is on guard. Birds catch on quickly though, so change your scare tactics regularly.

✔ **Deer:** Deer tend to travel the same routes day after day. If your yard is in the path of their customary travels from sleeping quarters to a water source, you'll be spending some evenings discussing deer-repellent strategies. Deer do, however, have some quirky tendencies that garden-ers can use to their favor. Try some of the following remedies:

- **Fencing:** Deer have been known to jump a 10-foot fence, but appar-ently, they are intimidated about jumping when they can't tell how much distance they have to clear. Deer are less likely to jump a fence over a narrow, long garden than a fence that surrounds a large, wide garden. The two long sides appear too close together for the deer to see a place to land. You can create the same illusion by installing a fence so that it slants outward away from the garden. This technique can intimidate the deer by making the fence appear wider than it really is. You can even make a 5-foot-fence more deer proof by using taller posts and attaching strands of wire above the fence, such as at 7 feet and 10 feet.

  If all else fails, you may need to resort to low-voltage electric fenc-ing, as shown in Figure 8-9. Place an electrified strand 3-feet high and 3 feet outside your other fence. Bait the strands of wire with peanut butter to encourage the deer to take a taste and get the message.

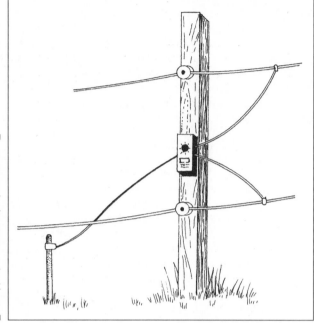

Figure 8-9:
Low-voltage electric fencing may be the only solution to foiling deer, raccoons, and other persistent pests.

- **Row covers:** In early spring, spread fabric row covers over tender new growth, supporting the covers with wire cages or hoops if necessary. This can deter the deer long enough to give your plants a head start and allow time for wild food plants to become plentiful.

- **Repellents:** Hang bars of soap from low tree branches or from stakes so that the bars are about 30 inches off the ground. Tallow-based soaps work best. Or spray plants with hot pepper solutions made from Tabasco pepper sauce or another hot sauce mixed with water and a little insecticidal soap or non-sudsing dishwasher detergent (to help the spray stick to the foliage). Another spray worth trying consists of three raw eggs in one gallon of water. This apparently smells worse to the deer than it does to you.

  You can purchase repellent sprays, such as Hinder, Deer-Away, Repellex, and Tree Guard, to spray on foliage. For best results, spray plants before the deer develop their feeding habits. You'll need to reapply most sprays after heavy rain. Avoid spraying fruit and vegetables because you don't want to eat the stuff yourself. Follow the label instructions carefully when using commercial repellents.

If you suspect that either a deer or rabbit is feasting on your plants, but you're not sure which one, take a close look at the partially chewed vegetation. Deer lack upper teeth, so they pull at the foliage, leaving torn and jagged edges. Rabbits leave a cleaner edge.

✔ **Rabbits:** Rabbits are homebodies. They tend to stake out a rather small territory — 10 acres or less — and not wander elsewhere. They make their homes in natural cavities in trees, other animals' abandoned burrows, brush piles, and under buildings. They nibble foliage of most any plant, returning again and again — day and night — to finish off the job. Here are some techniques to foil their feeding:

- **Fencing:** The best way to keep rabbits away from your plants is to fence them out. Because they burrow, a fence must also extend underground. Choose a 4-foot-high chicken wire fence with 1-inch mesh. Bury the bottom foot of the fence, bending the lowest 6 inches into a right angle facing outward.

- **Repellents:** I've had good luck repelling rabbits with hair gathered from hair salons and dog groomers. I sprinkle it around the boundary of a garden and replenish it every few weeks. You can also purchase commercial repellents that are made to spray on the ground or directly on plants.

✔ **Groundhogs:** These slow-moving rodents, also called *woodchucks,* live in an extensive system of underground dens and tunnels, and they defy you to find all of their tunnel entrances. A tunnel can extend nearly 70 feet. Groundhogs generally stay within about 100 feet of their dens, venturing out to find food — your tender veggies — usually in the morning and evening.

- **Fencing:** Groundhogs can climb up almost as well as they can dig down, so use a sturdy 4- or 5-foot fence and bury the bottom 18 inches underground. Bend the top of the fence outwards so the groundhog will fall over backwards if it attempts to climb over.

- **Repellents:** Spray plants with hot pepper solutions, such as the one recommended in the "Deer" section, earlier in this chapter.

- **Traps:** You can use a Havahart trap to capture a live groundhog and then release it into the wild. Be sure to check with local and state ordinances about restrictions on live trapping and releasing of wild animals.

✔ **Gophers:** These burrowing rodents live in underground tunnel systems extending as far as 200 yards. They feast underground on plant roots and bulbs, occasionally emerging to eat aboveground parts of those plants located near the tunnel openings.

You can plant gopher spurge *(Euphorbia lathyrus),* a natural repellent, as a protective border around the garden. Castor oil sprayed on the garden also repels them. Vibrating devices, such as large whirligigs, stuck in the ground near tunnels can send them packing. If gophers are a serious problem, you may want to go to the trouble of lining the sides and bottom of your garden (at a depth of 2 feet) with hardware cloth to keep the gophers out. Gopher-resistant wire baskets, which can be placed in planting holes prior to planting, are commercially available. For persistent problems, use traps.

- **Mice:** Mice cause the most damage to plants in the wintertime, when food is scarce and the bark of your favorite tree makes an easy meal. Even during the summer, if you have a thick layer of mulch surrounding the tree right up to the trunk, a mouse can hide in the mulch and feed undetected. To guard against this, leave a space of several inches between the trunk and the mulch to deter feeding. During winter, the snow cover provides a similar hiding place, so wrapping the trunk with a tree guard made of wire or plastic provides the best protection.

- **Moles:** These critters are the innocent bystanders or innocent burrowers of the garden pest realm. They simply love to burrow in search of grubs, earthworms, and other insects. In the process, they inadvertently expose plant roots to air or push the plants out of the ground, both of which kill plants. Field mice or voles also use the mole tunnels to reach plant roots and flower bulbs, which they eat. The best strategy is to control the grubs with some of the strategies discussed in Chapter 9.

- **Cats:** Roaming cats enjoy loose soil and mulch and frequently use gardens and landscaped areas as litter boxes. Laying rough-textured or chunky bark mulch or ornamental rocks on the soil may repel them because these materials are uncomfortable to soft paws. You can also lay chicken wire on the soil and cover it with mulch. Cats also don't like the smell of dog hair or anise oil, so these can be spread on the soil. Shredded lemon or grapefruit peels also deter cats. Look for a commercial product, such as "Bad Cat" for example, that contains citrus oils.

Chapter 9

Controlling Pests Safely

- -

In This Chapter

▶ Looking at all the organic pesticide options

▶ Selecting the least toxic controls

▶ Practicing safe and effective application

- -

*I*nsect pests often eat or spoil more than their fair share of your vegetable and fruit crops, and also spread diseases between plants, ruin blossoms, and mar your lawn. The effort to wipe out these pernicious pests has become the crusade of the agricultural chemical companies and a major concern of farmers everywhere. Unfortunately, the cure has turned out to be worse the sickness, so to speak, in many cases. As public, environmental, and financial pressures increase, farmers and researchers are seeking safer alternatives to many chemical pesticides.

Through these efforts, the system of integrated pest management (IPM) was born. In IPM, farmers follow a series of graduated steps, starting with good growing practices (see Chapters 2 and 3) and least toxic control methods, such as the traps, barriers, and beneficial insects discussed in Chapter 8. They move to more toxic or invasive steps only as needed. When more drastic measures become necessary, organic farmers and gardeners turn to pesticides that target only the specific pest that's causing the damage and avoid pesticides that harm innocent insects and other creatures. In this chapter, I take you through the organic options, one step at a time, from the least to most toxic methods of insect control.

Sorting Out the Products

An *insecticide* is any material used to kill insects. Some are non-toxic to all but the intended pest, while others affect any insect that comes in contact with it. Pesticides that kill a wide range of insects are called *broad-spectrum pesticides,* and they should be used only as last resort because they kill beneficial insects as well as the harmful ones.

The easiest way to classify all the different kinds of pesticides is to put them into groups based on how they work and, to some extent, where they come from. Organic pesticides come from plants, animals, minerals, and microorganisms, such as bacteria and fungi. Each of these pesticide groups — and individual products — kills pests in different ways. Some are more effective against insect larvae; others affect adults, for example. To get the best result from any product, you have to know as much as you can about the pest you hope to control: its life cycle, where it lives and at what times of the year, and when it's most vulnerable. Turn to Chapter 7 for information about pests; check out Part IV for plant descriptions, including major pests of each species.

Many people mistakenly believe that organic and non-toxic mean the same thing — I must lay this myth to rest. *Organic* simply means that the product came from naturally occurring sources, such as plants, animals, and soil minerals. But some organic pesticides — nicotine, for example — are highly toxic and every bit as dangerous to humans and other animals as they are to insect pests. Whether you grow plants organically or not, avoid the most toxic pesticides whenever possible.

Dust to dust

Insects don't have skeletons and skins like animals. Instead, a waxy cuticle covers their bodies, holding in moisture. Some insects have hard plates covering some of their body parts; others have almost entirely soft bodies. Dusts work by disrupting the waxy cuticle, which causes the insects to dry out and die. Unfortunately, these dusts harm beneficial insects, too. Although they are not toxic to humans, use them with caution to avoid harming the innocent bystanders of the bug world.

✔ **Diatomaceous earth:** Called *DE* for short, this well known and widely used white powder consists of the fossil remains of microscopic water creatures, called *diatoms,* and is mined from areas where ancient oceans or lakes once existed. DE resembles microscopic shards of broken glass, which pierce the soft bodies of insects, slugs, and snails. DE kills beneficial as well as harmful insects, so it may not be the best choice in all situations. Some DE products contain non-toxic bait that attracts pests and induces them to eat the dust, which is also fatal.

Apply the dust to damp foliage to control soft-bodied insects or sprinkle on the ground to target slugs, snails, ants, and earwigs. Reapply after a rain. Use an applicator, such as the Dustin Mizer, to spread the DE evenly. This useful tool, which is available from sources listed in Chapter 5, holds a pound of dust in a canister and dispenses with a hand crank.

Although it isn't toxic to animals, the dust can irritate your lungs — wear a dust mask to avoiding breathing the dust. The DE that gardeners use as a pesticide is not the same as the DE used in swimming pool filters; the two kinds aren't interchangeable.

✔ **Iron phosphate:** This mineral product, when mixed with bait, attracts and kills slugs and snails. You can find it as Escar-Go! at Gardens Alive!, Sluggo at Peaceful Valley Farm Supply, and Worry Free other outlets. (See Chapter 5 for a list of sources.)

✔ **Boric acid:** For cockroaches, ants, and silverfish, look for boric acid powder. If kept dry, the powder remains effective for years without harming animals, people, or the environment.

Watching the soaps and other oily characters

Insects breathe through pores in the cuticle that surrounds their bodies. If you plug up the pores, the insects suffocate and die. That's where horticultural oils enter the picture. Disrupt the cuticle with special soaps and — poof! — the insects can't maintain their internal moisture. Soaps and oils kill a wide range of pest insects, but affect beneficial insects, too. Use them with caution to avoid harming beneficial insects. See Chapter 8 for more on beneficial insects.

✔ **Horticultural oils:** Made from refined mineral or vegetable oils. Although oils effectively kill any insect that they cover, including eggs, larvae, pupae and adults, they don't differentiate between good and bad bugs.

Use horticultural oils in the winter to suffocate over-wintering pests, such as aphids, mites, and scales, on dormant fruit and ornamental trees and shrubs. During the growing season horticultural oils work against aphids, mites, lace bugs, corn earworms, mealybugs, leafminers, and many others, including tough-to-kill scale insects. Mix with water according to label instructions and then apply with a sprayer.

Oils do have several drawbacks. Don't use them when temperatures are likely to rise above 90°, when plants are suffering from drought stress, or if you have applied or plan to apply sulfur fungicide within 30 days. It will also remove the bluish waxy coating from Colorado blue spruce, so avoid using it on that species. Read the label carefully for other precautions.

Some products combine oil with additional ingredients, such as insecticidal soaps or botanical insecticides, which make them even more effective. Oil helps these other ingredients stick to the plant or penetrate the insect's cuticle.

✓ **Citrus oils:** The oils from the skin of citrus fruits kill a broad range of insects on contact by poisoning them. The oils continue to repel pests, such as fleas, ants, and silverfish, for weeks and are safe around people and pets. The *active ingredient* — chemical that does the damage — is d-Limonene. Look for it on the label or try the commercial product Orange Guard.

✓ **Plant extracts:** Many herbs, spices, and plants, including tansy, nasturtium, garlic, onions, marigolds, rue, mint, rosemary, sage, and geranium, contain chemicals that repel or kill insects. Garlic is one of the most well-known and effective extracts against thrips and other leaf-eating insects: The strong odor disguises the true identity of the host plant, so pests pass them by. Look for the commercial product Garlic Barrier.

✓ **Insecticidal soaps:** The active ingredient in insecticidal soap, called *potassium salts of fatty acids,* penetrates and disrupts the cuticle that holds moisture inside insects' bodies. When sprayed with soap, many soft-bodied insect pests, such as aphids, dry out and die. Some pests, however, especially beetles with hard bodies, remain unaffected. To make soaps more effective, products such as Safer's Yard & Garden Insect Killer, combine soap with pyrethrins, a botanical insecticide that's covered in the "Becoming botanically correct" section in this chapter.

Insecticidal soap is nontoxic to humans and other animals and breaks down quickly in the environment. If you use a concentrated product, dilute it with soft water before using for the best effect. Hard or mineral-rich water decreases its effectiveness.

The downside to insecticidal soap is that it also disrupts the waxy cuticle on some plants, making it toxic to young and thin-leafed plants, especially tomatoes. If you aren't sure of the plant's sensitivity to the product, always test it on a leaf or two and allow a couple of days to pass before spraying a whole plant. Follow the label directions carefully.

Getting small with microbes

Everybody gets sick at one time or another — and that includes bugs. You can help them along the path to their destruction with a variety of infectious microorganisms or *microbes* that target specific pests. The beauty of these disease-causing microbes is that they are completely harmless to most beneficial insects, humans, and other animals. Microbes take time to work, but often remain active in the environment long after you apply them.

✓ **Bacteria:** Several insect-infecting bacteria, or *Bacillus* species, that exist naturally in most soils have become important tools in the battle against damaging caterpillars, beetles, and other pesky bugs. In the 1960s, scientists began using the bacteria *Bacillus popilliae,* also called *milky spore disease,* to control the Japanese beetle and other closely related beetles. The disease affects the soil-dwelling larvae or grubs. After the grubs eat the bacteria, they become ill and stop feeding, dying within days. They often darken in color when infected. When the insects die, the disease organism spreads in the soil where it can infect others.

It takes several years for the bacteria to spread and achieve good control, however, and it is less effective in very cold-winter climates. In warmer climates, one treatment can remain effective for at least ten years. For best results, entire neighborhoods should participate in spreading the milky spore product.

Another very important group of bacteria, *Bacillus thuringiensis,* known as *B.t.* for short, infects many insect pests, especially their larval stages. Different strains or varieties of the bacteria affect different kinds of pests. One of the most widely used products contains the strain *B.t.* 'Kurstaki' or 'Aizawai', which infects and kills young caterpillars, including many major pests of vegetables, ornamentals, and trees. Product names to look for include Dipel, Thuricide, Javelin, Safer Bt Caterpillar Killer, and Caterpillar Attack.

The strains *B.t. tenebrionis* and 'San Diego' infect leaf-eating beetles, such as Colorado potato beetle. The bacteria are most effective against young larvae because the bacteria more easily rupture their stomach linings. Products include Colorado Potato Beetle Attack, M-One, and Novodor. Another strain, *B.t. israelensis,* is effective against mosquitoes, fungus gnats, and blackflies. Products include Bactimos Briquettes, Vectobac-G, and Mosquito Attack.

All bacteria-containing pesticides degrade when exposed to sunlight and high storage temperatures. Also, insects must eat the pesticide to become infected.

✔ **Fungi:** Many naturally occurring fungi infect and kill insect pests, and one of the most promising for farm and garden use is *Beauveria bassiana,* commonly known as the white muscadine fungus. The fungus lives in the soil and affects aphids, caterpillars, mites, grubs, whiteflies, and others. Insects don't have to consume the fungus — mere exposure can lead to infection. For this reason, avoid using it whenever bees and beneficial pollinators could be affected. It may also be toxic to fish and shouldn't be used around fish-containing waters. To encourage the native *Beauveria* population in your garden, avoid using fungicides. Products that contain *Beauveria* include Mycotrol and Naturalis H & G.

✔ **Viruses:** Two other groups of promising microbes include *granulosis virus* and *nuclear polyhedrosis virus,* which infect many caterpillar pests. Although still unavailable for home gardeners, granulosis virus is proving to be an important tool for commercial orchardists. These viruses can control codling moths, armyworms, gypsy moths, oriental fruit moths, and cabbageworms.

Becoming botanically correct

Insect and disease killers that come from plant extracts are called *botanical pesticides* or *botanicals.* Although derived from natural sources, botanicals are not necessarily safer or less toxic to non-pest insects, humans, and animals than synthetically derived pesticides. In fact, most botanicals are broad-spectrum insecticides, which kill both good and bad bugs indiscriminately. Some botanicals cause allergic reactions in people, others are highly toxic to fish and animals, and some may even cause cancer. All pesticides — including botanicals — should be used only as a last resort after thoroughly reading the label on the package. See the "Using Pesticides Safely" section in this chapter. The pesticides in this section are listed from least to most toxic to humans.

✔ **Hot pepper wax and powder:** The chemical *capsaicin* causes the heat in hot peppers and it's the active ingredient in these useful botanical products. In low doses, such as found in ready-to-use sprays and dusts, hot pepper wax repels most common insect pests from vegetables and ornamental plants. It doesn't cause the fruit or vegetables to become spicy hot, but instead stays on the surface of the plant where it remains effective for up to three weeks. Stronger commercial formulations kill insects as well as repel them. Hot pepper wax is even reportedly effective in repelling rabbits and tree squirrels.

✔ **Neem:** This pesticide is made from the seeds of the tropical neem tree, *Azadirachta indica,* and it comes in two forms — azadirachtin solution and neem oil. Unlike the other botanical insecticides in this section, neem does not poison insects outright. Instead, when insects eat the active ingredient, it interrupts their ability to develop and grow to their next life stage or lay eggs. It also deters insects from feeding and is effective against aphids, thrips, fungus gnats, caterpillars, beetles, leafminers, and others. Amazingly, plants can absorb neem so that any insects that feed on them may be killed or deterred from feeding.

It breaks down in the presence of sun and soil within a week or so. To discourage insects from eating your plants, spray neem before you see a large infestation. The product Safer BioNeem contains azadirachtin solution.

Neem oil, the other seed extract, also works against some plant leaf diseases, such as black spot on roses, powdery mildew, and rust diseases. Mix the syrupy solution with a soapy emulsifier to help it spread and stick to the plants. The neem oil products called Rose Defense and Fruit & Vegetable Defense from Green Light control insects, mites, and leaf diseases.

✔ **Pyrethrins:** These insecticidal compounds occur naturally in the flowers of some species of chrysanthemum plants. The toxins penetrate the insects' nervous system, quickly causing paralysis. In high enough doses or in combination with other pesticides, the insects die. Powerful synthetic compounds that imitate the natural chrysanthemum compounds are called *pyrethroids*. Pyrethroids are not approved for use in organic farms and gardens. Also avoid any pyrethrins that list "piperonyl butoxoid" on the label. This additive is not approved for organic use.

Although relatively harmless to humans, pyrethrins are very highly toxic to fish and bees and moderately toxic to birds. It kills both beneficial and pest insects. To keep bees safe, spray pyrethrins in the evening after bees have returned to their hives for the night and avoid spraying blooming plants. The compound breaks down rapidly when exposed to sun and air and becomes less effective if stored for longer than one year. Many commercial products contain pyrethrins.

✔ **Ryania:** This pesticide comes from the tropical *Ryania speciosa* plant. Although it controls fruit and codling moths, corn earworm, European corn borer, and citrus thrips, it is also moderately toxic to humans, fish, and birds. It is very toxic to dogs. Seek other botanical pesticides before considering ryania.

✔ **Sabadilla:** Made from the seeds of a tropical plant, sabadilla is a powerful broad-spectrum insect killer. It's especially useful for controlling thrips, aphids, flea beetles, and tarnished plant bugs, but it also kills bees and other beneficial insects, and some people have severe allergic reactions to the chemical. Use it only as a last resort.

Understanding Pesticide Toxicity

All pesticides are toxic, but some are more toxic than others. Some, called *acute toxins,* poison immediately upon exposure. Others, called *chronic toxins,* may accumulate in body fat or other organs and reach a toxic level after repeated exposure.

Acute pesticide toxicity is determined by feeding *(orally)* or applying the material to the skin *(dermally)* of laboratory rats, mice, or rabbits and determining the dosage (milligrams of product per kilograms of body weight) at which 50 percent of the animals die within 14 days. The acute toxicity is expressed as lethal dose or as LD_{50}. The lower the LD_{50}, the more acutely toxic the pesticide is. The LD_{50} doesn't measure chronic toxicity. In addition, the lethal inhalation dose is determined by exposing test animals to the chemical dust or vapors, and this toxicity is expressed as LC_{50} (parts per million). Many chemicals are more acutely toxic when inhaled because they enter the bloodstream very quickly.

Pesticides are categorized and labeled according to their acute oral and dermal toxicity as follows.

- **Class I:** The most highly toxic pesticides have an oral LD_{50} below 50 mg/kg or dermal LD_{50} below 200. Their labels always bear skull-and-crossbones and the words "DANGER" and "POISON" on the label. A special license is required for their use.

- **Class II:** Moderately toxic pesticides have oral and dermal LD_{50} levels of 51 to 500 and 201 to 2000 mg/kg, respectively. Their labels always say "WARNING."

- **Class III:** Slightly toxic pesticides have oral and dermal LD_{50} levels of 501 to 5,000 and 2,000 to 20,000 mg/kg, respectively, and the labels say "CAUTION."

- **Class IV:** Considered the least toxic, these pesticides have LD_{50} levels above 5,000 mg/kg oral and 20,000 mg/kg dermal and may say "CAUTION."

Many chemicals in our environment — both natural and synthetic — are toxic to one degree or another. Take a look at Table 9-1 to see the oral LD_{50} of some common household and garden chemicals, according to the Extension Toxicology Network and the Ball Pest & Disease Manual. Note the range for some chemicals, which can depend on the sensitivity of different test animals and on the way the pesticide is formulated. Not all of the materials listed in Table 9-1 are approved for organic use — I include them for general reference to show you the relative toxicity of some common chemicals. The ones marked with an asterisk (*) are considered safe to use in organic gardens.

Table 9-1	Acute Oral Toxicity of Some Common Chemicals
Chemical	*Acute Oral LD_{50} (mg/kg Body Weight)*
Nicotine	10
Copper sulfate	11 (human) to 472 (rats)
Kerosene	50
Chlorpyrifos (Dursban)	96 to 272
Phosmet (Imidan)	150
Ryania	150 (dogs) to 2,500 (guinea pigs)
*Caffeine	200
*Pyrethrins	200 to 2,600
Carbaryl (Sevin)	246
Aspirin	1,200

Chemical	Acute Oral LD_{50} (mg/kg Body Weight)
*Sabadilla	2,500 to 4,000
Table salt	3,320
*Azadirachtin (neem)	3,500
Glyphosate (RoundUp)	5,400
*Bacillus thuringiensis	>5,500
*Insecticidal soap	>5,500
*Sulfur	>5,500

Pesticide toxicity varies from one individual to the next and depends greatly on how you are exposed to the chemical. In some cases, such as sabadilla, the chemical may have low toxicity if ingested, but cause severe lung damage if inhaled. Some chemicals cause bodily harm other than acute poisoning. Treat all pesticides with respect and always read the label completely before using.

Using Pesticides Safely

As an organic gardener, you have already made the commitment to eliminate synthetic chemical pesticides from your garden and yard. Many of the insect, weed, and disease controls that organic gardeners use, however, are still toxic, especially if improperly used. Broad-spectrum botanical insecticides, such as pyrethrins and sabadilla, kill beneficial insects, destroy aquatic animals, and can injure pets and people. Knowing when, where, and how to apply these chemicals is part of responsible gardening.

Personal safety

Before you grab that spray bottle or can of dust off the shelf and head out to the garden, pause to check your personal attire. No matter how innocuous the pesticide, you must protect yourself from potential harm. Here's what you need:

- **Long-sleeves:** Cover your arms and legs completely. If you're spraying trees, wear a raincoat with a hood for extra protection.
- **Shoes:** No sandals, please, and don't forget the socks.
- **Hat:** Your scalp easily absorbs chemicals. Also, remember to cover your neck.

✔ **Gloves:** I use disposable rubber gloves, especially when measuring and mixing concentrated pesticides with water.

✔ **Goggles:** Eyeglasses aren't enough. Use safety goggles that enclose your eyes and protect them from spray.

✔ **Dust mask or respirator:** Protect your lungs and sensitive membranes from damage. Use a special respirator with filters (available from garden centers, farm supply outlets, and mail-order catalogs) when spraying pesticides. A dust mask is only helpful when applying non-toxic dusts to prevent inhalation.

Most pesticide injuries occur during mixing while you're preparing to spray. Put on your gear before you get started. Always mix and pour chemicals, including organic pesticides, in a well-ventilated area where accidental spillage won't contaminate or damage food or personal property. Even something as non-toxic as diatomaceous earth can irritate your lungs, while spilled oil can ruin your clothes. Don't use your kitchen measuring cups and spoons, either — buy a separate set for garden use.

Clear all toys and other stuff out of the area you plan to spray, including the areas where the spray may drift (check wind direction). Don't allow pets or other people into the area while you are spraying, and keep them out for the duration recommended on the product label.

Plant safety

Read the pesticide label carefully and apply the chemical only to listed plants. Relatively harmless pesticides can injure some plants. For example, horticultural oil isn't safe to use on Colorado blue spruce and many thin-leafed plants. Protect them from harm if you spray other nearby plants.

Consider weather and overall plant health, too. Some chemicals more easily injure drought-stressed and insect- or disease-weakened plants. High temperatures or intense sunlight can also increase the chances of plant damage.

Protecting the environment

One of the reasons I choose to garden organically is to keep the environment safe for the wild critters that live around me. Some botanical pesticides, such as pyrethrins, are very toxic to fish and beneficial insects. When you apply chemicals, follow the label directions very carefully. Never spray or dump pesticides near bodies of water or pour them into the sink or down the storm drain. Mix up only as much as you need.

Check the weather, too. Don't spray or apply dust in breezy conditions because the chemical may drift away from the target area and harm nearby plants or animals. If you expect rain, don't bother to apply pesticides that will wash off before doing their job.

Keeping records

I use a calendar with plenty of space on it to write notes and I record everything that affects my garden. Seed planting and first harvest dates, rainfall amounts, unusual temperatures and weather events, the appearance of pests and diseases — everything goes on the calendar. I also note which fertilizers and pesticides I used and on which plants. After keeping calendars for a couple of years, you may see patterns emerging that help you anticipate problems and keep them from becoming too troublesome. Good records show you what works and what doesn't, allowing you to make informed changes to your gardening practices. I think that keeping records is one of the easiest and most important organic gardening practices that you can do.

Chapter 10

Battling Plant Diseases

In This Chapter

▶ Figuring out the problem

▶ Preventing plant diseases

▶ Identifying the disease

▶ Using safe pesticides to treat disease

▶ Scouting out environmental problems

*P*reventing disease is the name of the game and it gets easier every year as plant breeders develop new plant varieties that resist common infections. You can do your part to prevent disease, too, through thoughtful garden and landscape planning and maintenance. But, what do you do when disease does strike? How can you tell whether the problem is a disease or some other malady?

In this chapter, I sort out the most common diseases (and environmental problems that sometimes look like diseases) and explain the most ecologically friendly ways to deal with them.

What's Wrong with This Picture?

The symptoms of many diseases, environmental stresses, nutrient deficiencies, and insect attacks look pretty much the same at first glance. Even something as simple as wilting has several possible causes, including too little water, stem or root disease, high temperature, and stem-boring insects. Fortunately, most problems have more than one symptom, which helps you pinpoint the trouble. Boring insects, for example, often leave a pile of sawdust or droppings at the entrance of the wound. Digging into the soil may reveal decaying or nematode-infested roots. So before you jump to any conclusions, look at all the possibilities.

The first step in diagnosing a problem is to gather all the facts that you can. Here's what I look for:

- **Environment:** Check soil moisture and pH (see Chapter 4), recall any fertilizers or other amendments you've used recently (see Chapter 5), rule out unusually hot or cold temperatures, consider wet or dry weather, and look for mechanical damage.

- **Insect activity:** Examine leaves and stems for obvious pests and sticky residue or droppings. Dig gently around the roots for grubs and nematode damage.

- **Compare to healthy plants:** Note specific differences between healthy specimens and troubled ones. Check leaf color and size and plant vigor. Look at the bark and stems.

Keep your notes and observations handy as you look through the pests in Chapter 7, the nutrient deficiencies in Chapter 5, and the plant diseases in this chapter. If you still can't identify the source of your plant's trouble, consult your local master gardeners, an expert at a local nursery, or call your local extension office.

And the Nominees Are . . .

Sorting out what ails your plant can be difficult, but the following sections give you a good place to start. Compare your observations to the disease and environmental problems in the sections that follow to narrow your list of suspects. I list symptoms, particularly vulnerable plants, along with prevention and control methods for each (more details about control methods in the "Understanding Disease-Control Methods" section near the end of this chapter).

Dastardly diseases

Several different kinds of organisms cause plant diseases, just as they do in people. Viruses are the toughest ones because they're incurable — all you can do is try to prevent them. Bacteria are nearly impossible to eliminate, too, after the plant is infected. Fortunately, fungi cause most plant diseases and they do have effective control chemicals, although prevention is still the best course of action. The following list describes some of the most common diseases of trees, shrubs, vegetables, flowers, and fruits:

- **Anthracnose:** This group of fungi can attack many plants (beans, vine crops, tomatoes, and peppers) and trees (dogwoods, maples, ash, and sycamores). Look for small, discolored leaf spots or dead twigs, especially on the youngest ones. The disease can spread to kill branches and eventually the whole plant. Many plant varieties are resistant to anthracnose fungi — choose them whenever you can. It spreads easily by splashing water and walking through wet plants. Prune off affected plant parts, if possible, and dispose of the debris in the trash, not the compost pile. Fungicides containing copper can help.

✔ **Apple scab:** This fungus attacks apple and crabapple trees, producing discolored leaf spots and woody-brown scabs on the fruit. The leaf spots start out olive colored, eventually turning brown. Plant scab-resistant varieties. Rake up and destroy fungus-infected leaves to prevent the fungus from reinfecting the trees in spring. Spray with copper- or sulfur-based fungicides during wet spring and summer weather.

✔ **Armillaria root rot:** This fungus infects and kills the roots and lower trunk of ornamental trees, especially oaks. Symptoms include smaller than normal leaves, honey-colored mushrooms growing near the base of the tree (see Figure 10-1), and declining tree vigor. Trees may suddenly fall over when the roots weaken and decay. Keep trees growing vigorously and avoid damage to their roots and trunks. If you live in an area where the disease is prevalent, plant resistant tree species. Consult local nursery or local extension office experts.

Figure 10-1:
Honey-colored mushrooms growing from the base of a tree indicate Armillaria root rot fungus.

Mycelial plaques

Armillaria on tree bark

✔ **Black spot:** This fungus causes black spots on rose leaves, as shown in Figure 10-2. Yellow rings may surround the spots, and severe infections can cause the shrub to lose all its foliage. The disease spreads easily by splashing water and overwinters in fallen leaves and mulch around the plant. Remove old mulch after leaf fall in the autumn and replace it with fresh mulch. Prevent black spot by choosing disease-resistant roses and cleaning up and destroying any diseased leaves that fall to the ground. Avoid wetting the foliage when you water.

Neem oil (not neem extract) is the best organic fungicide against black spot. Use it at the first signs of the disease, but spray either early or late in the day to avoid harming beneficial insects. Fungicide sprays containing copper or sulfur or potassium bicarbonate can also offer some protection.

Figure 10-2:
Black spot fungus on roses spreads easily by splashing water.

- **Botrytis blight:** This fungus attacks a wide variety of plants, especially in wet weather. It causes watery-looking, discolored patches on foliage that eventually turn brown. Infected flowers, especially roses, geraniums, begonias, and chrysanthemums, get fuzzy white or gray patches that turn brown, destroying the bloom. Strawberry and raspberry fruits, in particular, develop light brown to gray moldy spots and the flesh becomes brownish and water-soaked. Discourage Botrytis by allowing air to circulate freely around susceptible plants and avoid working with wet plants. Remove and destroy any infected plant parts.

- **Cedar-apple rust:** Rust diseases, including this one, often have complicated life cycles in which they infect different plant species and exhibit very different symptoms on each, depending on their life stage. Cedar-apple rust fungus appears as bright orange spots on the leaves and fruit of apples and crabapples. On its alternate hosts — juniper and red cedar — it develops yellow to orange-colored jelly-like masses in the spring. The fungus needs both hosts to reproduce and spread. Prevent the disease by planting resistant apple varieties and keeping the alternate hosts several hundred yards away from susceptible trees. A related fungus, western pear rust, affects pears similarly.

✔ **Club root:** This fungus mainly infects cole crops, such as cabbage, broccoli, and collards, and grows best in acidic soils. Symptoms include stunted growth, wilting, poor development, and swollen lumps on the roots. Practice good garden hygiene by keeping tools clean and picking up plant debris. Raise the soil pH to 7.2 and avoid planting susceptible crops in infected soil for at least 7 years. Some vegetable varieties are immune.

✔ **Corn smut:** You can't miss this fungus disease because it causes large mutant-looking, white to gray swellings on corn ears. When the swellings burst open, the fungus spreads. Prevent the disease by planting resistant corn varieties and rotating crops so that you don't grow corn in the same place year after year. Dispose of infected plant parts in the trash.

✔ **Cytospora canker:** Cankers appear as oozing, sunken or swollen areas on the bark of susceptible trees, such as peaches, apples, maples, spruces, and willows. The new shoots turn yellow and wilt, then die back. The disease attacks woody stems on susceptible plants, such as fruit trees, spruces, and maples, forming cankers that can kill infected branches. Plant resistant or less-susceptible plants and keep them growing vigorously. Avoid bark injuries that provide an entrance for infecting fungus. Remove and destroy infected branches, cutting back to healthy wood that doesn't contain any black or brownish streaks.

✔ **Damping off:** Mostly a problem in young plants and seedlings, this fungus rots stems off near the soil line, causing the plant to keel over and die. Prevent damping off by planting seeds and seedlings only in pasteurized planting soil and avoiding overwatering. Air circulation helps prevent the fungus, too. Clean your tools in isopropyl alcohol to prevent the spread.

✔ **Fusarium wilt:** This fungus is fatal to many vegetable crops. The first symptoms are yellowing leaves and stunted growth, followed by wilting and plant death (see Figure 10-3). In melons, the stems develop a yellow streak, which eventually turns brown. Choose Fusarium-resistant varieties. After plants are infected, there's no cure. If you build your soil's health so that it contains lots of beneficial microorganisms, you should rarely be bothered with this disease.

✔ **Galls:** These appear as swollen bumps on leaves, stems, and branches. Gall wasps, aphids, and mites infest oaks and other landscape trees and shrubs, causing unsightly swelling on leaves and twigs. In other cases, bacteria and fungi are the culprits. Usually the damage is simply cosmetic and not life-threatening to the plant. Control depends on what's causing the problem. Take a sample of the damage to a plant expert at your local extension office or contact your local master gardener program.

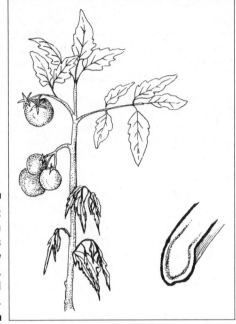

Figure 10-3:
Fusarium
wilt causes
yellow
leaves,
wilting, and
plant death.

✔ **Leaf spots and blights:** Several fungi show up first as circular spots on leaves of tomatoes, potatoes, peppers, and other vulnerable vegetables, flowers, and ornamental plants. The spots increase in size until the leaves die and fall off. The fungi spread easily in damp weather and in gardens where overhead watering wets the foliage, especially late in the day. The best control is to remove all plant debris at the end of the gardening season, clean tools between uses, practice crop rotation, buy disease-resistant varieties, and avoid contact with wet plants. Copper-based fungicides offer control as a last resort.

✔ **Mildew (downy and powdery):** These two fungi produce similar symptoms: white, powdery coating on leaves. They infect a wide variety of plants, including roses, vegetables, fruit trees, strawberries and raspberries, and lilacs. A different species of mildew attacks each kind of plant. A mildew that attacks lilacs, for example, won't harm roses. The fungi disfigure plants, but may not kill them outright. Instead, they weaken their hosts, making them unattractive and susceptible to other problems. Downy mildew attacks during cool, wet weather. Powdery mildew (shown in Figure 10-4) appears during warm, humid weather and cool nights, especially when the soil is dry.

Many vegetable and flower varieties are resistant to mildew — read package and catalog descriptions carefully. Remove infected plant debris from the garden and avoid getting the leaves wet. Use superfine horticultural oil or neem oil to treat infected plants. Use copper- and sulfur-based fungicides as a last resort.

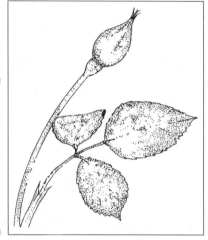

Figure 10-4:
Powdery
mildew
forms a
white or
gray coating
on leaves
and young
stems.

✔ **Root rots:** This broad term covers a number of fungal root diseases, which cause susceptible plants to turn yellow, wilt, and sometimes die. Nearly all plants are susceptible under the right conditions, such as excessive soil moisture, poor soil aeration, and wounding. The fungi can survive in the soil for many years without a host. Prevent root rot by building healthy, well-drained soil. Microbial fungicides, described in the "Understanding Disease-Control Methods" section in this chapter can help foil many root rot diseases.

✔ **Rust:** Many different fungi cause rust, and the symptoms of this disease vary widely, depending on the kind of plant they infect. Usually, the symptoms include yellow to orange spots on the leaf undersides, with white or yellow spots on the upper leaf surface. Susceptible plants include brambles, hollyhocks, roses, pines, pears, bluegrass and rye-grass lawns, wheat, barberry, beans, and many more. Each rust species infects a specific plant species, so that the rust on roses can't infect beans, for example. Some rusts, such as white pine blister rust, have complicated life cycles and must infect two different plants — in this case, white pines and *Ribes* species, such as currant and gooseberry. Symptoms of this disease include yellow, orange, reddish-brown, or black powdery spots or masses on leaves, needles, or twigs.

Rust fungus, shown in Figure 10-5, is most prevalent in humid and damp conditions. Provide good air circulation to keep foliage as dry as possible, remove and destroy infected parts, and keep your tools clean. Plant disease-resistant varieties.

✔ **Slime flux:** This bacterial rot inside infected trees, usually elms, maples, and poplars, causes oozing and often bad-smelling sap to run from old wounds or pruning cuts. There's no control after the symptoms appear.

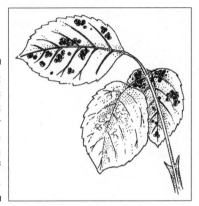

Figure 10-5:
Rust fungus forms yellow or orange bumps on leaf undersides.

✔ **Verticillium wilt:** This fungus affects many plants, including tomatoes, eggplant, potatoes, raspberries, strawberries, roses, Japanese maples, olives, and cherries. Look for wilting and yellow leaves, especially older ones. In some plants, the leaves curl up before falling off. Prevent future infections by cleaning up all garden debris, cleaning tools thoroughly with disinfectant, and avoiding susceptible species. Choose resistant varieties and practice crop rotation.

✔ **Viruses:** This group of incurable diseases infects vegetables, brambles, strawberries, trees, and flowering plants. Usually the leaves develop mottled yellow, white, or light green patches and may pucker along the veins. Flowers may develop off-color patches, and fruit ripens unevenly. Aphids, leafhoppers, nematodes, and whiteflies spread the virus as they move from plant to plant. Viruses often live in wild bramble plants and weeds. Smoking or handling tobacco products around susceptible plants can spread tobacco mosaic virus, which infects tomatoes, eggplants, peppers, petunias, and other plants. Prevention is the only strategy. Buy only virus-free plants and keep pests in check. Eradicate wild brambles near your garden.

Environmental diseases

Plants live intimately with their environment, which means that air, water, and soil quality, weather, and animals can take their toll. The way plants respond to environmental damage often mimics disease caused by microorganisms or insect pests; other times, the culprit is fairly obvious. Look through the following list of probable causes before you start blaming innocent viruses, aphids, and fungi:

✔ **Air pollution, ozone:** Automobile exhaust and other pollutants contain gases that injure susceptible plant leaves. Ozone gives foliage a white speckled appearance. Another common pollutant in urban areas is peroxyacyl nitrate (PAN), which causes silvery damage to leaf undersides. Sulfur dioxide, an industrial air pollutant, turns leaves yellow, especially between the veins. Beans, lettuce, spinach, tomatoes, sugar maples, pines, and English ivy are especially vulnerable to air pollutants.

✔ **Lawn mower, string trimmer damage:** Mechanical damage to the bark and stems of trees and shrubs poses a serious threat to their health. Water and nutrients flow through the stems just under the bark — breaking the bark interrupts this flow, causing stress, wilting, and even death. Even small wounds open the plant to insect and disease invasion. Maintain a wide weed- and grass-free area around trees, shrubs, and gardens so that you don't have to mow or weed whip close to them. Hard plastic or wire mesh tree guards also offer protection.

✔ **Leaf scorch:** When the edges of leaves turn yellow and then brown, as shown in Figure 10-6, suspect environmental damage from drought or heat. Trees in paved areas where heat rises from the pavement are vulnerable, as are any plants in very dry soil or unusually hot weather. Avoid planting susceptible trees, such as maples, in hot, dry locations.

Figure 10-6:
Yellow to brown leaf edges indicate leaf scorch.

✔ **Nutrient deficiency:** Although most natural soils contain enough nutrients to support healthy plants, disturbed soil around new homes and in improperly maintained gardens may have some nutrient shortages. Each nutrient has specific deficiency symptoms, but some resemble each other or mimic other problems or diseases. Nitrogen-deficient plants have yellow older leaves and stunted growth; lack of potassium causes yellow leaf margins; and phosphorus-deficient leaves usually have purplish streaks or overall appearance. Iron deficiency, caused by high pH, is especially prevalent in acid-loving plants, such as azaleas, blueberries, oaks, and hollies. The leaf veins remain dark green, but the rest of the leaf becomes yellow. Conduct a soil test (see Chapter 4) and flip to Chapter 5 for more information about specific nutrients.

✔ **Salt damage:** Salt used to de-ice roads poses a serious threat to perennials, trees, and shrubs. As water drains off the roads, salts in the water accumulate in the soil, burning foliage and roots and killing plants. Salt spray from passing cars can also damage or kill trees and shrubs. Injury appears as stunted growth, brown needles on conifers, and wilting. You can leach road salts out of the soil with heavy irrigation, but a better solution is to avoid planting within 20 feet of a frequently iced road and to divert drainage water from the road away from plants. If you live in a coastal area where salty air and soil is the norm year 'round, choose salt-tolerant plants recommended by your local nurseries.

✔ **Winter and frost injury:** Cold temperatures, frost, wind, and frozen soil combine forces to damage plants in several ways. Late-spring and early-autumn frosts injure tender plants as well as hardy plants that aren't sufficiently dormant and, therefore, able to withstand cold temperatures. Young, succulent, actively growing shoots and expanding flower buds are usually the most vulnerable. Avoid fertilizing and pruning plants in late summer, which can promote new growth that won't mature before freezing occurs. Injury symptoms include wilted, brown leaves, stems, and flowers. Protect vulnerable plants in spring and fall by covering them with row covers or cold frames, as described in Chapter 11.

Low winter temperatures cause the most damage to plants growing in containers, in areas where they are marginally hardy, and in places where winters bring little snow cover. Snow insulates the soil and prevents the soil temperature from dropping dangerously low. Even the roots of the hardiest shrubs and trees die at temperatures between 0° and 10°. Root damage may appear later in growing season when plants either fail to grow at all or sprout leaves, but then suddenly die in late spring. Spread 4 to 6 inches of loose mulch over the roots of perennials, strawberries, and vulnerable shrubs after the ground freezes in late autumn.

Sunscald is the cracking of tree branches and trunks caused by sudden and dramatic temperature fluctuations. The sun heats trees' bark during winter days, but the temperature drops rapidly at sunset. To protect vulnerable trees, such as citrus, paint trunks with whitewash made from a 1:1 mix of water and white water-based latex paint or wrap them in light-colored tree wrap.

The leaves and needles of evergreens face the challenge of drying out in the winter without being able to replace their lost moisture. When the soil freezes, the roots can no longer take up water to transport to the leaves. Winter sun and wind take their toll, and symptoms include bronze or brown needles and leaves. Surround vulnerable shrubs with burlap, plant them in protected places, or spray them with a chemical, called an *anti-transpirant,* that prevents them from drying out. See the "Understanding Disease-Control Methods" section in this chapter for more information.

Snow and ice can accumulate on tree and shrub branches and split them from the trunk, toppling whole trees. Protect shrubs by wrapping them with burlap and heavy twine, to hold the branches together, or covering them with plywood A-frames, especially if they are near a building where snow can slide off the roof or where snow plows dump their loads. Prune damaged limbs immediately to prevent further damage from bark tearing.

✔ **Woodpecker holes:** These birds eat insects that live in and around trees and they often make holes in the bark in pursuit of their prey. Some bird species also enjoy the sap of some trees and drill holes to get at it. The holes are usually small, round, and drilled in neat rows in the trunk. Unfortunately, there's not much you can do after the damage is done. Wrapping the tree may prevent further damage, but don't fill the holes or paint over them.

Preventing Problems

Your gardening methods can go a long way toward keeping diseases out of your vegetable and flower patch and away from your fruits and landscape trees. Many diseases, especially of trees and shrubs, are incurable and the plant values are high, so prevention is critical. I also discuss preventative practices in Chapters 2 and 3.

✔ **Choose disease-resistant plants.** Many popular flowers, vegetables, perennials, turf grasses, trees, and shrubs have varieties available that resist common diseases and even some pests. 'Liberty' apple, for example, resists apple scab fungus and the lilac 'President Lincoln' resists powdery mildew. One of my favorite tomatoes, 'Celebrity' is resistant to Verticillium and Fusarium wilts, nematodes, stem canker, and mosaic virus. Throughout Parts II and III, I describe other resistant plant varieties.

✔ **Mulch to reduce insects, weeds, and diseases.** A thick layer of organic mulch around your garden plants and shrubs keeps weeds from gaining an upper hand. It also helps to maintain consistent soil moisture and temperature, which keeps plant roots healthy and better able to resist disease. Soil and water-borne diseases, such as black spot on rose, have a harder time infecting plants, too, when mulch prevents puddles and water splashing onto leaves. But, to discourage fungus that attacks tree trunks and stems, keep mulch a few inches away from tree trunks and plants.

✔ **Choose plants that are adapted to your climate and site.** Avoid plants that struggle in your climate, moisture, sunlight, or soil conditions. If your soil drains poorly, for example, don't plant shrubs that require well-drained soil. See Chapter 2 for more about designing your garden and landscape for success; check out the plant descriptions in Parts II and III for specific plant requirements.

✔ **Space and prune plants to provide good air circulation.** Most fungus diseases described in this chapter thrive on moist leaves, but not on dry foliage. Fresh air helps leaves dry quickly and thwarts diseases. See Chapter 17 for more on pruning.

✔ **Water the soil, not the plants.** Early-morning watering is best because the sun will evaporate any water on the leaves. Avoid evening watering because the foliage will stay wet all night, giving fungus spores a chance to grow and infect plants.

✔ **Avoid working with wet plants because diseases spread easily when the foliage is wet.** Many diseases spread through splashed water. Beans, strawberries, raspberries, and other plants are particularly susceptible.

✔ **Avoid excess nitrogen fertilizer.** Nitrogen makes plants grow fast and juicy. As a result, the outer layers of the leaves and stems (similar to human skin) that protect the plant are thinner than usual and more susceptible to insect damage. Use organic fertilizers that release their nutrients slowly to avoid encouraging insects. See Chapter 5 for fertilizer suggestions.

✔ **Keep your yard clean.** Dispose of diseased leaves, fruit, and wood in the garbage, not the compost pile. Keep your yard tidy to discourage that pests live in dead plant debris, log piles, and other hidden places. Some insect pests — such as aphids, bark beetles, and tarnished plant bugs — can spread diseases between plants. Keep them under control, and you'll help prevent disease.

If you prune diseased plants, sanitize your pruning shears between cuts by spraying with isopropyl alcohol. Oil your shears regularly, too. It helps them cut easier and makes them a snap to clean. Clean your digging tools, too, and knock the dirt off your shoes to keep pests and diseases from traveling from one garden to another.

✔ **Inspect plants frequently.** You have a better chance of preventing a serious outbreak if you catch it early. Look for stem and leaf wounds and damage, off-color foliage, wilting, leaf spots, and insects whenever you work among your landscape and garden plants.

✔ **Practice crop rotation.** Many insects and diseases live in the soil from one year to the next, waiting for their favorite host plants to return. Foil them by planting something different in each spot each year. This method is especially effective for vegetables.

Understanding Disease-Control Methods

Preventing plant stress and environmental imbalances are the most important first steps in controlling disease. Beneficial microbes, especially in the soil, usually keep the populations of plant-disease-causing organisms in check, but environmental factors can tip the balance in favor of the bad guys. High humidity and soil moisture, as well as temperature extremes, encourage fungi to grow. Stress from transplanting, pruning, and insect infestation can weaken plants and make them more vulnerable to infection from fungi, bacteria, and viruses. And sometimes the pesticide you choose to use against one problem can make another problem worse. Broad-spectrum fungicides, such as copper and sulfur, for example, kill beneficial fungi as well as harmful ones.

The only plant diseases you can effectively control after the plants become infected are those caused by fungi. Except for solarization and copper, the following control methods target mainly fungi. The treatments are listed in order of toxicity, starting with the least toxic method.

- ✔ **Solarization:** Discussed in Chapter 6 as a weed control, heating the soil with the rays of the sun works to kill fungi and bacteria, too. Unfortunately, it kills both good and bad microbes. Use this technique in gardens where disease has been a problem in the past.

- ✔ **Anti-transpirants:** These waxy or oily materials are designed to help evergreens maintain leaf moisture during winter months. By coating the leaves, they also prevent fungus spores from attacking. Look for Wilt-Pruf and similar products and follow the instructions on the label.

- ✔ **Potassium bicarbonate:** This natural chemical controls powdery mildew on roses, grapes, cucumbers, strawberries, and other plants. It also supplies some potassium fertilizer when sprayed on foliage, which strengthens plant cell walls and makes them harder for pests and diseases to penetrate. Look for the products called Kaligreen by Toagosei and Remedy by Bonide Company. Mix the powder with water and spray all leaf surfaces thoroughly to ensure contact with the fungus. Note that repeated applications can burn or stunt the leaves.

- ✔ **Microbial fungicides:** Some of the newest fungicides are fungi themselves. These good guys grow in the soil on plant roots and protect the plants from harmful root-rot fungi. Apply them to the soil before planting or water them into lawns and gardens. Products to look for include AQ10, Mycostop, RootShield, TopShield, and TurfShield. These products contain viable fungi and must be stored properly and used carefully according to label instructions for best results.

- ✔ **Neem oil:** This multipurpose pesticide thwarts black spot on roses, powdery mildew, and rust fungi as well as insects and mites. Look for a product called Trilogy and others that contain neem oil, not neem extract. Warm the syrupy solution to make it easier to mix.

- ✔ **Sulfur:** Useful for controlling nearly all fungus diseases on leaves and stems, sulfur is one of the oldest pesticides known. You can dust the powder directly on leaves or mix finely ground dust with water and a soapy wetting agent that helps it adhere to leaf surfaces. It can cause leaf damage if applied within a month of horticultural oil, however, or when temperatures exceed 80°. It also lowers soil pH and harms many beneficial insects. Inhaled dust can cause lung damage. Take precautions to protect yourself. Products include Safer Garden Fungicide Liquid and Britz Sulfur Dust.

Copper: Copper sulfate is a powerful fungicide that controls a wide range of leaf diseases, including fungal and bacterial blights and leaf spots, but it is much more toxic to humans, mammals, fish, and other water creatures than most synthetic chemical fungicides. Use copper-containing products only as a last resort and take full precautions to avoid poisoning yourself and others. It can also build up in the soil and harm plants and microorganisms.

Flip to Chapter 9 for information about using pesticides safely. Look for products mentioned in this chapter, plus related products, at your local garden centers or check the catalogs and Web sites mentioned in Chapter 5.

Sources of information

As consumers and farmers demand more organic methods of disease control, alternatives to chemical pesticides are becoming more common. To keep up with the latest information, visit the following Web sites:

✔ Appropriate Technology Transfer for Rural Areas, known as ATTRA, offers in-depth information on many home, garden, and agricultural crops and focuses mainly on sustainable growing methods (Web site: www.attra.org).

✔ Ohio State University maintains a database of information from 46 North American universities and government agencies (Web site: http://plantfacts.ohio-state.edu).

Part IV

Growing Organically in Your Yard and Garden

In this part . . .

*E*ach chapter in this part is devoted to a special segment of your garden or landscape. Chapter 11 walks
you through the vegetable garden and Chapter 12 gives
you great growing tips for herbs. If you're leaning toward
fruits and nuts, I've got you covered in Chapters 13 and 14.

For a tiptoe through the tulips — or daylilies or zinnias —
prance over to Chapter 15. Think that you can't grow
organic roses? Think again after reading Chapter 16.

Make your landscape the envy of the neighborhood with
the tips on trees and shrubs in Chapter 17 and lawns in
Chapter 18. This part lists the most pest-free, low maintenance trees, shrubs, and turf grasses for your growing
conditions.

Chapter 11

Raising Organic Vegetables

. . . .

In This Chapter

▶ Putting your garden in the right place

▶ Preparing the soil

▶ Sowing and caring for vegetable plants

▶ Reviewing all varieties of vegetables, from asparagus to zucchini

. . . .

For most people, growing chemical-free vegetables is what organic gardening is all about. As more and more news comes out about the dangers of chemical pesticides and fertilizers, more people are choosing to grow their own food — and are finding that homegrown vegetables are fresher and taste better than store-bought. Nothing tastes better than a sliced red, ripe, sun-warmed tomato in a leafy salad or your own fresh peas picked right off the vine.

In the first half of this chapter, I talk about designing and starting your vegetable garden and give you some tips to make your garden more productive. The second half of the chapter describes the most popular home garden vegetables and varieties, tells you how to grow and harvest them, and describes which pests you can expect to show up for dinner.

Planning Your Vegetable Garden

When you're just starting your first garden, you may have more questions than answers — where to put the garden, when and how much to plant, which vegetables to choose. It's no wonder that problems can pop up before you know what's happening! In this section, I talk about how to get off to a good start and how to prevent troublesome pests, diseases, and other plant stress-related problems along the way.

A place to grow

You may dream of a big garden filled with all types of fresh and inviting vegetables, but getting to that stage takes experience and preparation. For the first timer, small is beautiful — take time to get it right on a small scale before launching a market-garden-sized project. Keep the following ideas in mind to save yourself a lot of work and frustration later in the season:

- ✔ **Start small.** Little plants and seeds turn into a big commitment as they grow. A 10-x-20-foot garden is plenty to grow a variety of vegetables such as lettuce, beans, carrots, tomatoes, and peppers. If you want to grow vining crops or space hogs, such as corn or pumpkins, you can expand it to 20 x 30 feet. Planting too large a space to keep well tended is probably the number one cause for gardener frustration and burnout.

- ✔ **Make it convenient.** Place the garden in a location where you'll see it daily. Mine is right outside the dining room window, and my garden gets more attention now than it did when it was in the corner of our backyard. Your garden is more likely to thrive when you visit it regularly.

- ✔ **Put the garden in full sun.** Vegetable plants need at least 6 hours of full sun each day. Orient and plan the garden so that tall plants, such as corn and tomatoes don't cast shade on shorter plants, such as beets and cabbage.

- ✔ **Choose a well-drained spot.** Vegetables are more prone to disease in soggy soil. See Chapter 3 for how to test and amend soil for proper drainage.

- ✔ **Grow a variety of crops.** Planting a number of different vegetables ensures that something will produce. Plus, diversity in the garden encourages good insects and helps to reduce problems from harmful ones.

Preparing the soil

Healthy soil is the key to the success of your vegetable garden and the logical place to start. Soil rich with fertile organic matter, beneficial microorganisms, nutrients, and air spaces produces the most vigorous and productive vegetable plants. Keep the soil pH between 6.0 and 7.0 and add a 3- to 4-inch layer of compost or composted manure, worked into the soil, before each planting season. Compost adds organic matter and it's the organic gardener's mantra (see Chapter 4)!

For all but the sandiest soils, I recommend that you grow your vegetables in raised beds. *Raised beds* are soil that has been mounded to form a large flat surface usually 3 to 4 feet wide, 6 to 12 inches tall, and as long as needed. Raised beds offer many advantages, especially if you have poorly drained or clay soil:

✔ **Soil drains faster.**

✔ **Soil warms up faster in the spring.** Drier soil warms more quickly than water-saturated soil.

✔ **Prevents soil compaction.** Because you don't step on raised beds, the soil doesn't compact as much and the roots grow better — especially on root crops such as carrots, beets, and radishes.

✔ **Concentrates and conserves fertilizer and water in the growing zone.**

✔ **Efficient and more productive plants.** More ideal growing conditions allow you to plant a little closer together than normal, which reduces watering and weeding.

You can build two types of raised beds — either contained or freestanding:

✔ *Contained raised beds* have permanent walls around them made from wood, bricks, or stone. These beds look neat and tidy and don't have to be reformed each year.

✔ You make *freestanding raised beds* from soil in the garden each year. They don't have walls made from other materials, so they tend to flatten and lower with time. Freestanding raised beds are good for flexibility and changing garden designs each year and to rotate crops.

Regardless of the type you make, amend the soil each year with several inches compost. Work it into the top 12 inches of soil with a garden fork. Smooth the top of the beds with a garden rake, as shown in Figure 11-1.

Designing your vegetable garden

You can be as creative or traditional as you like in your vegetable garden design. Plant everything in straight rows or create imaginative curved raised beds. My vegetable garden is oddly shaped so I frequently make rounded and triangular beds. I even made a heart-shaped raised bed one year and planted it with red-leaf lettuce and carrots!

In the winter, I sit down with a mug of hot tea and draw a diagram of my garden plan on graph paper, laying out rows and raised beds with a ruler and pencil. To figure out how many plants will fit into a row or bed, I follow the guidelines on the seed packets and make little dots or circles to indicate the larger veggies, such as broccoli, tomatoes, and squash. When you plan your vegetable garden, leave room for walking paths at least 24 inches wide to harvest and work the beds, and don't be afraid to mix in herbs and flowers. The more color and variety, the more beautiful the garden, and more likely you'll strike an ecological balance with birds and beneficial insects, helping to keep harmful pests in check.

Figure 11-1:
Rake the soil flat and smooth on top of raised beds before planting.

For even more garden success, try a few of the techniques I use in my garden. They may help you grow better and more vegetables, too.

✔ **Be creative with the garden design.** Don't plant all the same type of vegetables in one spot. For example, I plant two small patches of beans in different spots in the garden. This ensures that even if animals or insects destroy one patch, chances are, they may not find the other.

✔ **Rotate crops every planting season.** Follow crops that use lots of nitrogen, such as sweet corn and tomatoes, with crops that add nitrogen to the soil, such as beans and peas. Avoid planting crops from the same family, which tend to share the same insect pests and diseases, in the same spot, for example, tomatoes, eggplants, and potatoes or cabbage, broccoli, and kale. Allow at least 3 years before planting a vegetable family in the same spot again.

✔ **Use succession planting.** Crops, such as lettuce and beans, are quick to mature, so you can plant them several times throughout the growing season for a constant supply of tender new vegetables. This works best when you plant small patches of each vegetable every two weeks. That way you won't ever have a glut of lettuce, and it extends the growing season.

✔ **Try companion planting.** According to folklore and some gardeners' observations, some plants receive mutual benefit from growing near one another. Plants may benefit another plant by repelling certain insect pests, making nutrients more available, giving shade, or providing a habitat for beneficial insects. Table 11-1 shows some of the favorable and unfavorable combinations you might try. Keep in mind, most of this theory isn't scientifically proven, so experiment in your garden and see what happens. Chapters 12 and 15 have more on companion planting with herbs and flowers.

Table 11-1	Companion Planting Table*	
Crop	*Companion*	*Incompatible*
Asparagus	Tomato, parsley, basil	
Beans	Most vegetables and herbs	Onion, garlic
Beets	Cabbage, onion families, lettuce, radish	Pole beans
Cabbage	Celery, beets, onion family, spinach, chard	Pole beans, lettuce
Carrots	English pea, lettuce, rosemary, onion, sage, tomato	Dill
Celery	Onion and cabbage families, tomato, bush beans, nasturtium	Carrot
Corn	Potato, beans, pea, pumpkin, cucumber, squash	Tomato
Cucumber	Beans, corn, English pea, sunflower, radish	Potato
Eggplant	Beans, marigold	
Lettuce	Carrot, radish, cucumber	Broccoli, wheat, rye
Onion family	Beets, carrot, lettuce, cabbage, strawberry	Beans, English peas
Pea, English	Carrots, radish, turnip, cucumber, corn, beans	Onion, garlic, Irish potato
Potato, Irish	Beans, corn, cabbage family	Pumpkin, squash, tomato, cucumber
Pumpkins	Corn, beans on trellis	Irish potato
Radish	English pea, lettuce, cucumber, squash	
Squash	Corn, beans on trellis	Irish potato
Tomato	Onion family, asparagus, carrot, cucumber, parsley	Irish potato, dill
Turnip	English pea	Irish potato

Compiled from traditional literature on companion planting.

When to start?

Most vegetables are *annual plants,* which die after one season of growth and these generally fall into two groups — warm season and cool season.

- ✔ *Warm-season* crops such as tomatoes, peppers, sweet corn, melons, and cucumber, grow best in hot weather. Plant them 1 to 2 weeks after the last frost date for your area or when the soil is at least 60 degrees. These plants don't like the cold, so don't rush to plant them before the soil warms up. Contact your local weather service to determine your average last frost date, if you aren't sure when it usually occurs.

- ✔ *Cool-season* vegetables grow best during cool weather and include broccoli, spinach, lettuce, carrots, and potatoes. You can usually plant them in the garden 1 to 2 weeks before the last frost date. Not only can they tolerate cool weather, they need cool weather to grow and mature properly. If you plant these crops too late in spring, they won't thrive in the heat of the summer. You can even plant some, such as peas and lettuce, in mid-to-late summer for a fall harvest.

Winter is the quiet time between gardening seasons in most parts of the country. But in mild winter and hot summer areas of the country, such as southern California, Texas, and Florida, the cycle is reversed. There, you plant warm-season crops in spring and fall and cool-season crops in winter. Summer is the time for you and the veggies to take a break from the hot weather. In rainy, mild areas, you can grow some crops, especially those that enjoy cool weather, year 'round. Plant warm-season crops so that they mature during the warmest months of the year.

You can get vegetable plants started in your garden in two different ways. Some crops, such beans, peas, carrots, and squash, are normally sown directly in the garden soil where they'll grow. Other plants, such as tomatoes, peppers, and eggplants, which take a long time to mature their crops, grow best if transplanted — they're called *transplants.* They get an early start in greenhouses or indoors in your house 4 to 6 weeks before you set them in their permanent garden location. This head start is critical in cold areas with short summers.

Finally, some vegetables, such as cucumber, broccoli, onion, and lettuce, go either way. You'll find already started transplants of these at local garden centers or you can sow them directly in the garden. Base your decision on how much time you have and whether your favorite varieties are more readily available as transplants or seeds.

GARDEN JARGON

Sorting out seed types

When choosing vegetable varieties to plant, you may come across the terms *hybrid, open pollinated,* and *genetically modified.* The first two are important for home gardeners, while the third is a new type of plant that, to date, applies mainly to commercial farmers.

- ✔ *Open-pollinated* or *heirloom* varieties are those that produce offspring similar to the parents. The flowers are naturally pollinated in the fields with little or no interference from the farmer. Some classic open-pollinated varieties include 'Brandywine' tomato, 'Kentucky Wonder' bean, and 'Golden Bantam' sweet corn. Many of these varieties are locally adapted and have unusual colors, shapes, and flavors. Gardeners have relied on these for generations because they can save the seeds and grow the plants easily.

- ✔ *Hybrid varieties* have been around since the 1900s. Researchers found that breeding different corn varieties together resulted in offspring with better traits than either parent, plus they grew vigorously and more uniformly. Although you can't successfully save seeds from hybrids, many varieties exhibit important characteristics, such as

improved disease resistance, vigor, and consistent quality. Some classic examples of hybrid varieties include 'Big Boy' tomato, 'Gypsy' pepper, and 'Premium Crop' broccoli.

- ✔ *Genetically modified* plants are those bred through gene splicing where certain characteristics are taken from unrelated plants or even other organisms and inserted in the vegetable. Most of these varieties are in the corn, soybean, cotton, and potato groups and most are available only for farmers to purchase. While genetically modified plants offer many benefits, such as decreased dependence on pesticide sprays due to inserting an insecticide into the plant, many questions still exist about the long-term health risks and environmental safety of manipulating the gene pool so dramatically and quickly.

Which type of vegetable variety you grow is a personal decision based on trial and error and recommendations from fellow gardeners. The key is to experiment in your garden with a range of varieties to find the right ones that grow, produce, and taste best to you.

Growing Veggies 101

Growing a garden is like learning to run a marathon — start one step at a time, take it slowly at first, and build on your successes. The following sections give you the steps you need to follow — from seed starting to harvesting — to create a successful and abundant garden.

Sowing seeds

After your raised beds and garden soil are raked and ready (see the "Preparing the soil" section, earlier in this chapter), it's finally time to plant. The general rule for planting seeds is to plant them twice as deep as the seeds are wide. For big seeds, such as beans and corn, that means about 1 to 2 inches deep, while small seeds such as lettuce may be planted only ¼-inch deep. After they're in the soil, keep the soil evenly moist, especially the soil surface. If the surface dries out, it can form a crust that prevents seedlings from emerging.

You should see signs of life within a few days for quick sprouters, such as radish. It may take up to 2 weeks for slowpokes, such as carrots, to germinate. Be patient — as long as you used fresh seed, labeled for the current year, they should come up eventually. In unusually wet and cold or hot and dry soil, however, seeds may rot or fail to sprout. Replant, if necessary, when the weather improves.

When you put already started transplants into the garden, you can set them a bit deeper in the soil than they grew in their pots. I plant peppers, eggplants, tomatoes, and cabbage-type plants right up to their first set of *true leaves,* the ones that look like miniature adult leaves and grow above the fleshy *seed leaves.* Planting more deeply gives plants stability and, in some cases, a stronger root system. Loosely wrap a 2- to 3-inch wide strip of newspaper around each stem before planting to prevent cutworms from chewing through the tender stem. The paper should extend at least an inch above and below the soil.

Feed me

When seeds are up and growing and the transplants are planted, give them a dose of fertilizer. Mild, liquid organic fertilizers, such as fish emulsion and seaweed mix, provide nitrogen and other essential nutrients for early growth. Water your plants with 1 tablespoon each of liquid fish emulsion and liquid seaweed fertilizers mixed into 1 gallon of tepid water one week after seeds sprout and at planting time for transplants.

You may also consider applying a complete organic fertilizer, such as 5-3-3, to keep them growing strong. (See Chapter 5 for more on organic fertilizers.) *Heavy-feeding* vegetables, such as corn, tomatoes, and broccoli, may need monthly doses of fertilizer, while *light feeders,* such as beans, radishes, and peas, may need little or no additional fertilizer.

Use 1 to 2 tablespoons of granular fertilizer per plant or 1 to 2 pounds per 25 feet of row, depending on the size and type of plants. Sprinkle it 6 to 8 inches from the stems and scratch it gently into the soil. Water the soil to dissolve and disperse the fertilizer. If you use liquid fertilizer, follow the recommended dosage on the label and apply it with a watering can around the bases of the plants.

Don't go overboard on the fertilizer, however. Even organic fertilizers can accumulate in the soil, causing a harmful salt buildup that harms plant roots. And excess fertilizer can run off into streams, causing water pollution. If you give them too much nitrogen at the wrong time, you may even prevent some vegetables from forming fruit. Tomatoes, peppers, and eggplants, for example, grow loads of lush foliage, but few flowers or fruit.

Weeds and water

Almost as soon as you see signs of vegetables germinating, you're probably going to see weeds, too. Begin getting familiar with what your vegetables look like when they're small so you don't pull them out instead of the weeds.

The best way to control weeds is to hand pull or slice them off with a hoe when they're young because you disturb less soil and they're easier to pull at that time than when they're more mature. Then mulch around the vegetables, as follows:

- ✔ For heat-loving crops, such as tomato, cucumber, and squash, use black landscape fabric mulch to stop weed growth, heat the soil, and conserve moisture. Lay the fabric down on the planting bed *before* planting, then poke holes in the fabric with scissors or a knife to plant your transplants or seeds.

- ✔ For cool loving crops, such as lettuce, broccoli, and spinach, mulch with organic materials, such as hay, newspapers, grass clippings, or pine straw, after planting. A 3- to 4-inch thick layer keeps most weeds at bay throughout the summer, keeps the soil cool, and conserves moisture. In warm summer areas, you may need to reapply the organic mulch in mid-summer because it does degrade quickly in heat and moisture. See Chapter 6 for more on weeding and mulching.

Watering is critical during the early stages of plant growth, but it's also essential when the plants are forming and ripening fruits. Mulching is an excellent way to keep the soil moist throughout the summer, but you may need to do some supplemental watering, depending on your weather and where you live. Small, deformed fruits may be due to lack of water. Also, some conditions such as blossom end rot on tomatoes is due to fluctuating soil moisture, so be consistent about watering and mulching.

Garden tricks and season extenders

Experienced gardeners have picked up a few methods along the way that make certain crops grow better. Consider trying these nifty tricks — covered in the following sections — to help you save space, produce better quality veggies, and extend your growing season beyond the first and last frost dates.

Trellises, fences, and cages — oh my!

If you're short on space in your garden or perhaps want to plant more than you really have room for, go vertical! You can save space and energy by trellising, fencing, or caging certain vegetables. Climbing vegetables, such as peas and pole beans, need fences or poles to grow on. Not only do these save space, but these crops also produce best when allowed to climb. Set up a teepee of 6 to 8 foot poles, attach chicken wire to fence posts, or train on an A-frame. (If you use the teepee method, wind some twine around the poles at 6-inch intervals to give the vines something to cling to.)

Cucumbers, melons, and even some squash love to vine and ramble. You can direct their energy by growing them on a trellis. Place the trellis on an angle such as an A-frame design shown in Figure 11-2, instead of straight up and down. Be sure it's very sturdy if you're growing vines with heavy fruits, such as melons or squash.

Tomatoes, peppers, and eggplants all can be caged or staked with a pole to keep them growing upright, keeping their fruits off the ground (which can help prevent disease and damage from slugs, mice, and other ground-dwelling critters) and giving you more produce in less space. Commercial growers tie wire or twine between fence posts and weave the growing tomato plants through it. Four- to 5-foot-high wire cages made of hog fencing or concrete reinforcing wire work well, too. Secure them with a tall stake pounded into the ground to prevent the cages from blowing over.

Floating row covers

Floating row covers are one of best things ever to happen to veggie gardeners. This cheesecloth-like material is lightweight and lets air, light, and water through it, but blocks out insects that can attack vegetables. Also, when used as a cover in spring on newly sown plants, it keeps the air and soil a little warmer, which helps seeds germinate faster and young plants grow more quickly. I use floating row covers on my peppers in spring to ensure an early harvest of fruits because pepper flowers need warmer air temperatures for proper pollination. The row covers help at the other end of the season, too, by holding in heat and moderating the cool autumn night temperatures.

Figure 11-2:
Use an A-frame trellis to grow squash, cucumbers, or melons in less space. Inset shows weaving the net through the top support.

On vegetables, such as lettuce and broccoli, that don't need pollination from bees, you can also leave the row cover on all during the growing season — as long as it doesn't get too hot. The row cover prevents cabbage moths, aphids, and other pests from getting to your vegetables. You can support the row cover with wire hoops or just lay it right on the top of vegetables. It's so lightweight, the veggies will lift it as they grow.

Staying warm with cold frames

A clever way to start your growing season earlier in the spring and keep it going long into the frosty fall is to make or buy a cold frame. *Cold frames* are bottomless, insulated boxes made from wood, hay bales, metal, or plastic and they work like miniature greenhouses. The top of the box is angled slightly to increase its exposure to the sun and covered with a plastic or glass top, which keeps the inside much warmer than the outside air temperature. Even in the coldest climates, you can use a cold frame to grow food year 'round. In the spring, grow a crop of lettuce and get your other warm-season crops off to an early start. In the fall and winter, try cold-tolerant spinach, kale, and leeks. You can make your cold frame large enough to fit over a raised bed in the garden or keep it small and portable to move around as needed.

The key to using cold frames is to ventilate them properly by propping open the sash or top window. Even on very cool, but sunny days, the inside of the box really heats up, much like a car with its windows rolled up. Automatic vent openers, available from greenhouse suppliers, raise and lower the top automatically without electricity, depending on the air temperature. For more on gardening with cold frames, get a copy of Eliot Coleman's excellent book, *The New Organic Grower's Four-Season Harvest,* published by Chelsea Green Publishing Company.

Harvest time

Picking is one of my favorite activities, second only to eating. The temptation is to go out and harvest as soon as you see something growing. This works well for many crops, such as beans, summer squash, cucumbers, lettuce, and peas, that taste best when harvested young. The more you pick of these crops, the more they'll produce! In fact, if you let some vegetables become too mature on these plants they may stop producing altogether.

For many other crops, however, you have to be patient. Tomatoes, peppers, carrots, and beets taste best when allowed to ripen and grow to maturity in the soil or on the plant. Of course, when in doubt, take a bite. If it doesn't suit your taste buds, wait a few days and try again.

Most vegetables taste sweetest and most tender when freshly picked. In our house, I start the water boiling on the stove before I head outside to harvest the corn for supper. Peas, summer squash, and string beans, too, are sweet and juicy if picked just before eating. Some vegetables, on the other hand, such as most winter squash, need a week or two at 60 to 70 degrees to cure after harvest to develop their full flavor. Read the next section to get more specifics for each vegetable.

Vegetables From A to Z

Seed catalogs have so many delicious veggies to choose from that you may have a tough time knowing where to start — and stop! If you're growing your first garden, grow just a few different vegetables from among your favorites and stick to one variety of each. As you gain experience, add more kinds and experiment with one or two different crops each year. If something doesn't work out the way that you expected it to, try a different variety or growing method or abandon it and give the garden space to another crop. For me, that's one of the beautiful things about vegetables gardens — you get to start with a clean slate each year and have a chance to improve and change your garden based on last year's experiences.

In the following descriptions of each vegetable, I've included some choice varieties, plus planting and care recommendations, harvest tips, and specific pests you'll need to watch out for. Many organic gardeners prefer to buy seeds and young transplants that were produced organically. Although many seed companies don't grow organic seeds, some specialize in them and others offer them in addition to non-organically grown seeds. See the "Organic seed sources" sidebar in this chapter. Support your local organic growers by buying vegetable transplants from them if they offer them for sale.

Alliums: Onions, shallots, garlic, and leeks

Onions, shallots, garlic, and leeks all belong to a group of pungent plants called *alliums*. These plants generally form bulbs or enlarged below-ground stems. Many members of the allium family make lovely additions to the flower garden.

Choosing an onion variety is more complicated than choosing most other vegetables because they fall into different groups based on sulfur content and the day length they need to form bulbs. *Pungent* varieties contain more sulfur, which makes them keep longer in storage and produce more tears when you cut them. *Sweet* varieties don't have as much sulfur and need to be used sooner after harvest. Adverse growing conditions, such as weed competition, drought, and poor fertility can increase onions' sulfur content, even in the sweet varieties.

Onions are also referred to as short, long day, or intermediate. *Short-day* varieties form bulbs when they receive 11 to 12 hours of daylight. *Long-day* varieties need 14 to 16 hours of daylight to form bulbs. Choose long-day varieties, such as 'Walla Walla' (sweet) and 'Copra' (pungent) for northern climates. Go with short-day varieties, such as 'Granex' (sweet) and 'White Bermuda' (sweet) if you live south of 35 degrees latitude, which runs from northern

South Carolina through Oklahoma and Arizona to central California. When in doubt, try an intermediate variety, such as 'Candy' (sweet). You can start onions from seeds, transplants, or *sets,* which are small dormant bulbs.

Garlic varieties come in two types — soft-neck and hard-neck. *Soft-neck* kinds produce 12 to 18 small cloves and are best for long-term storage. *Hard-neck* types produce 6 to 12 cloves and don't keep as long in storage. Some favorite soft-neck varieties include 'Silverskin', while a good hard-neck variety is 'German Red'. Ask around at farmers' markets for advice and choose a variety that suits your climate and soil type.

Shallots are mild tasting, small onions and the easiest to grow of all the edible alliums. Try 'Gray' or 'Brittany' varieties. Another onion relative, leeks, are indispensable in European cooking and are easy to grow in raised beds. Varieties include 'King Richard' and 'Winter Giant'.

- **Planting and care:** Alliums like well-drained, fertile, loose soil and appreciate raised beds. They grow well in cool weather and can take a light frost. Sow onion seeds indoors a few months before transplanting into the garden and keep the tops trimmed to about 3 inches high until transplant time. In moderate climates, sow seeds in fall for a spring harvest. In colder climates, sow seeds in early spring for a summer harvest. Plant shallot and onion sets in the spring. Cloves of garlic are best planted in fall, even in cold climates, to overwinter and mature the following summer. Start leeks indoors in spring 8 to 10 weeks before setting transplants into the garden. They mature in fall.

  Keep your alliums weed-free, well watered, and fertilized with a high phosphorous fertilizer, such as bone meal, to promote large bulb growth.

- **Harvesting:** When the tops begin to yellow, the bulbs are usually ready for harvest. After pulling them out of the ground, either use fresh or allow them to cure in a warm, airy room for a few weeks before storing in a cold basement. Use sweet onion varieties within a few weeks. Shallots, pungent onions, and some garlic varieties, however, can last for months in storage. Pull leeks as needed in fall, after cool weather "sweetens" their taste. Many varieties can withstand 20-degree temperatures.

- **Pests and diseases:** Onion maggots are probably one of the worst pests of the allium family crops, feeding on onion roots and bulbs. Mulching, crop rotation, and row covers help reduce the risks from these pests.

Asparagus

Asparagus plants are either female or male and the best varieties of asparagus are the ones dubbed *all-male*. The female plants produce seeds, which reduce the amount of spears they produce. The males don't produce seeds and, therefore, produce more edible-sized spears. Good all-male varieties include 'Jersey Giant', 'Jersey King' and 'Jersey Knight'. 'UC 157' is a good one for California.

✔ **Planting and care:** Asparagus is a perennial vegetable that can live for 20 years, so take special care to create a proper planting bed. Choose a sunny location with well-drained soil. Dig a 1-foot-deep trench and add 6 inches of compost or well-rotted manure. Form 8-inch-high mounds, 18 inches apart, in the trench and lay the spider-like asparagus roots over the mounds, as shown in Figure 11-3. The *crowns,* where the roots meet the stems, should be about 5 to 6 inches below the soil surface. Cover them with 2 inches of soil and gradually backfill the trench, an inch or two at a time, as the asparagus spears grow until the trench is level with the surrounding soil. Fertilize the bed each spring with compost and a complete fertilizer. Keep the bed weed-free and well watered.

Figure 11-3:
Plant asparagus crowns in trenches and gradually fill them in as the plants grow.

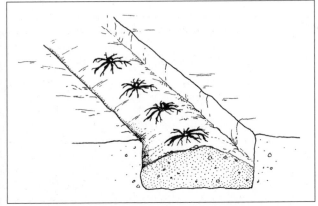

✔ **Harvesting:** Don't harvest any asparagus spears for the first year after planting. Let the crowns build up strength. The second year, harvest in spring only those spears larger than a pencil diameter for 3 to 4 weeks. In subsequent years, harvest pencil-diameter sized spears for up to 2 months. Let the remaining spears grow to rejuvenate the crown.

✔ **Pests and diseases:** Asparagus beetle is a hard-to-kill pest of asparagus. The adults damage the spears and larvae eat the fern-like asparagus leaves. Control them by removing the ferns in late fall and spray with pyrethrins in spring at first signs of this pest.

Cole crops: Broccoli, cauliflower, cabbage, and company

These closely related plants share the same growing requirements, diseases, and pests. All thrive in cool spring and autumn weather and tolerate frost. Some of the best broccoli varieties include 'Premium Crop', 'Packman' and 'Green Comet'. For good cauliflower, try 'Snow Crown' and 'Fremont'.

Cabbage varieties that perform well include 'Red Acre', 'Savoy Ace', 'Stonehead' and, 'Dynamo'. Some of my favorite kale varieties are 'Red Russian', 'Lacinato', and 'Vates Dwarf Blue Scotch Curled'. Other not-so-common cole crops to try include 'Bubbles' Brussels sprouts and 'Winner' and 'Superschmeltz' kohlrabi.

- ✔ **Planting and care:** Sow seeds directly into the ground or start transplants indoors 4 to 6 weeks before transplanting them outside. Cole crops need a moderate amount of fertilizer and water throughout the growing season to grow well, but also like well-drained soil. Fertilize at planting and one month later with a complete fertilizer. Organic mulch, such as straw, placed around plants after transplanting helps keep the soil cool and moist.

    Take advantage of cool weather by sowing cole crops in early spring for an early summer harvest or late summer for a fall harvest. Some varieties of broccoli, cabbage, and cauliflower can be grown through the winter in mild winter areas for harvest in spring.

- ✔ **Harvesting:** Harvest broccoli when the heads (clusters of flowers) are tightly packed and still green by cutting just below the head. In most cases, new, but smaller broccoli heads will grow further down the stem. If the yellow flowers begin to open, the taste becomes bitter and the plant will stop producing more heads. Harvest cabbage when they're firm when squeezed. Cut them as described for broccoli. To harvest white or *blanched* cauliflower, wrap the upper plant leaves around the developing, 3- to 4-inch heads. Harvest within 4 to 10 days. Harvest Brussels sprouts after cool weather in fall when the sprouts are still firm by twisting them off the stem. Pick kale leaves as needed.

- ✔ **Pests and diseases:** Cabbageworms and cabbage loopers are the two primary pests of cole crops. The larvae feed on the leaves, decimating the plants quickly. Hand pick the caterpillars or spray *B.t.* to control them. Cabbage maggots attack the roots of cole crops. Place row covers over the plants to prevent the fly from laying eggs at the base of the plant. Black rot and club root damage the roots and heads of cole crops — crop rotation is the best control for these diseases.

Eggplant

Eggplant, like its cousins, peppers and tomatoes, loves hot weather, plenty of water, and full sun. Eggplants come in many size and colored varieties. A few favorites include the large, oval shaped 'Black Beauty' (purple), and 'Rosa Bianca' (lavender streaked). Long, narrow varieties include 'Ichiban' (purple) and 'Thai Long' (green). For small, round eggplants try 'Easter Egg' (white) and 'Turkish Orange' (orange).

- ✔ **Planting and care:** Start seeds indoors 8 weeks before transplanting outside. Wait until the soil has warmed to at least 60 degrees before transplanting. In colder climates or in small space gardens, consider planting eggplant in large containers to save space and get them to grow faster. Eggplants in containers also are very ornamental and look great as a decorative plant as well. Here in cool Vermont, I grow the best eggplants by covering them with a floating row cover to hold in the heat.

  Eggplants like moderate fertility and water, so fertilizer monthly and mulch with black landscape fabric, but go easy on the nitrogen fertilizer or you'll have all foliage and few flowers and fruits.

- ✔ **Harvesting:** Harvest eggplant when they've reached the desired size for eating. Harvest before the skin color becomes dull-looking — a sign of over maturity and mushiness.

- ✔ **Pests and diseases:** Verticillium wilt disease is a main problem for eggplant. This disease causes the entire plant to wilt and die in summer. The easiest solution to this soil-borne disease is to plant in containers filled with sterilized potting soil. Colorado potato beetles also love eggplant leaves. Hand picking adults, crushing eggs, and spraying with *B.t.* 'San Diego' will control the larval stage of this pest. See Chapter 9 for more on *Bacillus thuringiensis (B.t.)* varieties.

Leafy greens: Lettuce, Swiss chard, spinach, and friends

Leafy greens are easy crops to grow because you don't have to wait for the flowers or fruits as with cucumbers or tomatoes — you just eat the leaves! Lettuce varieties are categorized by the way their leaves grow. *Head lettuces,* such as iceberg types, form compact balls of leaves. *Looseleaf lettuces,* at the other end of the spectrum, have loosely arranged leaves that don't form tight heads. Other types, such as butterhead, romaine, and oakleaf, fall somewhere in between. Some of my favorites include 'Buttercrunch' looseleaf, 'Rosalita' red Romaine, 'Summertime' crisphead, and 'Red Salad Bowl' looseleaf.

Other leafy vegetable garden staples include Swiss chard, spinach, and an array of less well-known salad and cooking greens. Swiss chard varieties include 'Ruby', 'Bright Lights' (with an array of multi-colored stems) and 'Fordhook Giant'. Good spinach varieties are 'Space', 'Tyee', and 'Bloomsdale Longstanding'.

In the specialty greens category, grow arugula, dandelion, cress, chicory, mache, and mustard to give salad a zippy flavor. Many of these are blended together in mixes called *mesclun*. These may be spicy or mild flavored, but I guarantee they'll have more flavor than just a simple bowl of lettuce.

For Asian cooking, grow pac choi, tatsoi, and mizuna. You can add these leafy vegetables to stir fries or mix them into the salad bowl. Pac choi forms a loose cluster of juicy stems and dark green leaves. Tatsoi grows in a low rosette of spoon-shaped leaves that will regrow if you cut the leaves. Mizuna has slender stalks and fringed leaves.

- ✔ **Planting and care:** Most are cool-season crops, so sow seeds or set transplants outdoors a few weeks before the last frost date. Some leafy greens, such as lettuce, can be started indoors 3 to 4 weeks before setting them outdoors, giving plants a jump on the growing season. Stagger your crops of greens by planting small patches a couple weeks apart throughout the season: These plants mature quickly and you'll want a consistent harvest of greens.

    Leafy greens need nitrogen first and foremost. Add compost before planting and add a supplemental nitrogen fertilizer, such as fish emulsion, every few weeks. Mulch the plants, after they're established, with an organic hay or straw mulch to keep the soil cool and moist. Keeping the plants well watered will help prevent leaf-tip burn on lettuce.

- ✔ **Harvesting:** Harvest lettuce and greens when you're hungry and whenever leaves are big enough to eat. Pick off the lower leaves first so that new, younger leaves will continue to grow from the center of the plant. When greens such as arugula and lettuce *bolt* (send up a flower stalk), the leaves are probably too bitter tasting for most tastes and you should pull up and compost them.

- ✔ **Pests and diseases:** Snails and slugs can devour a patch in no time. You can trap them, set up barriers, bait them, and of course, handpick them to keep the populations low. Rabbits and woodchucks can also be a problem and fencing is the best cure for them. Leaf miner insects, especially on spinach, can ruin individual leaves. Just pick off and destroy the damaged leaves and the plant will be fine. See Chapter 8 for more about how to discourage and prevent pests.

Legumes: Peas and beans

Legumes have a unique ability to make their own nitrogen fertilizer through a relationship with soil-dwelling bacteria called *rhizobia*. Beans enjoy warm weather, but peas produce better in cool weather. You can eat beans fresh or allow the pods to mature for dry beans used in cooking. Popular dry bean varieties include 'Pinto', 'Yellow Eye', 'Midnight' black turtle, and 'Red Kidney'. Bean plants grow two different ways, either forming low bushy plants or climbing up a pole or trellis. In some cases, you can find pole and bush versions of the same variety. Good varieties include 'Blue Lake', 'Kentucky Wonder', 'Romano', and 'Improved Golden Wax' bush beans and 'Blue Lake', 'Kentucky Wonder', 'Purple Pod' and 'Goldmarie' pole beans.

Pea varieties also fall into two camps — those with edible pods and those grown just for fresh or dried seeds, called English peas. Good English pea varieties include 'Alderman', 'Daybreak', 'Lincoln', and 'Green Arrow'. Peas with edible pods either have flat pods, called snow peas, or fat, juicy pods, called snap or sugar peas. Try 'Sugar Snap' and 'Sugar Ann' snap peas and 'Dwarf Gray Sugar' for the classic snow peas used in stir fries.

- ✔ **Planting and care:** Legumes are easy to grow because the seeds are so large and easy to plant. Sow directly in well-drained soil. Plant beans when the soil has warmed to at least 60 degrees. Peas, however, need to be planted as soon as the soil has dried out in spring because they grow best before the summer heat arrives. After they're growing, pole beans need poles for support, while tall pea varieties such as 'Sugar Snap', need a fence to climb on. Keep the beds well weeded and watered. They generally don't need supplemental fertilizer.

- ✔ **Harvesting:** Harvest bush and pole beans when the pods are about 6 inches long, before the pods get bumpy from the seeds forming. Harvest dry beans after the pods have yellowed and withered. If they don't dry in the garden, you can pull up the whole plants and hang them to dry in an airy garage.

    Harvest snap and English peas when the pods fill and are firm to the squeeze. Keep checking and tasting when the pods begin to size up to be sure you harvest at the peak of sweetness. Harvest snow peas at any point after the pods form.

- ✔ **Pests and diseases:** The Mexican bean beetle causes the most trouble. The adults are ladybug look-alikes, but they produce yellow colored young that love eating bean leaves. Hand pick or use predatory insects, such as soldier bugs, to control them. Pea aphids attack pea plants and are easy to kill with just a stream of water from a hose. Watch out for rabbits and woodchucks — fences work best.

    Rust fungal disease attacks beans and spreads quickly, especially if you work in the bean patch while the leaves are still wet. The plants and beans will develop yellow colored spots, which can kill the plant. Clean up plant debris in fall and stay away from the bean patch in wet weather.

Peppers

Peppers are warm-weather crops. Peppers are generally grouped according to their taste — sweet or hot. Hot peppers contain a chemical, especially in the seeds and ribs, called *capsaicin,* which makes peppers hot. This chemical can get on your hands during harvesting and processing and, if you rub an open wound or your eyes, can cause a painful burning. Harvest hot peppers with gloves and wash your hands after preparing to remove any capsaicin. Some hot pepper varieties to try are 'Ancho', 'Hungarian Hot Wax', 'Super Cayenne', and 'Super Chili'.

Sweet peppers lack the bite of their hot-seeded brethren. Both hot and sweet varieties come in a rainbow of colors when mature. Some sweet pepper varieties to try include bell-shaped 'Arianne', California Wonder', 'Golden Summer', and 'North Star'. Some elongated-shaped sweet pepper varieties are 'Corno di Toro', 'Gypsy', and 'Sweet Banana'.

Peppers are also great plants for container growing. Some varieties, such as 'Pretty in Purple' with its colorful purple to red fruit and purple-tinged stems and leaves, are very ornamental.

✔ **Planting and care:** Start seeds indoors 6 to 8 weeks before setting plants outside. Wait until the soil has warmed to 60 degrees before transplanting. Peppers need fertile soil and plenty of water to grow well. In cool areas, consider growing them in black fabric mulch to heat the soil and keep weeds away. Fertilize monthly with a complete fertilizer and add one tablespoon of Epsom salts to the water to help the peppers grow better. However, don't overfertilize peppers with nitrogen fertilizer or you'll have all foliage and few flowers and fruits.

✔ **Harvesting:** Pepper fruits will turn a rainbow of colors, depending on the variety, as they mature. The beautiful part about peppers is you can pick them at the green stage or let them mature, when they reach their sweetest flavor. Hot peppers also can be harvested at any stage, but the flavor is hotter and better developed when allowed to mature on the plant.

✔ **Pests and diseases:** The pepper maggot is one of the more frustrating pests on sweet peppers. The adult fly lays an egg on the developing fruits, which hatch into small, white worms that tunnel into the fruit. The tunneling causes the fruit to rot. Cover the plants with row covers early in the season to discourage the adult from laying eggs. Sprays are of little use because the worm is inside the fruit. Fruitworms (see the "Sweet corn" section) and wilt disease (see the "Eggplant" section) also cause trouble.

Potatoes

Look for early-, mid-, and late-season potato varieties to stretch out your harvest. Early potatoes are ready to harvest about 65 days after planting — perfect for summer potato salads. Mid-season varieties mature in 75 to 80 days, and late ones take 90 days or more to harvest. The later varieties keep longer in storage. Potatoes are also roughly divided into baking and boiling varieties. Baking potatoes, such as 'Butte' and 'Yukon Gold', have drier, more mealy textured flesh, while boiling potatoes, such as 'Kennebec', 'Carola', and 'Red Norland', are moist and waxy.

If you're looking for something new to try, plant some fingerling potatoes. These varieties produce long, slim, tasty tubers and tend to yield more per pound planted than regular potatoes. My personal favorites include 'Russian Banana', which has yellow flesh and skin, and 'French Fingerling' and 'Rose Finn Apple', which have pink skin and yellow flesh. Colorful varieties of regular potatoes include 'All Blue', 'All Red', and lavender-skinned 'Caribe'.

- **Planting and care:** Potatoes are another cool season root crop that can be planted a few weeks before your last frost date. They grow rather unpretentiously and without much maintenance until late summer when you dig the roots. Potatoes grow best in loose soil that hasn't been amended with fertilizer. Too much nitrogen fertilizer in particular can lead to poor tuber formation. Keep the soil moist by watering or applying organic mulches, such as hay or straw.

  Purchase potato tubers or *seed potatoes* and cut large potatoes into smaller pieces with at least one "eye" or bud. Place them in 1-foot deep trenches about one foot apart. Fill in the trench with soil as they sprout and grow, eventually mounding or hilling around the tops of the plants with soil, as shown in Figure 11-4. Hilling the soil around the plants allows the roots to form more potatoes, kills weeds, and protects the tubers from the light. Tubers exposed to light turn green and have an off flavor.

- **Harvesting:** When the potato tops turn yellow and begin to die back, it's time to dig up the tubers. With a shovel or iron fork, carefully dig around the potato plants and lift up the tubers. Let them cure in a dark, airy, 50-degree room for a few weeks, and then store them in a cool basement at about 40 degrees. Eat any damaged potatoes immediately and never store potatoes and apples near each other because apples give off ethylene gas, which causes potatoes and other vegetables to spoil.

- **Pests and diseases:** The Colorado potato beetle is the most famous pest. This yellow and black-striped beetle lays orange eggs on the undersides of leaves, which hatch into voracious orange-red larvae that devour potato and eggplant leaves. Hand pick the adults and crush the eggs. Spray *B.t.* 'San Diego' to control the larvae. Wireworms attack potato tubers under ground, causing tunneling and rotting. They're mostly a problem in new gardens created from lawns.

Fungal diseases, such as potato scab and blight, can ruin a crop. Your first defense is to buy resistant varieties. Control potato scab by lowering the soil pH to below 6 and avoid using manure fertilizer. Control blight by planting your potato crop in a new place every year, buying certified disease-free tubers, mulching, and keeping weeds under control.

Figure 11-4:
Hill soil around young potato plants to increase yield and prevent weeds.

Root crops: Carrots, beets, and radishes

Root crops provide good eating well into the fall and winter and are easy to grow. Raised beds filled with loose, fertile, stone-free soil provide just the right environment. Some great carrot varieties to try include 'Scarlet Nantes', 'Danvers Half Long', 'Sweetness II', and 'Sweet Sunshine'. Some good beet varieties include 'Detroit Dark Red', 'Ace', and 'Chioggia'. A few choice radish varieties to grow include 'Easteregg', 'Cherry Belle' and 'French Breakfast'.

✔ **Planting and care:** Root crops generally need a loose soil, well-amended with compost, weed-free growing conditions, and water to thrive. Directly sow root crop seeds a few weeks before the last frost date for your area. Sow them lightly and cover with sand, potting soil, or grass clippings and keep moist. Radishes germinate within a few days, while carrots may take 2 weeks. I usually mix radish and carrot seeds to help mark the row and harvest the radishes before the carrots need the space.

Thin the seedlings so the eventual spacing is about 2 to 4 inches apart, depending on the crop. If you don't thin root crops when they're young, they won't get large enough to eat. You can eat the thinned beet greens.

✔ **Harvesting:** Pull up radishes when the roots get large enough to eat. Leave carrots and beets in the ground to harvest as needed. Their flavor gets sweeter after the soil cools. You can even cover carrots in late fall with a cold frame and fill it with hay mulch and harvest carrots all winter.

✔ **Pests and diseases:** Other than four-legged critters such as rabbits, which love to eat the carrot and beet tops, the biggest pest of carrot is the rust fly. The adult fly lays an egg near the carrot and the small larvae tunnels into the carrot root. Cover the crop with a row cover to prevent the fly from laying an egg. Swallowtail butterfly larvae also like to munch on carrot tops, so try to grow enough for both of you!

Sweet corn

As soon as you harvest corn, the sugars in the kernels begin to turn to starch, making the corn less sweet as time goes by. But many new sweet corn varieties stay sweeter longer after harvest because plant breeders breed them to contain *supersweet* characteristics. These varieties, which include 'Bodacious' (yellow), 'Honey N'Pearl' (bicolor), and 'How Sweet It Is' (white), must be planted at least 25 to 100 feet from other, non-supersweet varieties. If another variety pollinates a supersweet variety, the kernels may be tough and starchy.

If you're satisfied with regular, old-fashioned varieties, choose from those with yellow, white, or both-colored kernels, called *bicolor*. If you plant yellow and white varieties near each other, you may get bicolor corn, anyway. Some of my favorites include 'Silver Queen' (white) and 'Early Sunglow' (yellow).

✔ **Planting and care:** Sweet corn needs a well-drained, highly fertile soil and warm weather to grow well. Sow seeds in blocks of 4 to 5 short rows after the soil has warmed to 65 degrees. Separate blocks of different corn varieties from each other by at least 25 feet so that no cross-pollination occurs. Hoe soil up around the plants when they're 8 inches tall to support them during windy days and to destroy young weeds that compete with the corn plants. Fertilize at planting (with compost) and again when the corn is knee-high (with a high nitrogen fertilizer, such as soybean meal). Fertilize a final time with the same fertilizer when the silk emerges at the tips of the ears.

✔ **Harvesting:** Start checking for maturity when the corn ears feel full and the silks are brown. You can take a peek under the husks at the corn ear tip to see if the kernels have matured. Pick the ears on the young side for the sweetest and most tender flavor.

✔ **Pests and diseases:** Major corn pests include the corn earworm and corn borer. The earworm larvae tunnel into the tip of the corn ear, causing only cosmetic damage. The ear is still edible. Either spray *B.t.* on the silks or apply a few drops of mineral oil when ears are young to kill the earworm larvae. Varieties with extra tight husks, such as 'Tuxedo' resist damage.

The corn borer larva causes more major damage to a plant by tunneling into the leaves and stalk. *B.t.* sprays and crop rotation can help lessen the problems from corn borers. Raccoons are the other major corn pests. Raccoons love corn and seem to know when it's ripe. An electric fence is the best — and maybe the only — defense against these clever animals.

Tomatoes

Tomato, easily the most popular garden vegetable, boasts varieties with fruit available in many sizes, shapes, and colors. The plants, however, fall into two categories. *Determinate* varieties stop growing taller when they reach a certain height and need minimal support, making them ideal for containers. *Indeterminate* varieties just keep on growing taller and taller, like Jack's beanstalk! Indeterminate tomatoes require trellising, but yield more fruit per square foot of garden space.

Most gardeners grow tomatoes for three main purposes — slicing, snacks, and sauce. Some of my favorite standard, round-shaped, slicing tomato varieties include 'Celebrity' and 'Early Girl' (red), 'Brandywine' (pink), 'Lemon Boy' (yellow), 'Big Rainbow' (striped yellow and red), and 'Big Beef' (red). For snacking, I like cherry tomato varieties 'Sun Gold' (gold), 'Super Sweet 100' (red), 'Sweet Million' (red), and 'Yellow Pear' (yellow). My favorite plum-shaped tomatoes, which I use to make sauce, include 'Amish Paste', 'Roma', 'Bellstar', 'Heinz 2653', and 'Viva Italia'.

- ✔ **Planting and care:** Tomatoes grow best when transplanted into 60-degree soil and kept warm. Mulching with black landscape fabric in cool areas helps speed along their growth. They need fertile soil, so amend the soil with compost before planting and then side-dress plants monthly with a complete fertilizer. Keep plants mulched and well watered to avoid blossom end rot (rotting of the end of maturing tomatoes) as fruits mature.

    Plant tall and leggy tomato transplants up to within 4 inches of their tops in a deep hole or lay them on their side in a trench, as shown in Figure 11-5, and the stem will root. Place a tomato cage or trellis support around the plants at planting time. Tie or wind indeterminate varieties around their supports as they grow and prune off extra side shoots to keep the plant from getting too bushy.

- ✔ **Harvesting:** Let the fruits turn red (or yellow, gold, or whatever color was intended). The longer you leave them on the vine, the deeper the color and sweeter and fuller the fruit flavor. However, even if you pick too early, fruits will continue ripening indoors if placed in a warm, airy room.

- ✔ **Pests and diseases:** The main insect pests are tomato hornworms and tomato fruitworms. Both of these caterpillars can be controlled with *B.t.*, although you can easily handpick hornworms. Nematodes can also attack tomato roots, causing the roots to be deformed and the plants to be stunted and unproductive. Choose nematode-resistant varieties if these microscopic soil pests are a problem in your area.

    Leaf blight diseases often start as small spots on leaves and then expand to yellow areas, killing leaves and the plant if unchecked. To control these, clean up crop debris at the end of the growing season, rotate crops, and mulch to prevent the disease spores from splashing onto leaves during rains. Wilt diseases, such as Verticillium and Fusarium, can cause plants to suddenly wilt and die in midseason. Purchase plants that are wilt resistant (usually indicated in the variety description) and remove and destroy infected plants as soon as you can to prevent the disease from spreading.

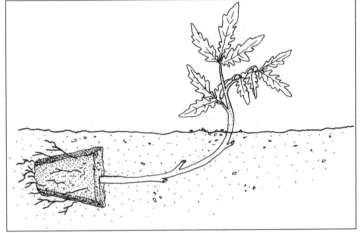

Figure 11-5:
Plant leggy tomato transplants horizontally in a trench.

Vining crops: Cucumbers, squash, pumpkins, and melons

All these crops share the common trait of growing their fruits on long, trailing vines, although some varieties now grow more compact and bush-like. Many of these species can pollinate each other, too, making it nearly impossible to get seeds that grow fruit resembling the original varieties.

Cucumbers are classified as either *slicers* (long and thin) or *picklers* (short and prickly). Good slicing varieties include 'Fanfare' and 'Suyo Long'. For pickles, try 'Bush Pickle' or 'Calypso'.

Squash are grouped as either summer squash, such as 'Black Zucchini', 'Sunburst' patty pan, 'Yellow Crookneck', or winter squash such as 'Table King' (acorn), 'Burgess Buttercup', and 'Waltham Butternut'. Winter squash fruits develop hard skin and dense flesh, making them good for storing through the fall and early winter.

Pumpkins range in dimension from apple-sized to something resembling a small Volkswagen Beetle. Some are used for cooking, while others are better for carving and ornament. For pies and soup, grow 'New England Pie', 'Baby Pam', or 'Small Sugar'. For carving, 'Howden' and 'Connecticut Field' are among the standards. Grow 'Atlantic Giant' or 'Big Max' for the big pumpkin contest at the county fair.

Organic seed sources

One way to support organic farming is to purchase organically grown vegetable seeds for your garden. Some seed companies and mail-order catalogs specialize in organic seeds or at least offer as many organically grown seed varieties as they can. Here are a few sources to get you started:

✔ **Fedco Seeds** is organized as a cooperative with workers and customers sharing in their profits. They sell seeds, potato tubers, and lots of gardening supplies. In their very informative and extensive catalog, they disclose the sources of the seeds they offer, some of which are grown specifically for them. Send for a catalog at Fedco Seeds, P.O. Box 520, Waterville, ME 04903-0520. You can leave a message on their answering machine at 207-873-7333 or fax a catalog request to 207-872-8317.

✔ **Abundant Life Seed Foundation** is a not-for-profit organization that works to preserve heirloom seeds and promote sustainable agriculture worldwide through the World

Seed Fund. They offer seeds through their mail-order catalog. Write them at P.O. Box 772, Port Townsend, WA 98368, call 360-385-5660, or visit their Web site for more information about their mission at http://csf.colorado.edu/perma/abundant/index.html.

✔ **Seeds of Change** sells only organic, open-pollinated seeds and plants and is dedicated to preserving sustainable agriculture. Visit their informative Web site at www.seedsofchange.com, call them for a catalog at 888-762-7333, or write them at P.O. Box 15700, Santa Fe, NM 87506-5700.

✔ **Seed Savers Exchange** is a not-for-profit organization that preserves and offers over 11,000 varieties of heirloom seeds through its membership exchange program. Nonmembers can also order seeds through their catalog. Write to them at 3076 North Winn Road, Decorah, IA 52101 or call 319-382-5990. Visit their Web site at www.seedsavers.org.

And finally, a few good melons include 'Earli-Dew' and 'Burpee Hybrid' muskmelon, 'Crimson Sweet' and yellow-fleshed 'Yellow Doll' watermelon, and 'French Orange', a muskmelon/Charentais cross. Cantaloupes, by the way, have smoother skins and smaller seed cavities than muskmelons, but they taste pretty much the same. Charentais are orange-fleshed French melons that resemble muskmelons. For something delicious and unusual, grow green-fleshed 'Passport' cantaloupe.

✔ **Planting and care:** These warm-weather crops need heat, water, and fertility to grow best. Directly sow these vegetables 1 to 2 weeks after your last frost date when the soil is at least 60 degrees. In colder areas, start seedlings indoors 3 to 4 weeks before setting them outdoors to get a head start.

Even though many bush varieties are available, most squash-family plants need room to spread their vines, so space them according to seed packet instructions. Amend the soil at planting with a layer of compost and side-dress the plants with a complete fertilizer when they start vining. Keep the plants well watered.

Squash-family crops need bees to pollinate the flowers in order to get fruit. Plant bee-attracting flowers around the garden to ensure fruit polli- nation. If fruits form but rot and drop off before enlarging, it's probably due to poor pollination.

- **Harvesting:** Pick cucumbers when they are 4 to 6 inches long, before the seeds enlarge. Harvest summer squash when they're small and the flow- ers are still attached for best flavor and to keep the plants producing well. Harvest winter squash and pumpkins when the varieties turn the desired color and your thumbnail can't puncture the skin when pressed.

  Harvest muskmelons when they easily slip off the vine when lifted. Watermelons are harvested when the skin color turns from shiny to dull and the spot where it rests on the ground turns from white to yellow. Also, check the last *tendril* (curlicues coming off the stems) before the fruit. When it turns brown, it's harvest time. Protect all squash family plants and fruits from frost.

- **Pests and diseases:** Squash-family vegetables have their own whole set of insects and diseases — many named after the plants they attack. The most prominent ones include cucumber beetles, which are yellow and black-striped or spotted beetles that feed on young cucumbers, melons, and squash; squash vine borers, which attack mostly squash and pump- kins; and squash bugs. Turn to Chapter 7 for more detailed information on these bad guys.

  Bacterial wilt disease attacks mostly cucumber and melons. The plants wilt during the day and are slow to recover even if well watered. Control this disease by planting resistant varieties and controlling cucumber beetles that spread the disease.

For more about growing vegetables, check out *Vegetable Gardening For Dummies* by Charlie Nardozzi and the Editors of the National Gardening Association (IDG Books Worldwide, Inc.).

Chapter 12

Herbs for Home and Garden

• •

In This Chapter

▶ Understanding plant life cycles

▶ Growing and using the most common herbs

▶ Choosing herbs that attract helpful insects

• •

Defining herbs is no easy feat when you consider that this group includes plants from every continent and climate and refers to everything from shrubs and trees to short-lived annuals and tough-as-nails perennials. Throughout history, herbs have served as food, medicine, fragrance, ornament, and even magical ingredients. In the days before refrigeration, people used strongly flavored chives, thyme, sage, rosemary, savory, basil, and mint to flavor meats. Aromatic herbs with scented flowers and leaves bring pleasant fragrance to homes today and still help protect woolen and linen fabric from insect damage. Some medicines consist primarily of herbal preparations.

Many traditional uses for herbs continue to grow in popularity, while other uses have passed into the realm of folklore. Early gardeners no doubt recognized that some herbs had beneficial effects on other food crops growing nearby. Modern gardeners and farmers have rediscovered that many herb plants attract beneficial insects that prey on damaging pests. See Chapter 8 and the "Herbs for companion planting" sidebar in this chapter for descriptions of the beneficial insects.

The Herb Society of America defines herbs as plants valued for their "flavor, fragrance, medicinal and healthful qualities, economic and industrial uses, pesticidal properties, and coloring materials." That seems to cover just about every cultivated plant in existence plus a large chunk of the wild plant population! For this chapter, though, I focus on plants commonly grown to flavor foods, to add color and fragrance to the garden, and to make helpful companions for other crops.

Herban Development

Herbs come in a wide variety of shapes, sizes, colors, and habits, making each one unique. Knowing something about plant characteristics in general and getting familiar with their descriptive terms makes choosing and using herbs easier and more satisfying. In the individual plant descriptions in this chapter and others, I describe how and when plants grow, the shapes of their flowers and leaves, and how they make new plants.

Life cycles

Herbs, like all other plants, have different life cycles, which is the amount of time its takes for them to become mature enough to bloom and produce seed and, ultimately, die. Plants belong in one of three categories:

- **Annuals** complete their life cycle in a single growing season. They typically sprout from seed in the spring, bloom, produce seed, and die before winter comes again.

- **Biennials** live for two growing seasons. In the first year, they sprout and grow leaves and roots. The flowers and seeds come in the second growing season and then the plant dies. With biennial herbs grown for their leaves, such as parsley, you want only the first year plants. Caraway, on the other hand, needs the second growing season to produce its pungent seeds.

- **Perennials** live for at least three seasons and many live much longer. (Some, in fact, are nearly impossible to get rid of.) Perennials with stems that die to the ground in winter but grow back from their roots are called *herbaceous* perennials. Some, like rosemary, have tough, persistent stems and are referred to as *woody* perennials.

  Perennial plants live from year to year only in the right climate, however. *Hardy* perennials, such as comfrey and horseradish, generally survive cold winters, while *tender* perennials, such as bay and rosemary, may succumb to freezing temperatures. Chapter 3 has more information about hardiness and climate zones.

Parts is parts

If you're familiar with some of the terms used to describe the different plant shapes and parts, you'll have an easier time picturing an herb in your mind or finding the right place for it in the garden. Pick up a book, such as *Herb*

Gardening For Dummies by Karan Davis Cutler, Kathleen Fisher, and the Editors of National Gardening Association (IDG Books Worldwide, Inc.), to help you identify and use herb plants.

Botanists, people who study plants, have scores of words to describe leaves. I won't bore you with all of them, but here are a few useful terms:

- **Deciduous plants** grow new leaves each spring, and those leaves die in the autumn and fall off.

- **Evergreen plants** keep their leaves year round.

- **Simple leaves** have a single stem and blade, or flat part. Basil and oak trees have simple leaves, for example.

- **Compound leaves** are made up of more than one stem and leaf, called *leaflets.* Parsley and palm trees have compound leaves.

When you're planning how to use a plant in your garden or landscape, it helps to know something about how it grows. A few more terms to clarify the issue:

- **Climbing** plants, like hops and morning glory, cling or twine around a support as they reach for the sky.

- **Upright** plants stand tall on their own and include dill and bee balm.

- **Mounding** plants, such as basil and parsley, form a low cushion.

- **Prostrate and creeping** plants stay close to the ground and some may spread themselves around the garden. Examples include creeping thyme and German chamomile.

Roots don't get much attention — out of sight, out of mind. But the kind of roots a plant has can give you hints about its culture. Plants generally have two kinds of roots. *Fibrous roots* are finely branched and grow close to the soil surface. Plants with fibrous roots are easy to transplant and divide into new plants, but are more easily damaged by drought and cold weather. *Taproots* are usually thick and long, reaching deep into the soil. After they're established, taproots are difficult to move but tolerate temporary drought.

The last batch of terms describes flowers. Knowing what a plant's flowers look like can help you find the most complementary place for it in your garden. Some plants, like daffodils, have *single* flowers, which come one to a stem. Others produce clusters of flowers in a wide array of shapes.

- **Spike:** Small flowers attach to a stiff, upright stem. Examples include basil and lavender.

- **Umbel:** Think of an upside down umbrella with each of its ribs ending in a little burst of tiny flowers. Dill and Queen Anne's lace have this kind of flower cluster.

> ✔ **Panicle:** Flowers, such as oregano, lilac, and hydrangea, grow on a loose cluster of branched stems.
>
> ✔ **Composite:** These often look like single flowers, but actually contain many flowers packed tightly together. Sunflowers, daisies, and clover have composite flowers.

To complicate matters, some plants can produce seeds on their own, but others need *cross-pollination,* or input from another plant of the same kind to make seeds. You can find out more about cross-pollination in Chapter 14.

Go forth and multiply

Some herbs have a very bad habit. They just don't know when to stop growing; when to say enough is enough. These so-called *invasive* plants travel in several of the following ways:

> ✔ **Seeds:** In an effort to take over the world or at least ensure the continuation of their species, some plants produce way more seeds than you need. Their little seedlings pop up everywhere, like weeds. Examples of prolific plants include German chamomile, fennel, and garlic chives. Keep them in check by removing the flowers before they disperse seeds.
>
> ✔ **Roots:** With some herbs, such as comfrey and horseradish, your eradication efforts may lead to an even larger patch of the confounded plant. Any bit of root left in the soil may grow into a new plant. Introduce these unruly herbs to your garden with caution.
>
> ✔ **Rhizomes and stolons:** Some herbs take off cross-country, growing horizontal stems from their crowns that creep over or under the soil, forming new plants along the way. *Rhizomes* grow under and *stolons* on top of the soil. This habit is useful for covering large areas or filling in between paving stones, but rapidly becomes a nuisance in other situations. Watch out for tansy, mint, and artemesia. Plant in containers or in gardens surrounded by 12-inch deep barriers that prevent the roots from getting out. Pull up escapees as soon as they appear.

Don't be afraid to look the proverbial gift horse in the mouth. Be leery of any herb that your friends and neighbors give away freely or that you find in abundance at local plant swaps. You may be inviting a more long-term guest to your garden than you planned for.

Growing Herbs

How and where you choose to grow herbs is limited only by your imagination and, of course, the needs and characteristics of the plants themselves. Most herb plants aren't too fussy about the soil they grow in as long as it's well drained (see Chapter 4). Soggy soil spells trouble for herbs, but young plants need moisture after transplanting until they begin growing vigorously. Water mature plants during times of drought to prevent wilting and stress. If you're growing herbs simply for their ornamental flowers or foliage, give them fertile garden soil. Herbs grown for fragrance and flavor, however, are more pungent if grown in less fertile soil, so go easy on the fertilizer.

You can fit herbs into your garden and landscape in myriad ways. Tuck herbs into your flower garden, plant them among your vegetables, or give them a special garden of their own. Take advantage of their flowers or leaves to add spark to container gardens and window boxes. Use creeping kinds between paving stones or let them trail over retaining walls. Even if you're challenged for space, you can grow some herbs on a sunny windowsill as houseplants. If you need a few ideas on where to grow herbs, here's a list for inspiration:

- ✔ **Herb garden:** Take an herbs-only approach and design an intricately patterned garden. A typical arrangement consists of a geometric border of tidy, compact plants, such as basil or lavender, which surrounds groupings of herbs with contrasting foliage colors and textures. For a simple, utilitarian herb garden, try a four-patch design that features four same-size triangles, squares, or rectangles separated by 2-foot walkways.

- ✔ **Ground covers:** Creeping herbs, such as thyme and mint, can cover large areas quickly or fill in the gaps between stones in a path. Let them trail over a wall to add color and soften the effect of the stone.

- ✔ **Vegetable gardens:** Some herbs make natural companions for vegetable plants. Basil, for example, is said to improve tomatoes, while dill and cabbages complement each other. Stick to well-behaved herbs that don't spread by roots or rhizomes, however, or else your garden may be over-run by too much of a good thing (see the "Go forth and multiply" section earlier in this chapter).

- ✔ **Flower gardens:** Many herbs have beautiful flowers or foliage that add color and texture to flower borders. As a bonus, some attract butterflies and provide food for their larva. Good additions to your flower garden include catnip, lavender, chamomile, borage, and oregano.

- ✔ **Containers:** Treat them as ornamental plants or bring your culinary herbs closer to the kitchen by planting them in pots, tubs, or baskets. Use trailing thyme or rosemary to hang over the side, and add colorful sages, parsley, oregano, and chives. In cold climates, grow tender herbs, such as rosemary and bay in pots that you can bring indoors for the winter. Be sure to give these Mediterranean-climate plants 14 to 16 hours of bright light year 'round to keep them happy. Be careful to keep the soil moist, but never soggy.

Using Herbs

Although many herbs are ornamental, most people grow them to harvest. Most herbs have fragrant or pungently flavored leaves or flowers that make them useful for cooking, crafts, and potpourri, and adding aroma to cosmetics. Some have attractive stems, leaves, or other plant parts that can be dried or preserved for wreaths and arrangements. Consider the following ways to use harvested herbs:

- **Food and drink:** Herbal teas from soothing chamomile to refreshing mint offer alternatives to stronger brews, and no supper is complete without seasonings for soup and salad, meat, and vegetable. Indispensable edible herbs include basil, chives, coriander, dill, horseradish, marjoram, mint, oregano, parsley, sage, and thyme.

- **Fragrance:** Homes and people haven't always smelled as pleasant they do today. In the days before frequent bathing, central vacuum cleaners, and indoor plumbing, herbs played a large role in odor control. Sweet Annie, peppermint, chamomile, and lavender, for example, can scent a room or a closet, masking the odors of cooking, wet dogs, or any other smelly aroma. *Aromatherapy,* the art and science of affecting mood with scent, makes liberal use of dried herbs in little pillows and bowls of potpourri.

- **Crafts:** Dried wreaths, arrangements, and other crafts depend on herbs for color, structure, and fragrance. The long silvery stems of artemesia, for example, make excellent wreath foundations. Dried lavender flower spikes add elegance to everlasting arrangements. Some herbs lend their colors to fabric and paints.

- **Medicine:** Far be it from me to advise anyone on the medical use of herbs, but rest assured that people have used herbs to treat every ailment known to mankind. Many herbs do contain chemicals, such as those used for heart medicine and to treat pain, cough syrups, headaches, which modern doctors find useful. Laymen can safely use aromatic herbs to add zip or tranquilizing effects to ointments, massage oils, and baths. Check out *Herbal Remedies For Dummies* by Christopher Hobbs (IDG Books Worldwide, Inc.) for ways to use herbs as medicine.

Another, often overlooked way to use herbs, is as landscape and garden plants. They serve several important functions:

- **Ornament:** Flowers, attractive leaves, and shapes from sprawling to towering give herbs a place in any garden. Several varieties of sage, for example, have colorful golden, purple, white, or gray-green leaves. Rue and compact artemesia varieties with silvery leaves are prized in decorative herb gardens.

- **Companion plants:** Some herbs reputably aid the growth of other plants by repelling insect pests, discouraging disease, and helping nutrients become more readily available. Members of the onion family, such as chives, for example, may keep bugs away from roses and other flowers.

✔ **Insect habitat:** Most insects are good for your garden and it pays to encourage them to come on in and stay awhile. Herbs with small, nectar-rich flowers, such as dill, fennel, thyme, caraway, and parsley, attract some of the most important beneficial insects mentioned in Chapter 8.

Encyclopedia of Herbs

Useful herbs number in the hundreds, at least. In this section, I highlight a few of the most commonly grown herbs. For more herbs and in-depth discussions, pick up a copy of *Herb Gardening For Dummies* by Karan Davis Cutler, Kathleen Fisher, and the Editors of the National Gardening Association (IDG Books Worldwide, Inc.).

Basil (Ocimum basilicum)

Easily one of the most popular culinary herbs grown, basil is an annual that comes in over 30 varieties which include both ornamental and tasty forms. For plenty of pesto, grow sweet basil varieties, such as 'Mammoth' or 'Large Leaf' in your vegetable garden. Or try some with unusual foliage, such as purple-leafed 'Dark Opal' and 'Purple Ruffles' or frilly 'Green Ruffles'. To edge a garden or spice up a patio planter, grow compact, small-leafed varieties, such as 'Spicy Globe' or 'Green Globe'. For an alternative taste sensation, grow lemon, anise, cinnamon, and Thai basil varieties.

✔ **Planting and care:** Give basil moist, fertile, well-drained soil and space plants about 1 foot apart in full sun. Water them in dry weather and pinch off young flower buds to prevent bloom and encourage more leaves. Sow seeds directly in the garden or start indoors and protect from frost, which will kill it.

✔ **Special uses:** Plant with tomatoes to discourage tomato hornworms. Dry the leaves or use fresh to flavor food.

Caraway (Carum carvi)

Caraway is a biennial that produces its aromatic seeds in its second growing season, although some may bloom the first year. A member of the carrot family, the plants share the fine, lacy foliage topped by umbels of tiny white flowers.

✔ **Planting and care:** Sow seeds directly in the garden in full sun where they can remain for two growing seasons. In hot climates, give caraway part shade. Seeds germinate slowly and have deep taproots, which bring minerals to the surface and loosen the soil. Plants grow 1 to 2 feet tall.

✔ **Special uses:** Add leaves to salads or add to soup. Use the distinctively flavored seeds in breads, stews, and other foods. Flowers attract many beneficial insects.

Chamomile (Matricaria recutita, Chamaemelum nobile)

Choose from 2- to 3-foot-tall German chamomile *(Matricaria recutita)* or creeping, 9-inch Roman chamomile *(Chamaemelum nobile),* depending on your garden desires. The perennial Roman species is hardy through Zone 3 and thrives in cool, damp climates. German chamomile is an annual. Both plants have lacy, aromatic, apple-scented foliage and small, daisy-like flowers.

✔ **Planting and care:** Sow seeds directly in the garden and keep moist until well established. Chamomile can tolerate some drought after that and appreciates full sun. Harvest the flowers when fully open and dry them on screens in an airy place. Plants self-sow prolifically, so after you plant some, you'll have chamomile for a long time.

✔ **Special uses:** The dried flowers make a popular tea for relieving stress and heartburn. They're also used in many cosmetics and toiletries. Roman chamomile makes an excellent ground cover or mowed lawn in mild, moist climates similar to England or the Pacific Northwest.

Chives (Allium schoenoprasum)

Grassy, onion-flavored foliage make chives popular in the culinary arts, but this perennial plant makes a good 1-foot-tall addition to the ornamental landscape and vegetable garden, too. The dense tufts of lavender-purple flowers bloom in early summer. The related species, garlic chives, grows about 2 feet tall and has starry white flowers in late summer to early fall. Both species self-sow freely.

✔ **Planting and care:** The best way to obtain chives is to divide a clump into groups of slender bulbs and plant in any well-drained garden soil. It prefers full sun, but isn't fussy. If you sow from seed, cover the seeds lightly with soil, keep moist, and be patient — they may take 2 to 3 weeks to sprout. Keep weeds away to make harvesting easier. Harvest by shearing the stems to within a few inches of the ground.

✔ **Special uses:** The pungent foliage reportedly repels some injurious pests, especially around roses, tomatoes, carrots, grapes, and apples. Puree the leaves in the blender with water, strain, and use as a spray to prevent powdery mildew. The flowers attract beneficial insects. Use in cooking as you would onions or serve fresh in salads, dips, and sauces.

Herbs for companion planting

The idea of growing certain plants near each other for mutual benefit is well-rooted in folklore and gaining some ground in scientific circles. Some plants, such as marigolds, emit a chemical that repels certain pests — in this case, soil nematodes. Other plants, notably legumes, increase the fertility of the soil, which benefits the plants growing nearby or following the crop. Herbs, with their fragrant leaves and history of magical uses, are especially singled out for this treatment.

One of the most useful ways that plants help each other is by providing habitat for insects and other creatures that prey upon damaging pests. Many herbs excel in this role because many have small, nectar-rich flowers and aromatic leaves. Those in the carrot family, especially dill, caraway, tansy, fennel, and parsley, attract the following beneficial insects:

✔ Lacewings

✔ Braconid wasps

✔ Aphid parasites

✔ Syrphid flies

✔ Spiders

✔ Mealybug and spider mite destroyers

✔ Trichogramma wasps

✔ Minute pirate bugs

Researchers continue to look for ways to use plants to increase crop harvests and improve plant health without the use of harmful chemicals. Simply by diversifying the plant environment — planting more than one species of plant in an area — the number of pest problems decrease because beneficial insects find more shelter and food, and harmful pests find less.

You can find more plants for companion planting in Chapters 11 and 15.

Coriander and cilantro (*Coriandrum sativum*)

This herb is so versatile that it bears two names — cilantro for the roots and leaves and coriander for the seeds. The flat, parsley-like leaves add pungency to Latin American and Asian dishes. The seeds play a major role in curry and other Middle Eastern fare. It's an annual herb that ancient Mediterranean people prescribed for many medical ailments.

✔ **Planting and care:** Sow directly into fertile garden soil where seeds will sprout in a couple of weeks. Plant every 2 to 3 weeks for continuous harvest because the plants tend to set seed quickly, especially in hot weather, and stop producing new foliage. Harvest young tender leaves before plants send up flower stalks. Harvest seeds when seed heads turn brown, but before they scatter, and dry thoroughly before using for best flavor.

✔ **Special uses:** Use leaves and seeds in cooking. Plant near aphid-prone crops to help repel pests. The flowers also attract beneficial insects.

Dill (Anethum graveolens)

Another member of the aromatic carrot family, dill's seeds are an essential ingredient in pickles, breads, and other savory dishes. The fine, thread-like foliage is rich in vitamins and flavor for fish, sauces, and dips. Tall, narrow plants of this annual herb grow 2 to 3 feet tall. Choose the variety 'Bouquet' for seeds or 'Dukat' or 18-inch-tall 'Fernleaf' if you want mainly leaves.

- ✔ **Planting and care:** Sow seeds directly into fertile, sunny garden soil. Barely cover the seeds and sow again every few weeks for continuous harvest. Protect from strong winds.

- ✔ **Special uses:** Flowers attract beneficial insects and the foliage is a favorite of swallowtail butterfly larvae. It reputedly makes a good companion for cabbage crops and can be planted with low-growing lettuce and cucumbers. Use seeds and leaves in cooking.

Fennel (Foeniculum vulgare)

Useful in cooking and in the garden, 4- to 8-foot-tall fennel has a tropical look and resembles giant dill plants. The common fennel is hardy in Zones 6 through 9, but you can grow it as an annual in cooler climates. It self-sows and can become a nuisance weed in warm climates. Try the bronze-red-leafed variety 'Purpureum' as an ornamental plant. If you want to eat the root, look for the annual or biennial plant called finocchio or Florence fennel.

- ✔ **Planting and care:** Sow directly in fertile, sunny soil where you want it to grow. Its long taproot makes it difficult to transplant. Protect from strong wind.

- ✔ **Special uses:** You can use all parts of fennel — from the bulb-like root to the leaves, stalks, and seeds. Harvest seeds when they turn brown and snip leaves and stems as needed and use fresh or cooked lightly in soups and sauces. Flowers attract many beneficial insects.

Horseradish (Armoracia rusticana)

Take care where you plant this tenacious perennial herb — its pungent roots extend 2 feet into the soil and the smallest piece can sprout into a new plant. The 1- to 3-foot-long wavy leaves have an attractive appearance, however, and small white flowers add to its appeal. It's hardy through Zone 5.

- ✔ **Planting and care:** Plant the roots in deep fertile soil about a foot apart and 2 inches deep in full sun. Wait a year or so before harvesting the roots in the fall.

✔ **Special uses:** The roots are sharply pungent and valued for the zip they give to sauces and tomato drinks. The young spring leaves are edible when cooked like spinach. Try a little horseradish to open your sinuses next time you have a head cold. Some biodynamic farmers (see Chapter 1) believe that horseradish is beneficial in fruit orchards and around potatoes, but if you hope to contain it, keep it corralled in a bottomless trashcan sunk into the ground.

Lavender (Lavandula)

One of the most recognized and popular scents for cosmetics, toiletries, and aromatherapy, lavender also adds drama to your flower garden. A number of different species exist, but all have needle-like foliage and spikes of purplish blue flowers. The English lavender varieties, such as purple 'Hidcote' and 'Munstead', grow up to 24 inches high and are hardy through Zone 5. Pink-flowering varieties include 'Hidcote Pink' and 'Miss Katherine'. Other species are less hardy, but equally appealing and include spike, French, and fringed lavenders.

✔ **Planting and care:** Start from stem cuttings because seeds may not give you plants of uniform quality. Plant in compost-enriched, very well-drained, even gravelly soil in full sun. Space plants 2 to 3 feet apart for a low hedge or mass planting. Prune in early spring to encourage bushy growth.

✔ **Special uses:** Harvest flowers as they begin to open. Dry them in bundles hung upside down in an airy place. Flowers attract bees and beneficial insects.

Mints (Mentha)

With 20 or so species and more than 1,000 varieties, you should find a mint to suit any taste. Peppermint and spearmint are the most popular, but other fruit-flavored varieties exist. Some also have variegated foliage, including pineapple mint 'Varieagata'. Some mints creep along low to the ground, such as Corsican mint, and others grow 2 to 3 feet tall. Hardiness varies with the variety and species.

✔ **Planting and care:** Start new plants from stem cuttings of the varieties you want to be sure you get the flavor or scent you expect. Plant just below the soil surface and keep them moist until they begin to grow. Mints can be invasive, so contain them or plant where you don't mind a carpet of fragrant foliage.

✔ **Special uses:** Harvest the fresh leaves and add them to Middle Eastern dishes, soups, vegetables, and beverages. Mint flowers attract beneficial insects, and the fragrant plants reportedly repel some damaging insects and improve the health and flavor of nearby cabbages and tomatoes.

Oregano (Origanum vulgare)

Small fragrant leaves on sprawling 1- to 2-foot stems topped by loose spikes of white to pink flowers give oregano a casual appeal for planting in vegetable and flower gardens or trailing over a wall or basket. Choose plants carefully by pinching a leaf to test flavor and pungency. Some varieties, such as 'Aureum Crispum' and 'Compactum' are more ornamental than edible. It's a hardy perennial in zones 5 and warmer.

✔ **Planting and care:** Start new plants from stem cuttings to guarantee the best flavor. Seed-grown plants may lack their parents' pungent flavor. Any average, well-drained soil in full sun will do. Harvest leaves as needed or cut the plant down to a few inches from the ground and hang the sprigs to dry.

✔ **Special uses:** The tiny flower clusters attract bees, butterflies, and other beneficial insects. The fresh and dried leaves add classic flavor to many Latin American and Mediterranean dishes. Some varieties look good in hanging baskets, patio containers, and flower gardens.

Parsley (Petroselinum crispum)

A common garnish on restaurant plates, parsley is probably the most recognized herb. The leaves contain loads of vitamins A and C and help sweeten garlic breath. Although both varieties are edible, the flat-leafed variety has stronger flavor while the curly-leafed kind is more commonly used as garnish. Plants are biennial, hardy through Zone 5, and bloom only in their second year. The 1-foot-tall plants form tidy bright green mounds of ornamental foliage. Plant in vegetable and flower gardens or in container gardens.

✔ **Planting and care:** Soak seeds overnight before sowing and plant directly in the garden. If you start seeds indoors, plant them in *peat pots* (biodegradable compressed peat moss containers) so that you don't have to disturb their taproot when transplanting them later. Give the plants fertile garden soil and a cool, slightly shady spot in hot summer climates. Snip fresh leaves as needed or cut the whole plant to a few inches high and dry the leaves on screen.

✔ **Special uses:** Use for cooking, especially in Greek and Middle Eastern dishes. Makes an attractive ornamental garden plant and serves as food for swallowtail butterfly larvae. Flowers attract beneficial insects.

Rosemary (Rosemarinus officinalis)

Two species of this tender perennial evergreen shrub exist — upright and prostrate — and both are fragrant and edible. The short, needle-like foliage gives off a heady, distinctive aroma when lightly bruised. Ornamental varieties include those with golden or variegated leaves, pink or bright blue flowers, and especially sprawling or upright forms.

✔ **Planting and care:** Start from rooted stem cuttings and plant in well-drained garden soil. Rosemary doesn't tolerate soggy soil or complete drought. Although hardy only to Zone 8, you can grow rosemary in a greenhouse or indoors under strong light. Plant it in a pot at least 1 foot deep to accommodate its taproot and maintain humidity by setting it over moist pebbles or misting the plant a few times a week.

✔ **Special uses:** As an ornamental, rosemary excels in the low shrub border or trailing over a low wall. Its aromatic foliage is said to repel flying insects from cabbages and other vegetables. Use fresh sprigs in meat stews; use dried rosemary for either culinary use or to scent rooms and linens.

Sage (Salvia officinalis)

In Zones 5 and warmer, sage is a perennial that grows into a shrubby mound of fragrant leaves. It can grow up to 2 feet tall. The 2- to 3-inch-long leaves are fuzzy and oval and range in color from silver-green, purple, golden to mixed white, green, and pink, depending on the variety. Sage is equally at home in the herb garden and amongst the ornaments in a container or flowerbed. In late spring, sage has spikes of blue flowers, although some varieties have white flowers. A number of different sage species exist and they range in hardiness, pungency, and size. One of my favorites, pineapple sage, is only winter hardy to Zone 8, but its soft-textured, fruity pineapple-scented foliage and red flowers make a beautiful addition to my flower garden.

✔ **Planting and care:** It's easier to start sage from stem cuttings, but it will grow slowly from seeds. Plant in organically rich, well-drained garden soil and give it full sun. Avoid soggy soil. Prune to keep the growth compact.

✔ **Special uses:** The spiky flowers attract bees and other beneficial insects and look great in the garden. Use it to scent dresser drawers and to help prevent damaging clothes moths. Use the leaves, either fresh or dried, in poultry and meat dishes.

Sweet marjoram (Origanum majorana)

A tender perennial shrub in Zones 9 and warmer, most gardeners have to be satisfied to grow this oregano relative as an annual. It tends to sprawl and is best confined in a container or planted in an herb garden.

- ✔ **Planting and care:** Start from seed in late spring indoors or buy rooted cuttings to be sure that you get the plant that you expect. It prefers full sun and fertile garden soil. Remove the flowers to encourage more leaves. Harvest and dry the leaves for year-round culinary use.

- ✔ **Special uses:** The light-purple flower clusters attract many beneficial insects. The leaves taste similar to oregano and are used extensively in cooking, especially in vegetable and egg dishes.

Thymes (Thymus)

Hundreds of thyme species and varieties exist and they range in height from creeping, 1-inch-high mats to 18-inch shrubs. They all have tiny, roundish leaves and their colors range from wooly gray to smooth green to golden to white-edged. Even their fragrance varies from very mild to pungent and includes lemon, caraway, coconut, and more. Creeping thyme makes a fragrant and attractive groundcover and excels between paving stones, while shrubby types are useful low hedges. Clusters of tiny white, pink, or crimson flowers bloom in summer, sometimes covering the plants. The creeping thymes are the hardiest and survive in Zone 4.

- ✔ **Planting and care:** Start with rooted stem cuttings to guarantee the flavor and appearance of your thyme. Plant in organically enriched, well-drained soil in full sun. Divide the plants every few years and keep them pruned to encourage dense growth.

- ✔ **Special uses:** Flowers attract bees and many beneficial insects. Much folklore exists on the use of thyme as a helpful companion plant for roses and vegetables. Use between patio and walkway stones or plant as a groundcover to replace lawn in small areas. The trailing kinds look good in hanging baskets and planters. Harvest the leaves and young stems for cooking.

Hand-pick pests into a bowl of soapy water (Chapter 8).

Use a row cover to keep pests away (Chapter 8).

© Crandall & Crandall

This wire cage keeps above-ground pests from snacking on your plants, while the concrete blocks line the sides and bottom to keep burrowing animals from invading (Chapter 8).

© Michael S. Thompson

Plant flowers, such as clover, that attract beneficial insects (Chapter 8).

This kitchen garden gets high yields from a small space. A plastic-covered cold frame extends your growing season (Chapters 3 and 11).

Use water jackets to keep early-season plantings from freezing (Chapter 3).

Plants such as peas and beans add nitrogen to the soil (Chapter 4).

Chapter 13

Picking from the Berry Patch

• •

In This Chapter

▶ Planning where to plant

▶ Preparing the planting site

▶ Choosing the best fruits for your area

▶ Anticipating common pests and problems

• •

*F*ew plants give you more bang for your buck than berries. Homegrown raspberries, strawberries, blueberries, and grapes take little space and return months of mouthwatering fruit salads, pies, pancakes, and fresh-eating goodness. Although less commonly grown, elderberries, currants, and some other small fruits make excellent landscape specimens and turn out fruit fit for delicious jellies and other homemade treats.

Some of these berries are easy to grow organically, while others present a real challenge. Choosing disease-resistant varieties, using pest and disease control methods described in Part III, and planting correctly goes a long way toward producing healthful, pesticide-free berries.

Berry Patch Basics

Site selection and preparation is more critical with berries than with nearly any other food crop you may grow, because most of these plants stay in place for years. The varieties you choose, where you plant them, and how you prepare and maintain the soil determines whether your berry patch produces bumper crops or becomes a disappointing chore.

As you make decisions about where to plant your berry patch, keep the following requirements in mind.

- ✓ **Sun:** All fruits need at least 6 hours — preferably more — of full sun each day to produce large, flavorful crops.

- ✓ **Air circulation and drainage:** Moving air helps prevent disease organisms from settling on vulnerable fruits and leaves, so choose a slightly breezy site, if possible. High winds cause damage, however, so protect crops with a windbreak, if needed.

   Cold air settles at the bottom of slopes, where it may damage early blooming flowers in the spring or ripening fruit in the fall. Plant your fruits on the slope of a hill instead of at the bottom.

- ✓ **Soil moisture and drainage:** With the exception of elderberry, all small fruits need well-drained soil. Soggy soil encourages root diseases, which are among the most serious problems for fruits. If your soil drains poorly, however, you can still grow fruits in raised beds. Make beds 6 to 10 inches high and 4 feet wide and amend with plenty of organic matter.

- ✓ **Soil amendments and fertility:** Fruiting plants need fertile, moist, richly organic soil to produce the best crops. Improve the soil with several inches of compost or composted manure and any needed pH amendments and nutrients before planting. If you must significantly alter the soil pH, allow several months to a year before you plant. Do a soil test for pH and fertility before you plant and again each year, especially if fruits fail to produce well or plants look stressed. See Chapter 4 for more on soils and drainage.

- ✓ **Locally adapted varieties:** Some plant varieties grow better in particular situations than other varieties. Check with your local extension office or nurseries in your area for recommendations. See Chapter 3 for information about taking an inventory of your site.

Another consideration that many people fail to consider is what I call the "convenience factor." Plant your fruits close to the kitchen door, garage, or some other place that you visit daily. Frequent inspection helps you see potential pests and diseases before they become a problem. Picking and maintenance feel like less of a chore, too, when the patch is just outside the door. Many of these plants can also do double duty as landscape specimens — use them in mixed borders and foundation plantings whenever you can.

Weed control

Controlling weeds is more critical for small fruits than for nearly any other crop (except vegetables). Many fruits have shallow roots, which can't compete for water and nutrients with more aggressive weeds. Weeds also harbor insect pests that feed on your fruits. Perennial weeds often cause the most trouble because their roots persist from year to year and often sprout if even a small piece remains in the soil. Annual weeds come in the form of seeds blown by the wind or carried by people, pets, birds, and rain.

Weed control needs a double-barreled approach to succeed.

- ✔ **Before you plant:** To beat the weeds, get rid of them completely before you plant your fruits and allow yourself plenty of time. If you have a year to prepare, grow weed-smothering cover crops and till them into the soil. Got only a few months? Use soil solarization with clear plastic (see Chapter 6).

- ✔ **After planting:** Mulch, mulch, and mulch again. Use materials that add organic matter to the soil as they decompose. Pull individual weeds by hand and hoe only in footpaths.

Weeding a mature berry patch is a strenuous chore because most of these plants have shallow roots that don't allow cultivation, or grow in such a way that hand pulling each weed is the only solution. Weeding thorny brambles is an especially onerous job. Using a propane-powered flame weeder can make this job easier. See Chapter 6 for details.

Buying plants

It really pays to buy the best quality plants that you can find. If you're fortunate enough to have a local nursery that grows its own fruit plants, by all means, pay them a visit. They usually offer the best varieties for your area and can give you valuable advice on growing them in your particular situation. Local nurseries usually sell potted plants, which transplant well, provided that they've been well cared for and not allowed to dry out before you buy them.

Specialty mail-order nurseries are often the best source of virus-free, disease-resistant fruits in many parts of the country, however. They carry the widest selection and usually offer the most complete description of each variety and its requirements. When shopping for virus-prone fruits, such as raspberries and strawberries, buy only those guaranteed to be virus-free. Also read the catalog carefully to find varieties that resist common diseases, especially those prevalent in your area.

Mail-order nurseries ship most plants *bareroot;* that is, without soil around their roots, when they are dormant in the fall through spring months. Plants quickly recover and begin growing soon after planting. See Chapter 17 for how to plant bare-root shrubs.

A last piece of advice from someone who's been there and done that — don't plant more than you have time to harvest and maintain. It's easy to get excited about all the promising fruits that you can grow and end up buying more plants than you need. Luckily, small fruits freeze very well, but you still have to weed and pick them.

Small Fruits Guide

Growing berries is one of my most rewarding gardening activities. The season begins with strawberries. Then, raspberries, blueberries, elderberries, and grapes ripen in succession through the summer and early fall. Pick your own favorites from this chapter and get growing!

Beautiful blueberry

I'd be hard pressed to name a shrub that I like better than blueberry (*Vaccinium* species). As an ornamental plant, it offers small white flowers in spring, glossy green leaves in summer, and spectacular crimson fall foliage. As an edible fruit, it can't be beat for fresh eating, pies, pancakes, dessert sauce, and jam.

Blueberries grow in Zones 3 to 10, but the species and best varieties vary from one extreme to the other. Choose one of these three species to suit your climate.

- **Lowbush blueberry** (*V. angustifolium*) is the hardiest for Zones 3 to 6. These 8- to 18-inch tall plants form spreading mats and produce small, intensely flavored berries. Grow them as ground-covering landscape plants in well-drained acidic soil and enjoy the fruits as a bonus or leave them for wildlife. Prune only to remove dead, damaged, or diseased plants. Varieties include 'Northsky' and 'Putte'.

- **Highbush blueberry** (*V. corymbosum* and hybrids) can grow from Zones 4 to 10, but some varieties are better suited to either extreme. If you want plenty of large, flavorful, easy to pick fruit, choose highbush blueberries. Shrubs grow 2 to 6 feet tall and produce more fruit when you plant at least two different varieties. In the northern U.S., try 'Bluecrop', 'Blueray', 'Earliblue', 'Northblue', 'Patriot', and 'Northland'. In the south, plant 'Gulf Coast', 'Misty', 'O'Neill', and 'Reveille'.

  Flower buds, which appear larger and rounder than leaf buds, form in the summer the year before they bloom. Prune in late winter to remove unproductive canes, leaving the most vigorous 15 to 18 canes.

✔ **Rabbiteye blueberry** *(V. ashei)* grow in the warmer Zones 7 through 9. Growing up to 10 feet tall, the varieties of this species have thicker-skinned berries. You need to plant two different but compatible varieties to get fruit. Good companions include 'Beckyblue' and 'Bonitablue' or 'Powderblue' and 'Tifblue'.

Blueberries belong to a group of plants that have very specific soil needs, including lots of decomposed organic matter and an acidic pH of 4.5 to 5.2. They grow where azaleas and rhododendrons naturally thrive, but you can also alter your soil with acidifying peat moss and sulfur to accommodate their needs. It takes at least six months to a year or more for amendments to significantly lower soil pH, so plan ahead and test the soil before planting. See Chapter 4 for more on soil amendments and pH.

All blueberries have shallow roots and need moist, well-drained soil. Mix ½ cubic foot of peat moss per plant into the soil at planting time. Cover the soil around the shrubs with organic mulch, such as pine needles, shredded oak leaves, or hardwood bark, to maintain the soil moisture and prevent weeds. Keep the soil moist throughout the growing season. Avoid deep cultivation.

Blueberries have relatively few serious pests or diseases, but good sanitation practices are a must. Mummy berry fungus causes trouble in some areas and spreads from fallen fruit. You can avoid other fungus diseases by pruning to encourage air circulation through the plant and keeping the foliage dry. Birds are the most serious pest — cover the plants completely with bird netting before the berries turn blue.

Ramblin' brambles

If you love fresh raspberries or blackberries, you'll be glad to know how easy they are to grow. These delicate and perishable fruits are expensive in the market, but you can plant your own small patch and produce enough for fresh eating and freezing, too.

When planning your patch of *brambles* (as these fruits are known), thoroughly follow the instructions in the "Berry Patch Basics" section earlier in this chapter. Pay special attention to air circulation and soil drainage. Taking weed-control precautions before you plant is also important because most brambles sport hooked thorns that make weeding the mature plants difficult and shallow roots that hoes easily damage. Raised beds work well with brambles. Allow at least 8 feet between rows of plants. Don't plant where other brambles or potatoes, tomatoes, or eggplant have grown in recent years due to risk of Verticillium root disease infection. It's also best to eliminate nearby wild brambles, if possible, because they often spread disease.

Brambles range in growth habit from upright to sprawling — some stand up on their own, but most need trellis supports to keep the fruiting canes off the ground. A typical arrangement consists of a T-shaped post and crosspiece at either end of the row with taut wires or heavy twine running between them down the length of the row. Trailing varieties of blackberry can also be tied to wire fence or other flat support.

Shoots called *canes* grow from either the roots or crown of the plant. Brambles are biennial, which means that plants flower on second-year canes, which subsequently die. Canes are called *primocanes* the first year they sprout and *floricanes* in their second year. Floricanes die after fruiting and should be pruned out. Most raspberries and blackberries produce fruit only on the floricanes, but some raspberry varieties, often referred to as *everbearing,* also produce on primocanes in the fall.

Depending on your personal preference and climate, you can choose from several bramble types and many different varieties for your garden:

✔ **Red raspberries:** This delicate fruit grows best in cool climates where plants will receive the 800 to 1800 hours of chilling they need to produce fruit (see Chapter 14). Most varieties bear one crop per year, but others produce two. *Summer-bearing* varieties produce fruit in the summer on floricanes. *Everbearing* types fruit in the summer on floricanes and again in the fall on new primocanes. Although most raspberries produce red berries, some varieties have yellow or purple fruit.

Prune summer-bearing raspberries twice a year. After summer fruiting, remove all the floricanes. In early spring, prune out winter-damaged and weak canes, leaving about 3 to 4 vigorous canes per square foot or roughly 6 to 9 inches between canes. Cut these remaining canes back to about 3 to 4 feet high. See Figure 13-1. You can treat the everbearing types similarly or prune all the canes to the ground in late autumn or early spring. This severe pruning forfeits the summer crop, but yields a bumper crop in autumn.

Summer-bearing red varieties include 'Latham', 'Boyne', 'Killarney', 'Milton', 'September', 'Canby' (nearly thornless), and 'Nordic'. Everbearing varieties include 'Heritage', 'Autumn Bliss', and 'Indian Summer'. Yellow varieties include 'Fall Gold', 'Amber', and 'Honeyqueen'. Purple varieties share red and black raspberry parentage and may resemble either one. 'Royalty' is the most common variety.

✔ **Black raspberries, black caps:** The fruits of this plant have a rich flavor and lack the core that characterizes blackberries. Plants grow new primocanes from the crown instead of the roots, and thus are easier to contain within a row because they don't grow shoots several feet from the mother plant as red raspberries do. Plant 3 feet apart in raised hills.

To control their length and encourage *lateral branches* or side shoots to form, prune 3 to 4 inches off the primocane tips when they reach 24 to 30 inches high in mid-summer. The following spring, prune the lateral side branches to about 6 to 10 inches in length. At that time, also remove all but the strongest 4 to 6 canes. Black raspberry varieties include 'Black Hawk', 'Mac Black', 'Bristol', and 'Jewel'.

Purple raspberries result from crosses between red and black raspberry varieties, but they are much less commonly grown. Their growth habit is similar to black raspberry and the fruit is excellent for jams. 'Royalty' is the most common variety.

✔ **Blackberries:** Preferring hot southern summers, blackberries grow in Zones 6 and warmer, although some varieties make it into Zone 5 and warmer parts of Zone 4. Prune blackberries as described for summer-bearing raspberries, but leave the floricanes about 4 to 5 feet high.

Blackberries fall into two main categories — bush or upright types and trailing. The trailing varieties make less appealing plants for most home gardeners because they require more trellising and maintenance, have more thorns than the uprights, and are less cold hardy. Thornless blackberries are now available, including 'Arapaho', 'Black Satin', 'Chester', 'Navaho', 'Hull', and 'Triple Crown'. Of the thorny upright varieties, 'Illini Hardy', 'Darrow', 'Lowden', and 'Ebony King' are among the cold hardiest.

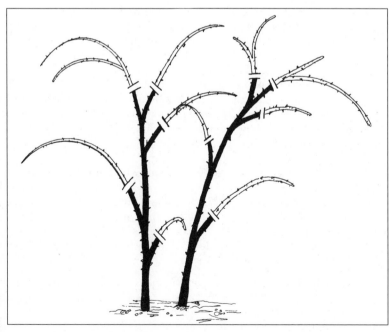

Figure 13-1:
In spring, prune raspberry canes to 3 or 4 feet to encourage more fruit.

Some diseases cause serious damage to raspberries and blackberries, leading to their decline and reduced fruiting. Root rots, Verticillium wilt, and leaf rust are among the worst, but some varieties are less susceptible than others to disease. Choose a resistant variety whenever possible, such as the ones listed in this section. Another way to prevent the spread of disease is to plant the different kinds of brambles away from one another. Black and purple raspberries, for example, can get mosaic virus from red raspberries, which can get it from blackberries. If possible, burn or shred prunings and remove them from the site to prevent the spread of diseases and pests. Don't prune, harvest, or walk among plants when the foliage is wet.

Keeping current with currants and gooseberries

A mainstay in European gardens and gaining popularity in North America, currants and gooseberries (*Ribes* species) make excellent jams, jellies, and dessert berries. The U.S. government at one time banned growing this group of ornamental and delicious fruits because *Ribes* species contribute to a deadly white pine disease called white pine blister rust. A number of states still restrict the sale and transport of *Ribes,* although disease-resistant varieties, which eliminate the problem, are now available.

Use currents and gooseberries as ornamental landscape shrubs — they bear attractive flowers and fruit, have maple-shaped leaves, and remain 3 to 4 feet high. Gooseberries do have thorns, however, so choose their planting locations carefully. Plant 3 to 4 feet apart in fertile, well-drained, compost-enriched soil with a pH of 6 to 7. Full sun to light shade is best. Most plants in this group are hardy to Zone 3, but spring frost may damage the early flowers. In very cold regions, plant on the north side of a building or other location that warms slowly in the spring to delay bloom. Their high chill requirement (see Chapter 14) makes them unsuitable for climates with warm or very short winters and hot summers.

The most commonly grown *Ribes* fall into two major groups:

- **Currants** don't have spines and bear ⅜-inch fruit in clusters, called *strigs,* that look like miniature bunches of grapes. Red and white currants have a mild flavor, while black currants have a stronger taste. Disease-resistant red currants include 'Red Lake' and 'Redstart'. The most disease-resistant black currants are 'Consort' and 'Crandall'.

- **Gooseberries** have a spine at the base of each leaf. The fruit is larger than that of currants and varies in color from greenish white to red and is borne singly or in small clusters. Popular varieties include 'Hinnonmaki Red', 'Invicta', and 'Poorman'. Jostaberries have black currant and gooseberry parentage and have red or black fruits that are larger than currants.

Currants and gooseberries can pollinate themselves and don't need another variety to produce fruit. Prune the shrubs in late winter and remove only canes older than 3 years. Thin younger canes, if necessary, to prevent crowding. Red currants produce fruit on 2- and 3-year-old canes. Gooseberries produce fruit on 1-, 2-, and 3-year-old canes.

Elegant elderberry

This underutilized shrub *(Sambucus canadensis)* is native to eastern North America. It has few serious pests or diseases, thrives in poorly drained soil, lives in Zones 3 to 9, and produces clusters of Vitamin C-rich fruit. If groomed to remove dead wood and wayward shoots, elderberry makes an attractive small landscape tree or large shrub, which grows up to 8 feet tall and 8 to 12 feet wide. Elderberry tends to send up new shoots from its roots and create a thicket, but individual stems usually live for only a few years. Prune these out when they become unproductive.

Elderberry blooms in the late spring, producing 8- to 12-inch-wide, flat-topped clusters of flowers that nearly cover the plant. Elderflowers are used to make wine and a delicate liquor. You can also dip them in batter and fry into fritters. The dark purple berries ripen in late summer. You can eat the berries raw, but they contain large seeds. I boil and strain the berries to collect the juice for jelly. Mixed with apple juice, they make a beautiful, clear, deep pink to wine-colored jelly. The St. Lawrence Nursery (see Chapter 14) catalog suggests boiling a pint of juice with 2½ cups of sugar and 10 whole cloves and serving it over ice for stomach ailments and colds. I mix a similar concoction with sparkling water for a natural soft drink. Of course, elderberry wine is another possibility.

Plant elderberry in moist soil and full sun. For best fruiting, plant two different varieties or seedlings. Wild seedlings are adequate for my garden, but several good improved varieties exist, which have larger and more numerous fruit. These include 'Kent', 'York', 'Nova', and 'Johns'.

Going ape for grapes

Growing organic grapes *(Vitis* species) successfully depends on your climate, cultural strategies, and the varieties you choose. Arid climates provoke fewer diseases than humid climates. You can grow grapes nearly anywhere in Zones 3 through 10 and they tolerate a wide range of soil conditions; well-drained soil in the pH range of 5.5 to 7.0 is best. Grapes need full sun and very good air circulation to hamper diseases.

At least three different grape species and countless varieties exist in North American gardens and vineyards. The European grape, *V. vinifera,* grows best in a Mediterranean climate, such as California and parts of the southwestern U.S. In hotter, humid climates, many people grow muscadine grapes, *V. rotundifolia,* which thrive in Zones 7 through 9. The native North American species, *V. labrusca,* and its hybrids are the hardiest and best for most other regions of the country.

To sort out the complicated lineage, divide grapes into two broad categories — table grapes and wine or juice grapes. Table grapes have tender skins suitable for fresh eating and may contain seeds or be seedless. Wine and juice grapes may have tougher skins, but plenty of sweet juice for liquid consumption or making into jelly. Ripe fruit colors range from green to pink and red to deep purplish black.

Before planting young grapes, prepare the soil thoroughly as described in the "Berry Patch Basics" section (earlier in this chapter) and install a sturdy trellis consisting of 2 or 3 heavy wires strung 24 inches apart on sturdy posts. Brace the end posts.

Several pruning and training systems exist, but the basic idea in all of them is to establish 1 or 2 main trunks per vine. Each trunk grows horizontal lateral branches, as described for kiwi (see the following section), which you attach to the wires. The flowers and fruit appear on wood that grows in the current year from the laterals that grew in the previous year. Starting in winter after the first growing season, begin the pruning and training as follows.

1. **In the first winter, choose two healthy, vigorous canes to keep and remove the rest.**

   Prune these main trunks back to 3 or 4 buds each.

2. **The next summer, select the most vigorous shoot from each trunk and remove competing shoots.**

   Train the shoots on a string until they reach the top wire, then pinch them to encourage lateral branching, as shown in Figure 13-2.

3. **In the second winter, remove all growth from the trunk and lateral branches.**

   Cut laterals back to 10 buds. Let vines grow unpruned through the summer.

4. **In the third winter and subsequent years, choose the laterals for the current year as well as replacement laterals for next year.**

   Leave 10 buds on the current year laterals and 2 buds on the replacements. Remember that grapes grow fruit on wood that grows in the current year from last season's laterals. Prune off all other wood, removing as much 90 percent of the previous year's growth.

Prevalent diseases and pests include berry moth, mites, leaf hoppers, and Japanese beetles, as well as Botrytis bunch rot, powdery mildew, and black rot. Some varieties are less sensitive to infection than other varieties.

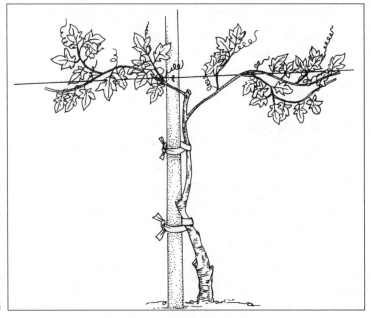

Figure 13-2:
Train grapes
on a trellis
and prune to
a main stem
with lateral
branches.

Grape varieties often grow best in specific regions of the country. Consult your local extension office or reputable nursery for recommendations. Also take a look at the "Surfing for small fruits" sidebar in this chapter.

Have a hardy kiwi, mate?

Unless you happen to live in Zone 8 or warmer, you can forget about growing the subtropical kiwis that appear in grocery stores. Luckily, if you live in a climate as cold as Zone 5 and even Zone 4, you can grow hardy kiwis. The hardy species, *Actinidia arguta,* produces very sweet, smooth-skinned, green fruit about the size of a large cherry, which ripens in late summer to early fall. You can eat them skin and all and many people consider them more flavorful than the less hardy, store-bought kiwifruit. Male and female flowers occur on separate plants, so you need one male plant for every 5 female plants. The ornamental flowers smell sweetly like lily-of-the-valley.

The hardy kiwi plant is a very vigorous vine that can grow 20 feet or more in length and requires a strong trellis. A mature, properly pruned kiwi vine can produce over 100 pounds of fruit per year. To make a trellis, set 4- to 6-inch diameter, 8- to 9-foot high posts at least 2 to 3 feet into the ground and run heavy gauge wire between them 6 feet off the ground. Train the vines up the posts and along the wire. Avoid planting where strong wind may damage the vines or blow down the trellis.

Space plants about 15 feet apart in full sun. Soil must have a pH around 6.5 and be well drained, but moist, especially as new plants become established and while fruit develops. Root rot is common in overly wet soil. Mulch to suppress weeds and maintain soil moisture.

Pruning is critical to control rampant growth and encourage maximum fruiting. Plants produce flowers and fruit on shoots that grow in the current spring.

- **Summer pruning:** Establish from 1 to 4 main trunks, using more in colder climates and fewer where cold damage is less likely. Train these up the center post and prune to 6-foot lengths when they reach the top to encourage them to sprout lateral shoots along the wires. These lateral shoots become the permanent *arms* from which fruiting wood will grow. In the summer, as the laterals branch, prune off 4 inches of new growth whenever it reaches 8 inches in length. The result should be a series of 4-inch sections of vine, called *spurs,* that will send out fruiting wood the following spring.

- **Winter pruning:** In late winter, remove fruiting wood older than 3 years, as well as very tangled or twisted vines. Shorten any vines that may reach the ground when growth resumes, but avoid cutting the spurs or arms.

Harvest the fruit in late summer when it softens and becomes sweet. You can store it for a short time in the refrigerator. You may have to beat the squirrels to the harvest.

Sublime strawberries

Probably the most popular small fruit for the home garden, strawberries are also among the hardest to grow organically. Strawberries have many insect pests and diseases that damage plants and berries alike. Establishing your planting in well-drained, fertile soil, and maintaining a weed-free patch is essential for success.

You can choose from three different kinds of strawberries, depending on when you want fruit. Consult your local extension office or nurseries for the best varieties for your area. See the "Surfing for small fruits" sidebar in this chapter.

- **June-bearing** varieties produce one large crop of berries in late spring to early summer.

- **Everbearing** varieties produce two smaller crops — one in the early summer and another in early fall.

- **Day-neutral** berries, the newest type, can produce fruit continuously throughout the growing season.

Plant dormant, bare-root strawberry plants 18 to 24 inches apart in 3- to 6-inch high, 3- to 4-foot wide raised beds. Set the plants so that soil covers the roots, but the crown remains above the soil, as shown in Figure 13-3. Keep the soil moist, but not saturated. Pinch off all flowers until mid-summer for the first season to encourage strong root and top growth.

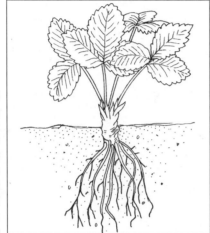

Figure 13-3:
Plant
strawberry
plants so
that crowns
are just
above
the soil.

The plants that you set out are called the *mother plants*. They send out runners that take root and develop new *daughter plants* in mid to late summer. Space the daughter plants evenly around the mothers to give each plenty of space to grow. Daughter plants flower and fruit the year after they grow. In the second summer, you can remove the original mother plants to make room for new daughter plants. Another method is to rotary till the sides of the bed in mid-summer of the second or third year, leaving plants only in the 18- to 24-inch wide center strip. Train new daughter plants into the tilled soil. Plan to replace your strawberry planting every 3 to 5 years. Cover the planting with straw mulch after the ground freezes in cold-winter climates and remove as the weather warms in spring.

One of the most serious insect pests that affect strawberries is the tarnished plant bug, which can severely damage the developing fruit. These insects spend the winter in plant debris and live on weeds in and around your yard. Covering the strawberry plants in the fall with a floating row cover can offer some, but not complete protection from the bugs in the following spring and early summer. Early ripening varieties often suffer less damage than late-season berries.

SOURCE

Surfing for small fruits

The Internet offers a wealth of information about any topic that you care to know about (and some that you don't), and small fruits are no exception. Government and university-sponsored sites feature advice and how-to instructions as well as links to other related sites. Commercial mail-order nurseries sell their plants and offer on-line planting and care guides that help ensure your success. Here are a few of my favorites:

✔ **www.attra.org/attra-pub/fruitover.html:** Funded by the U.S. government, the Appropriate Technology Transfer for Rural Areas, known as ATTRA for short, has an excellent Web page with advice for establishing a small fruit patch for home use or commercial-sized production. Lots of good links and cultural instructions for specific crops, too.

✔ **www.noursefarms.com:** Nourse Farms offers a good assortment of small fruits and perennial vegetables. I drove by this large and well-established nursery frequently while attending college in western Massachusetts. You can also write to them

at 41 River Road, South Deerfield, MA 01373 or phone 413-665-2658.

✔ **www.raintreenursery.com:** Raintree Nursery specializes in fruits for the Pacific Northwest. You can also write to them at 391 Butts Road, Morton, WA 98356 or call 360- 496-6400.

✔ **www.inberry.com:** Indiana Berry & Plant Co. offers a wide variety of small fruits as well as planting and care guides on their Web site. Write them at 5218 West 500 South, Huntingburg, IN 47542 or phone 812-683-3055.

✔ **www.eat-it.com:** Edible Landscaping offers in-depth care guides as well as many different fruit and nut plants. Write them at P.O. Box 77, 361 Spirit Ridge Ln., Afton, VA 22920 or call 800-524-4156.

✔ **www.qnet.com/~johnsonj/:** Visit Cyndi's Catalog of Garden Catalogs, which lists over 1,850 catalogs, to find more small fruit sources.

The strawberry clipper or bud weevil is another significant pest in some areas. This insect flies into the planting from neighboring woodlots and hedgerows about the time that the flower buds swell. Adults destroy the developing buds by laying eggs in them. Many other insects, slugs, mites, and nematodes attack strawberry fruits and plants, reducing vigor and production and introducing disease. Birds and ground squirrels will also take their share.

Strawberries are also subject to many fungus, bacteria, and virus diseases. Fungal infections include leaf spot, leaf scorch, leaf blight, powdery mildew, red stele, Verticillium wilt, root rot, and several berry rots. Avoid planting strawberries where tomatoes, eggplants, or potatoes previously grew to avoid wilt diseases. Buy only virus-free plants from a reputable nursery. See Part III for more control strategies.

Chapter 14

Fruits and Nuts for Your Organic Orchard

In This Chapter

▶ Selecting tree size

▶ Cultivating fruits

▶ Growing nut trees in the landscape

▶ Choosing disease-resistant varieties

*F*reshly picked fruit from your own trees and shrubs is juicy joy — and easier to grow than you may think. Sure, some fruit and nut trees need more attention than many other plants, but the harvest is worth the effort. Many fruit varieties that you can grow at home taste far better than supermarket fruit. Commercial growers have to choose varieties that ship and store well and often pick fruit before it's really ripe, which means that flavor suffers.

Better flavor is reason enough to grow your own fruit. But if you're concerned about pesticides, you have another compelling reason, as well. Cherries, peaches, apples, and apricots are among the 12 most pesticide-contaminated foods, according to research done by the United States Food and Drug Administration.

Even if you have nothing more than a large patio planter, you can grow your own fruit; on a half-acre lot, you can plant an orchard large enough to provide fruit for yourself and half the neighborhood. As an added bonus, most fruit trees and shrubs are ornamental, too, especially when blooming.

Anatomy of a Fruit Tree

Fruit and nut trees resemble other trees in most ways, but differ in one important aspect: Unlike ornamental plants, most people grow fruit trees primarily to produce food. To make these fruit factories more and more efficient, plant breeders continue to develop special techniques, such as reducing the size of the trees, to make trees produce at an earlier age and yield more fruit per acre. That's good news for home gardeners.

Size does matter

Trees are easier to harvest and maintain when all of the branches are within arm's reach. Unfortunately, many fruit trees can grow up to 40 feet tall or even higher when left to their own devices. To keep them in bounds and to produce more high quality fruit, most fruit varieties and many nuts are *grafted* onto roots of smaller-growing varieties. Tree nurseries slip a bud, called a *scion,* from a desirable fruit variety, such as 'Delicious' apple or 'Bing' cherry, under the bark of a *dwarfing rootstock* variety in early spring. The two grow together and, when the scion bud starts growing vigorously, the nursery prunes off the dwarfing rootstock's top growth to just above the bud. The place where the two parts meet is called the *bud union* and usually shows as a bulge, bend, or scar, as shown in Figure 14-1.

Plant breeders and tree nurseries graft fruit and nut trees for a variety of reasons:

- ✔ **Reproduce exact copies of desirable trees:** Nurseries can make as many trees as they need by grafting buds of a desirable variety onto uniform rootstocks.

- ✔ **Influence the mature size of the tree:** Reducing the tree size has many advantages, especially for home gardeners.

- ✔ **Encourage fruit bearing at an earlier age:** Some standard-sized apple trees can take up to ten years to begin bearing fruit, while a dwarf bears fruit in two years.

- ✔ **Increase disease and pest resistance:** Some rootstocks resist soil-borne diseases and harmful pests better than others.

- ✔ **Adapt to different soils:** Some, for example, grow better in clay soils, while others prefer loam.

- ✔ **Determine hardiness to particular climates:** Roots are one of the most cold-sensitive parts of a tree. Some rootstocks increase the trees' hardiness to cold temperatures.

Some rootstocks influence the size that the tree will ultimately attain, although the mature size of the tree also depends on the standard height that's normal for the scion or main variety. Dwarfing rootstocks are categorized by the amount of dwarfing they provide. Apple tree sizes, for example, fall into several categories:

✔ **Standard-sized** apple trees, grown on seedling or non-dwarfing roots may reach 25 feet.

✔ **Semi-dwarf** is about 75 percent of the standard height or about 18 feet at maturity.

✔ **Dwarf trees** are about 50 percent as high as standard or 12-feet tall.

✔ **Miniature trees** are only about 15 percent of the standard size. At a mere 4 feet in height, these make the best trees for growing in containers.

As an organic home gardener, consider dwarf to semi-dwarf size trees for several reasons. It's easier to monitor and control pests when you can reach the top of the tree. On very small trees, you can even use a barrier fabric to help prevent insect infestations (see Chapter 8). You can also harvest fruit years sooner and pick the fruit more easily.

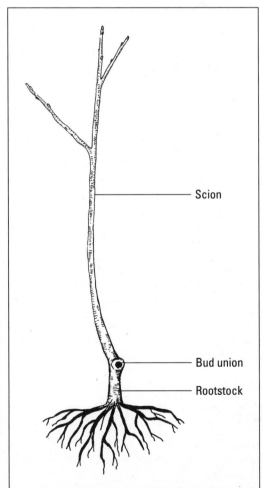

Figure 14-1:
Most fruit trees are made of two parts — a desirable variety grafted onto a dwarfing rootstock.

Scion

Bud union

Rootstock

Whether you have a large yard or a half whiskey-barrel container, you can find a fruit or nut variety that fits your available space, soil, and climate by choosing the right rootstock. Specialty nurseries that ship by mail have the largest selection of varieties and rootstocks, while local garden centers usually offer only dwarf or semi-dwarf trees in a handful of popular varieties.

Sex and the single tree

Many fruit and nut species, such as apples, sweet cherries, European pears, Japanese plums, walnuts, pecans, and filberts require *cross-pollination* to bear fruit. That means that you need two different, but compatible varieties planted near one another so that the pollen of one fertilizes the flowers of the other.

The trees must bloom at the same time for cross-pollination to occur, and some varieties are fussy about with whom they mix. Other fruit and nut species are *self-fruitful,* which means that they can pollinate their own flowers, but even those often produce larger crops when they mix pollen with a friend. Reputable nurseries can tell you which varieties can pollinate each other. See the "Where to find fruits and nuts" sidebar, later in this chapter.

Chill out

Fruits and nuts have another peculiar requirement — most need a certain number of hours below 45 degrees — called *chill requirement* or *chill factor* — in order to produce lots of flowers and fruit. As you may guess, fruits, such as oranges, that grow mostly in the warm climates have lower chilling requirements than some cold-climate fruits, such as apples. The chill factor is not related to cold hardiness, however. Even some frost-tender plants, such as fig trees, need some time below 45 degrees to bear fruit properly.

Crops fall into several categories, depending on how many hours of chilling that they need. Each variety is different, however. Some peach varieties need only 200 hours, while others require more than 1,000. Look for specific varieties that match your climate.

- **Low chill** fruits need fewer than 400 hours below 45 degrees. In the U.S., warm pockets in California, southern Texas, and Florida fall into this category.

- **Moderate chill** fruits need between 400 and 700 hours of chill. Look for varieties with this requirement if you live along the Gulf coast, southeastern seaboard, or Pacific coastal areas.

- **High chill** varieties need more than 700 hours and often more than 1,000 hours of temperatures below 45 degrees. Most of the U.S. and Canada easily fall into this range.

Low winter temperatures and timing of autumn and spring frosts play important roles in your selection of fruit species and varieties for your organic orchard. Local nurseries generally sell plants best suited to your local climate. Reputable mail-order nurseries and your local extension office can also steer you toward appropriate varieties.

Budding genius

Fruit trees grow different kinds of buds and it helps to be able to recognize the various types. The *terminal bud* grows at the end of branches, and that's where new branches and twigs grow from each spring. When the terminal buds expand, they leave *bud scars,* which look like slightly raised rings around the twig. You can measure how much a tree has grown each year by looking at the distance between bud scars. *Leaf buds* appear along the twigs and expand into leaves. *Flower buds* are usually fatter than leaf buds and swell first in the spring. Some trees, such as most apples, pears, cherries, plums, and apricots, produce their fruit on *spurs,* which are short, modified twigs. Spurs usually live and produce flower buds for several years or longer before becoming unproductive. See Figure 14-2 for examples of these bud types.

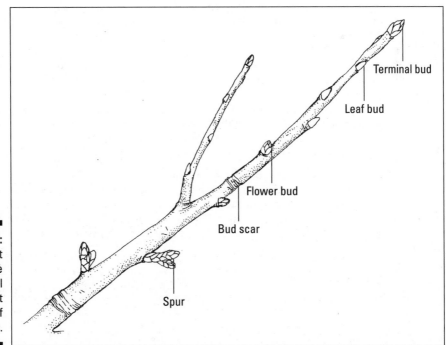

Figure 14-2: Fruit and nut trees have several different kinds of buds.

For the best-quality apples and pears, leave only one fruit on each spur and pinch off the others in early summer. Spurs and flower buds develop best on limbs that are angled slightly above horizontal. Branches that grow upright and those that dangle below horizontal produce little, if any, fruit.

Cultural Exchange

Choosing the best kinds of fruit and nut plants for your climate is only one part of establishing a successful, low-maintenance, organic orchard. You also have to plant your trees and shrubs where they can thrive, give them the fertile soil they need, prune them for health and maximum production, and plan your strategies for dealing with the inevitable pests and diseases.

Planting for success

All fruits need moisture-retentive, but well-drained soil. (Flip to Chapter 4 for more on soil testing and drainage.) Soggy sites spell doom for these species. Adequate water is also critical, especially when the fruit is developing and expanding. If you live in a drought-prone area, consider irrigating your fruit trees for the best yield. Drip tubes, which deliver water directly to the soil around the trees, are best. Avoid sprinklers that spray water on the leaves and contribute to disease.

Professional fruit growers also consider air movement when they plan their orchard placement and layout. Air affects fruit and nut plants in several ways:

- ✔ **Wind:** Too much wind can keep pollinating insects, such as bees, from flying and pollinating the flowers at critical times. It also knocks fruit off the tree and can damage the branches. Plant a windbreak, if necessary, or put the trees where a building shields them.

- ✔ **Frost pockets:** Cold air flows downhill and collects at the bottom of a slope. Trees that bloom in early spring are especially vulnerable to cold temperatures at that time and the flowers maybe severely damaged if planted where cold air collects. Plant fruit trees and shrubs on the slope instead of near the bottom, but avoid the windy top of a slope.

- ✔ **Circulation:** Constantly but lightly moving air helps prevent disease organisms from getting a foothold on your trees. Many fungus diseases that infect leaves need water and moisture to spread and grow, so keeping the leaves dry is important.

If you buy your plants locally, they will usually be already growing in a container. If you order them from a mail-order nursery, however, they will arrive in a *dormant* or non-growing state and *bareroot,* without any soil around their roots. Be sure to plant bareroot trees and shrubs right away. Skip to Chapter 17 for information on how to plant trees and shrubs.

After planting, establish a wide ring of organic mulch around your trees to conserve soil moisture, prevent grass and weeds from competing with the tree roots, and reduce insect pests. See Chapter 6 for the lowdown on mulch and its benefits.

Because producing heavy crops of fruit stresses trees and shrubs, fruit and nut-bearing species need additional nutrients. The texture of your soil, its current nutrient levels, plant age and type, climate, and amount of fruit your tree bears all have an effect on the amount of additional nutrients you need to add to the soil. Soil tests and leaf analyses are the most accurate methods used to determine which nutrients your trees need. See Chapter 4 for soil testing and Chapter 5 for more on fertilizers. Consult your local extension office for information on how and when to take leaf samples and where to send them.

Pruning fruit trees

Producing bushels of high quality fruit and developing a sturdy tree that can support the crop are the twin goals of pruning and training fruit trees. If you end up with an attractive landscape specimen, too, that's a bonus! Although you use the same basic pruning techniques on all fruit trees, each kind of fruit tree has unique timing and methods for reaching your goals. For an introduction to basic pruning techniques and tools, flip to Chapter 17.

You need to prune fruit trees regularly for several reasons. Keep these goals in mind as you make decisions about which limbs to remove:

- ✔ **Removing dead, damaged, and diseased wood:** Do this before any other pruning and whenever necessary.

- ✔ **Controlling tree and shrub size:** Keep fruit down where you can harvest and care for it without a ladder.

- ✔ **Providing air circulation:** Circulation helps ward off pests and diseases. Crowded limbs invite fungus diseases and provide habitat for damaging insects.

- ✔ **Increasing exposure to sunlight:** Sunlight makes fruit develop a sweeter flavor and deeper color. Fruit that's exposed to direct sunlight tastes better than fruit shaded by leaves and branches.

- ✔ **Increasing the quality and quantity of fruit:** Branches trained to 60-degree angles where they meet the trunk develop the most flower buds. Spacing the limbs up and down and around the trunk provides the best conditions for the fruit to mature.

Professional fruit growers use several different pruning and training methods, depending on the type of fruit they grow. The following styles apply mainly to temperate-climate fruit — tropical fruits, such as citrus, are trained differently. See Figure 14-3 for examples of each style.

- **Central leader:** Used mainly with apples, European pears and plums, large nut trees, and dwarf cultivars, this method yields trees with single, upright trunks, as shown on the left in Figure 14-3. The main limbs should be spaced about 8 inches apart and extend in all directions around the trunk so that no limb is directly above another. If you looked straight down from the top, the limbs should resemble a spiral in which no two branches are at exactly the same level on the trunk. To maximize sunlight penetration, prune the limbs so that those at the top of the tree are shorter than branches under them.

- **Modified central leader:** In this system, trees are trained to a single, upright trunk, called a *central leader,* with evenly spaced limbs until they reach a desired height, usually 6 to 10 feet. At that point, you prune out the leader and maintain the tree at that height. All fruit trees can be trained to this form and it's especially useful for keeping fruit within picking distance of the ground.

- **Open center (also called vase shape):** Peaches, nectarines, sour cherries, apricots, Asian pears, and Japanese plums produce easy-to-reach, high quality fruit when pruned to this form. In this style, shown on the right in Figure 14-3, you select four or five well-placed main branches and then prune out the central leader. This limits the height of the tree and creates a spreading crown. You can use this method with any fruit tree, especially those that normally grow too tall to harvest comfortably.

Figure 14-3: Train deciduous fruit trees to one of three forms, depending on the type of fruit and desired tree size.

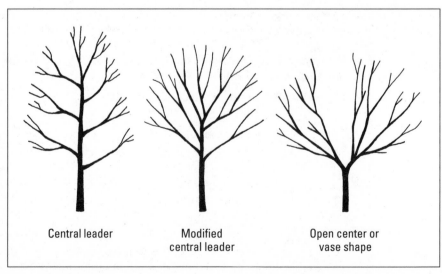

Central leader   Modified central leader   Open center or vase shape

Choose young *deciduous* fruit trees — trees that lose their leaves in the autumn — with good structure to start with, and shape them as they grow. The first few years are the most critical time to develop a healthy tree structure that will provide years of tasty fruit. Here's how to get your trees off to a good start:

- ✔ **At planting time:** Remove damaged and dead limbs, those under 25 inches from the ground, and any with narrow crotch angles of less than 45 degrees. Leave branches with crotch angles between 45 and 80 degrees. If the tree has two shoots competing to be the leader, choose one and remove the other.

- ✔ **First winter:** In mid to late winter, select 3 to 4 limbs to keep as main branches. They should be about 8 inches apart vertically, be well spaced around the trunk, and have approximately 60-degree angles at the trunk. Prune off all other limbs. Prune remaining limbs back by one-third of their length to encourage side branching. Prune the central leader to 24 to 30 inches above the uppermost limb for a central-leader-style tree. If pruning for an open center or vase shape, remove the central leader just above the top branch.

- ✔ **Second summer:** In mid-summer, remove *water sprouts* that grow upright from the branches and *suckers,* which grow up from the base of the tree. In central-leader trees, choose the strongest, most upright leader and remove competing ones. Using the criteria mentioned for the first dormant season, choose the next tier of limbs beginning about 15 to 18 inches above the top branch of the lower tier. Remove undesirable limbs. In open center trees, remove competing, crowded, and upright shoots.

- ✔ **Second winter:** Remove undesirable limbs, competing leaders, water sprouts, and suckers and prune the new growth of side branches back by one-third. Use notched sticks, called *spreaders,* to spread the remaining limbs to 60-degree angles where they meet the trunk. Leave the spreaders in place until mid to late summer. In open center trees, prune new shoots by one-third to *outward-facing buds* — buds that face away from the trunk — to encourage branching. Thin out crowded shoots by removing the weakest ones. See the "Where to find fruits and nuts" sidebar for sources of spreaders. Many nurseries offer them.

- ✔ **Continuing care:** Continue to follow the directions for the second season year after year. To develop a modified leader tree, remove the central leader just above the uppermost branch you wish to keep. Do this in the summer to inhibit vigorous sprouting.

Preventing pests and diseases

Humans aren't the only ones who love fruit — insects, diseases, and other creatures appreciate these trees and shrubs, too. Some insects damage the fruits while others concentrate their efforts on the foliage and wood. Insects take a toll, but you can control many of them without resorting to pesticides.

Sticky traps, baited either to resemble a ripe red apple or with hormones that the bugs find sexy, capture many codling moths, apple maggots, borers, and some scale and leafminer species, for example. White and yellow plastic rectangles covered with sticky glue also attract several species of harmful insects. See Chapters 8 and 9 for more information on natural pest controls and purchasing sources.

Non-toxic horticultural oil spray applied in late winter and during the summer, as needed, can control aphids, pear psyllas, mites, leafminers, and caterpillars. Other insects can be trickier to deal with, but luckily, you can fool many pests with traps and barriers and well-timed plant-based pesticides. Timing is everything when controlling many of these bad guys. Contact your local extension office to find out the most effective time to use pest controls on your particular crops.

Plant breeders have developed many modern fruit varieties that resist or at least tolerate some of the most devastating diseases: Choose these for your organic orchard. Remember that prevention is the first and most important key to fighting pest and disease problems!

Unfortunately, most old-time favorite fruit varieties aren't resistant to disease and, therefore, not as suitable for home growing. Trying to grow organic Macintosh apples, for example, is just an invitation to heartbreak. Many less well-known, but equally yummy varieties are nearly care-free, however, and I mention them in the remaining sections of this chapter. Thorough clean-up of fallen foliage and fruit and other cultural strategies can also help control many pests and diseases — see Part III of this book for more good ideas.

Temperate-Climate Trees and Shrubs

Popular and easy-to-grow in USDA Hardiness Zones 8 and northward, these fruits find their way into lunch boxes, fruit salads, and pies from coast to coast. All require some dedication to their cultural needs, but richly reward your efforts. If you have limited space or just don't need bushels of fruit, try growing dwarf or even miniature versions of these trees. I grow peaches and nectarines in tubs on my deck, for example, even though I live in a colder climate than these trees normally withstand. I can easily protect my miniature trees from pests and extreme weather and move them into a sheltered barn for safe winter storage.

Help for growing organic fruit

One book that I can't do without is *The Orchard Almanac* by Steve Page and Joe Smillie, published by agAccess, Davis, California. It contains valuable, organic pest control calendars and strategies for temperate-climate fruits.

Another book that I use frequently is *Designing and Maintaining Your Edible Landscape Naturally* by Robert Kourik. The author provides lots of charts and illustrations plus detailed information on a wide variety of plants.

Apples (Malus sylvestris)

With hundreds of varieties available, you can find at least one apple to match nearly any climate and set of taste buds. Apples are among the most popular fruit trees to grow, but to harvest high-quality fruit, you must be prepared to regularly prune, feed, and deal with pests. Apples require cross-pollination, but some nurseries offer trees with two or more varieties grafted onto one rootstock. You can also use ornamental crabapples to pollinate apple trees.

Apples have several serious pests that make them a challenge to grow organically. Plum curculio, apple maggot, and codling moths damage the developing fruits, frequently making them inedible. See Chapter 7 for more on these pests and how to control them.

As trees increase in size, they become harder to prune and spray, so choose trees on semi-dwarf and dwarf rootstocks that reach only 8 to 12 feet tall. You can also use pruning techniques to control tree height. Prune apple trees in late winter, while they are dormant, and follow up in mid-summer to remove overly vigorous sprouts.

Disease resistance is key when choosing apple varieties for organic orchards. Apple scab, cedar apple rust, powdery mildew, and fire blight devastate many common and older varieties, which makes them unsuitable for home orchards. Although the names of improved varieties may be unfamiliar, the fruit is just as flavorful. Some disease-resistant apple varieties worth seeking out, listed from those that ripen earliest (late summer) to latest (mid to late autumn), include 'Redfree', 'Prima', 'Novamac', 'JonaFree', 'Priscilla', 'Freedom', 'Liberty', 'Nova Easygro', 'Enterprise', and 'GoldRush'. Although you may not see these varieties in the supermarket, many farmers' markets and organic cooperatives offer the fruit in season, so you can do a taste test before you buy your own trees.

Apples ripen from late summer through late autumn, so choose a variety that ripens its fruit before freezing temperatures in your area have a chance to damage the crop. Varieties also vary considerably in their chill requirements, with some better suited to colder climates and others to milder seasons. Take a look at the "Where to find fruits and nuts" sidebar, later in this chapter, for sources of trees that are best suited for your area.

European and Asian pears (Pyrus)

Pears (*Pyrus* species) share many of apple's quirks and characteristics, and they grow in similar climates. Like apples, pears are usually sold as grafted trees and require similar pruning and training. Pears, with their glossy dark green foliage, make especially good landscape specimens in addition to providing delicious fruit.

Unfortunately, pears also share many of apple's diseases and insect pests. Fireblight is its most devastating disease, while pear scab can render the trees and fruit unsightly. Avoid planting fireblight-prone varieties and keep insect pests, which spread the disease, under control. Pear psylla, an insect that resembles a winged, yellow- to orange-colored aphid, sucks the juice out of new foliage and excretes sticky droppings that support a black, sooty-looking fungus. You can control it with dormant spray oil.

You can choose from two kinds of pears — European and Asian. They share most cultural attributes, but differ in some other ways:

- **Pollination:** Most European pears require another variety planted within 50 feet for cross-pollination. Asian pears are mostly self-fruitful, but produce heavier crops when cross-pollinated.

- **Shape:** European pear fruits have the traditional pear-shape, with a wide bottom tapering to a narrower top. Most Asian pears resemble round apples.

- **Texture:** European pears have soft, melting flesh when ripe. Asian pears have crisp, apple-like flesh.

Fireblight-resistant varieties of European pear, listed in order of ripening, include 'Harrow Delight', 'Harvest Queen', 'Starking Delicious', 'Moonglow', 'Stark Honeysweet', 'Magness', 'Seckel', and 'Harrow Sweet'. The earliest varieties begin ripening in mid-August in Zone 5, with the latest finishing up in late September.

Disease-resistant Asian varieties include 'Shinko', 'Shinseiki', 'Large Korean' (also known as 'Dan Beh'), 'Korean Giant', and 'Olympic', all of which ripen from September through October. Ripening begins earlier in Zones 6 and 7.

Pears are best picked when still somewhat hard and allowed to ripen at room temperature or in the refrigerator. Fruit that overripens on the tree develops hard, gritty spots in the flesh and may turn brown and mushy near the core. Asian pears and late-season European pears keep for months in the refrigerator if picked just before ripeness.

Sweet and sour cherries (Prunus)

Cherries are glorious in their spring bloom — the fruit seems just like an added bonus. In Zone 5, cherries ripen from June into July, providing the first fruit of the season. Most cherries are red when ripe, but some sweet cherries are yellow. Cherries belong to the *Prunus* genus along with peaches, almonds, and plums.

Although sweet and sour or tart cherries are similar in many respects, they differ from each other in significant ways.

- **Pollination:** Sweet cherries need cross-pollination, except for the variety 'Stella', so you need two compatible varieties. Sour cherries, also called pie cherries, are self-pollinating. Sour cherries can pollinate sweet cherries, but may not bloom at the same time. Trees must bloom at the same time for them to cross-pollinate.

- **Hardiness:** Sweet cherry trees grow reliably only in Zones 5 to 8, but some sour cherries thrive in Zone 4.

- **Culinary use:** Sweet cherries, common in supermarkets in early summer, are best when eaten fresh. Sour cherries make the best pies and jams, but you have to grow your own — markets rarely offer them. Some varieties are sweet enough to eat fresh, too.

The pests that plague apples, including plum curculio and apple maggot, also infest cherries, as do the cherry fruit fly and Oriental fruit moth. Birds will also take a portion of the crop, if not the whole thing, unless you cover the ripening fruit with a net. Birds tend to bother tart cherries less than sweet cherries, but its better to be safe than sorry. Fruit of some varieties tend to crack in the rain as they ripen, but others resist this bad habit. Of the diseases that affect all *Prunus* species, black knot fungus, bacterial canker, and leaf spot are the most serious. Practice good sanitation by raking up foliage and dropped fruit, and prune out any infected wood immediately.

 For best flavor, let sweet and sour cherries fully ripen on the tree before picking, but keep them covered to prevent bird theft! 'Montmorency' is the most widely grown commercial sour cherry, but other varieties, such as 'Morello', 'Meteor', and 'Northstar' are good choices for home orchards.

Good sweet cherry varieties for home-grown fruit include 'Stella', 'Lapins', 'Glacier', 'Surefire', and 'Sunburst', which are self-pollinating. 'Bing', which is the most common commercial variety, is susceptible to canker and fruit splitting. Good varieties that require cross-pollination include 'Van' and yellow cherries 'Emperor Francis', 'Stark Gold', and 'Rainier'.

Peaches and nectarines (Prunus persica)

Peaches and nectarines are actually the same species, but peaches are fuzzy and nectarines are smooth-skinned. They share the same diseases and pests as cherries, but are worth growing for the juicy flavor and aroma that comes only from freshly picked, sun-ripened fruit. They are self-pollinating, so you only need one tree.

Peaches, nectarines, apricots, and plums are called *stone fruits* after the seed pit in their centers. These fruits fall into one of two camps, called *freestone* and *clingstone,* depending on whether or not the flesh separates easily from the seed. In general, freestone fruit has softer, melting flesh and is best for fresh eating, while clingstone fruit has firmer flesh that holds up well in baking and canning. Generally, fruits ripen from mid-July through August, depending on the climate and variety.

Geography and climate influence peach growing rather significantly. Diseases and pests that are prevalent in some parts of the U.S. cause little concern in other areas. Plum curculio, bacterial leaf spot, and fungus diseases, for example, present problems for peaches in the eastern part of the U.S., from a line that runs approximately from Fort Worth, Texas to Fargo, North Dakota. Gardeners west of that line have an easier time growing peaches organically, except in the Pacific Northwest where the damp climate encourages diseases. If you're in the eastern U.S., vigilant housekeeping, pruning, and choosing a site that encourages air circulation, as well as using natural pesticides, can help you grow this problem-prone crop.

Peaches and nectarines grow reliably only in climates with mild winters and fairly dry summers, preferably Zones 6 to 9, although some varieties produce fruit in warmer parts of Zones 4 and 5. The hardiness of their overwintering flower buds is the limiting factor in cold-winter climates — several consecutive nights of –13 degrees will kill them. Mild weather in winter or early spring followed by a return to freezing weather also spells disaster for their blooms. Plant breeders have developed varieties, such as 'Reliance' and 'Veteran', that withstand temperatures as low as –25 degrees but they are usually less flavorful than peaches grown in warmer climates. If you want to try growing peaches in Zones 4 or 5, choose varieties with high-chill requirements because they bloom later in the season.

Gardeners in Zones 9 and 10 can successfully grow peaches if they choose varieties with low chill requirements. Some varieties developed for Florida, for example, need only 150 to 400 hours below 45 degrees to bear fruit.

Peaches and nectarines bloom on wood that grew in the previous year, so prune them in June after flowering. Maintain an open-centered form and encourage lots of new growth each year. Maintain a vigilant pest- and disease-control program, too, because peach and nectarine trees are among the most susceptible to attack of all fruit trees. Peach leaf curl — a serious fungus disease — causes leaves and fruit to drop prematurely. Look for varieties that resist canker, brown rot, bacterial leaf spot, and pit splitting. Catalog or plant-tag descriptions will usually tell you whether a variety is resistant to particular diseases.

Peach varieties that resist bacterial leaf spot include 'Harrow Diamond', 'Harrow Beauty', 'Delta', 'Southern Pearl', 'Desert Gold', 'Candor', 'Sweethaven', 'Redhaven', 'Reliance', 'Harbrite', 'Harken', and 'Veteran'. Nectarine varieties include 'Sunraycer', 'Fantasia', 'RosePrincess', 'Mericrest', 'Hardired', and 'Harko'.

European and Asian apricots (Prunus)

Members of the *Prunus* genus, European and Asian apricots enjoy the same mild climates and well-drained soils as peaches and sweet cherries. Although plum curculio, codling moth, and brown rot can infest the fruits, the trees are more vigorous and resistant to disease than peaches. Prune apricot trees to a modified central leader or open-center form. If you can grow them in your climate, give apricots a try because they have beautiful early spring flowers followed by luscious fruit that supermarkets just can't match. Unfortunately, spring frosts damage the tender blooms in cold regions.

European apricots that you may see in your grocery's produce section grow on 10- to 30-foot trees that thrive in the warmer, drier parts of Zones 6 to 8. Trees grown in cool, humid climates produce less fruit, and it tends to be of poorer quality. Choose varieties that are suitable for your specific climate. Local nurseries and your local extension office can make knowledgeable recommendations. Choose a freestone variety (discussed in the "Peaches and nectarines" section), if you wish to dry the ripened fruits for storage. Good varieties include 'Harcot', 'Harglow', 'Hargrand', 'Harlayne', 'Puget Gold', 'Veecot', and 'Goldcot'. For best flavor, allow the fruits to ripen on the tree before picking in July and early August.

Plums and prunes (Prunus)

This is one of the most genetically complicated fruits in the *Prunus* group because a number of species share the name of plum and all of the various species commonly interbreed. The resulting fruits fall into several broad categories, including European, Japanese, and prune plums. They differ in important ways:

✓ **Japanese plums** are round, usually require cross-pollination to set fruit, and are pruned to an open-centered shape. They are generally hardy to Zone 6 and warmer parts of Zone 5, although some hybrids are hardier. Varieties include 'Shiro', 'Early Golden', 'Burbank', 'Redheart', 'Santa Rosa', 'Methley,' and 'Beauty'. Hybrids 'Elite', 'Superb', 'Tecumseh', 'Perfection', and 'Brookgold' are hardy through Zone 4.

- ✔ **European plums** are oval and most don't need a second variety for pollination. Train these to a modified leader form. Most varieties are hardy through Zone 5 and some produce fruit even in Zone 4. Varieties include 'Damson', 'Seneca', 'Verity', and 'Green Gage'.

- ✔ **Prune plums** are European plums with drier flesh and a high sugar content that makes them suitable for drying. Common varieties include 'Stanley', 'French Prune', 'Fellenberg' or 'Italian Prune', 'Valor', 'Earliblue', 'Sugar', and 'Mount Royal', which is hardy in Zone 4.

Japanese and European plums can't pollinate each other, so if your trees require cross-pollination, be sure to choose compatible varieties. Thin the fruits to hang 4 to 6 inches apart, 5 to 8 weeks after bloom. Fruits ripen from July through September, starting with Japanese plums and ending with prune plums, depending on the variety.

Plant breeders have also crossed apricots with plums to create hybrids called apriums, plumcots, and pluots. These are hardy wherever European apricots grow, require cross-pollination, and otherwise have characteristics of both parents.

Where to find fruits and nuts

Look to specialty catalogs for the widest assortment of fruit and nut varieties:

- ✔ Stark Brothers Nursery is one of the largest and oldest temperate-climate fruit nurseries in the U.S. and offers a comprehensive catalog. Phone 800-325-4180 or visit their Web site at www.starkbros.com.

- ✔ To purchase warm-climate fruits, try your local nurseries or, on the west coast of the U.S., contact Pacific Tree Farms at 4301 Lynwood Drive, Chula Vista, CA 91910. Phone 905-468-7262.

- ✔ In the southeastern U.S., try Garden of Delights at 14560 SW 14th Street, Davie, FL 33325-4217. Phone 954-370-9004 or e-mail godelights@aol.com.

- ✔ If you live in Zones 3 to 5, contact St. Lawrence Nurseries at 325 State Hwy. 345, Potsdam, NY 13676. Phone 315-265-6739 or e-mail trees@sln.potsdam.ny.us for a catalog of cold-hardy fruits and nuts.

- ✔ In the Pacific northwest, contact One Green World at 28696 South Cramer Rd., Molalla, OR 97038-8576. Phone 503-651-3005, fax 800-418-9983, or visit their Web site at www.onegreenworld.com. They offer a variety of fruits and nuts.

- ✔ Another good nursery for the Pacific northwest, Raintree Nursery, offers fruit and nut trees, as well as unusual fruits. Write to them at 391 Butts Road, Morton, WA 98356; call 360-496-6400; fax 888-770-8358; or visit them on the Web at www.raintreenursery.com. Their Web site offers handy maps, charts, and detailed growing instructions.

- ✔ If you're looking for nearly any plant in existence, visit Cyndi's Catalog of Garden Catalogs at www.qnet.com/~johnsonj/. This site lists over 1,850 catalogs devoted to plants of all kinds, plus nifty links to various societies, organizations, and international sources.

Warm-Climate Fruit Trees

These trees grow where winter temperatures remain mild — generally in Zones 8 and warmer. Evergreen species, such as citrus, perish when the thermometer reaches or goes more than a few degrees below freezing, although some citrus varieties can grow in colder climes. Deciduous fruits, like figs and persimmons, are somewhat hardier, especially if you give them a favorable site. Gardeners in colder climates can grow some of these fruits successfully in containers, moving them to sheltered places in the winter or growing them as houseplants.

Citrus (Citrus)

This large *tropical* and *subtropical* group covers a wide range of juicy fruits from tiny kumquats to huge pummelos, which require almost frost-free climates to produce fruit (most can take 25 to 28 degrees for several hours) and hot summers to help ripen and sweeten the fruit. These trees need temperatures between 70 and 90 degrees for best growth. In the U.S., the citrus-growing region is limited to Florida, coastal areas of the Gulf coast states, and parts of Arizona and California.

Citrus trees have evergreen foliage and most have thorny limbs. Trees are usually grafted. (See the "Size does matter" section earlier in this chapter.) Most species bloom in early spring and don't require cross-pollination. Fruit ripens from autumn to spring, but some everbearing trees produce fruit year 'round. Allow fruit to ripen on the tree for best flavor.

- ✔ **Grapefruits:** Grown primarily in Florida and southern Texas, the trees reach 30 feet in height. Varieties include both seeded and seedless types and those with red, pink, or white flesh.

- ✔ **Kumquat:** A bit hardier and smaller than most citrus trees, kumquat can tolerate temperatures as low as 18 to 20 degrees and also make good houseplants. You can eat the small fruit whole — rind and all.

- ✔ **Lemons and limes:** Among the most cold-sensitive citrus, this group grows best in frost-free climates. Some varieties do well as houseplants, producing the sour fruit indoors.

- ✔ **Mandarins:** Members of this large group have somewhat flattened shapes and loose, easy-to-peel skins. Varieties include tangerines, clementines, and tangelos. The 'Calamondin' variety makes a good houseplant or container shrub and produces loads of small fruit with edible rinds. Most mandarin varieties need Zone 9 and warmer, although 'Calamondin' and 'Satsuma' varieties tolerate temperatures down to 20 degrees.

✔ **Oranges:** You can choose from many varieties, which vary in ease of peeling, sweetness, number of seeds, hardiness, quality of the juice, color, and time of ripening. Although most types ripen during December and January, some are ready to pick in November, while others, such as juicy Valencia varieties don't ripen until late winter to spring. Navel oranges are among the hardiest varieties.

Annual pruning isn't necessary for citrus trees, which is a good thing — most of these trees sport long, sharp thorns. They require pruning mostly just to keep the centers of the trees open to light and air and to remove dead branches. If trees get too big to pick easily, you can cut back the limbs with thinning cuts (see Chapter 17) every year or two. Wait to prune frost-nipped trees until new growth shows the extent of damage. To prevent sunburn after pruning, paint exposed branches that were previously shaded by foliage with whitewash made from a 1:1 mix of water and a white, water-based paint.

Citrus demands moist, but well-drained soil and regular applications of nitrogen fertilizer beginning in January and ending in late summer. Adequate water is especially needed when the trees are actively growing and developing fruit. Pests and diseases infrequently cause problems, except when trees are stressed from drought or other weather-related factors. Scale, mites, thrips, and whiteflies may infest these trees, in addition to cankers that infect the wood. You can easily control most pests with fine oil spray, as described in Chapter 9.

Figs (Ficus carica)

These attractive trees have smooth, gray bark and large, lobed, tropical-looking leaves. Figs can take winter cold down to 15 degrees, but freezing temperatures kill the upper branches and even the trunk of the tree. When this happens, the tree sprouts up from its roots and forms a shrub with several stems. Following such a freeze, the plants may not produce fruit in the following season, depending on the variety. Figs grow best in subtropical climates with mild winters and long, hot summers to ripen their fruit. They need well-drained soil.

Figs make good container specimens for climates where they can't survive outdoors year 'round. Move the containers into a cool, protected location where temperatures remain above freezing. Bring the plants into a warm, sunny location in early spring when the buds begin to swell.

Figs typically ripen two crops per year in warm climates. Leave the fruit on the trees to fully ripen before picking, but protect them from hungry birds. Prune to encourage new shoots, prevent branch crowding, and remove dead wood. Encourage the plant to form 3 to 5 main stems. If you prune when the trees are dormant, you'll decrease or eliminate the first crop, but increase the second crop of the year.

Fig trees have no serious pests except for fruit flies and ants, which attack the fruit in some climates. In some areas, the trees are prone to fig rust, which can be controlled with Bordeaux mix sprayed on the leaf undersides every 2 to 3 weeks from June through August. (See Chapter 10 for more on Bordeaux mix.) 'Brown Turkey', 'Celeste', 'Magnolia', and 'Mission' are common varieties.

Persimmon (Diospyros kaki, D. virginiana)

This lovely landscape tree grows up to 25 feet tall and wide, with bright yellow, red, and orange fall foliage and gracefully drooping branches. Its orange fruit dangles from the ends of the limbs as they ripen. Although this tree can withstand winter temperatures to 0 degrees, in colder regions, it tends to break dormancy and begin growing before the cold weather has fully departed.

Plant persimmons in well drained, acidic soil, but keep the soil moist, especially during the summer when the tree is carrying fruit. Prune only to establish a modified central leader branching structure of young trees and to remove dead and damaged limbs from mature trees. Persimmons have few serious pests or diseases, although fungus disease can affect the fruit late in the season and trees are susceptible to wilt disease in some areas. Control scale insects with dormant oil spray in late winter.

Oriental persimmon (Diospyros kaki) fruit fall into two different categories — astringent and non-astringent. Fruit of the astringent varieties are eaten when the flesh is soft and almost jelly-like, while non-astringent varieties can be eaten when firm. Some varieties have seeds and others are seedless. The best astringent varieties include 'Saijo', 'Tanenashi', and 'Yomato Hyakume'. Good non-astringent varieties include 'Fuyu', 'Hanagosho', and 'Hana Fuyu'. Female trees don't need male trees to set fruit and, in fact, produce seedy fruit with dark streaks in the flesh when pollinated. Harvest in autumn when the fruit feel slightly soft. Protect from birds.

The common persimmon (Diospyros virginiana), which is native to the U.S., grows vigorously from Zones 4 to 9 and spreads easily from seeds eaten by birds and animals. The trees tend to form thickets of suckers. Fruits measure 1 to 2 inches across. Some varieties exist with larger fruit.

Oh, Nuts!

Plant these ornamental or shade trees and enjoy the nut harvest as an added treat. Most nut trees need little care, but can be messy when the fruit and foliage drop. Plant the large-nut species, such as walnuts and pecans, where you can enjoy their beauty without worrying about falling nuts. Use smaller species, such as filberts, as hedges or small landscape trees. Most nut trees and shrubs require cross-pollination, which means you need two compatible varieties to produce nuts.

Filberts (Corylus avellana, C. americana)

Also known as hazelnut (*Corylus* species), you can grow this delicious nut as an ornamental 20-foot high tree or large shrub in Zones 5 to 8. Several species exist, but the one most commonly grown is the European filbert (*Corylus avellana*). Native North American species (*C. americana*) have smaller nuts, which make excellent wildlife food, but can be harvested, as well. European filberts like moist, well-drained soil and climates where late spring frosts don't damage their flower buds, but native species tolerate a wider range of conditions from Georgia into Canada. Commercially, European filberts grow best in the coastal valleys of the Pacific Northwest where summers are cool and winter mild.

Filberts require cross-pollination with another filbert variety to set fruit, which is ready to harvest in late summer. Variety pairs that can pollinate each other include 'Barcelona' with either 'Daviana' or 'Casina' and 'Royal' with 'Hall's Giant'. Prune and train to a central leader tree or maintain as a shrub. Collect the nuts as they fall from the trees and dry them in the sun until the kernels snap when bitten, and then store them in a cool, dry place. Squirrels and nut-eating birds are the most serious pests. Eastern filbert blight, however, is a devastating disease that has no known cure. The native North American species is less affected than the European filbert.

Almonds (Prunus amygdalus)

Almonds are related to peaches, plums, and apricots and require similar growing conditions. Although the trees are hardy to Zone 6, they have a chilling requirement of only 300 to 500 hours (see the "Chill out" section, earlier in this chapter), which results in early spring flowering. Warm spring weather followed by a cold snap ruins their lovely pink flowers and damages their developing fruits. Warm, dry summers in Zones 6 to 9 ensure a good harvest of sweet, oval nuts. Trees range in height from 10 to 40 feet depending on the rootstock and variety. They require cross-pollination to set fruit, except for the varieties 'All-in-One' and 'Garden Prince'.

Pests and diseases are the same as for peaches. Train trees to an open-centered shape and remove limbs that become unfruitful. Almonds fruit on spurs up to 5 years old. Harvest the nuts in early- to mid-autumn by shaking or knocking them from the tree when the hulls begin to split. Let them sun dry for a day or two, and then store in a cool, dry place.

Pecans (Carya illinoensis)

Pecans grow best in peach country in Zones 6 to 9, but need at least 140 to 200 or more frost-free days to develop their fruit, depending on the variety. Although these trees may live in cool climates, they may not produce fruit unless temperatures remain in the 75- to 85-degree range. High humidity encourages disease and other problems. They can serve as 60- to 100-foot shade trees in large home landscapes, although the dropping fruits can make quite a mess on the lawn.

Choose varieties that grow well in your climate and look for varieties with thin, easy to shell nuts. Pecans are grouped according to growing conditions:

- **Warm, humid climates:** Look for scab-resistant varieties that tolerate humidity. Varieties include 'Stuart', 'Candy', ' Chickasaw', and 'Choctaw'.

- **Cold winter climates:** Choose pecans that can mature their nuts within the shorter growing season, such as 'Colby', 'Starking Hardy Giant', and 'Fritz'.

- **Arid climates:** These varieties, including 'Cheyenne', 'Sioux', and 'Western Schley', are often susceptible to scab disease, but grow in more alkaline soil.

Pecans require cross-pollination and adequate water to set good crops. Keep the soil moist during the growing and fruiting season. Train the young trees to a modified central leader form (see "Pruning fruit trees" in this chapter) and prune older trees to remove dead or undesirable limbs.

Walnuts (Juglans)

These stately 50- to 150-foot shade trees grow from Zones 4 to 9, depending on the species, variety, and origin of the seedling. They enjoy fertile, deep soils with adequate moisture and require cross-pollination to produce good fruit. English and black walnuts are the two most commonly available types.

- **English walnuts** (*Juglans regia*) grow primarily in Zones 5 to 9 and have thin shells. They are susceptible to walnut blight on early spring foliage, especially in cool, damp climates. Codling moths and walnut husk flies damage developing young nuts. To ensure high-quality nuts, choose grafted varieties, such as 'Lake', 'Stark Champion', 'Hartley', and 'Franquette'.

✔ **Black walnuts** (*J. nigra*) are native North American trees that grow as far north as Zone 4. They have hard shells and intensely flavored nuts. The lumber from these huge trees is valuable for fine woodworking. Choose locally adapted trees to ensure their hardiness in your area. Although often grown from seed, cultivated varieties include 'Thomas' and 'Ohio'. Black walnut roots produce a chemical that inhibits the growth of many other trees and plants. Flower and vegetable gardens may not grow readily within the root zone of these trees.

You may have to fight off the squirrels, but collect the nuts as they fall and remove the husks as soon as possible to hasten drying. The hulls contain a yellow-orange dye that readily stains everything they touch so take care when handling them.

Chapter 15

Say It with Flowers

In This Chapter

▶ Choosing healthy flowering plants and bulbs

▶ Designing with annuals, perennials, and bulbs

▶ Picking the best varieties

▶ Planting and maintaining flower gardens

Trees and shrubs give your landscape structure, and vegetables and fruits put food on the table. But flowers are pure fun. You plant them to bring your landscape to life — to add color, vibrancy, drama, and romance. Daffodils, tulips, and other spring bulbs cheerfully greet the end of winter, while annual and perennial flowering plants put on a constantly changing and colorful show from one end of the growing season to the other. (*Annuals*, by the way, complete their life cycle in a single year, while *perennials* grow from one year to the next, usually sprouting from their over-wintering roots. *Bulbs* are perennial plants that store food in special swollen stems or roots.)

Flowers are among the easiest crops to grow organically. Yes, insects and diseases do bother some of them, but you have many control strategies from which to choose. Keeping them well fed isn't hard, either. This chapter covers all the basics you need to grow happy flowers almost all year 'round.

Mixing It Up

Flowers are diverse, resilient, and compatible with each other. You can mix them up any way you like and, as long as you give them their basic food, soil, water, and sun requirements, you can reasonably expect loads of bloom or attractive foliage. But even if a plant dies or gets eaten by bugs, it usually costs little to replace. And, in the case of annuals, which only live for the summer anyway, you can always try again next year.

Strength through diversity

Promoting diversity in any garden and landscape is a crucial part of organic gardening, and nowhere is it easier than in the flower garden. Except for large formal plantings or commercial-cut flower fields, most gardeners grow only a few plants of each flower species or variety and tend to mix them up their gardens. Here are a few good reasons to continue that practice:

- **Beneficial insects** and other organisms, which fight harmful pests and diseases, thrive in diverse environments.

- **Season-long color** is easier to manage when you plant perennials, annuals, and bulbs that bloom at different times throughout the spring, summer, and fall. You can mix and match color schemes, too.

- **Save garden space** by planting ornamental vegetables and herbs in your flower beds or planting flowers in your vegetable or herb garden. You can plant bulbs right under the root zones of annuals and perennials and extend the season of color.

- **Fool pests** by planting only a few of each species in spots around the garden or landscape. They may find some — but not all — of your zinnias or lilies!

Designing for year-round beauty

Flowers come in a rainbow of colors and a vast array of shapes and sizes. Mixing and matching them with creative flair is the part of gardening that gets me excited every winter when seed and plant catalogs land in my mailbox and when the soil warms in the spring. I have several different perennial and bulb flower gardens around my yard, plus containers and baskets. Oh, yes, and the rows of annual cutflowers in the vegetable patch. When shopping for new plants to add to your garden or rearranging the ones that you have, keep the following design elements in mind:

- **Season of bloom:** A big mistake that many gardeners make is to buy only what they see blooming in the garden center in the spring. Their gardens end up looking lovely in spring and early summer, but lack color during the rest of the summer and fall.

 A balanced flower garden has about one-third of its plants in bloom at any given time. Divide your flowering season into thirds (or fourths, if you live in a long-growing season climate) and choose plants that bloom in each part of the season. Visit garden centers in mid- and late-summer to find attractive plants that bloom in those seasons.

- **Flower color and form:** Gardeners usually make flower color their top priority when deciding which plants to purchase. Popular garden themes that revolve around color include single-color plantings, such as white gardens, soft pastels, bright crayon box colors, or motifs to match the color of your house. Although you really can't go wrong in mixing flower colors, some hues naturally go well together.

  Color wheels, which you can find in the local art supply store, show the rainbow as a circle of colored slices. Color wheel opposites, such as red and green, orange and blue, purple and yellow complement each other. Colors that form triangles on the color wheel, such as blue, green-yellow, and red-purple, also make good combinations. A single hue (such as red) has many lighter and darker colors (such as pink and deep red) within its family, and combining these make single-color theme gardens more interesting.

  Red, yellow, and orange — called *hot colors* — jump out in the landscape and can appear closer than they are. Blue, green, and purple — called *cool colors* — blend into the garden and look farther away. Use these colors to achieve certain effects. Cool colors in a small garden can make it appear larger, for example, while hot colors draw more attention to street-side plantings. White also stands out in the landscape, especially in dim light, and is useful for planting with more-colorful flowers to brighten or moderate the mix.

  Flower size and shape contribute to the plant's overall appearance, too. Add variety and interest to your garden by blending plants that produce masses of small flowers with those that bear larger or single blooms.

- **Foliage color and texture:** Although often overlooked, the shape, size, and color of your plants' leaves have a greater influence on the season-long look of your garden than do the flowers. Consider that most perennials and bulbs only bloom for a few weeks at best; however, you see their foliage from early spring to fall frost. Mix different textures and colors for best effect.

  Some plants feature variegated, golden, or purple leaves. *Variegated* plants have white or yellow streaks, spots, or margins on their leaves. Use these as accent plants, keeping in mind that they tend to stand out in the landscape.

- **Plant height and spread:** Most gardens have a front, back, and middle. To arrange plants by height, put the shortest ones in the front and tallest in the back, just like the lineup for your class photograph. Pay attention to the mature width of your plants and give them the space they need. But watch out for aggressive plants that travel unbidden throughout your garden. These usually creep rapidly above- or underground or spread by numerous seeds.

✔ **Season-extending attributes:** In addition to flowers, some plants offer good-looking seedpods, flower buds, leaves, or growth habits. Flower arrangers prize poppy seed heads, strawflower, statice, and other ever-lasting flowers for dried bouquets, for example. Plants with an extra-long blooming period or that bloom twice in a season, such as new reblooming bearded irises, offer good garden value. Dried grasses and flower stalks add interest to late autumn and winter gardens, too.

Growth habit can also make a particular plant more or less suitable for a garden. I enjoy climbing vines because they take up little room in the garden and give an extra vertical dimension to the space. I grow clematis vines on a fence and climbing hydrangea up an old maple, for example. Creeping and trailing plants, such as periwinkle *(Vinca minor)* and petunia, carpet the ground with color and compete with weeds.

✔ **Cultural considerations:** I look for disease-resistant varieties, especially in species vulnerable to particular problems. Phlox, for example, is prone to powdery mildew, but many newer varieties resist the fungus (see Chapter 10). After taking an inventory of your garden site (see Chapter 3), select plants that match the soil, sun, water, and climate conditions you have to offer. Trying to grow plants where they won't be happy is just asking for extra work and potential problems. If you have a shady garden, look for shade-loving plants. Gardening in a hot, humid climate? Seek out plants that won't melt in the mid-summer sauna.

When you design your flower garden, whether you choose annuals, perennials, bulbs, or combinations of each, keep in mind that plants have a greater impact when you plant them in groups of the same kind. For example, a single petunia looks lost in a 5-x-20 border, but six petunias of the same color make a bold statement. The same goes for perennials — always plant at least three and preferably five or more of each kind, especially the smaller varieties. With bulbs, I consider a dozen the bare minimum for tulips and daffodils and two dozen for crocus and small bulbs. Plant in circular or free-form groups and avoid rigid rows.

Buying and Planting

The first warm and sunny days of spring always beckon me to the garden center where promises of summer flowers await. Impulse shopping strikes! Before I know it, my cart is overloaded with pots and flats. Even after all these years of gardening, I'm not immune to the Siren's song of spring, but I have learned how to shop more wisely. And, more often than not, now I bring my new plants home to prepared garden beds and planting containers. Having a plan — and a list — in hand before seeing the dazzling nursery choices helps keep my garden healthier and more organized and my own peace of mind intact.

So before you fill out the catalog order form or head out to the garden center, take time to plan your garden for success (Chapters 2 and 3) and prepare your soil (Chapter 4). Remember that annual flowers grow rapidly from seedling to mature flowering plant in just a few short weeks, so they need plenty of good nutrition. Perennials and bulbs, too, need to put down roots and develop leafy tops to make food for their roots, which live from year to the next. Adequate soil fertility, moisture, and organic matter keep your flowers growing robustly, producing more and larger blooms, and fending off pests and diseases.

When you're done, make a list of plant combinations that suit your site, then boldly go forth to make your selections.

Buying the best

It seems as though everyone sells plants — from the traditional greenhouse/nursery to the drug store. You can buy plants locally or order them from a catalog or off the Internet. How do you choose? Here are some tips:

- **Locally owned garden center:** Plants are adapted for the local climate and growing conditions and probably grown nearby or onsite by experienced and knowledgeable people. Plants haven't been subjected to shipping and handling stress. Usually the size-to-price ratio is excellent. I often find a good blend of favorite "bread-and-butter" varieties and newer, more exotic offerings.

- **National chain store:** Garden centers attached to home improvement and mass-market department stores are known for their cheap prices and vast quantities of merchandise, but watch out for neglected plants. For the best-quality plants, show up when the delivery trucks do. More and more chain stores now sell some of the newest plant varieties available, along with the old tried-and-true petunias and geraniums. Just be sure that the nifty new perennials you find are truly hardy in your climate. The staff may or may not have a clue.

- **Mail-order catalog:** The glossy pictures look so perfect, so enticing, and the descriptions sound like dreams come true. In many cases, you can find your perfect plants through the mail, but be aware of the caveats. Due to shipping costs, plants are usually smaller and more expensive than locally grown specimens. Plants also have to undergo the rigors of hot, cold, and bumpy travel. To be fair, mail-order nurseries pack their plants very well, but they can't control what happens to them after they leave the loading docks. Catalogs, however, expand the universe of available plant varieties and offer a cornucopia for the specialist and the connoisseur.

✔ **Internet company:** Buying plants online is similar to buying from a mail-order catalog and, in fact most catalog companies now offer Web sites in addition to their traditional paper-and-ink offerings. The same rules apply whether you mail in the order form or click a digital box.

Where you buy your plants matters less than choosing vigorous, healthy specimens, but you do have to know what qualities to look for when shopping in garden centers and nurseries. Here's how I pick the winners from the losers:

✔ **Look for disease-free foliage.** Avoid plants with yellow, brown, or black spots, or wilted, yellow, or mottled leaves. See Chapter 10 for more on diseases.

✔ **Check for pests.** Pass your hand gently over a flat of flowers. If a cloud of whiteflies or tiny gnats swirl up out of the foliage, pass them by. Peek under leaves for aphids, thrips, and spider mites, and check stems for scale insects. See Chapter 7 for pest descriptions.

✔ **Consider compact growth in proportion to pot size.** If the top of the plant appears too big for the pot, the roots may be squished, too, compromising the plant's health and vigor.

✔ **Small is beautiful.** Large plants make a more immediate impact in your garden, but they cost more and recover from transplanting more slowly than smaller ones. Small plants often catch up in growth to larger plants within a few weeks, anyway, and may even surpass them by season's end. And although they're tempting, avoid plants that are already in full bloom. Plants with plenty of unopened buds give you longer garden performance.

It goes without saying that buying wilted plants is a no-no. Plants need water to survive and even a short drought when they are small and growing rapidly can affect how they perform in your garden in the coming months. If you see widespread wilting in the nursery, take your business elsewhere.

Breaking ground

After you get your plants home, you want to pop them right in the ground, right? Not so fast. Plants have a better chance of survival if you follow a few steps first:

✔ **Check the calendar and the weather forecast.** If the ground is still frozen or very cold (below 60 degrees), summer-loving plant roots are going to be shocked and unhappy at their plight. Potential frost may undo all your carefully laid plans, too. Although some tough perennials don't mind a little chill, you're better off waiting until the soil warms and the last expected frosts have passed before setting out your annuals.

Planting in the fall is best in warm, dry climates, but may be tricky in freezing winter climates. Perennials need at least six weeks before the soil temperature drops below 50 degrees to establish strong roots. Here in Vermont (Zone 4), I try to finish transplanting perennials by mid to late September, but in warmer zones you can safely plant into October or even November. A 4- to 6-inch layer of straw or raked leaves protects them after the ground freezes.

If you live in a warm, but dry climate, time your planting to coincide with naturally cool and damp weather. Those tender transplants resent scorching heat and just won't survive drought. If you must plant when it's hot, provide some shade and keep everyone well watered until they can survive on their own.

✔ **Prepare plants for outdoor life.** If you're planting tender, greenhouse-grown annuals, you need to give them a week or two to gradually toughen up and adjust to the natural wind and sun conditions in your garden. Introduce them to the great outdoors on cloudy, calm days and bring them inside when temperatures drop toward freezing. Gradually allow them more direct sun and wind over a period of 10 days or more. Allow the soil to dry between waterings, but don't let the plants wilt. When they can tolerate full sun and wind, they're ready for the garden. Remember to cover them, though, if frost threatens.

✔ **Prepare the soil.** The perfect garden soil is weed-free, well drained, and loosened and fertile to a depth of at least 12 inches. See Chapter 4 for more on soil preparation.

If you're starting with an empty new planting bed, set the plants (still in their pots) on the ground and test different arrangements before tucking them into the soil. Be sure to give each plant enough space to mature without crowding its neighbors.

Actually putting the plants in the ground is pretty straightforward, and most plants are quite forgiving. Water the plants a few hours prior to planting, then follow these simple steps to get your annuals and perennials off to a good start:

1. **Dig a hole that's twice as wide as the pot.**

   Use a shovel or trowel and make it deep enough to keep the plant at the same soil level as it was in its container.

2. **Tip the plant out of the pot.**

   Cup your hand around the stem of the plant and tip the pot gently, supporting the soil with your fingers and the heel of your hand and protecting the stem and leaves from bruising. Push or tap on the bottom of the pot if the plant resists, but don't pull on the stem.

   If the plant is large, lay the container on its side on the ground and slide the plant out. Squeeze the pot if necessary to dislodge the rootball. If you can't loosen it, cut the pot away.

3. **Check for tangled roots.**

   If the roots are tightly wound around the ball of soil, tease them out gently to encourage them to venture out into the soil in the planting hole.

4. **Put the plant into the hole.**

   The *crown* of the plant — where the roots meet the top of the plant (usually the soil level in the pot) — should be at ground level. Add or remove soil from the hole to get it right.

5. **Backfill with soil.**

   Gently fill the hole with soil, working it around the roots and keeping the crown at the soil level. Press the soil gently to make a slight depression to hold water.

6. **Water the plant.**

   Saturate the soil gently, being careful not to displace the soil. Add more soil to the hole if needed.

If you purchased perennial plants from a mail-order nursery, the plants may have arrived with no soil around their roots. Plant these *bare-root* perennials as you would potted plants, except make a cone of soil in the hole over which to spread the roots. Be sure that the plant crown is just at soil level.

When you have finished planting your garden, give all the transplants a boost with manure tea or liquid fish/seaweed fertilizer, diluted to one-fourth strength (see Chapter 5). Spread an inch or two of mulch over the garden, pulling it away from the plant stems. If frost, high winds, or a scorching heat wave threaten, protect your tender transplants with a floating row cover or shade-providing structure.

Caring for your flower garden

Consistent maintenance throughout the growing season guarantees plenty of flowers and lush, healthy plants. Perennials and bulbs, which live for more than one year, are better prepared for winter, too, when they've had adequate nutrition and water during the summer and fall.

Keeping your garden looking good and growing strong doesn't have to be a lengthy chore if you take a few minutes each day or on the weekend. My favorite time to fuss with flowers comes at the end of my workday — it's a relaxing reward that reconnects me to the natural world. Here's what I do to keep my garden looking it's best:

- ✔ **Deadhead:** Removing spent flowers, called *deadheading,* before they go to seed keeps annuals and some perennials blooming longer. Snip or pinch the dead flower off, making the cut just above a bud or a leaf.

✔ **Pinch:** Flowers that get tall and floppy, especially perennial asters and chrysanthemums, stay more compact if you pinch back their early summer stems to encourage them to grow shorter and more numerous shoots. When the plants reach a foot high in spring, snip off the top 3 to 4 inches. Repeat once more in mid-summer, but not after you see flower buds forming.

✔ **Support:** Some tall, floppy flowers, such as delphiniums and peonies, need a little help to stay upright. Use bamboo stakes to tie up individual delphinium or lily stalks. Surround peony clumps with purchased circular wire or homemade stake-and-twine supports. I often use branches left over from tree and shrub pruning to support plants, too.

✔ **Scout for problems:** As you walk through the garden, keep sharp eyes out for anything unusual — holes in flowers or leaves, wilting, insects, off-color foliage. Catch the problem early and you have a better chance of solving it without drastic action.

✔ **Fertilize:** Plants need plenty of fuel to keep pumping out the flowers. Supplement your fertile soil with composted manure in the spring and feed again in mid-summer with a mild complete fertilizer, such as fish emulsion.

✔ **Water:** If Mother Nature provides regular, gentle rainfall from spring through fall, you've got it made. Otherwise, you may have to supplement. Dig into the top 6 to 8 inches of soil and, if it's dry, irrigate your garden until the water reaches an 8-inch depth. Shallow watering that only wets the top few inches encourages roots to grow close to the surface where they're more vulnerable to drought.

✔ **Weed:** No, it's not the most fun, but it's necessary. Pull up or hoe small weeds as soon as they appear, disturbing the soil as little as possible. Try corn gluten meal (see Chapter 5) as a fertilizer because it also prevents weed seeds from sprouting. Replace or add more mulch as needed to smother weeds, but keep the mulch an inch or two away from plant stems.

If you grow flowers in gardens surrounded by lawn, as I do, you face the additional chore of edging. *Edging* means keeping the lawn and the flowers separated by a barrier. I use a half-moon edging tool to cut away a slice of lawn around the entire perimeter of the garden in the spring and again in mid-summer. To use the tool, push the blade straight down into the turf about 4 to 6 inches and pull the handle back toward yourself to pop out the wedge. Other edging options include flexible plastic edging (available at garden centers) that you install around the garden, or bricks, landscape timber, or stones. If you use these materials, bury them so that they are flush with the ground level, which makes mowing easier.

Annual Events

Annual plants live short but spectacular lives, because they have to accomplish their entire life's purpose — perpetuating the species — in only one growing season. Most annuals bloom nonstop from spring to autumn or until they succeed in setting seed. The secret to keeping annuals blooming all summer is preventing the plants from forming seeds by deadheading (see the "Caring for your flower garden" section). Some plants, such as *Vinca rosea,* ivy geraniums, and begonias, that you may consider annuals, however, actually are perennials in non-freezing climates. Count yourself lucky if you can enjoy these plants year 'round.

Use versatile annuals anywhere you want nonstop color. Plant them in mixed gardens with perennials to provide constant bloom, in the cutflower garden for bouquets, or in hanging baskets and patio planters for portable color. You can also dedicate a garden just for them. The beauty of annuals is that you can change the garden completely from one year to the next, as my neighbor does, to suit your current taste and whim.

Some annuals, especially those with large seeds, are easy to start yourself from seed, either right in the garden or in the house prior to transplanting. The easiest to grow from seed include calendula, cosmos, marigold, zinnia, aster, nasturtium, morning glory, sunflower, and sweet pea. Plants with tiny seeds, such as begonia, petunia, and impatiens, are tough to start or need several months of pampering before they're ready for the garden. For more on annuals and starting them from seed, look for *Annuals For Dummies* by Bill Marken and the Editors of the National Gardening Association (IDG Books Worldwide, Inc.).

Hundreds of annual flowering plants exist in every shape, form, color, and size imaginable, and it's beyond the scope of this book to describe them all. I've divided a few of the most popular annuals into categories to help you find the best ones for each landscape use. Consult the label that comes with each particular plant for spacing and cultural requirements.

- **Bedding plants for mass planting:** Gardens devoted to just annuals make a big impact along streets, sidewalks, and other places where the mass of color is more important than the individual plants. Look for plants that grow fairly low, usually up to a foot high or so, and that bloom for at least 2 to 3 months with little maintenance. Bright red, yellow, orange, and white work best in plantings viewed from a distance. Cool blue and purple are better for close-range viewing. To find the number of plants you need to fill a 100-square-foot garden (10 feet x 10 feet or 9 square meters), consult Table 15-1.

Table 15-1	Plants Needed to Fill 100 Square Feet	
Space between Plants		
Inches	*Centimeters*	*Number of Plants*
6	15	400
9	23	178
12	30	100
18	46	45
24	61	25

Popular bedding plants include ageratum, calendula, celosia, coleus, coreopsis, dahlia, dusty miller, impatiens, marigold, nasturtium, nicotiana, pansy, petunia, salvia, snapdragon, sweet alyssum, verbena, *Vinca rosea,* and wax begonia.

✔ **Cutting flowers for bouquets:** Plants that produce long stems for cutting, as well as colorful or fragrant flowers, are tops in my garden. Many of these plants mix well in a perennial border or you can devote a row in your vegetable garden to them. If you have space and a passion for bouquets, give them a garden of their own. Don't forget to add some *everlasting* flowers, such as statice and strawflower, which have papery petals that remain colorful for months or even years when dried. Use them for making dried bouquets and craft projects.

For the freshest and longest lasting bouquets, cut the flowers in the morning before the sun heats up and plunge the stems right into a bucket of water. Use a sharp knife or scissors to cut stems at a 45-degree angle and choose stems with only partially opened buds. Strip the leaves from the submerged parts of the stems. Use clean vases and change the water daily, adding a floral preservative or 2 to 3 drops of bleach per quart.

Great annuals for cutting include aster, baby's breath, calendula, campanula, cosmos, sweet William, gloriosa daisy, larkspur, lisianthus, pincushion flower (scabiosa), salpiglossis, salvia, snapdragon, stock, sweet pea, sunflower, and zinnia. For dried flower bouquets, try strawflower, statice, cornflower, salvia, celosia, ageratum, globe amaranth, larkspur, baby's breath, and love-in-a-mist. Cut them before the flowers fully open, bundle the stems into a rubber band and hang them to dry in a cool, dry, airy place away from the sun.

✓ **Foliage fillers:** Flowers usually take center stage, but you need supporting players, too. Plants with attractive foliage provide a soothing foil for their more flamboyant companions, although some plants have foliage colorful enough to stand alone. Popular favorites include dusty miller, coleus, Kochia (or firebush), Persian shield, nasturtium 'Alaska', ornamental cabbage and kale, amaranthus, and polka dot plant.

✓ **Best for baskets and containers:** These plants stay small enough to live in confinement all summer without complaint. In containers, you can plant everything closer together than usual, but their limited soil space means that plants need more attention to watering and fertilizing and pruning than other landscape and garden plants.

Although it's tempting to use your own garden soil to fill containers, consider a pasteurized, lightweight alternative instead. When you put garden soil into a container, it loses its loose, well-aerated structure and becomes too compact for healthy root growth. In most cases, a soil-less peat and perlite mix is best. I usually add up to 25 percent pasteurized topsoil or composted manure to the mix, plus some water-retaining gel crystals, which help the soil hold more moisture.

For the best design effect, combine trailing, upright, and low-growing plants in each container. Good trailing plants include browallia, creeping zinnia, lobelia, nasturtium, nierembergia, petunia, scaevola, sweet alyssum, and verbena. Choose bedding plants to fill in most of the container. Consider adding a trellis to larger containers to hold an annual vine, such as canary creeper, morning glory, or thunbergia.

Perennial Favorites

Perennial plants, by definition, live from year to year, but *herbaceous perennials* actually die to the ground in the fall and sprout from their roots again in the spring. Happy perennials increase in size and bloom potential with each growing season that passes. Unlike with annual flowers, however, your USDA Hardiness Zone and AHS Heat Zone make a difference in your garden's success (see Chapter 3). Use the information as a guide when buying plants.

Popular myth claims that perennial gardening is low-maintenance compared to other types of gardening — you know, plant it once and forget about it. That's simply not true, as any experienced perennial gardener quickly points out. While it is true that many plants live for a long time, they also require regular maintenance. See the "Caring for your flower garden" section, earlier in this chapter, to see what your perennials need to flourish.

Making more perennials

One of perennials' best features is that you can start with one plant and divide it into more plants as it grows. *Dividing* a plant means separating its roots and their attached stems into smaller pieces to form new individual plants. This trick doesn't work with all perennials, especially those with *taproots* that grow straight down, deep into the soil. The best plants for dividing form clumps of stems and have fibrous roots. Easy plants to divide include daylilies, hosta, bee balm (*Monarda* species), Siberian iris, ornamental grasses, and almost anything that creeps over the ground, rooting as it grows.

The best time to divide perennials depends partly on their season of flowering and your climate. I find it easier to divide mid- to late-summer-flowering plants, such as asters, in the spring as soon as they start growing. Spring and early summer-bloomers, such as peonies and iris, recover better if divided later in the summer. A few, such as daylilies and Siberian iris, can be divided anytime you have a shovel handy.

Here's the basic method for dividing perennials with fibrous roots:

1. **Soak the soil to make digging easier.**

   Water the day before, if possible, so that soil isn't still muddy.

2. **Cut down some or all of the stems to within 6 inches of the ground unless you're dividing newly sprouted plants in the spring.**

   The roots won't be able to support big leafy tops until they fully recover.

3. **Dig up the whole clump and drag it onto a tarp.**

   Check it over, looking for groups of rooted stems that could form new, self-supporting plants. Blast the clump with spray from the hose to wash away soil that obscures the crown or soak the whole clump to make root separation easier.

4. **Pry, tease, cut, or pull apart the clump.**

   Some perennials come apart easily, while others may require a sharp knife or other drastic measures. For large, tough grasses, Siberian irises, and daylilies, push two garden forks into the clump back-to-back and pry the handles apart to divide the clump in two, as shown in Figure 15-1. Repeat as needed to reduce the clump into manageable pieces.

5. **Discard dead and less vigorous pieces.**

6. **Replant the pieces as soon as possible.**

   See the "Breaking ground" section earlier in this chapter.

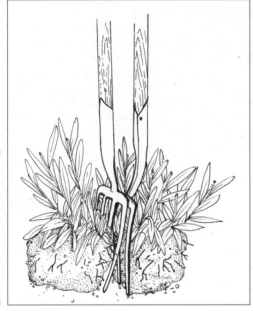

Figure 15-1:
Insert two garden forks back-to-back and pry apart to divide perennial clumps.

GARDEN JARGON

Some perennial plants, such as bearded iris, get bare spots in their centers as they expand outward, so they need dividing to keep them vigorous. Bearded irises need slightly different treatment during division. After the plants finish blooming, proceed with Steps 1 through 3. Then choose the fattest sections of fleshy roots, called *rhizomes,* with the most vigorous fans of foliage and roots. Using a sharp knife, cut the rhizomes apart into one- or two-fan sections, as shown in Figure 15-2. Discard woody and insect-damaged pieces as well as the oldest parts. (The newest rhizomes are firm and grow at the outer edges of the clump.) Plant immediately in fertile soil, draping the roots over a ridge of soil so that the top of the rhizome is just at the soil surface when watered.

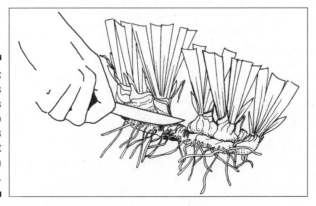

Figure 15-2:
Cut iris rhizomes into sections with at least one fan each.

Popular perennials

You have hundreds, if not thousands, of perennial plants from which to choose. Instead of trying to memorize all those plants, think of them in groups. You can divide them into groups based on garden placement, cultural requirements, flower color, season of bloom, use, or any number of other criteria. I've chosen the following categories with organic gardeners in mind. For more information on gardening with perennials, look for *Perennials For Dummies* by Marcia Tatroe and the Editors of the National Gardening Association (IDG Books Worldwide, Inc.):

- **Butterfly and bee attracting plants:** Butterflies and moths glide from flower to flower looking for energy-rich nectar. Some of their favorites include butterfly weed, aster, butterfly bush, *Centaurea,* purple and orange coneflowers, Joe-pye weed, *Penstemon,* goldenrod, verbena, salvia, and bee balm.

- **Shade-loving perennials:** Shade is a relative concept — it ranges from dense to dappled. Most of these perennials prefer a few hours of direct sunlight each day, but can survive in all but the deepest shade. For your shady nook, try hosta, forget-me-not, pachysandra, lungwort, meadowrue, foamflower, myrtle, coral bells, lily-of-the-valley, foxglove, *Bergenia,* wild ginger, and Solomon's seal.

- **Deer-resistant perennials:** Although it seems that deer will eat anything, it's really not true. Plants with strong scent or flavor repel them, as do some toxic plants. Resistant plants include alliums, artemesia, black-eyed Susan, lupine, catmint, delphinium, hellebore, tansy, and yarrow.

- **Hard-to-kill perennials:** If you're just starting out or need low-maintenance plants, give these tough customers a try. Perennials that can survive in well-drained soil almost anywhere include yarrow, *Artemesia,* tickseed (*Coreopsis* species), *Euphorbia,* blanket flower, *Heliopsis,* catmint, Oriental poppy, sedum, and feverfew. If your soil tends to run on the damp side, try Siberian iris, daylily, bee balm, and mint.

- **Foliage friends:** Flowers aren't everything and these lovely-leafed perennials prove it. Although some of these also have nice bloom, for fabulous foliage try hosta, dead nettle *(Lamium),* lungwort *(Pulmonaria),* coral bells, astilbe, peony, thyme, sage, liriope, amsonia, artemesia, ginger (*Asarum* species), *Bergenia,* crane's bill geranium, ornamental grasses, and many others.

Perennials work well in containers, too. See the section called "Annual Events," earlier in this chapter, for ideas on how to use them in patio planters and baskets.

Blooming Bulbs

Some plants form swollen underground roots or stems, which people tend to lump together and refer to as *bulbs*. Not all these fleshy appendages are the same, however, and the differences affect how you plant and use them. *True bulbs,* including onions, lilies, tulips, and daffodils, have pointed tops and flat bottoms, called *basal plates,* from which roots grow. If you cut one open, you see that a bulb consists of rings or layers with developing leaves, flowers, or stems in the center. The bulb itself lives from year to year and develops new daughter bulbs from its base.

Other bulb-like plants form corms, tubers, or rhizomes. *Corms,* such as crocus, colchicum, crocosmia, and gladiola resemble bulbs, but their flesh isn't layered when cut open. Each corm lives for a single year, but it produces *offsets* or new corms around its basal plate. *Tubers,* such as potatoes, caladiums, and tuberous begonias, don't have a basal plate and sprout from several *eyes* or growing points. They just grow larger and form more eyes each year, but don't produce offsets. *Rhizomes,* such as bearded iris and canna, are simply swollen, creeping stems. They grow from the tip, which may branch and root, forming new plants.

To simplify bulbs and bulb-like plants, I divided them into two broad groups — spring flowering and summer flowering.

- ✔ **Spring-blooming bulbs** include tulips, narcissus (daffodils), crocus, fritillaria, snowdrops, winter aconite, hyacinths, bluebells, glory of the snow (*Chionodoxa* species), and others. These bulbs survive in the ground in cold-winter climates and bloom when the soil warms in the spring. Plant them in early autumn to allow them time to root before winter.

- ✔ **Summer-blooming bulbs** include lilies, alliums, canna, caladium, dahlia, gladiola, tuberous begonia, crocosmia, amaryllis, and others. Many of these bulbs are frost-tender and must be dug up at the end of the growing season and stored in a non-freezing place. Many species and varieties of lilies and alliums, however, are perfectly winter-hardy throughout most USDA hardiness zones. Plant tender bulbs in the spring and hardy ones in the fall.

Finding the best source

You can buy bulbs from so many sources, it's downright confusing to know where to get the best value and quality. Here's my take on the choices:

- ✔ **Mail-order bulb suppliers** have selling down to an exact science. Although you can't find tulip and daffodil bulbs in the local stores until fall, when do the promotional catalogs appear in your mailbox? In the spring, of course, when the bulbs are in bloom! To be honest, I think that's the best time to order spring-flowering bulbs, too, because you can see exactly where your existing bulbs are in your garden and where new ones would look best. (If you go this route, place markers in your garden to remind you where to plant when the bulbs arrive.) Most catalogs offer a hefty discount if you order early, which results in big savings. Specialty bulb suppliers also carry the widest assortment, including rare, unusual, and hard-to-find bulbs as well as the most popular varieties.

Avoid catalogs that give inadequate information or offer prices significantly lower than similar catalogs. They may be offering smaller bulbs, which produce smaller and fewer flowers.

✔ **Garden centers** usually start selling bulbs shortly after the bulb farmers harvest them, which is the right time to plant them in your garden. When the bins of bulbs appear in the stores, they're as tempting to a gardener as candy to a chocoholic! Go ahead and indulge, but keep a few tips in mind. Boxes of loose bulbs may get mixed up (think of playing children), the selection is relatively limited, and the bulbs are often smaller in size than those available from specialty catalogs. On the other hand, you can usually inspect the bulbs before you buy. Bulbs stored in sunny windows or hot corners may not grow as well as those stored at cooler (50 to 65 degrees) temperatures. The selection is relatively limited, too, and bulbs are often smaller in size than those available from specialty catalogs. On the other hand, you can usually inspect the bulbs before you buy.

When you shop for bulbs, look for firm, heavy, unblemished specimens. Avoid those with gouges or signs of withering, softness, or decay. Bulbs vary enormously in size from one species and variety to the next. In general, you want to buy *top-size* bulbs, which usually are the largest bulbs available for the particular variety. *Landscape-size* bulbs are smaller and produce fewer stems and smaller blooms.

After you get your bulbs home, plant them as soon as possible. If you must store them — evenly briefly — keep them cool (50 to 65 degrees) and dry. Don't store them with apples or other fruit, however, because ripening fruit gives off ethylene gas, which is deadly to dormant flower buds inside the bulbs.

This side up — putting down roots

Bulbs appreciate the same loose, fertile, well-drained garden soil that your other plants enjoy. If you're planting bulbs in an existing, well-maintained garden, you only need to add a bit of fertilizer to the hole at planting time, otherwise, turn back to Chapter 4 for more on soil preparation. Slow-release, complete, granular fertilizer works best at planting time. Mix it into the soil at the bottom of the hole, covering it with a thin layer of unamended soil before setting in the bulbs.

A word of caution is in order here — contrary to tradition, bone meal is not the best fertilizer choice for bulbs. It also attracts skunks and other scavengers willing to dig up a tasty meal. If it's well mixed in small quantities with composted manure and other nutrient-rich fertilizers, however, your garden is less likely to have nocturnal visitors.

How deeply you plant your bulbs depends on whether you have true bulbs, corms, tubers, or rhizomes. Each is handled a little differently.

- ✔ The general rule for true bulbs and corms is to plant them so that the top is buried twice as deep as the bulb is tall. For example, a daffodil that measures 2 inches from base to tip needs a hole 6 inches deep so that 4 inches of soil covers the top of the bulb. Bulb companies always provide handy charts, too, with specific instructions for each type of bulb. Depending on your soil type, you can vary the planting depth a bit — set bulbs an inch or two deeper in sandy soil and 1 to 3 inches more shallowly in heavy clay. Gardeners in warm winter climates who wish to grow daffodils can plant the bulbs twice as deeply as northern gardeners.

- ✔ Tubers and rhizomes get special planting treatment because they prefer to grow closer to the soil surface. Tuberous begonias and cyclamen, for example, only need 1-inch depth, while gladiolas and cannas prefer 2 to 3 inches of soil over them. Plant bearded iris rhizomes so that the top of the rhizome is just barely exposed after watering the planting site.

Determining which end goes down and which points up is easy for bulbs with a pointed top or roots clinging to the bottom. But what do you do with shriveled, featureless anemone tubers? If you can't tell which side is up, plant them on their sides — the plants will figure it out.

Planting methods vary depending on whether you're putting in a handful of bulbs or planting dozens. The most efficient system is to dig a hole large enough to accommodate a group of bulbs. I dig it to the proper depth, amend the soil (see Chapter 4), space the bulbs around the hole, backfill, and water. Bulbs grow best in the loosened soil. I find those little bulb planters that look like open-ended tin cans with handles to be useless. You can't amend the soil effectively, planting takes longer, and the soil around sides of the hole remains compact.

Protecting your assets

Bulb-producing plants need leaves to make food and keep their bulbs fat and happy during their dormant season. Although yellowing leaves look unsightly after the flowers bloom, leave the foliage alone (and resist the urge to braid it) until it naturally withers away. If you cut the blooms of lilies, gladiolas, and other leafy stemmed plants, leave as much foliage behind as you can. Bulbs robbed of their food source will produce fewer — if any — blooms in subsequent years.

In climates where the ground freezes, gardeners must dig up and store tender tropical bulbs, corms, tubers, and rhizomes for the winter. (Tulips, daffodils, lilies, and other hardy bulbs can remain in the ground.) You can keep cannas, dahlias, tuberous begonias, and other tubers and bulbs from one year to the next by putting them in a cool, nonfreezing place. Dig up the bulbs after the leaves die back, brush off loose soil, and trim off the leaves and stems. After letting them dry for a few days in a non-freezing place, brush off more soil and place in dry wood shavings or peat moss in a cardboard box. Don't let the pieces touch each other. Cover with more shavings or moss and store in a cool, dry place until spring.

Gladiola and similar corms are even easier to store. After brushing off the soil, place them in a mesh bag (like the ones that onions come in) and hang in a cool (35 to 41 degrees) place where mice can't reach them.

Bulb-munching rodents and deer can take a bite out of your bulb garden, but you can take preventative action. My favorite method is to plant bulbs that they won't eat, such as narcissus, fritillarias, snowflakes (*Leucojum* species), and snowdrops (*Galanthus* species). These bulbs are toxic and may give some protection to surrounding non-toxic species. Animals seem to stay away from alliums, too.

If you want to succeed with tulips, crocus, lilies, and other tempting morsels, plant your bulbs in a wire cage, as shown in Figure 15-3, that excludes the troublesome animals. Bend hardware cloth into a shallow cage and bury it at the appropriate depth to keep out voles and mice. For the top, choose a wire opening large enough to allow the shoots to grow through. Use chicken wire for woodchucks and other large diggers.

Figure 15-3:
Plant bulbs in wire mesh baskets to protect them from hungry rodents.

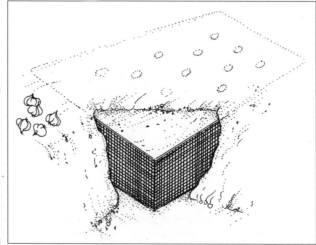

Chapter 16

Run for the Roses

● ●

In This Chapter

▶ Choosing trouble-free roses

▶ Getting roses off to a good start

▶ Caring for roses organically

▶ Preparing roses for winter

▶ Dealing with common rose pests

● ●

*R*oses have an undeserved reputation as temperamental, demanding, pest-prone plants. That's why you may have assumed that in order to grow roses successfully, you have to use pesticides and fertilizers and other materials that you don't want to use.

The key to growing roses organically is really quite simple. First, choose varieties of roses that grow best in your region. Look for more information about these roses in the "Making the Right Choice" section, later in this chapter. Second, get the plants off to a strong start by carefully selecting disease and pest-resistant plants and planting them properly. Skip to that section, "Planting Roses," if you'd like.

Those classic, long-stemmed, fragrant roses — the kind that made roses so popular in the first place — attract the most insects and dastardly rose diseases. You may, perhaps, decide to throw good sense to the wind and plant one of these, despite my good advice to the contrary. Many disease-prone roses are among the most popular and readily available varieties at some garden centers. These include 'Climbing America', 'Apricot Nectar', 'Chrysler Imperial', 'Don Juan', 'Double Delight', 'Fragrant Cloud', 'Mister Lincoln', 'Queen Elizabeth', 'Pristine', and 'New Dawn'. Nevertheless, you can try to grow them "organically," that is, with an ecological perspective. If you decide to attempt to grow one of these, see the "Solving Common Rose Trouble" section near the end of this chapter.

Making the Right Choice

Over the years, rose fanciers have developed many different categories of roses, such as *hybrid tea* and *antique* roses. Although they share the rose name, each has unique features and garden merit. Sorting out the many different kinds of roses gets confusing, and, as an organic gardener, the names don't really mean as much to me as whether they are trouble-free to grow.

I prefer to grow plants that don't need lots of extra care, and you probably do, too. So, to help you choose the easiest roses for your garden, I've compressed all the kinds of roses into only two groups — easy and hard. For this chapter, I'm calling pest- and disease-prone types, *show* roses and the carefree types, *garden* roses. Show roses produce those beautifully shaped, long-stemmed flowers for cutting and arranging. Show roses, however, need plenty of TLC to maintain their stylish good looks. Garden roses, on the other hand, are more like other flowering shrubs — laid back and easy going. They add lots of color and fragrance to the garden without too much fuss, but aren't really grown for their dramatic bouquet potential.

Depending on where you live, you must also consider hardiness (the rose's ability to survive cold winter temperatures — see Chapter 4). Hardy roses stay healthier because they aren't struggling for survival when spring warmth — and pests — return.

Recognize the difference between your rose garden friends and the pests. Don't assume that any insect you spot in the garden is the perpetrator of some damage. Nothing could be further from the truth! Most of the insects you see in your garden are harmless and only a few cause damage. Some actually help! The "Solving Common Rose Troubles" section, near the end o this chapter, has more information about harmful and helpful bugs.

If you'd like to know more about all the kinds and varieties of roses, I highly recommend *Roses For Dummies,* 2nd Edition, by Lance Walheim and the National Gardening Association (IDG Books Worldwide, Inc.). It's one of the most complete and up-to-date guides available, not to mention the most fun.

Choosing disease-resistant roses

If you absolutely must grow show roses, skip to the "Solving Common Rose Troubles" section, later in this chapter. But if you're planning to start a new rose garden or replace your pest-prone varieties, try garden roses instead, because many of them are among the most trouble-free plants you can own. Some of my favorite disease-resistant garden roses include pink-flowered 'Baby Blanket', 'Bonica', 'Carefree Delight', 'Carefree Wonder', 'Cécile Brunner', 'Flower Carpet Pink', 'Lady of the Dawn', 'Pink Meidiland', 'Simplicity',

'The Fairy', and red-flowered 'Red Meidiland' and 'Red Ribbons'. Good white roses include 'Alba Meidiland' and 'Sea Foam'. Also try orange 'Livin' Easy' and 'Ralph's Creeper' and 'Lavender Dream'.

Picking a winter survivor

Gardeners in warm climates, where temperatures rarely drop below 15 degrees, don't have to worry whether their roses will survive the winter. But if you live in colder places, you may have greater success if you stick with the roses that can put up with plenty of snow and frosty weather.

If you live in USDA Zone 5 or colder, you can still grow most any kind of rose, but your plants will need winter protection, as described in "Preparing Roses for Winter" section, later in this chapter. Unless you really must have a particular rose variety, regardless of its hardiness, I advise you to stick to the hardier roses. In the long run, they're easier to live with and give you more gardening satisfaction. Cold-hardy stalwarts over 5 feet tall include pink-flowered 'Applejack', 'Carefree Beauty', 'John Cabot', 'Moss rose', 'Prairie Dawn', 'Prairie Princess', and 'William Baffin'. Tall white varieties include 'Blanc Double de Coubert' and 'Henry Hudson,' and for yellow try 'Agnes' or 'Harrison's Yellow'. Hardy roses that grow 3 to 5 feet tall include pink 'Bonica', Carefree Wonder', and 'Stanwell Perpetual'. Low-growing varieties that stay under 3 feet include 'Flower Carpet Pink', 'Frau Dagmar Hastrup', 'Morden Blush', 'Sea Foam', and 'The Fairy'.

Buying Roses

Everybody sells roses — from grocery stores to hardware stores to mail-order nurseries. Impulsively grabbing a four-dollar rose with a pretty picture on the wrapper and dropping it into your cart, however, won't guarantee you the best value. You've heard it before — you get what you pay for. It may sound obvious, but it really does pay to buy your rose plants from nurseries that promote their high-quality plants.

You can buy roses in two different forms — *bareroot* and potted. Bareroot plants are dormant and have no soil around their roots. Nearly all roses are made of two parts, grafted together. The top part, called the *scion,* is the desirable flowering rose. The *rootstock,* on the bottom, adds hardiness and tolerance to a wide range of soil types. Where the two parts meet is called the *bud union,* as shown in Figure 16-1.

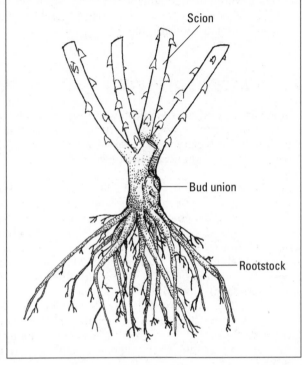

Figure 16-1:
Most roses
consist of
two parts —
scion and
rootstock —
which join
at the
knobby
bud union.

Stores usually have large bins full of these bareroot roses in plastic-wrapped packages at the start of the growing season. Mail-order nurseries also sell bareroot plants because they cost less to ship than potted plants and survive transport more easily. Bareroot roses grow vigorously after planting, as long as they remain cool and moist before you buy them.

Generally, local nurseries and garden centers are good sources. Different nurseries often sell exactly the same rose varieties, but the difference is in how they handle the plants. Buy from stores that take good care of their roses. Don't buy plants that have shriveled canes or wilted leaves or dusty dry packing material around their bare roots.

Mail-order nurseries can also provide a good selection of high quality plants. Reputable mail-order organizations will send you catalogs, listing the plants that they sell. Most guarantee their plants to grow and bloom given normal care. Look for catalogs that list the recommended winter-hardiness zones, too, if you live where winters get frigid. Both bareroot and potted roses are graded to insure quality, with Grade 1 indicating the highest quality.

The American Rose Society offers a listing of where to buy roses, plus lots of other information. Visit their Web site at www.ars.org/buyroses.html. If you become a member of the ARS, you'll also receive their *Handbook for Selecting Roses,* which compiles ratings of how different varieties performed from rose growers throughout the country.

The other rose organization you'll hear about is the All-America Rose Selections. A nonprofit organization, they evaluate new roses under actual garden conditions, then select and recommend superior varieties to the rose-buying public. You can find out more about AARS and their recommendations at www.rose.org. To obtain a partial listing of AARS recommendations, send requests to All-America Rose Selections, 221 N. LaSalle Street, Suite 3500, Chicago, IL 60601 or call 312-372-7090.

Members of local garden clubs and rose societies are always good sources of specific information regarding varieties of roses that do well in your area. Most every rose you can buy will grow throughout North America, but some are more or less tolerant of heat, cold, or wind. Local rose growers are happy to share their knowledge about varieties that grow best where you live and garden.

Planting Roses

Growing beautiful roses begins with putting them in the right place and planting them properly. The following sections show you how to get your new roses off to the best possible start.

Picking an ideal time and place

Roses establish quickly and resist pests and diseases better when you plant them in an ideal location. Roses require at least six hours or more of direct sunlight for good flowering and growth. An eastern exposure, which receives morning sun, is ideal. To maximize the amount of sunshine the plants receive, choose a planting location away from shady buildings or trees. Also avoid trees and shrubs with roots that will compete with the roses for moisture and nutrients.

Make sure the site is open to allow the summer breezes to blow through — that helps keep leaf diseases to a minimum. Also choose a location from which water drains promptly. Roses don't grow well where soil stays wet or where water puddles on the surface.

You can plant roses any time from early spring into early fall, but the best planting time depends on where you live and how your plants are packaged.

Plant bareroot roses in early to mid-spring before the new shoots start to develop and before daytime temperatures rise above 70 degrees — usually late March to early April in the middle latitudes of North America, although timing varies farther north and south (see Table 16-1). You can plant container roses anytime from spring to early fall, after danger of spring frost and a month or so before danger of fall frost.

Table 16-1	When to Plant Bareroot Roses
Your USDA Hardiness Zone	*When to Plant*
Zones 1 to 3	June
Zones 4 to 5	May
Zones 6 to 7	April to May
Zones 8 to 9	March to April
Zones 10 to 11	February

Preparing the planting site

Roses thrive in a loamy, well-drained garden soil with a pH of 5.5 to 7.0 (see Chapter 4). Begin with a soil test to determine pH and nutrient levels so that you can make corrections, if needed, while you prepare the soil.

Most soils, whether clay or sandy, benefit from the addition of organic matter, which improves drainage, aeration, and nutrient holding capacity. Spread a 2- to 4-inch layer of organic matter — such as compost, rotted manure, shredded leaves, dampened peat moss, or finely ground potting bark — on the soil surface and work it into the top 8 inches of soil.

To plant a rose, dig out enough soil to form a hole approximately 15 inches deep and at least 18 to 36 inches wide. (It's important to improve the soil in the entire future root zone.) Mix approximately three to six shovels of your chosen organic matter with the soil removed from the hole. Add to that about 10 cups of fertilizer made of a half-and-half mixture of alfalfa and cottonseed meals and mix thoroughly. This becomes the backfill soil for the new plant. Repeat the alfalfa and cottonseed meal fertilizer applications every ten weeks, mixing it lightly into the top inch or two of the soil. For more details about fertilizing roses, see the "Fertilizing" and "Watering" sections, later in this chapter.

Plant spacing varies according to the growth habit of the rose plant. Plants growing too close together will be tall and spindly and produce only a few small flowers. For a guide to plant spacing by rose type, see Table 16-2. The plant description in the catalog or on the plant tag should tell you what type of rose you have and also recommend the proper spacing.

Table 16-2	Rose Plant Spacing
Type of Rose	*Spacing*
Hybrid tea	30 inches
Grandiflora	36 inches
Floribunda	24 inches
Climbing roses	8 to 12 feet
Shrub roses	4 to 5 feet
Ground cover roses	36 inches
Miniature roses	12 inches

Planting a bareroot rose

Plant bareroot roses as soon as possible after purchasing or receiving them through the mail. Unwrap plants from the packaging and soak the root system in a bucket of tepid water for about an hour prior to planting. If you must delay planting for a few days, keep the plants moist and in a cool, dark location, or place them into a temporary soil trench in a shaded location. Don't store them with any ripening fruit, such as in a refrigerator or root cellar, however, because the fruit gives off ethylene, which harms growing plants. Prune out any damaged or dead roots and stems before planting.

Be sure your planting hole is twice as wide as your plant's root spread. Loosen the soil in the bottom of the hole and make a cone of soil, using the prepared backfill soil discussed in the "Preparing the planting site" section. Set the plant on top of this cone, spreading out the roots. Now check its *planting height* or place where the knobby bud union is relative to the ground at the top of the hole.

In most parts of the country, adjust the height of the cone until the bud union is just above the level of the surrounding soil, as shown in Figure 16-2. In cold-winter climates (USDA Zones 3 to 5), set the bud union 3 to 6 inches below ground to help protect it from freezing.

After the rose is properly positioned, begin filling the planting hole with the prepared backfill. Work the backfill around each root with your hands, and after you're about halfway done, add water to the hole to settle and moisten the soil around the roots. After the water drains away, finish backfilling. If you live where irrigation is a necessity, build a water-retaining ring of soil around the outside edge of the planting hole and water again. See Figure 16-3.

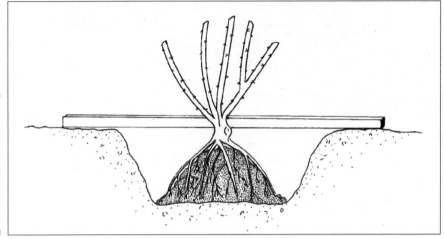

Figure 16-2:
Place the roots over a cone of soil and adjust the depth of the bud union.

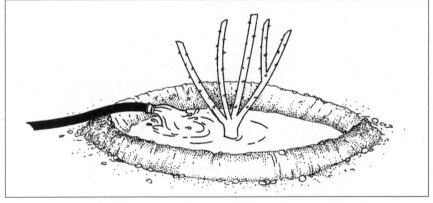

Figure 16-3:
Make a raised ring of soil around the planting hole and fill with water.

After the plant is set, mound the canes with an additional 4 to 6 inches of soil or mulch to prevent the canes from drying out before roots start growing (see Figure 16-4). After the new shoots appear and the danger of frost is past, remove this soil slowly, over a week's time.

Planting a container-grown rose

Keep container-grown plants watered and in a sunny location until they can be planted in the garden. Be sure that the soil in the pot is moist, but not sopping wet at planting time to make handling the plant easier. Prune out any damaged, dead, or broken stems before planting.

Remove the potted rose from its container and hold it in the planting hole so the top of the soil ball is at ground level. A common problem is planting too deep, so make sure the plant is placed at the same depth it was previously growing in the container. Fill the hole with the prepared soil mixture, described in "Preparing the planting site." Water the plant well to settle the back-filled soil around the root ball. Add more soil, if necessary.

Water as described in the "Planting a bareroot rose" section, making sure the entire root mass is wet. Plants require an inch of water weekly. If rainfall is insufficient, apply water by irrigation through the first growing season to aid plant establishment. Soak the soil to a depth of 12 inches at each watering to encourage deep rooting. Don't overhead sprinkle, which encourages disease problems; water at soil level.

Mulch your rose after planting by applying a 2-inch layer of mulch, such as shredded bark or leaves, to reduce water loss from evaporation during the summer months. Mulch also increases the organic matter content of the soil, moderates soil temperature, and suppresses weed growth.

Figure 16-4: Protect the bud union from drying out with a mound of soil for the first few weeks.

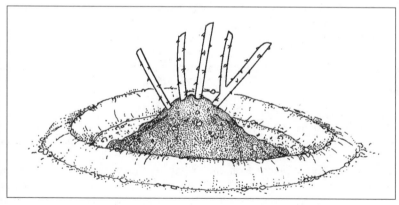

Cultivating Roses

Roses grow best in soil that's moderately to slightly acidic, meaning a soil pH of 5.5 to 6.5. See Chapter 4 for information about testing and changing your soil pH.

Roses need plenty of nutrients and regular watering to grow vigorously and flower profusely. You don't need the synthetic chemical rose fertilizers, though — many organic options exist.

Fertilizing

Organic fertilizers, such as fish emulsion, bat guano, composted manure, and dried blood meal, not only contribute nutrients to soils, but also provide organic matter that has positive, long-term benefits on soil health. Compared to chemical fertilizers, organic fertilizers also release their nutrients slowly over a longer period of time and feed the beneficial soil microorganisms. Therefore, don't expect fast results when you first apply the fertilizer. Follow recommendations and allow the soil and plants time to respond.

The fertilizer elements most likely to be deficient in garden soil are nitrogen, phosphorus, and potassium. In addition, roses often need extra calcium, magnesium, and sulfur. To supply these nutrients, use a *complete fertilizer,* which contains all three major elements, such as 1-2-2, or one with a similar analysis (see Chapters 4 and 5). Specially formulated organic fertilizers for vegetable gardens supply nutrients in roughly the same proportions that roses need. Spread the fertilizer evenly around the plant, work it into the soil, and then water.

My favorite organic fertilizer for roses is a half-and-half mix of alfalfa and cottonseed meals. Use about 10 cups per plant every 10 weeks through the growing season. You can save a lot of money if you shop for organic fertilizers like alfalfa and cottonseed meal at feed stores rather than at garden centers. Animal feed dealers sell much greater quantities of these materials compared to garden centers, so they can offer them at a much lower price per pound.

If you can't find the selection of organic fertilizers you like, check with Peaceful Valley Farm Supply at www.groworganic.com or Gardener's Supply Company at www.gardeners.com.

Apply fertilizer when new spring growth is well-established and all danger of frost has passed. Make a second application 4 to 6 weeks after the first or monthly at lower rates if plants show evidence of mineral deficiencies, such as yellowing of leaves from lack of nitrogen. Don't apply any type of nitrogen fertilizer within 6 weeks of the expected frost in fall. When applied late in the season, nitrogen may stimulate fresh growth and delay hardening of the wood before winter.

Watering

How much and how often you need to water roses depends on three things: the type of rose, where you live, and the weather. But if you're looking for a rule to remember, figure that a mature rose bush needs about 1 or 2 inches of water per week applied over its root zone. Start with a schedule, such as watering once every five days or so, and then watch the plants carefully and check the soil. Whatever the calendar says, if the soil is dry 2 or 3 inches down and the plant looks a little piqued, water.

Water enough to soak the entire root zone. If your soil is crumbly and water passes through it quickly, an inch of water will penetrate and soak about 12 inches down. But if your soil is a heavy clay soil, an inch of water will only soak about 4 or 5 inches deep. You can check the water penetration in the soil by digging out a shovel-length wedge of soil, but try not to damage the plant roots in the process.

Drip irrigation, shown in Figure 16-5, is particularly useful for organic and conservation-minded gardeners because it delivers the water to the root zone under the rose bush without waste. Additional benefits include fewer weeds to contend with and dry foliage, which reduces the incidence of many diseases. See Chapter 6 for more ways to prevent and control weeds.

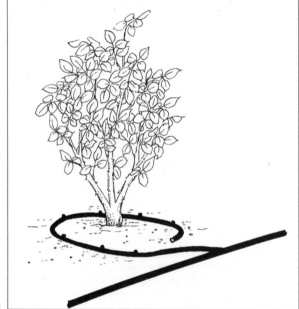

Figure 16-5: Drip irrigation conserves water and prevents disease by keeping the foliage dry.

For more about drip irrigation, see "Drip Irrigation in the Home Landscape," Publication 21579 from the University of California. You can buy the publication online at http://anrcatalog.ucdavis.edu/ or by calling 800-994-8849.

Pruning

While some kinds of roses don't absolutely require pruning to remain in good health, most do. Pruning improves the plant's health by letting more air and light reach all the leaves and stems, which discourages insects and some diseases. Left unpruned, roses become a tangled mess of barbed, disease-prone canes. Reaching into such a thorny thicket to weed and prune takes nerves of steel and heavy leather gloves! Some vigorous roses just don't know where to stop, and you need to prune them to keep their stems within bounds.

Well-pruned roses give you more bang for your buck because you remove the weak and unproductive shoots and spent flowers that divert the plant's energy away from making new flowers. *Show roses,* the kind with the long stems and big, luscious blooms, respond especially well to pruning by growing even bigger flowers with longer stems. *Garden roses* that produce clusters of flowers bloom more prolifically when you keep them groomed.

Making the cut

Use only sharp, clean tools to prune roses. Dull blades crush stems and tear and fray the edges of the cut, making it easier for diseases to gain a foothold. Also disinfect your tools between plants to prevent the accidental spread of disease. Just give the blades a wipe with a cloth dampened in isopropyl rubbing alcohol.

Bypass hand pruners are the tool I use most frequently because they snip everything from dead flowers to canes up to ½-inch thick. Loppers take care of canes up to an inch thick, plus the long handles let me reach into a prickly tangle without endangering my arms. If you're dealing with big, old roses bushes with large dead canes, use a fine-toothed saw.

Your three primary pruning goals are to remove weak, dead, and undesirable canes; to open up the center of the bush to air and light; and to remove old flowers. If you don't know where to start, remove the dead wood first, cutting back to healthy tissue. Living wood is beige or white. If you see dark brown tissue in the stem, cut back a little farther.

Most people start getting cold feet when cutting into living wood. Following a few simple rules and keeping your goals in mind should alleviate your fears:

- ✔ **Prune most roses right after they bloom.** Cut the flowers off just above a healthy 5-leaflet leaf, as shown in Figure 16-6. Cut farther down the stem to encourage stockier growth or to shorten over-long canes.

- ✔ **Make cuts at a 45- to 60-degree angle about ¼-inch above a bud.** The angle and proximity to a bud is important because the cut heals more quickly and sheds water away from the bud. See Figure 16-7.

- ✔ **Cut to a bud that points away from the center of the bush.** Imagine a "V" or vase-shape with the center of the bush mostly free of stems and branches. As you prune, keep in mind that buds grow in the direction that they point.

✔ **Remove suckers that grow from the rootstock.** Most roses consist of a scion of a desirable flowering variety grafted onto a rootstock of a more vigorous type of rose. Suckers often arise from this rootstock, and because they are more vigorous than the scion variety on top, they eventually crowd out the flowering rose. It's easy to distinguish sucker growth because the leaves and flowers look very different. Cut or pull them off below the soil line.

Figure 16-6:
Remove dead flowers by cutting just above a healthy 5-leaflet leaf.

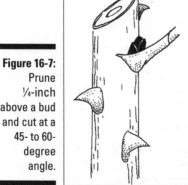

Figure 16-7:
Prune ¼-inch above a bud and cut at a 45- to 60-degree angle.

Pruning climbing roses

Roses with very long canes, called *climbing roses* (which I consider garden-type roses), offer a special challenge to rose growers because they have two different kinds of shoots — the main structural canes and the flowering shoots, called *laterals,* that grow from them. For the first 2 or 3 years after planting, let the structural canes grow with abandon, removing only dead or damaged canes. Tie them to a trellis or other support as desired.

Some climbing roses bloom just once in the spring. The time to prune them is right after flowering, as you would for other garden roses.

Another kind of climbing rose, called *everblooming,* blooms throughout the summer and these need a different pruning strategy. Tie their structural canes at a nearly horizontal angle to encourage them to sprout flowering lateral branches. In the winter or early spring, when the plant is dormant, prune these laterals back to about two to three buds above the structural canes. These buds will grow vigorously and produce flowers. After blooming, remove the flowers as you would for other roses.

Preparing Roses for Winter

If you live where winter temperatures rarely dip much below 15 degrees — USDA Zones 9 through 11 — you can skip this section entirely. Just about any rose you may plant can handle typical winters without any special attention.

Zones 6 through 8 are transition zones for winter hardiness. If you live here, you can grow most any kind of rose, but the more tender ones may be damaged by some winters. Often, it's not the absolute cold that does them in, but the wide temperature swings from cold to warm and back to cold again. That's why gardeners in these zones are likely to take measures to protect their favorite plants.

If you live in Zones 5 or colder, expect the harshest winter cold and wind and protect all but the hardiest of roses.

The bud union is the most cold-sensitive part of most rose plants. Covering the bud union with soil protects it from the cold. Follow these steps:

1. **Tie all the canes together to keep them from being wind-blown and loosening the soil around the base of the bush.**

   Or shorten canes to reduce wind whipping. Don't cut the canes to the soil level, though, because you want the buds near the bottom of the canes to sprout into new canes in the spring.

2. **Mound soil 8 to 10 inches high around the base of canes after the first hard frost, but while you can still work the soil.**

   Bring soil from another part of the garden for mounding because you may injure roots if you remove soil from around the rose plant or bed. Avoid using clay or heavy soils to build these mounds because they hold too much moisture.

3. **Pile hay, straw, horse manure, leaves, or similar loose material over the mounded canes.**

   To prevent mice invasion, wait until after the ground has frozen in late fall, around Thanksgiving in northern areas. Hold the material in place by covering with some soil. These materials help to keep the soil temperature constant. For additional protection, place twiggy branches or evergreen boughs over the top of the bushes. (I use limbs from my Christmas tree.) These branches help accumulate snow between the bushes, which may help reduce injury to the roots while still allowing for some air circulation.

You can also make or buy cylinders, such as styrofoam cones, to place around your rose bushes, but these work only for small plants. Set the cylinders in place after two hard frosts have occurred, usually after Thanksgiving. If you use an open-top cylinder, tie canes together, place the cylinder, cut the canes even with the cylinder's top, and then fill with dry organic matter, such as leaves or straw. Don't use peat moss. Cover the top with polyethylene film to keep the insulation material dry and anchor it in place to keep it from blowing over. Check the plants occasionally in winter for mouse, wind, or other damage.

Remove protective materials in spring as soon as danger of hard frost passes, but before new growth appears. Carefully remove the soil mounded around the bases of plants to avoid breaking off any shoots that may have started to grow. Never uncover the bushes in spring before the ground has thawed because the tops may start to grow before the roots can provide water.

The most important thing you can do to help prevent winter injury is keep your roses healthy during the growing season. Roses that were free of disease and properly nourished during the summer are less likely to suffer damage come winter.

Solving Common Rose Troubles

Choosing disease-resistant roses in the first place eliminates many common problems, but many of the most widely popular roses need intervention to keep them healthy. Show roses regularly fall prey to the common diseases, especially in climates with humid growing seasons. If you're in a low humidity region, where summer rainfall is rare, you have the best chance of growing disease-free show roses without fungicides.

As in all areas of organic gardening, planning and prevention are the keys to growing success. Many diseases and pests live on rose leaves and debris, including mulch, around your plants. Rake up fallen leaves and replace bark mulch at the beginning of every growing season to foil harboring villains. See the "Planting Roses" section, earlier in this chapter, for information on choosing the best site and getting your roses off to a great start.

Rose diseases

Diseases that damage leaves look unsightly and prevent plants from making enough food to flower and grow robustly. The two most common diseases throughout most of the U.S. are black spot and powdery mildew. My observation from years of growing and watching roses is that the favorite show roses — dark red and richly scented — are more prone to powdery mildew than others. Similarly, roses with yellow flowers or yellow-flowered ancestors are also somewhat more disease-prone. Other common rose diseases include downy mildew, rust disease, and rose mosaic virus. You can find out more about diseases and control methods in Chapter 10.

Insect pests of roses

Many insect pests will feed on roses, but few cause really devastating harm. Vigilance and a strong blast of water or hand picking takes care of most pests, such as the common aphids, Japanese beetles, rose slugs, rose curculios, and caterpillars. Other common pests include spider mites, scale insects, and thrips. You can read more on pests in Chapter 7 and find out how to control them in Chapters 8 and 9.

Chapter 17

Managing Landscape Trees and Shrubs

In This Chapter

▶ Finding the right trees and shrubs for your yard

▶ Planting trees properly

▶ Fertilizing and pruning landscape plants

▶ Looking at a list of popular ornamental shrubs and trees

Trees and shrubs lend structure to the landscape — they form the framework around which you plan your flower and vegetable gardens. As these long-lived plants mature, they become like old friends. Losing one to accident or disease leaves a hole in your landscape, a gap in the hedge. Taking care of these irreplaceable assets and using them to best advantage starts with choosing the right plants in the first place, planting them correctly, and caring for them to keep them thriving.

Planning for Low-Maintenance

I like to have a map in hand when I set out into unfamiliar territory. Knowing the lay of the land — what to expect around the next bend in the road — saves me missteps and valuable time and energy. Using a map of your yard works the same way when choosing the best trees and shrubs. Miss a turn and you may not get where you intended to go. In Chapter 3, I talked about how to assess your growing conditions — that chapter is a good reference as you browse through the rest of this one.

A place for everything and everything in its place

Trees and shrubs live for a long time when they're happy and suffer from fewer problems. So what makes a plant happy? The right soil, climate, moisture, and sun exposure are key ingredients. Even before you begin shopping for these long-term landscape investments, assess the conditions of your planting site, as described in Chapter 3, so that you know what your yard has to offer. Use your assessment to narrow the list of potential plants to those that thrive in your particular situation. If your planting site is damp and shady, for example, you can cross drought-tolerant sun-lovers off your list.

One aspect that many people fail to consider when placing trees and shrubs in their landscapes is the plants' mature sizes. Most of these woody plants grow so slowly that it's easy to forget that the spindly twig you planted by the mailbox will grow wide enough to divert traffic within a few years. Play it safe by spacing trees where they can grow to full size without overhanging buildings and roads, growing into utility wires, or crowding the house. Choose shrubs that won't cover the windows or sidewalk. If the space between your small, newly planted shrubs looks too bleak and barren, plant some colorful annual or perennial flowers in the gaps until the shrubs fill in.

Avoiding troublemakers

Buying trees is like entering into any long-term relationship — the characteristics that attracted you in the first place may loose their appeal in time if their bad habits outweigh the good ones. When you choose the trees and shrubs for your landscape, consider the attributes that you want your plants to have. It's easy to focus on color, texture, shape, and flowers, but keep other factors in mind, too. If you want a shade tree to plant in the lawn, look for deeply rooted species, avoiding those with shallow roots. No time for raking? Stay away from trees that drop copious twigs and leaves. The following is a list of some notorious troublemakers:

- **Invasive roots** wreak havoc in septic fields and often grow close to the soil surface, making lawn mowing difficult. Trees to avoid in lawns include red *(Acer rubrum)* and silver maples *(A. saccharinum)*, boxelder *(Acer negundo)*, birches *(Betula* species), beech *(Fagus* species), *Ficus* species, poplars *(Populus* species), and willows *(Salix* species).

- **Weak-wooded trees** frequently break under ice and wind stress, causing property damage. Home wreckers include red *(Acer rubrum)* and silver maples *(A. saccharinum)*, boxelder *(Acer negundo)*, horsechestnut *(Aesculus hippocastanum)*, *Catalpa* species, *Eucalyptus* species, poplars *(Populus* species), and willows *(Salix* species).

✔ **Messy trees** drop leaves, sap, fruits, nuts, and twigs frequently, adding to yard maintenance. Those to avoid include boxelder *(Acer negundo),* oaks *(Quercus* species), walnuts *(Juglans* species) and other nut-bearing trees, *Catalpa* species, sweetgum *(Liquidambar styraciflua),* pine *(Pinus* species), magnolia *(Magnolia* species), and planetree or sycamore *(Plantanus* species).

If you have space to let some of these troublesome trees grow without endangering or inconveniencing you, by all means, plant them. They do have some endearing traits, but it pays to be forewarned. Learn as much as you can about a species before you buy and choose varieties that offer disease resistance, if available. I mention disease-resistant varieties in the plant descriptions in this chapter.

Planting for Success

How you plant your tree or shrub may determine whether it thrives, merely survives, or dies. Not long ago, a neighbor asked me to look at a young crabapple tree that he had planted several years earlier. It wasn't growing well and looked a little sadder each year. After digging around the trunk a bit, I discovered that he had planted it about 6 inches too deep — the tree was suffocating! We replanted that tree and now it's blooming reliably every spring. Six inches seems like such a small thing and yet it meant life or death to a tree. Read the following sections to get your plants off to the best possible start.

There is a season . . .

The best time of year to plant trees and shrubs depends mostly on your climate and the type of plant you're installing. Newly transplanted trees and shrubs have small root systems that need time to grow before they can support lots of leafy twigs and flowers. Roots grow best in cool, moist soil, making spring and fall the ideal planting times in most parts of the United States. Identify your climate in order to find the best planting times for your trees and shrubs:

✔ **Cool, rainy winters:** Plant in autumn at the beginning of the rainy season to take advantage of the natural moisture.

✔ **Freezing, snowy winters:** Plant in early spring as soon as the ground thaws or in late summer to early autumn. Roots continue to grow until the ground temperature approaches 40 degrees.

✔ **Warm year 'round:** Plant at the beginning of the coolest, wettest season.

Deciduous and evergreen plants have somewhat different needs in the months following transplanting, which can affect the best time to plant in your area.

- **Deciduous:** Plant when they have an opportunity to grow roots without the added stress of leaves, usually early autumn to spring.

- **Evergreen:** These plants lose water through their leaves year 'round, but can't take up water through their roots when the ground is frozen. Avoid planting just prior to winter in cold climates.

How your tree or shrub was harvested and shipped also determines the best time to plant it. Nurseries sell woody plants in three different ways:

- **Containers:** Plants grow right in the container, so they have plenty of roots. Plant these at any time of year when they are available, but preferably at the best time for your climate.

- **Bareroot:** Plants are dug from the growing field during their dormant season and shipped without any soil. Plant in late autumn through early winter in mild climates and early spring in cold climates.

- **Balled and burlapped (B&B):** Plants are dug from the field with a ball of soil around their roots, which is wrapped in burlap or plastic. Plant in late fall to early winter in warm climates and early spring in cold climates or whenever they become available.

You can plant at less-than-ideal times of the year, too, but you will have to be more vigilant in your watering and care until the plant begins growing normally again. Stressed plants are more prone to disease and insect attack — and that's something you want to avoid.

Picking out a healthy plant

My mantra throughout this book is prevention, prevention, prevention. One of the key first steps to low-maintenance, problem-free trees and shrubs is picking out healthy specimens. Here's what to look for when you go shopping:

- **Wilting and water stress:** Don't buy a wilted tree or shrub. Period. Water stress symptoms include wilted or pale-colored foliage, brown edges on the leaves, and unusually small or sparse leaves. Choose a well-cared-for plant, or if it's not available, shop elsewhere. Water-stressed plants may not recover from transplanting or grow as well in the future as plants that receive adequate care in the nursery.

- **Diseases and pests:** Check the leaves and stems for sticky residue; off-colored spots; distorted or chewed leaves and twig tips; and sunken, oozing, or discolored spots on the bark.

- **Mechanical damage:** A few broken twigs is usually not a reason to reject a plant, but avoid those with gashes on the trunk and main limbs and any with torn limbs. Balled and burlapped plants should have a solid, unbroken root ball, which indicates intact roots.

✔ **Normal leaf color and size:** Some varieties are supposed to have unusual foliage, but if you see plants with smaller-than-normal leaves for their variety, watch out. Water stress may be a culprit. Off-colored foliage, except in autumn, may signal nutrient deficiency or other trouble.

✔ **Branch and trunk structure:** Look for trees with straight, evenly tapered trunks and evenly distributed limbs. Unless the tree is supposed to have several trunks or large main branches, such as ornamental cherries and crabapples, choose trees with a single, main trunk that doesn't fork. Avoid trees with crowded or lopsided branches. Trees, such as birch, sold in clumps should have similarly sized trunks that don't rub against each other. Remember that they will become larger and more crowded as the tree grows. Figure 17-1 compares trees with good and poor structure.

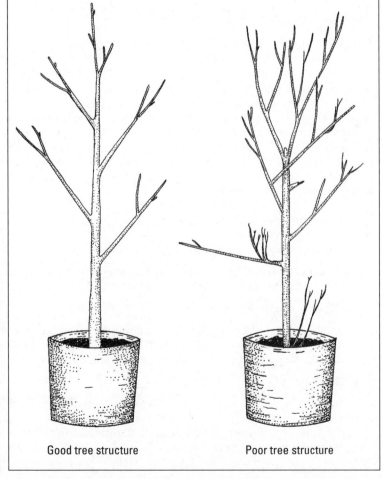

Figure 17-1:
Trees with healthy structure (left) have straight trunks and evenly distributed branches. Poorly structured trees (right) have lopsided, rubbing, or damaged limbs.

Good tree structure   Poor tree structure

Shrubs vary considerably from species to species — desirable structure in one may be undesirable in another. In general, choose shrubs with symmetrical branches that don't rub against one another. Avoid shrubs with roots growing on the surface or out of the drainage holes of their pots.

If you shop at a nursery with helpful, experienced, and knowledgeable staff, ask someone to help you choose the best specimens. Ask how they determined the quality, so that you can make your own good decisions in the future.

When you transport your trees and shrubs from the store to your planting site, protect them from wind, heat, and cold. Never carry them uncovered in the back of a truck — it's the equivalent of a hurricane — and don't let them cook in a closed vehicle. Keep them in a cool, shady place and water as needed until planting time.

Digging the ten-dollar hole

In some circles, controversy has surrounded the proper way to dig a hole. What's the big deal, you ask? Plenty, if you ask someone who installs trees for a living. If you plant trees too deep or too high, or crowd the roots into a small hole, they'll fail to thrive. People who study these things have also discovered that adding peat moss and other amendments to the planting hole is not only unnecessary, but can even contribute to trouble in the long run: As it turns out, roots tend to stay where the soil is most fertile and may not venture outside the walls of the original hole. Plants with such small root systems are more prone to drought stress and likely to blow over in strong wind. (A few exceptions to this rule include shrubs, such as rhododendrons and blueberries, that need very acidic soil.)

Here's the right way to plant a tree or shrub:

1. **Measure the diameter of the rootball or root spread.**

   Multiply the result by 3 to find the diameter of the hole. If the rootball is 1 foot wide, for example, you need a 3-foot wide hole.

2. **Measure the depth of the rootball.**

   Dig the hole no deeper than this result. If planting a bareroot tree or shrub, leave a pedestal of undisturbed soil in the middle of the hole and dig deeper around it to accommodate the root spread.

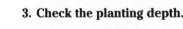

3. **Check the planting depth.**

   Set the tree into the hole. The *trunk flare,* where the trunk widens near the base, should be just at the soil surface or slightly above it, as shown in Figure 17-2. Shrubs should be at or slightly above the same soil depth as they previously grew.

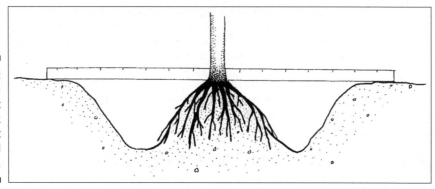

Figure 17-2:
Position the tree so that the trunk flare is at the soil surface.

4. **Prepare the roots.**

   Slip the plant out of its pot or remove the plastic burlap from the rootball. (Natural burlap can be left on the rootball and will degrade in the soil, but should be carefully sliced and rolled down below the soil surface to help the decay process.) Prune off broken roots and gently unwind tangled roots, preserving as many roots as possible.

5. **Backfill the hole.**

   Put the plant back into position in the hole, draping the roots over the pedestal, if needed. Fill the hole with the soil you removed from the hole, working it gently around the roots and holding the tree in position. Stop when the hole is about three-quarters full.

6. **Add water.**

   Fill the hole with water to settle the soil around the roots. Let it drain and finish filling the hole with soil.

7. **Make a watering basin.**

   Build a low ring of soil around the perimeter of the planting hole to hold water for the first few months. Knock it down when the tree begins growing actively.

8. **Mulch and water again.**

   Spread a 2-inch thick layer of bark or shredded leaf mulch over the planting hole. Pull mulch 3 to 4 inches away from the trunk, however. Water the tree again.

After planting your tree or shrub, water it only when the soil dries out to a depth of 4 to 6 inches. Bareroot trees, in fact, usually don't need watering again until they begin to sprout leaves.

Unless your tree has a trunk greater than 3 inches in diameter, or you live in a windy area, you probably don't need to stake it. Trees develop stronger roots and trunks if allowed to move in the wind. If you must stake it, use two stakes and place them opposite one another and perpendicular to the prevailing wind. Cut the stakes equal to half the height of the tree plus 18 inches. Loosely attach loops made from strips of soft cloth to the tree and stakes so that the tree can gently sway in the wind. Remove the stakes and ties after one year.

Long-Term Care for Landscape Trees and Shrubs

Established trees and shrubs need less attention than just about any other landscape plant. Except in unusual circumstances, they rarely need watering. They need little fertilizer. All they ask for is observation for potential problems and occasional pruning to keep them healthy and looking respectable.

Fertilizing follies

Unless your soil is unusually infertile or you want your trees to grow extra fast, you don't need to fertilize them regularly. If you do choose to fertilize, don't apply more than 1 pound of nitrogen per 1000 square feet per year. (Never add it to the hole at planting time, however.) You can either apply organic granular fertilizer or spread composed manure over the root zone. The *root zone,* where the roots grow, is usually at least twice as wide as the branch spread. If the branches measure 10 feet from the trunk to the tips, figure that the roots stretch about 20 feet. To calculate the square feet in the root zone, use this formula: 3.14 × (root radius) × (root radius). In this case, 3.14 × 20 × 20 = 1,256 square feet. See Chapter 5 for more on using organic fertilizers.

Runs with scissors

You need a good reason to prune a twig or remove a limb from a tree or shrub — every time you cut into a plant, you open a wound that's vulnerable to disease. Having a goal in mind helps guide you toward the right cuts and minimizes the size and number of cuts you need to make. Common reasons to prune include the following:

- **Establishing healthy structure:** Removing poorly placed, crowded limbs when they are small avoids major pruning cuts down the road. Limbs that rub against one another, emerge too close together from the trunk, or have very narrow crotch angles where the limb meets the trunk are all candidates for removal.

✔ **Controlling growth:** Part of your annual yard maintenance includes shaping shrubs that grow out of bounds, removing old and unproductive shoots, and trimming limbs that get in the way.

✔ **Increasing flowers:** Fruiting and ornamental flowering trees and shrubs produce more flowers and better-quality fruit when pruned properly. As a rule, prune spring-flowering shrubs right after they finish blooming. Prune summer-blooming shrubs and most trees when they're dormant in the winter.

✔ **Removing dead, damaged, and diseased wood:** Prune any time you see these three Ds to prevent the damage or disease from spreading. If the trunk or major limbs are affected, call an arborist for help.

The tools you need to do a good pruning job include hand pruners for cuts up to ¾ inch in diameter and loppers for cuts between ¾-inch and 1½-inches in diameter or for limbs that are just out of arm's reach. Use a pruning saw with a curved 8- to 12-inch blade for larger cuts. If the pruning job is too high to reach from the ground, use a pole pruner with a telescoping handle or call a professional. Never climb a tree when using power equipment, such as a chain saw, or cut limbs near utility wires. To prevent the spread of disease, always clean your tool blades with isopropyl alcohol between prunings of trees and shrubs. Don't coat the wounds with paint, tar, or any other material — it actually slows the healing process.

You only need to know two basic pruning cuts to maintain your trees, shrubs, and flowering plants — heading and thinning.

✔ A *thinning cut* removes a branch back to its origin, as shown on the left in Figure 17-3. Use thinning cuts to maintain plants' natural appearance while decreasing its height, width, or branching density.

✔ A *heading cut,* shown on the right in Figure 17-3, removes shoots or branches back to stubs or buds. Plants usually respond to heading cuts, such as hedge shearing, by sprouting new shoots near the pruning site, resulting in denser growth. *Deadheading,* a technique used to remove spent flowers, helps increase future flowering. Pinch or prune off the flowers to a point just above healthy-looking buds.

When you make a thinning cut, it's really important to cut at the right place. If you look closely where a branch joins the trunk or a larger limb, you should see a series of raised ridges, called the *branch collar.* That's where the scar tissue begins to form when the limb dies or is removed. Make your cut just outside that collar without leaving a stub. Stubs invite infection that may lead to the death of the tree. Never cut a limb flush with the trunk, either. And always support the limb you're removing to avoid tearing the bark on the trunk.

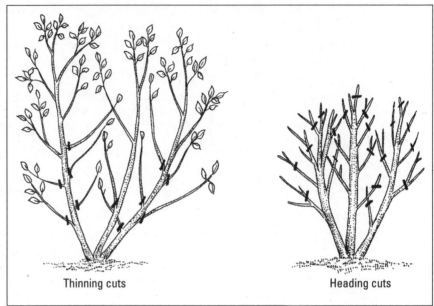

Figure 17-3:
Thinning
cuts remove
a limb to its
point of
attachment.
Heading
cuts remove
shoots back
to buds or
stubs.

Thinning cuts

Heading cuts

Choosing the Perfect Trees and Shrubs

When you choose new trees and shrubs, think about what you want these plants to do in your landscape. Do you need shade or shelter from the wind? Does a corner of the yard need a spark of color? Consider all the seasons of the year when you make your decision — the best shrubs and trees have practical or decorative value in several seasons, not just one. A Japanese maple, or example, may have ornamental leaves in spring and summer, colorful fall foliage, and interesting branching patterns and bark in the winter. I've chosen some of the best and most versatile landscape trees and shrubs for this section.

Shade trees

Shade trees frame the landscape, cool the space around them, and provide a backdrop for colorful flowering trees and shrubs. Most of these trees grow too tall for you to treat for pests or diseases, so if you are planting new trees, your best bet is to choose species that suffer few problems in the first place. If you already have large shade trees with chronic pests or you suspect disease, call an arborist who can diagnose the trouble and offer advice and treatment.

✔ **Maple:** *Acer* species. A large and diverse group of valuable landscape trees, maples range in mature size from 20 to 100 feet, depending on species. The larger species serve as shade trees, while smaller ones make good specimens and street trees. Many maples are renowned for their brilliant autumn foliage color; some also have attractive bark.

Maples that grow 25 to 30 feet high include trident *(A. buergeranum),* hedge *(A. campestre),* fullmoon *(A. japonicum),* Japanese *(A. palmatum),* Amur *(A. tataricum),* and Shantung *(A. truncatum).* All have yellow, orange, or crimson fall foliage. Larger species for shade include paperbark *(A. griseum),* red *(A. rubrum),* and sugar *(A. saccharum)* maples.

Most maples prefer well-drained, fertile soil and regular moisture. Some maples, including hedge and trident, tolerate drier and less fertile soil, such as occurs near roads. For damp soil, try red or Amur maples. Prune only to remove dead, damaged, or diseased limbs or any that rub or hang over buildings. Prune in early summer, avoiding late winter through spring.

Leaf spots, cankers, caterpillars, borers, leaf hoppers, and scale insects injure maples, especially those growing in stressed conditions or in unsuitable soils. Some species are also more prone to insects, disease, and structural damage than others, including boxelder *(A. negundo),* silver *(A. saccharinum),* and sycamore *(A. pseudoplatanus)* maples. In hot, dry climates, look for brown leaf edges that signal leaf scorch. Give additional water to moisten the soil to a depth of at least 12 inches.

✔ **Birch:** *Betula* species. When you think of birches, you likely picture a clump of white-barked trees. Not all birches have white bark, however. Many of these actually make better landscape specimens, especially for organic gardeners, because they resist the most common and devastating pest — the bronze birch borer — and tolerate a wider range of growing conditions. Birches cast light shade, making them good choices for cooling a shady seat. Most birches thrive on moist, well-drained, acidic soils, but try gray birch in drier situations and river birch in damp soil. Prune birches in late spring to early summer after the leaves have fully emerged. If pruned too early or late in the season, they bleed sap excessively. Avoid disturbing the soil around their shallow roots.

Birches are subject to attack from many insects and several diseases, including leaf miners, canker, and leaf diseases. The bronze birch borer decimates the white-barked birches, especially the European white birch, throughout the eastern and midwestern United States, targeting stressed trees and older specimens first. The first symptom of infestation is dead branches near the top of the tree.

Choose species that resist the bronze birch borer insect, such as Asian white *(B. platyphylla japonica),* gray *(B. populifolia),* and river *(B. nigra)* birches. If the pest is not a problem in your area, try white-barked paper *(B. papyrifera)* and European white *(B. pendula)* birches. All of these birches are hardy in Zones 3 to 6, except Asian white birch, which grows north to Zone 4, and river birch, which grows south to Zone 9.

✔ **Hackberry:** *Celtis* species. These native North American species thrive in adverse conditions, tolerating wet to dry soil and urban to open prairie situations. They grow 40 to 60 feet tall and form an elm-like silhouette. Common hackberry *(C. occidentalis)* grows in Zones 3 to 9, tolerates Midwestern wind and dry soil, and has wildlife-attracting berries. Sugar hackberry *(C. laevigata)* grows in Zones 5 to 9, prefers low wet areas, and has smooth gray bark and resists some common hackberry diseases.

Common hackberry is prone to a disfiguring disease called witches' broom that makes the twigs grow abnormally. The cultivar 'Prairie Pride' resists the disease. Other problems include leaf spots and galls. The Mourning Cloak butterfly larvae enjoy its foliage.

✔ **Ginkgo:** *Gingko biloba.* Growing 50 to 80 feet tall and 30 to 40 feet wide, ginkgo is best suited to large yards. Young trees have a pyramid shape, but older trees become widely spreading. Varieties also differ significantly in width and shape. Ginkgo's pollution tolerance and neat habits make it attractive for planting along streets, in parks, and other urban and sub-urban areas. Not fussy about soil, the gingko thrives in Zones 4 to 8. It needs little care and has no significant pests or diseases. Choose a male cultivar, such as 'Autumn Gold', 'Fairmount', or 'Princeton Sentry' to avoid the unpleasant smelling fruits that drop from female trees.

✔ **Katsura:** *Cercidiphyllum japonicus.* This tree has so many good things going for it that's it hard to go wrong by choosing it for your yard — as long as you have the space to accommodate it. It grows 40 to 60 feet high and spreads just as wide from several branched trunks. The nearly round leaves are attractive from spring to their final fall blaze of apricot-orange.

Katsura prefers moist, slightly acidic, well-drained, fertile soil, and full sun. Keep the soil moist, but not saturated for the first few years after transplanting. Mulch to hold soil moisture. It has no significant pests or diseases. For something different, look for the cultivar 'Pendula', which grows cascading limbs that reach 15 to 25 feet high with a wider spread.

✔ **Oak:** *Quercus* species. The queen of trees, oaks suggest majesty wherever they grow. Oak species fall into three broad categories:

- White oaks have leaves with rounded lobes and grow 80 feet high — too large for most home landscapes.

- Red oaks have leaves with pointed lobes and make better landscape specimens.

- Narrow-leafed oaks don't have lobed leaves and many are suitable for home landscapes.

Plant dormant, balled and burlapped or container-grown specimens in well-drained soil. Pin oak *(Q. palustris)* and swamp white oak *(Q. bicolor)* can grow in wet soils. Preferred soil pH varies widely. Pin oak is especially sensitive to high pH soils and leaves will turn yellow if the soil isn't acidic. Oaks suffer from many insect pests that eat their leaves, including gypsy moth, oak moth, mites, and borers, plus various fungus diseases. Few pests prove fatal to otherwise healthy trees.

Flowering and ornamental trees

Flowering trees give your yard a colorful exclamation point whenever they bloom. The anticipation of cherry or crabapple blossoms marks the changing of the seasons, often highlighting the start of the gardening season. Some of the most beloved trees, crabapples and cherries among them, are prone to diseases and insect pests that spoil their appearance and performance. Choose disease-resistant varieties or select a native, locally adapted tree species. To prevent some insects from recurring year after year, clean up fallen fruit and destroy it.

- **Serviceberry:** *Amelanchier* species. These trees grow about 20 feet high in Zones 3 to 7 and often form multiple-trunked trees with silvery bark. In spring, they produce clouds of white flowers, which ripen to delicious deep red to black fruits similar to blueberries by early summer. Their glossy, deep green, oval foliage turns brilliant yellow to orange in the fall. They have a few diseases, such as leaf spots and rust, and while insects pester them, none are serious. Plant in moist, acidic soils.

- **Redbud:** *Cercis canadensis.* Although hardy in Zones 5 to 9, individual trees may have a much narrower range, depending where their fore-bearers grew. If possible, choose trees from a similar climate to your own. Trees grow up to 25 feet tall and tend to form wide-spreading, multi-trunked canopies. Leaves are heart-shaped and follow the pink, early spring flowers. Plant in moist, well-drained soil and full sun to light shade. Canker disease is the only serious problem — prune out infected limbs. Varieties with unusual foliage include 'Forest Pansy', which grows in Zones 6 to 9, has dark purple new leaves that mature to deep burgundy, and 'Silver Cloud' with creamy-white, variegated leaves. Other varieties have flower colors ranging from white to reddish purple.

- **Dogwood:** *Cornus* species. Distinctive horizontal branching, clouds of spring flowers, and fiery autumn foliage make this group of landscape trees well loved. The most commonly planted species is flowering dog-wood *(C. florida)*, which is hardy in Zones 5 to 9. Many good varieties exist, including 'Cherokee Princess', which is very cold hardy and disease-resistant. Another under-appreciated species is kousa dogwood *(C. kousa),* which grows in similar conditions, but stays smaller and blooms later than flowering dogwood, and is more resistant to anthrac-nose disease.

  Plant dogwoods in well-drained, moist, humus-rich soil. In hot climates, give midday shade. Canker, twig blights, anthracnose, and wood-boring insects frequently damage these trees. Prune out diseased wood when you see it. Dogwood is also prone to rot diseases if the bark is damaged — take care with the mower and string trimmer!

✔ **Hawthorn:** *Crataegus* species. This group of trees tolerates urban pollution and poor, dry soil and, in return, offers clouds of spring bloom, followed by crabapple-like fruits. Most have thorny branches and grow in Zones 4 to 7 or 8. Fireblight, leaf rusts, blights and spots, apple scab, leaf miners, and aphids plague hawthorns. A few, such as green hawthorn *(C. viridis),* Lavalle hawthorn *(C. × lavellei),* and English hawthorn 'Crimson Cloud' *(C. laevigata)* are more resistant to leaf diseases.

✔ **Magnolia:** *Magnolia* species. Ranging in size from shrubs to magnificent trees, magnolias include both evergreen and deciduous species. Some grow only in warmer climates from Zones 6 to 9, while others tolerate Zones 5 and even 4. Magnolias prefer moist, well-drained, slightly acidic soil with plenty of organic matter and full sun to light shade. Protect the shallow roots from drought and weed competition with a layer of organic mulch. Prune only to shape the tree and remove undesirable limbs. Magnolias as a group suffer from few pests or diseases, except for saucer magnolia *(M. × soulangiana),* which is prone to several leaf diseases.

For shrub to small tree-sized magnolias, look for lily magnolia *(M. lili-iflora);* any of the Kosar-DeVos hybrids, such as 'Ann' or 'Betty'; sweetbay *(M. virginiana);* and star magnolia *(M. stellata).* Species that grow up to 30 feet tall include Yulan *(M. denudata),* Loebner *(M. × loebneri),* and many hybrids.

✔ **Flowering crabapple:** *Malus* species. One of the most widely grown flowering trees in Zones 4 to 7 for home and public landscapes, flowering crabs have a lot to offer. Spring bloom, persistent and colorful fruit, and attractive branching and bark make them justifiably popular. Hundreds of varieties exist, and many of the newest ones have built-in disease resistance. Plant in nearly any well-drained, moderately fertile soil and full sun. Prevent weed and grass competition with organic mulch. Prune while dormant, in late winter to early spring.

Choose the best varieties by first looking at disease resistance. Crabapples suffer from many serious diseases, including leaf scab, cedar-apple rust, powdery mildew, and fire blight. Expect aphids, mites, and caterpillars, as well as rodents and deer, to take a bite, too. After selecting disease-resistant cultivars, select for flower color (white to deep pink), height and growth shape (column to wide and low), leaf color (green to reddish), and fruit size and color (red to yellow). Some also have fragrant blooms or double flowers with extra petals. If you want to know more about crabapples, look for the book *Flowering Crabapples* by Fr. John L. Fiala.

✔ **Stewartia:** *Stewartia* species. If you have moist, well-drained, acidic soil, consider stewartia for its flaky, mottled bark, late summer bloom, and striking fall foliage. Trees stay 20 to 40 feet tall, making them ideal for most home landscapes. They suffer from few pests or diseases and need little pruning.

Flowering and ornamental shrubs

The seasonal stars of the show, flowering shrubs, light up the landscape with drifts and spots of bloom. Butterflies, moths, and hummingbirds flock to their nectar, and countless other birds and wildlife depend on their fruit and berries. The best shrubs, however, offer more than a week or two of flowers — attractive foliage, stems, and colorful berries can carry the show through the rest of the year.

- **Japanese barberry:** *Berberis thunbergii.* This tough, thorny plant grows in soil from soggy to drought-prone, doesn't mind pollution or city conditions, thrives in full sun, and rarely needs pruning, except to shape it. It is prone to some leaf diseases and insects, but these rarely prove fatal. Use for low hedges and barriers. Many varieties exist and include reddish-purple leafed 'Crimson Pygmy' and 'Rose Glow', and yellow-leafed 'Aurea' and 'Bonanza Gold'.

- **Butterfly bush:** *Buddleia davidii.* Although hardy in Zones 5 to 9, this shrub often dies to the ground in its colder range, but sprouts from the roots in the spring. Large trusses of white, yellow, pink, to red flowers attract butterflies in great numbers. Depending on the variety and climate, plants range in size from 5 to 15 feet high. Prune in early spring to encourage lots of new growth on which the flowers appear. Plant in moist, fertile soil in full sun. In dry conditions, spider mites can be problematic.

- **Summersweet:** *Clethra alnifolia.* This North American native offers spikes of fragrant, white to pink, late-summer flowers that attract butterflies and many other pollinating insects. It grows 6 to 10 feet tall and wide, but the award-winning cultivar 'Hummingbird' grows only 36 inches high. It grows in Zones 4 to 9 and prefers moist, acidic soil and part shade to full sun, but tolerates less hospitable seashore conditions. It has few pests except for mites in overly dry sites. Prune to maintain shape and to remove spent flowers.

- **Cotoneaster:** *Cotoneaster* species. Deciduous members of this group have small leaves, attractive fruits, and distinctive, herringbone-patterned branches. Some, such as spreading cotoneaster *(C. divaricatus),* grow upright to 5 or 6 feet, but most species remain under 3 feet tall. Creeping *(C. adpressus),* cranberry *(C. apiculatus),* and rockspray cotoneaster *(C. horizontalis)* spread up 6 feet wide, making them useful as groundcovers.

  Plant cotoneasters in nearly any well-drained soil, including sandy, heavy clay, drought-prone, salty, and those with high or low pH. Prune to shape or remove damaged limbs. Pest and disease problems can include fire blight, leaf spots, canker, and spider mites.

- **Euonymus:** *Euonymus* species. This group includes the popular deciduous burning bush *(E. alatus)* as well as many species of evergreen shrubs and groundcovers. Nearly all of them do fine in nearly any soil, as long as it isn't waterlogged. Problems include aphids, thrips, and scale insects, plus a variety of bacterial and fungal diseases. Popular euonymus include spreading euonymus *(E. kiautschovicus)* and many varieties of evergreen wintercreeper *(E. fortunei),* such as 'Emerald 'n' Gold', 'Emerald Gaiety', and 'Sunspot'.

✔ **Forsythia:** *Forsythia* species. Cheerful, yellow, bell-shaped flowers welcome spring, but the shrubs frequently become straggly and overgrown unless pruned regularly. Prune after flowering in the spring, choosing ¼ of the oldest stems and cutting them right to the ground. To ensure consistent flowering in the most northern parts of its Zone 4 to 8 range, choose hardy varieties, including 'Northern Sun', 'Northern Gold', and 'Meadowlark'. Plant in nearly any soil in full sun. Although a number of insects attack forsythia, none are serious. Prune out twigs that die back.

✔ **Hydrangea:** *Hydrangea* species. Popular for their huge balls of white, pink, and blue flowers, this group of shrubs grows in nearly any soil and sun conditions. Most do prefer some mid-day shade in hot climates, however. As a rule, hydrangeas are tough as nails, although some are prone to powdery mildew in humid climates, and aphids, mites, and scale can cause some damage. Prune smooth hydrangea *(H. arborescens)* and panicle or 'PeeGee' hydrangea *(H. paniculata)* in the late winter or spring because they bloom on new growth. Bigleaf or French hydrangea *(H. macrophylla)* and oakleaf hydrangea *(H. quercifolia),* however, bloom on last year's wood, so prune them right after they bloom in the summer and avoid spring pruning.

✔ **Holly:** *Ilex* species. This huge group of mostly evergreen trees and shrubs includes everything from the classic English holly *(I. aquifolium)* to the less well-known inkberry *(I. glabra)* and hundreds of species and varieties in between. Hardiness ranges from inkberry's Zone 4 to 9 span to the tender Chinese holly *(I. cornuta),* which prefers Zones 7 to 9. Most hollies produce large crops of attractive, persistent berries, but most species bear male and female flowers on separate plants. Plant at least one of each, if you want berries, and look at the plant names for clues about the sex of the shrub. For example, Blue Boy and Blue Girl make good companions, as do China Boy and China Girl.

Hollies, in general, enjoy moist, well-drained soil and full sun, although Chinese holly withstands drought and flooding with aplomb. In windy areas and climates where the soil freezes, protect the foliage from drying out by covering with burlap or other windbreak material. Hollies suffer from many pests and diseases, including scale, spider mites, nematodes, leaf miners, various bugs and caterpillars, as well as mildew and leaf spots. The most problem-free species include Yaupon *(I. vomitoria),* inkberry, and the Foster hybrids.

Winterberry *(I. Verticillata),* one of my favorite hollies, grows in Zones 3 to 9. It loses its leaves in winter but retains the characteristic masses of red berries. Winterberry has male and female plants — you need one of each to get the berries, but one male can pollinate several females. Plant in moist, acidic soil, if possible, although winterberry can tolerate drier conditions. Prune only to shape plants and to remove old, unproductive shoots. It has few pests or disease problems. 'Jim Dandy' (male) and 'Red Sprite' (female) make good companions in colder regions. 'Southern Gentlemen' (male) and 'Winter Red' (female) in the South and Midwest.

✔ **Spirea:** *Spirea* species. These easy-going shrubs are useful for informal hedges, foundation plantings, and mixed shrub borders. Most have flat clusters of little white to pink flowers and some, such as 'Magic Carpet' and 'Goldflame', even offer three seasons of interest with their brilliant yellow foliage, floral display, and autumn color. Plant in any well-drained soil and give them full sun and regular watering in dry spells. Spireas come under attack from many pests and diseases, but these rarely prove fatal. After flowering, cut the weakest or oldest one-fourth of the shoots to the ground each year right to keep shrubs vigorous and tidy.

✔ **Lilac:** *Syringa* species. If you give your lilac moist, fertile soil and full sun, and prune it to remove spent flowers and weak growth, you can expect it to live for many years. Varieties now exist that can grow in any Zone from 3 to 9. Major problems include lilac borer, scale insects, lilac blight, and powdery mildew. The common lilac *(S. vulgaris)* offers the widest range of flower colors from white to pink and blue to deep purple. Some varieties have double flowers or extra fragrance. Meyer lilac *(S. meyeri)* and Manchurian lilac *(S. patula)* 'Miss Kim' stay smaller than the common species. Japanese tree lilac *(S. reticulata)* grows 20 to 30 feet tall and has white blooms in June.

✔ **Viburnum:** *Viburnum* species. This diverse group shares the attribute of profuse flowering and some, such as Korean spice viburnum *(V. carlesii)* and fragrant viburnum *(V. × carlcephalum),* have intoxicatingly fragrant flowers. Many also produce attractive berries, although with some species, such as Korean spice viburnum, you have to plant both male and female shrubs. Birds appreciate some native species for food. Most of these shrubs grow in any well-drained, but moisture-retentive soil. Some prefer acidic soil, while others are less fussy. Full sun to part shade suits them fine, depending on the species and climate. Species that grow in dry soils include wayfaring tree *(V. lantana),* arrowwood viburnum *(V. dentatum),* and blackhaw viburnum *(V. prunifolium).* Few pests or diseases cause serious damage.

Conifers

Needle- and cone-bearing trees and shrubs, called *conifers,* provide the backdrop for more colorful garden elements and serve as hedges, screens, and windbreaks. Their imposing size and stiff formality make many evergreen trees difficult to integrate into small home landscapes. Think twice before planting a potentially 50-foot tall Colorado blue spruce in your front yard! In larger settings, where the trees can attain full size, evergreen trees add grandeur and provide refuge for wildlife.

Shrub-sized conifers are invaluable for the year-round color and texture they add to the landscape. Some creep over the ground and drape over walls, while others grow into neat cones, pyramids, and rounded cushions. Foliage colors range from gold through a wide range of greens to silver and even purplish. Some plants appear fuzzy and soft; others, stiff and bristly.

Although you can shape many conifers into geometric and fanciful forms, most don't really require pruning at all, except to remove dead, diseased, or damaged limbs and undesirable growth that detracts from the plant's appearance. In fact, pine, spruce, and fir trees that grow in *whorls,* or have layers of branches around the trunk, will not sprout new limbs in response to pruning. To control their growth, pinch or prune their new, soft growth in late spring before it hardens, cutting into only the new tissue. Arborvitae, false cypress, cypress, juniper, and yew plants with random branching can tolerate more pruning, however, and usually will sprout new limbs to replace the ones that you remove. Conifers that usually grow into a pyramid shape with one central trunk sometimes develop additional *leaders,* or competing main trunks, at the top of the tree. Remove all but one to retain the tree shape.

As a group, conifers suffer from their share of pests and diseases. The most troublesome pests include spruce budworm, bagworms, and various caterpillars. Bacterial and fungal diseases cause blights, cankers, and root rots. See Part III for more information about these pests and diseases. The best defense against disease is to plant your trees and shrubs in the soil and sun conditions they prefer and keep them growing strong. Protect evergreens from drying winter winds wherever the ground freezes.

- **Fir:** *Abies* species. Imagine the perfect Christmas tree and you probably picture a fir. Firs have short, bristly needles, and a pyramid shape. Although popular for home landscapes, balsam *(A. balsamea),* white or concolor *(A. concolor),* and frasier *(A. fraseri)* firs grow from 30 to more than 40 feet tall and spread up to 25 feet or more at their bases when mature. Use as windbreaks or plant as groups in large areas. Firs prefer cool, moist, acidic soils and don't readily tolerate dry, alkaline soil. They require no pruning, except to remove damaged limbs. Insect pests include spruce budworm, bagworm, spider mites, and scales. Diseases include leaf and twig blights and rust fungus.

- **Cypress and falsecypress:** *Cupressocyparis* and *Chamaecyparis* species. These two closely related groups share many features, but differ in their preferred growing conditions. Falsecypress *(Chamaecyparis)* prefers cool, moist, humid conditions, while cypress *(Cupressocyparis)* enjoys heat and drier soil found in more arid climates. The hybrid between the two groups, Leyland cypress, tolerates a wider range of soils and climates than either of its parents. Cypresses have flat, scale-like foliage that's compressed against the twigs, giving the branches stringy or fan-like textures.

  Hundreds of varieties exist, including low-growing shrubs to stately trees. Leyland cypress is used widely for hedges because it grows up to

3 feet per year and tolerates salt spray and any soil except poorly drained. Hinoki *(C. obtusa)* and threadleaf *(C. pisifera)* falsecypresses have many popular varieties used in home and commercial landscapes. Cypresses require no pruning except to shape the plant or remove damaged limbs. Bagworms are the only troublesome pest. Twig blight occurs in some areas, but isn't prevalent.

✔ **Juniper:** *Juniperus* species. Versatile and tough-as-nails, junipers are justifiably among the most popular landscape shrubs. They tolerate poor, dry soil and urban and roadside conditions, and come in a seemingly infinite number of shapes, sizes, colors, and textures. Depending on the species and variety, you can find a juniper to grow in any climate from coastal Florida to the Canadian plains. Ground-hugging forms make excellent carpets for slopes and lawn substitutes. Taller varieties serve as shrubs for hedges and planting around buildings.

In cold-winter Zones 3 or 4 and warmer, look for Chinese *(J. chinensis, J. × media)*, creeping *(J. horizontalis)*, savin *(J. sabina)*, and Rocky Mountain *(J. scopulorum)* juniper varieties. Shore juniper *(J. conferta)* enjoys the heat in Zones 6 to 9 and tolerates coastal conditions. Junipers can suffer from a number of insect pests and diseases, including bagworm, scale, webworm, and borers, as can twig blight and cedar-apple rust. Creeping juniper is more disease-prone than others, but savin juniper varieties 'Calgary Carpet', 'Arcadia', 'Scandia', 'Blue Danube', and 'Broadmoor' resist juniper blight. In wet, poorly drained soils, junipers are prone to root rot.

✔ **Spruce:** *Picea* species. Give spruce trees plenty of room if you plant them in your landscape because they tend to spread widely at the base as they mature, often measuring 20 feet or more across at the ground. Most spruce have a stiff, formal, pyramid shape, which looks best in large landscapes or when the trees grow in groups. Use for windbreaks or large screens. A few dwarf varieties exist, which grow into small mounds or weeping specimens suitable for planting in home landscapes. For dwarf varieties, look for Norway *(Picea abies)* 'Little Gem', 'Pumila', 'Nidiformis' or 'Bird's Nest Spruce'; black *(P. mariana)* 'Nana'; or white spruce *(P. glauca)* 'Conica', also known as 'Dwarf Alberta Spruce'.

Spruces prefer cool climates and well-drained, but moderately-moist soil. Avoid them in dry soil and polluted urban situations. They often suffer from aphids, spruce budworm, bagworm, and other pests, as well as canker and twig blight.

✔ **Pine:** *Pinus* species. Most pines grow into large, picturesque trees up to 100 feet tall, but a few dwarf varieties stay small enough to serve in home landscapes. For small pines, seek out Japanese red pine *(Pinus densiflora)* 'Umbraculifera', Japanese white pine *(P. parviflora)* 'Glauca', Japanese black pine *(P. thunbergii)*, and mugo pine *(P. mugo)*.

Pines have long needles that give them a softer texture than most other conifers. The needles occur in bundles of two, three, or five. Pines with the same number of needles in a bundle often share other common characteristics, such as growth habits and cultural requirements. *Two-needled pines,* such as Scotch pine *(P. sylvestris),* for example, tolerate drier soil and more heat than the *five-needled species,* such as white pine *(P. strobus).* Pines don't tolerate air pollution or road salt spray, and common diseases and pests include white pine blister rust, spruce budworm, and white pine weevil.

✔ **Yew:** *Taxus* species. Yews, among the most widely grown conifers for hedges and shearing into fanciful shapes, respond to pruning by sprouting ever-denser growth. Keep in mind that most yews will grow into 30- to 60-foot trees if allowed to do so. They grow best in well-drained, fertile, moist soil and full sun to part shade, and may need protection from the winter wind in cold climates. In hot, muggy climates, look for the variety 'Tauntonii', which tolerates the summer heat better than most other yews. Pests include deer, weevils, and mealybugs, as well as blights and root rot.

✔ **Arborvitae and white cedar:** *Thuja* and *Platycladus* species. These tough trees and shrubs grow in a wide range of soils and climates, from soggy to well drained and Zones 3 to 11. They need full sun to grow lush and full. Few pests or diseases cause them serious trouble, although bagworms, spider mites, blight, and canker can show up when plants are stressed. Protect them from road salt spray and drying winter winds. As trees, arborvitae grows up to 50 feet high, but many varieties stay shrub-sized and come in many shapes, including globe, cone, column, pyramid, and weeping. Some have yellowish foliage; others are deep green. Choose a variety that matches your climate, soil, and specific landscape needs. Arborvitae makes a classic tall hedge without shearing and smaller varieties are suitable for planting around buildings.

If you want to know more about flowering and shade trees, shrubs, and conifers, and how to care for them, pick up a copy of my book, *Trees and Shrubs For Dummies* (IDG Books Worldwide, Inc.). The book also lists many of the most attractive and disease and pest-resistant varieties of each tree and shrub.

Chapter 18

Caring for Your Organic Lawn

. . . .

In This Chapter

▶ Selecting easy to care for grasses

▶ Getting your lawn started right

▶ Maintaining a lawn organically

▶ Considering lawn alternatives

. . . .

"**O**rganic lawn" seems like a contradiction in terms. Many people think that in order to grow grass, you have to douse it with herbicides, insecticides, and fungicides. That, of course, is a fallacy. It's possible — and even easy — to grow a great-looking lawn organically.

An organic lawn-care program requires an attitude adjustment, however. The secret is to think of your lawn as a mixed garden of grass and other compatible, low-growing plants that tolerate mowing (see the "Mixing it up" sidebar, later in this chapter). And, as in any other kind of gardening, your success depends on how well you lay the groundwork by preparing the soil, choosing the right grass varieties, and giving the plants what they need.

Grass plants have some unique needs that make them a bit different than other garden plants. This chapter gives you the tips you need to know about your lawn's growth habits, fertilizer needs, and pests and diseases. But after you understand the basics, you may find that organic lawn care is easier than you ever imagined.

Getting Down to Grassroots

If you dig out a wedge of turf and soil and look at it, you'll see several layers. At the top is the mostly flat grass blade, which should be bright green. That's the part of the plant that you mow every week. At the next lower level, you see rounder grass stems, then the *crown,* where the roots meet the stems. The new grass growth emerges at the ground-hugging plant crown. Under the soil, you'll find miles of roots for each grass plant. The root length is directly proportional to the plant health: The longer the roots, the healthier the plant.

Grass plants come in two basic forms — clump-forming and creeping. With *creeping* or sod-forming grasses, such as Kentucky bluegrass or Bermuda grass, horizontal stems, called stolons and rhizomes, grow out of the crown, take root, and form new plants. *Stolons* grow on top of the soil, while *rhizomes* grow underground, as shown in Figure 18-1. *Clump-forming* or noncreeping grasses, such as chewings and hard fescue, don't spread by stolons or rhizomes. If allowed to grow without mowing, these and other grasses send up a tall flowering stalk, which may produce seed.

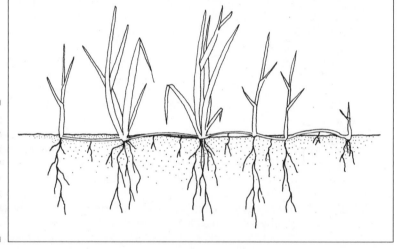

Figure 18-1:
Many grass types spread by stolons and rhizomes, which make a dense turf.

Choosing the Right Grass

Lawns are all about the grass. That may seem obvious, but very few lawn owners know the species, let alone the variety of the grass in their lawn. If you think that grass is just grass, and as long as it's green and creeps along the ground, it'll work, you may want to think again.

Organic lawn care gets a lot easier if you grow the right grass for your climate, sun, and soil conditions. You can find grasses that thrive under nearly every combination of lawn conditions. Some like it hot and dry; others prefer cool and wet. Some grasses grow in shade, while others love the sun. Finding the right grass variety for your lawn is easier than ever, too, because plant breeders have created a virtual grass seed explosion over the last half of the twentieth century. In the 1950s, fewer than half a dozen varieties of Kentucky bluegrass and perennial ryegrass existed. Now you can find hundreds of each.

Turfgrass species (grasses that are used for lawns) are classified as either cool season or warm season. The *cool-season grasses* grow best north of the so-called *bluegrass line* — an imaginary border that stretches from the middle of North Carolina, through the centers of Arkansas and New Mexico, and into southern California. The *warm-season grasses* grow best south of that line.

Too cool, man

Cool-season grasses prefer moist, cold-winter climates with short summers. Grasses that thrive in such climates grow most actively in the cool spring and fall months and may turn brown and become dormant during extended hot, dry periods in summers. Although traditionally grown north of the bluegrass line, cool-season grasses also grow well at higher elevations and in other cooler microclimates south of the bluegrass line. (Jump to Chapter 3 for information about microclimates.)

Trying to grow cool-season grasses outside of their preferred climate, however, adds up to more maintenance and trouble. These species need frequent watering in arid climates and are prone to disease and insect attack in hot summer spots.

The main grass species and recommended varieties of each that grow in the north include the following. See the "Reading the seed label" sidebar for an explanation of grass varieties.

- **Kentucky bluegrass** is known for its cold hardiness, fine-textured blades, and rich green color. Recommended varieties include 'Glade', 'Eclipse', and 'Midnight'.

- **Perennial ryegrass** is tough enough to be used on athletic fields. Best new varieties include 'Manhattan II', 'Pennant', and 'Repell'.

- **Tall fescue** is a good low-maintenance grass that can be allowed to grow tall. Look for 'Amigo', 'Rebel II', and 'Wrang'.

- **Chewings fescue** grows well in light shade and tolerates cold and drought. Good varieties include 'Banner II', 'Jamestown II', and 'SR5000'.

- **Hard fescue** is a low-maintenance species good for the far north. Best varieties include 'Aurora', 'Biljart', and 'Scaldis'.

- **Red fescue, also known as creeping fescue,** withstands shade and drought well. Best varieties include 'Claudia', 'Flyer', and 'Shademaster'.

- **Bent grass** is the very fine textured (and very fussy) grass used mainly on golf putting greens. Best varieties include 'Penncross', 'Regent', and 'Bardot'.

Reading the seed label

Plant breeders have worked hard to produce grasses that thrive under different conditions. But one particular variety can't do it all. For that reason, most grass seed and turf is sold as combinations of grasses that complement each other. Grass combinations are described as one of the following:

✔ **Straights** are seed packages or sod that are made up of a single grass variety, such as 'Tiffway II' Bermuda grass or 'DelMar' St. Augustine grass.

✔ **Blends** contain several varieties of only a single species, such as 'Amigo', 'Rebel II', and 'Wrangler' tall fescue.

✔ **Mixtures** contain more than one grass species. Typical mixtures of cool-season grasses include Kentucky bluegrass, fescue, and perennial ryegrass.

Blends and mixtures offer you the most uniform and versatile lawn because some of the grasses will thrive in sunny spots, for example, while another succeeds in the shade under a tree.

Improved varieties are the best value for your organic lawn because they resist disease, stay darker green with less fertilizer, and tolerate a wider range of moisture and temperature conditions.

The labels on grass seed all look pretty much the same and by law must contain consistent information. The label lists the percentage of each seed by weight, its name, place where it came from, and what percent of the seed you can expect to sprout. In addition, the label tells you what percentage of weed seed and inert matter the package contains and when the seed was tested for germination. The most important things to look for are improved varieties, current year test date, and weed content of less than 1 percent.

Some like it hot

Warm-season grasses thrive where winters are mild and summer temperatures stay above 85 degrees for months on end. Most don't appreciate freezing weather and respond by turning brown. They grow vigorously, especially during the summer.

Warm season grass species and recommended varieties for the South include the following:

✔ **Bahia grass** makes a thick, drought tolerant lawn in the Gulf states. Good varieties include 'Pensacola' and 'Wilmington'.

✔ **Bermuda grass** is the workhorse grass of the South. It grows fast and can withstand hot and dry weather. Good varieties include 'Midiron', 'Tiffway II', 'NuMex', and 'Sahara'.

✔ **Centipede grass** is called lazy man's grass because it needs less mowing and water than other grasses. Try 'AU Centennial' and 'Oklawn'.

✔ **Carpet grass** has thick and coarse blades, but it grows well in the coastal plain region. There are no improved varieties.

✔ **St. Augustine grass** may be the most attractive of all warm season grasses, but it does require frequent watering and feeding to stay that way. Look for 'DelMar', 'Floralawn', and 'Jade'.

✔ **Zoysia grass** stands more shade than most warm season southern grasses, but is slow to establish. Improved varieties include 'Emerald' and 'SR 9100'.

Regional preferences

Dividing all the grasses into simple warm and cold-season categories leaves out the fact that climates vary in many ways other than temperature. For that reason, it helps to divide the United States into nine different turf-growing zones, as shown in Figure 18-2. Each zone has specific grass species best suited to grow in its climate.

Best grass for trouble spots

Sure, anybody can grow a lawn when conditions are perfect. But when they're not so great, you can stack the odds in your favor by choosing grasses proven to succeed under less than optimal conditions.

Shade: Many grasses tolerate at least a bit of shade. The best grasses include the following:

✔ Cool-season: Rough bluegrass, fine fescue, tall fescue

✔ Warm-season: St. Augustine grass, centipede grass, Bahia grass

Drought: Vigorous, deep-rooted grass species tolerate drought the best. They include the following species:

✔ Cool-season: Tall fescue, perennial ryegrass, fine fescue

✔ Warm-season: Bermuda grass, zoysia grass, Bahia grass

Heat: Of course, warm season grasses are, as a rule, more heat-tolerant than cool-season grasses. But some cool-season grasses are more heat-tolerant than others, as follows:

✔ Cool-season: Perennial ryegrass, tall fescue, fine fescue, Kentucky bluegrass

✔ Warm-season: Bermuda grass, centipede grass, zoysia grass, St. Augustine grass

Cold: Some cool season grasses excel in their ability to survive winter. Warm-season grasses differ quite a bit in their ability to withstand cooler temperatures in the southern U.S.:

✔ Cool-season: Kentucky bluegrass, Canada bluegrass, fine fescue, creeping bentgrass

✔ Warm-season: Bermuda grasses, zoysia grass, hybrid St. Augustine grass

Figure 18-2:
The U.S.
can be
divided
into nine
different
turf-growing
zones, based
on climate.

✔ **Zone 1, the coastal west,** is characterized by dry summers and cool wet winters. Grow cool-season grasses, such as Kentucky bluegrass, tall fescue, fine fescue, and perennial ryegrass.

✔ **Zone 2, the western transitional zone,** has long dry summers and moderate winters. You can grow either warm- or cool-season grasses here. Hybrid Bermuda grass is popular for the summer. For winter color, sow seeds of a cool-season grass, such as ryegrass or tall fescue, over your warm-season grass lawn when it starts to turn brown or yellow in the fall.

✔ **Zone 3, the arid southwest,** has long, hot, dry summers and dry winters, as well. Plant Bermuda grass or zoysia grass for summer in low elevation areas and overseed with ryegrass or fescue for winter color. In high elevations, plant drought-resistant buffalo grass.

✔ **Zone 4, the Great Plains,** is the home of two native turfgrasses — buffalo grass and blue grama grass. Plant them for a low-maintenance lawn. Use Bermuda grass or zoysia in the southern area of the region, and northern grasses, such as Kentucky bluegrass or perennial ryegrass in the northern regions.

✔ **Zone 5, the Midwest,** offers moist, humid summers and cold winters. Any cool season grasses will grow here, such as Kentucky bluegrass, perennial ryegrass, or any of the fescues. Warm-season zoysia may be grown in southernmost areas.

✔ **Zone 6, the northeast,** has a climate similar to the Midwest, except with cooler summers and the longer winters. Grow the same types of grasses — all cool season species, especially Kentucky bluegrass and perennial ryegrass.

✔ **Zone 7, the eastern transitional zone,** is an area where the border between north and south blurs. Both warm-season grasses, such as Bermuda grass, and cool-season grasses, such as Kentucky bluegrass grow here.

✔ **Zone 8, the central southeast,** has a warm, humid, and wet climate year 'round. Although the cool-season grass tall fescue may be grown in high elevation areas, this is primarily warm-season country, best suited for Bermuda grass, zoysia, and centipede grass.

✔ **Zone 9, the Gulf coast,** is even warmer and wetter than the central southeast. Along with Bermuda grass and zoysia, you can grow centipede grass, Bahia grass, and St. Augustine grass.

Preparing the Soil

When you're planting a new lawn, you have only one chance to get it right. After you plant the grass, you can't easily improve the soil or add amendments as you can with your flower or vegetable gardens. That's why it's so important to start with the best soil possible. Prepare your soil well in advance of your actual planting day and give yourself and your soil plenty of time — you won't regret it. Here are the basic soil preparation steps to follow:

✔ **Test for pH.** It should be neutral to slightly acidic — pH 6 to 7 is best. Add enough lime or sulfur to bring the pH to the proper level. See Chapter 4 for instructions.

✔ **Add organic matter.** Starting the lawn from scratch offers you a perfect opportunity to improve drainage and moisture-holding ability and possibly even disease-fighting power. Spread a 1-inch layer of peat moss or shredded compost and till in to a depth of 6 inches.

✔ **Correct any potential drainage problems.** Install drain tiles if necessary. Wet spots attract disease.

✔ **Remove every single weed root.** If you don't, you can be sure that every one of them will sprout. Better to take the time to deal with them once than to struggle with them over and over during the life of your lawn. For the best results, let the prepared soil rest for a week or two to allow weeds and weed seeds to sprout, then use a hoe (see Chapter 6) to slice them off just under the soil.

✔ **Rake it smooth and level.** Hollows, ruts, and dips cause uneven turf growth and result in wet or dry patches that encourage disease and attract insect pests.

For more about improving your soil, changing pH, and adding organic matter and other amendments, flip to Part II of this book.

Planting the Lawn

Planting a lawn is like standup comedy: Timing is everything. If it's at all possible, plant during the prime grass-growing time for your area. In the northern U.S., late summer or early spring is best. In the south, the best time is late spring or late summer. As a rule, it's okay to plant anytime when you can count on about a month of temperate and moist weather to follow. That should give your grass enough time to get off to a good start.

If you need a lawn in a hurry, but it's the wrong time to plant, borrow a trick that many building contractors use around new homes. Sow a temporary crop of annual ryegrass. It will come up fast and hold your place against weeds until you can replace it with a permanent lawn. Annual ryegrass won't survive a freezing winter, but it can help prevent erosion and discourage weed seeds from sprouting.

Choosing seed versus sod

You can plant a lawn in two primary ways — from seed or sod. *Sod* is already established turf that's grown on a sod farm, harvested in strips with a thin layer of soil, and sold for instant lawns.

Most people assume that starting a lawn from sod is easier, faster, and more reliable than seeding. Well, at least one of those assumptions is true. It is faster. With sod, you can have a great-looking lawn in one day. But *sodding* (installing sod) still requires just as much soil preparation work as seeding. And sodding requires even more aftercare. Sod costs much more than seeds. Variety selection is more limited than with seed, too. You won't find the same number of shade tolerant, disease- and insect-resistant varieties available in sod. And sod is a *monoculture,* which consists only of grass without other beneficial low-growing plants. Monocultures tend to have more disease and pest problems than lawns containing a mix of plant species. On the other hand, if you plant sod properly and nurse it through its establishment period, your lawn will start out entirely free of undesirable weedy plants, such as dandelions and thistle.

If you start your lawn with seed, weeds can and will sprout along with the grass. That's the major disadvantage to seed versus sod. But you have many more improved varieties of seed to choose from and that's very important when you want to avoid pest and disease controls on your organic lawn. Choosing seed also allows you to add the seeds of other desirable lawn plants, such as clover and white yarrow. (See the "Mixing it up" sidebar in this chapter.) Seed is much less expensive than sod, too.

A third planting option exists for some southern grasses — sprigs or plugs. *Sprigs* are individual pieces of stolons or rhizomes that grow into plants that spread to form a continuous lawn. *Plugs* are just tiny patches of sod that are spaced out along the soil. Although less expensive than complete sod cover, plugs and sprigs still require thorough soil preparation and aftercare.

Installing sod

For best results, sodding has two important rules to follow: Get the soil thoroughly moist and work quickly. It's also a good idea to get the ground as level as possible and make sure the soil is good to go before the sod arrives. You don't want to let it sit and dry out in a heap.

Store sod in a cool area out of the sun and cover it lightly with a tarp to keep it moist until you can install it. Mist it with water, if necessary, but don't soak it. Wet sod is heavy to work with and may fall apart. It's best to get it on the prepared ground within a day or two after delivery.

To lay the sod, start at a straight edge, such as a driveway or sidewalk. Lay the sod pieces end to end, making sure they butt up against each other tightly with no bare soil showing. When you've finished one row, offset the beginning of the next row so that the starting ends of each row are staggered instead of in a line.

Mixing it up

Historically, lawns were not composed solely of grasses. Many other low-growing plants, including herbs and wildflowers, grew in lawns, adding color, drought tolerance, and habitat for beneficial insects and microorganisms.

Researchers at Oregon State University, along with the owners of Nichols Garden Nursery of Albany, Oregon, have developed several seed mixes for what they call low-maintenance, ecologically sound lawns — or *ecolawns* for short. The blends contain 80 to 90 percent grass seed and the rest is made up of clovers, herbs, and wildflowers that withstand mowing and foot traffic. For more information check the following sources:

✔ Contact Nichols Garden Nursery at 1190 Old Salem Road NE, Albany, Oregon 97321-4580,

by phone at 866-408-4851, by fax at 800-231-5306 or via the Internet at www.nicholsgardennursery.com).

✔ Visit the Oregon State University's information page at http://eesc.orst.edu/agcomwebfile/garden/Lawn/ecolawn.html.

✔ Contact Hobbs & Hopkins, Ltd., which also sells ecology lawn mixes. Write them at 1712 SE Ankeny St., Portland, OR 97214, phone 800-345-3295, or visit their Web site at www.teleport.com/~lawn/index.html).

Even after the entire area has been covered, your job is far from over. Aftercare is critical for success. Follow these steps:

1. **Roll the entire area with a lawn roller to make sure the sod is in good contact with the soil beneath it.**

   You can rent a roller from any tool rental agency.

2. **Spread a small amount of topsoil over the sod, and work it into the cracks between strips with a broom.**

3. **Now water — and keep watering!**

   The sod needs pampering until the roots dig deep into the soil to forage for their own water. Don't let the sod dry out for four weeks.

4. **Mow the grass when it starts growing vigorously.**

Seed-sowing basics

How much seed do you need? That depends on the type of grass you're planting. The seed of various lawn grasses vary tremendously in size, and thus in the amount of seed needed to cover a square foot. Use the number on the box to figure how much you need, and buy about one-quarter again as much as you think you need.

Prepare the soil as described in the "Preparing the Soil" section in this chapter, and then go over it one more time with a rake to remove all rocks and make the surface as level as possible. Water the area thoroughly.

You can sow the seed with a broadcast or drop spreader. A *broadcast spreader* spins the seeds out in a wide pattern. A *drop seeder* places the seeds in a band between the wheels. If the lawn area is small, you can also sow the seed by hand. No matter how you do it, be careful to get uniform coverage. Here's how:

1. **Divide the seed into two equal lots.**

   If you need to spread 20 pounds of seed, for example, divide the seed into two 10-pound applications.

2. **Adjust your spreader to deliver seed at half the rate recommended on the seed package.**

3. **Sow the first half of the seed across the lawn in rows.**

4. **Sow the second half of the seed in rows at right angles to the first until the whole lawn has been covered.**

5. **Rake very lightly to mix seeds into the top $\frac{1}{8}$ to $\frac{1}{4}$ inch of soil.**

6. **Roll with a water-filled roller.**

To speed germination, mulch the area with organic materials, such as finely shredded compost or dried manure, topsoil, finely chopped straw, or even a thin layer of sawdust. Apply it at no more than ¼ inch thick and as evenly as possible. Avoid hay and other mulches, which contain weed seeds.

For complete germination, you must keep the top layer of soil constantly moist. This is crucial. Soak the soil to a 6-inch depth after sowing, then lightly sprinkle by hand or with a sprinkler as often as three to four times daily until the young grass is established. Letting the tender grass seedlings dry out will kill them.

Allow the young grass to reach its maximum recommended height before mowing. Read the "There's more to mowing" section to find the best mowing height for your lawn grass.

Maintaining an Organic Lawn

Organic lawns require a little more attention than chemically treated lawns. Maintaining turf without chemicals requires that you understand a little bit about the habits of grass and the problems that plague it. After that, it's simply a matter of applying the organic principles that you use in the rest of your garden to the lawn.

There's more to mowing

The lawn mower is your most important turf-maintenance tool. Yes, you use it every week to whack the grass back, but a mower can accomplish much more than cutting the grass down to size. Using the mower properly helps the grass to grow thicker. It can reduce the weed population and even feed the turf.

Your lawn likes to be mowed. The grass plant has evolved to benefit from regular trimming. Grass grows from the base of the plant down near the soil, so the tops of the plants are old growth. Trimming them off triggers the release of chemicals inside the plant that encourage the plant to spread. That's why regular mowing makes a good thick lawn.

For organic lawn care, hauling out the mower once a week on Saturday and mowing at two inches just won't cut it, if you'll pardon the pun. Every type of grass has its own preferred height, as shown in the "Best mowing heights" sidebar. For the best results, mow when the grass is no more than 50 percent taller than its optimal height, as shown in Figure 18-3. For example, if your grass should grow to 3 inches, mow it when it reaches 4½ inches tall.

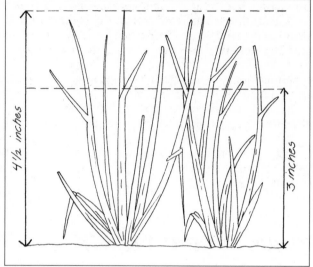

Figure 18-3:
Mow the
grass when
it reaches
50 percent
taller
than the
recom-
mended
height.

The best mowing height for each grass also varies from season to season. You may tend to mow at the same time and at the same height every week, but that practice ignores a vital fact — the lawn doesn't grow at the same rate from month to month. In the northern U.S., the grass spurts in spring, slows in summer, and resumes vigorous growth in fall. In the southern U.S., warm-season grasses start slowly in spring, increase in vigor though the summer, and begin a slow decline in late summer. You should mow more often when the grass is growing faster. The alternative is to cut off more blade with each mowing, but that's not a good idea. Cutting more than ⅓ of the blade in a single mowing damages the plant.

Vary the height of the cut slightly according to season, as well. Mow higher by about ½ inch in times of stress. That's summer in north, spring and fall in south. That helps the plant to survive.

Here's how to get the best cut from your mower:

- ✔ **Make sure the blade is sharp.** Sharpen your blade at least twice per season.

- ✔ **Vary the mowing direction once a month to avoid soil compaction.**

- ✔ **Don't mow when the grass is wet.**

- ✔ **Overlap by about ⅓ of the width of the deck with each pass**

- ✔ **Clean the grass off the mower after each mowing.**

One of the best things to happen to the organic lawn was the *mulching mower,* which pulverizes grass clippings into smaller pieces than a conventional mower. That's because grass clippings are probably the best fertilizer your lawn can get. When they've been chopped up in to little bits, they begin to break down into useful nitrogen almost as soon as they hit the ground. Grass clippings provide free and natural nitrogen, about one pound of it per 1,000 square feet per year.

Watering

People spend a lot of time, effort, and money keeping their lawn watered. In many parts of the country, that effort is totally wasted because the lawn can survive the summer without any supplemental water.

Many types of turfgrass have developed a mechanism to withstand periods of drought — they enter dormancy. They stop growing and turn brown. But after the rains return, the grass springs back to life. Sometimes, raising an organic lawn means putting up with an unattractive lawn for a while instead of using precious water resources.

If and when you do irrigate your lawn, you must water deeply and slowly. Standing out on the front lawn in the evening with a hose in hand does more harm than good. You'd have to stand out there for hours and hours to apply an adequate amount of water. Shallow sprinkling makes the roots lazy — if they get a little bit of water regularly, they become conditioned to staying near the surface of the soil. If you stop watering, your lawn will die of drought because the roots haven't grown deep enough to forage for their own water.

Every time you water your lawn, water long enough to moisten the soil to a depth of 6 to 12 inches. The amount of time that takes depends not only on the sprinkler, but also on the type of soil under the lawn. For example, it may take only an hour for 1 inch of water to penetrate sandy soil, but it can take as much as 10 hours for the same amount of water to soak into clay soil (see Chapter 4).

It's a good idea to push a shovel down into your lawn to check the depth of water penetration once in awhile until you figure out how long it takes to water your lawn thoroughly. Simply dig out a wedge of soil, look at the water level, and replace the wedge in the lawn.

It's also important to apply water slowly enough so that it doesn't puddle or run off your lawn. For that reason, the heavier your soil, the more slowly you should water. Look for a sprinkler with a low flow rate of less than ¼ inch of water per hour, especially if you have clay soil. On such heavy soils, you may need to cycle your watering by turning the water on for 15 minutes, off for 15 minutes, then on again, and so on.

Best mowing heights

Each grass species prefers to grow within a particular height range. In general, mow at the lower end of the range when the grass is actively growing and at the upper end of the range during times of stress or slow growth.

Cool-season grasses:

- Bent grasses: ¼ to ¾ inches
- Chewings fescue: 1 to 2 inches
- Hard fescue: 1 to 2 inches
- Red fescue: 1½ to 2 inches
- Sheep fescue: 2 to 4 inches
- Tall fescue: 2½ to 3 inches
- Kentucky bluegrass: 2 to 3 inches

- Perennial ryegrass: 1½ to 2½ inches

Warm-season grasses:

- Bahia grass: 2 to 3 inches
- Bermuda grass: ½ to 1 inches
- Blue grama grass: 2 to 3 inches
- Buffalo grass: 2 to 3 inches
- Carpet grass: 1 to 2 inches
- Centipede grass: 1 to 2 inches
- St. Augustine grass: 1 to 3 inches
- Zoysia grass: ½ to 1 inches

What kind of sprinkler should you choose? In general, high-quality oscillating and impulse sprinklers offer the most uniform coverage and cover the most ground.

Feeding the lawn

Grass needs more nitrogen than any other nutrient for strong growth. And, because it grows almost continuously, it needs a constant supply. Grass clippings themselves provide some natural fertilizer, but you can use several other organic materials to feed your lawn, as well. Natural fertilizers contain nitrogen that doesn't dissolve readily in water, but require a little help from soil microorganisms to become available for plants. That's good. It means that the nitrogen is released slowly, and, consequently, the lawn grows slowly and steadily. The problem with most synthetic chemical lawn fertilizers is that they tend to release lots of nitrogen all at once, which makes the lawn grow fast at first, adding to your mowing chores. Chemical lawn fertilizers are also one of the largest sources of water pollution in the country.

Your lawn probably needs less nitrogen than you think. You can figure out how much nitrogen to apply by using the following steps:

1. **Find the amount of actual nitrogen required by the type of grass in your lawn.**

Cool-season fescues need 1 to 3 pounds of nitrogen per year per 1,000 square feet. Kentucky bluegrass and perennial ryegrass need 2 to 3 pounds, and bent grasses prefer 2 to 6 pounds. Warm-season blue grama and buffalo grasses need only ½ to 1 pound of nitrogen; Bermuda and carpet grasses need 1 to 3 pounds; Bahia, centipede, and zoysia need 2 to 3 pounds; and St. Augustine grass needs 3 to 6 pounds.

If you don't know the predominant type of grass in your lawn, dig up a sample and take it into your local extension office or a full-service nursery for identification. Or start with one pound of actual nitrogen per 1,000 square feet twice a year. That's a safe maintenance dose.

2. **Find the percent of actual nitrogen in the fertilizer you want to use.**

   See Chapter 5 for naturally nitrogen-rich fertilizers and the percent nitrogen they contain.

3. **Plug those numbers into the following formula to determine exactly how much material you need to feed your lawn: Pounds of nitrogen that grass requires per year ÷ percent of nitrogen in the fertilizer = pounds of fertilizer required per year per 1,000 square feet.**

   For example, Kentucky bluegrass requires 2 pounds of actual nitrogen per year, per 1,000 square feet. A bag of 10-6-4 organic lawn fertilizer contains 10 percent actual nitrogen. And 2 divided by .10 (10 percent converted to decimal) equals 20. So 1,000 square feet of Kentucky bluegrass would require 20 pounds of 10-6-4 fertilizer per year.

4. **Divide the pounds of fertilizer required per year by the number of applications you plan to make.**

   For example, if you will fertilize your lawn twice, divide the answer you get in Step 3 by 2 to find the amount you need for each application.

You can find a good supply of organic turf fertilizer in nearly any garden center. Many stores offer bagged mixes containing compost, manures, rock powders, and perhaps leather or cottonseed meals. One of the best, and least expensive, turf fertilizers is dried poultry waste. You can also mix your own, using alfalfa meal or dried blood for nitrogen, rock phosphate to provide phosphorus, and greensand for potassium. See Chapter 5 for more on fertilizers and how to read a fertilizer bag.

Knowing when to feed

Most folks go into a lawn feeding frenzy at the first sign of spring, but for most of the country, that's not the best time to feed the grass. Sure, early season fertilizing gets your lawn off to a fast start, but it will do the same for the weeds that are sprouting at the same time. It's better to fertilize in autumn in cold climates. That helps the grass grow strong and packs away some nutrients for the following year.

In warmer climates, the best time to feed is late spring, after the grass breaks out of dormancy and begins to grow again. Warm-season grasses need regular feeding to survive the stressful summer months. Cold-season grasses can usually get by with just one or two feedings per year.

If you want to green up your lawn quickly and naturally, use a hose-end sprayer to apply liquid seaweed. The iron in the seaweed encourages a rich green color.

Thinking about thatch

As grass plant parts die, they can form a tangled mat of undecomposed or partially decomposed organic matter on the surface of the soil called *thatch*, as shown in Figure 18-4. A little thatch is a good thing. In fact, if it's less than ¼ to ½ inch thick, thatch may even be helpful because it helps to cool and cushion the soil and conserve moisture. Thick thatch may cause problems, however. If the layer is more than ½ inch thick, it blocks water and nutrients from reaching the soil and provides a cozy home for turf-destroying insects and diseases.

Figure 18-4:
Thatch is a layer of undecomposed plants that blocks water and nutrients from reaching the soil.

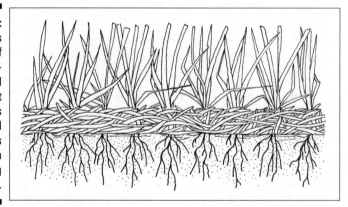

What causes thatch to become a problem? Usually, it's chemicals. On an organic lawn, the soil teems with decomposing microorganisms and earthworms. They work hard to break down the organic matter and improve the soil in the process. But on a lawn that's been fed a steady diet of herbicides and pesticides, the soil activity is decreased, if not totally halted. With nothing to break down the thatch, it builds up to harmful levels, which in turn prevents water and chemicals from reaching the roots, which in turn makes the grass look bad, which in turn causes lawn owners to add more chemicals. You get the picture.

If thatch builds up on your lawn, remove it, or *de-thatch,* the lawn. For small areas, you can use a thatch rake, sometimes called a *cavex rake,* to scratch the thatch from the soil. This is backbreaking work, however, so try it only on small lawns. For large areas, rent a *dethatcher* — also called a vertical mower. This gasoline-powered device cuts the thatch and lifts it to the surface where you can easily rake it up and haul it away.

Loosening up the soil

Sometimes thatch is the result of compacted soil because, as you probably know, the soil under a lawn takes a lot of abuse. You walk and run over it, stand on it, run a heavy mower over it regularly, and sometimes even drive over it. The result is compaction that slows the growth of the grass. With lawns, we don't get the opportunity to turn and condition the soil every year. But there's a specialized way to cure lawn compaction and invigorate the soil. It's called aeration, and it's especially useful for the organic lawn.

Aeration is simply the process of poking holes in the turf. When it's done right, you remove cores of compacted soil, leaving room for air, water, and nutrients to penetrate. On small lawns, you can aerate by hand. For under $20 you can buy a hand aerator that uses foot power to remove cores of soil. For large lawns you can rent a power aerator from the local tool rental shop, as shown in Figure 18-5. Steer it over the lawn like a lawnmower as it jams its tines into the turf, removing cores of soil in the process. With either implement, you can then break up the cores and leave them on the surface of the lawn, or toss them into the compost heap. If you use your lawn heavily, aerate once a year — just like they do down at the ball field.

Topdressing

There's one very important organic lawn care practice that most lawn owners neglect — *topdressing,* which is simply spreading a thin layer of organic matter over the lawn. No, it's not fertilizing per se, but it does improve the soil and can provide nutrients, depending on the topdressing material used. Topdressing is vital because you don't normally get an opportunity to improve the soil under the lawn the way you do with annual vegetable and flower gardens. Because you don't dig up the lawn every year, the only way to do it is from the top down.

Topdressing is a simple process: In autumn, spread a very thin — about ¼ deep — layer of organic matter over the lawn. Use topsoil, shredded compost, peat moss, or any other organic matter. The material works its way down through the sod, with the help of earthworms and other critters, to improve the texture of the soil. You can make the process even more effective by aerating the turf first. See the "Loosening up the soil" section.

Figure 18-5:
Rent a gas-powered core aerator to open up compacted soil.

Weeding

For some reason, folks get agitated about weeds in their turf. They pour on the herbicides, often before weeds even show up. But weeds in the lawn can be managed using many of the techniques that you use on weeds in other parts of your landscape.

The best way to defeat weeds is to grow a healthy, thick sod. Fertilizing, watering, and mowing properly all make the grass thicker, which makes it tougher for weeds to get a foothold. In fact, correct mowing alone can help to control certain types of weeds. University experiments show that mowing a bluegrass lawn at a height of 2 inches helps to reduce the amount of crabgrass in a lawn significantly. Mowing your lawn higher helps the grass outcompete low-growing weeds, such as crabgrass and creeping Charlie.

You can also use old-fashioned elbow grease. When you find weeds in the vegetable garden or perennial bed, what do you do? You pull 'em or chop them out. You can do the same in the lawn. Long-handled, specialty weeding tools for the lawn, such as the Houn Dog Weeder and the Speedy Weeder, make a surprisingly fast and easy job of pulling dandelions, plantain, and other lawn weeds.

Take the time to learn a little bit about your weedy enemies. Study the weeds in your lawn and discover what they want — then try to deprive them of it. Here's a lowdown on the usual suspects:

- ✔ **Annual weeds reproduce by seeds.** One way to control the spread of annual weeds is to bag the clippings when annual weeds are setting seed, rather than letting them fall to the turf and germinate. If you see weeds with flowers on them, their seeds won't be far behind!

- ✔ **Perennial weeds spread by roots, tuber, stolons, or rhizomes, as well as seeds.** Hit perennials where they live by digging out the roots and underground parts to remove them. You may be surprised at how easy that can be with a long-handled weeder.

Recently, some natural herbicides have become available that give organic lawn care owners a lucky break. In the mid-1980s, researchers discovered that corn gluten meal, which is used in pet and livestock food, is a highly effective natural turf herbicide. It works as a pre-emergence to kill sprouting plantain, creeping bentgrass, dandelion, and many other weed seeds. Apply 25 pounds per 1,250 square feet in spring before weeds begin to sprout. Don't apply it to newly seeded lawns, however.

For already growing weeds, you can also try Sharpshooter — a broad-spectrum, soap-based organic herbicide that kills all vegetation on contact. Use it with caution because it kills grass as well as weeds. For more on weeds and weeding, turn to Chapter 6.

Perhaps the best way to deal with weeds is to change your definition of them. Take clover, for example. Today it's a weed to most people, but not too long ago it was considered an important part of a good lawn. Just because it's not a grass plant doesn't mean it doesn't belong in the lawn. It stays green through tough weather, recovers nicely from mowing, is soft and cushiony, and, unlike grass, it increases the fertility of the soil by taking nitrogen from the air and making it available to plant roots in the soil. Other so-called weeds, such as yarrow and Roman chamomile, attract beneficial insects. See the "Mixing it up" sidebar for more on mixed lawn plantings.

Managing pests

Although a long list of insects, including billbugs, turfgrass *Ataenius,* and chinch bugs, may chow down on grass, only a few pests really do serious damage to turfgrass. And organic treatments exist for all of them.

The most notorious and damaging turf pest is the grub, which is an immature beetle that lives in the soil. Grubs, especially the larvae of Japanese beetles, can do a number on turf. They feast on grass roots and kill the plants in the process. Pull up a patch of sod and if you see a dozen grubs per square foot it's time to take action. What can you do organically? Plenty.

First, there's *milky spore disease,* which is a bacteria that infects and kills grubs. Also known as *Baccillus popilliae,* it was one of the first biological insecticides. Although it's been used for 50 years, grubs have not yet developed a resistance to it. Apply at a rate of 4 ounces per 1,000 square feet any time the grubs are active. It works best in areas where the soil temperature remains above 70 degrees for several months a year. Flip to Chapter 9 for more on milky spore disease and other safe pesticides.

Beneficial nematodes are the latest control to be enlisted against grubs. Spray these microscopic worms onto the soil and they begin killing grubs within 48 hours and continue their grub-killing duty for months. In the process, they also eliminate cutworms and armyworms. The only drawback is that they are rather expensive. For more on beneficial nematodes, see Chapter 8.

Intensive turfgrass breeding has yielded several new varieties of grass that actually resist damage from greenbug, armyworm, billbug, cutworm, and sob webworm. Look for tall fescue variety 'Apache', and several perennial ryegrass varieties, including 'Premier', 'All Star', 'Cowboy', 'Prelude', 'Sunrise', 'Pennant', 'Citation II' and 'Repell'.

Getting rid of diseases

There's no excuse for putting up with disease on the home lawn. For every turf disease, you can find a grass variety resistant to it.

Ironically, highly maintained, chemically treated lawns are more susceptible to disease. Why? Because in rich, natural organic soil, beneficial organisms keep disease-causing fungi in check. Applications of pesticides, fungicides, and herbicides, however, kill off the beneficial microorganisms, which allows the disease fungi to grow unchecked. So the first step in disease prevention is to stop applying chemicals.

Other disease prevention strategies include the following:

- **Cut your lawn properly.** Keep the mower blades sharp, mow high, cut when the grass is no more than 50 percent taller than optimum, and mow only when the grass is dry. See the "There's more to mowing" section in this chapter for more tips.

- **Eliminate excessive shade.** Turf grasses like full sun, although some will tolerate light shade. Deeper shade, however, weakens the grass and makes it more vulnerable to insects and diseases.

- **Don't over-fertilize or over-water.** Too much of a good thing can lead to soft, weak growth, which invites trouble.

✔ **Aerate the soil.** Grass roots, water, nutrients, and air can't easily penetrate compacted soil. Loosen it up with an aerator (see the "Loosening
up the soil" section earlier in this chapter).

✔ **Topdress with compost.** Composted organic matter contains natural
disease-fighting organisms. Compost also improves the drainage and
water-holding capacity of soil and provides food for soil-building worms
and other microorganisms. You can also use compost or manure tea on
your lawn. See Chapter 5 for details on how to make it.

If disease does strike, you can use a soap-based organic fungicide, such as
Soap Shield, to eliminate many fungus diseases. Research has shown that
the microorganisms called *Actinomycetes* are especially effective at battling
diseases. They are naturally present in compost and may be found in some
natural fertilizers. Check out Chapter 10 for more on lawn diseases and how
to control them.

It's also important to correct the environmental conditions that allow the
disease to strike. Those conditions may include shade, poor drainage, and
infertile soil. Go back to the "Preparing the soil" section in this chapter for
tips on getting your lawn off to a healthy start.

Lawn Alternatives

Lawns just don't belong in some places, and trying to grow grass where it won't
thrive is just going to cause heartache. Grass doesn't like shade. It doesn't
like wet roots. Sometimes it can't stand too much foot traffic. It doesn't like
hard and dry soil. In situations like these, you may do better to find a substitute
for turfgrass that enjoys the conditions you have.

Using low-maintenance grass

If you really want a lawn, but your conditions just don't suit most turfgrasses,
consider a tough-as-nails native grass instead. Two native grasses — buffalo
grass and blue grama grass — work well in hot dry conditions with little
maintenance. You can mow and maintain them as a lawn or let them grow
as meadow grasses.

✔ Buffalo grass is a Plains native and, as such, has adapted to survive with
very little water. It makes an attractive fine-textured lawn when watered
and mown and also as an ornamental prairie grass when allowed to go
dormant in periods of low rainfall. For the best-looking lawn, mow it
high — 2 to 3 inches high — to discourage weeds. Despite it's tolerance
to heat, sun, and dry, hard soil, buffalo grass doesn't like shade or sandy,
wet soils.

✔ Blue grama grass is another North American native. This bunch-type grass forms a dense sod of fine-bladed grass. During drought, it goes dormant and turns brown. It requires little fertilizer, no watering, and only infrequent mowing while still surviving extreme heat and cold.

Uncovering ground covers

Although breeders have made some species of grass more shade tolerant, turfgrass is still basically a sun-loving plant. Trying to grow grass in deep shade is just an invitation to aggravation. You're better off giving up on grass in those areas and growing a shade-loving ground cover instead. Good choices include the following:

✔ **Ajuga** grows only about 2 to 6 inches high and has slender, deep-green or purplish leaves on mounding plants with blue, purple, red, or white blossoms.

✔ **Lily of the valley** spreads by underground runners in heavy shade, forming large colonies of 8- to 10-inch-long leaves. It produces very fragrant blooms in late spring and is hardy in the coldest climates.

✔ **Liriope** sports narrow, grass-like leaves. It forms creeping mounds and blooms in clusters of lavender flowers in summer.

✔ **Pachysandra** is an easy-to-grow, spreading, attractive foliage plant that does best in damp shade.

✔ **Periwinkle** creeps over the ground, forming large mats of shiny, oval, dark green leaves. It has blue flowers in spring and summer, and some varieties have white-edged leaves or white flowers.

The problem with lawns is that they need frequent mowing. That's enough of a hassle on flat ground, but mowing on steep banks is frustrating and downright dangerous. Instead of inviting disaster, grow a plant that covers the ground but doesn't need mowing. Good choices include the following:

✔ **Crown vetch** is commonly used as a cover crop on farms because it actually contributes nitrogen and improves the soil.

✔ *Phlox subulata* forms low, creeping mats of needle-like foliage and are covered with blooms of white, pink, or lavender in spring. It's hardy in cold-winter climates.

✔ **Vinca** offers glistening foliage and attractive white or pink blossoms in mild climates, but dies with freezing weather. It's considered invasive in some areas, such as parts of California, so check with your local extension office before covering large hillsides.

Making a meadow

Meadows and prairies sound too good to be true, and, in a way, they are. Despite the common belief that making a meadow involves little more than sowing some seeds and letting nature takes it's course, meadows require more work than that.

It's true that after it's established, a meadow or prairie takes less time and labor than a lawn or a flowerbed. But getting a meadow started takes just as much preparation and labor as establishing a lawn. You can plant a meadow or prairie in one of two simple ways. If you start with bare ground, follow this procedure:

1. **Prepare the area as you would for a lawn.**

   Rotary till the top few inches of soil and rake smooth, removing as many weed roots, stolons, and tubers as possible.

2. **Sow a low-maintenance clump-forming grass, such as sheep fescue in cold climates or buffalo grass in warmer areas.**

   Avoid grasses that spread by runners or stolons. Sow it at one-half the recommended rate.

3. **Plant transplants or sow wildflower seed at random spots, about two or three feet apart, throughout the area.**

   Keep those spots grass-free until the wildflower plants are established.

A less labor-intensive way to establish a meadow is to plant in existing turf. Remove patches of turf throughout the lawn and replace it with wildflower plants or seeds. Gradually remove more and more of the lawn each year.

Good meadow plants for the eastern and Midwestern U.S. include the following:

- ✔ **Purple coneflower** *(Echinacea purpurea)*
- ✔ **Queen of the prairie** *(Filipendula rubra)*
- ✔ **Butterfly weed** *(Asclepias tuberosa)*
- ✔ **Meadowsweet** *(Spirea latifolia)*
- ✔ **Bee balm** *(Monarda didyma)*
- ✔ *Eulalia* **grass** *(Miscanthis sinensis)*

Prairie plants for the Plains states and far western U.S. include the following:

- ✔ **Pale lobelia** *(Lobelia spicata)*
- ✔ **Boneset** *(Eupatorium perfoliatum)*

  ✔ **Prairie coreopsis** *(Coreopsia palmata)*

  ✔ **Pale purple coneflower** *(Echinacea pallida)*

  ✔ **Big bluestem grass** *(Andropogon Gerardii)*

  ✔ **Prairie dropseed** *(Sporobolus heterolepsis)*

  ✔ **Flowering spurge** *(Euphorbia corollaata)*

  ✔ **Prairie smoke** *(Geum trifloorum)*

If you want to know lots more about choosing the right grasses, starting a lawn, and keeping it lush and beautiful, look for *Lawn Care For Dummies* by Lance Walheim and the Editors of the National Gardening Association (IDG Books Worldwide, Inc.) If you're intrigued by lawn alternatives, check out *The Wild Lawn Handbook* by Stevie Daniels.

Part V
The Part of Tens

In this part . . .

If you like lists as much as I do, start here. It's also a good place to get started if you want to be an organic gardener, but really don't know what to do first. This part gives you some great ways to achieve your goals and sums up the major principles and techniques of organic gardening in a few short pages.

Chapter 19

Ten Best Organic Gardening Practices

In This Chapter

▶ Combining the best strategies

▶ Beating the pests naturally

▶ Promoting plant health

*T*he most successful organic gardeners use a combination of strategies to grow healthy food and ornamental plants. They monitor and increase soil fertility, observe and emulate nature, and make planting decisions based on the needs of the plants and opportunities of their site. Organic gardeners see their gardens as a small part of the larger natural world and understand that their gardening practices have an impact that goes far beyond the borders of their yards.

If you're just getting started, though, all these practices can seem daunting — even discouraging. Keep in mind that gardening is a process and take it one step at a time. Add the ten (er, nine) practices in this chapter, one at a time, and you'll be gardening organically before you know it.

Enrich Your Soil

Plant health starts with the soil so it makes sense to put this organic gardening practice at the top of the list. Enriching your soil instead of pouring on fertilizer is similar to eating healthy foods instead of popping vitamin tablets. Get your diet and soil right, and many other potential problems are apt to be less troublesome.

Soil is composed of various sizes and shapes of mineral particles, which give it *texture.* Clay, sand, silt, and loam are common terms that describe soil texture. You can't do too much to alter your soil's texture, except in limited areas, such as raised beds, but you can change the other soil components — organic matter, air, water, and soil organisms.

Organic matter, which decomposes into humus, increases soil's ability to hold moisture and drain efficiently, feeds the beneficial soil organisms, and adds important plant nutrients. You can increase the amount of organic matter in your soil by adding compost and using plant-based mulches, such as shredded leaves, bark, and straw. Make your own compost, as described in Chapter 4, or buy it in bags or bulk from a local nursery.

You can improve the ratio of air and water in your soil, too, by avoiding excessive tilling, compacting it as little as possible, and adding organic matter.

Let Nature Do the Weeding

Preventing weeds is so much easier than getting rid of them when they're all grown up. Weeds flourish on open ground, but mulch can slow them down — even stop them in their tracks. Surround your garden and landscape plants with bark, pine needles, grass clippings, shredded leaves, straw, and other organic materials to shade the ground and keep weeds from sprouting. Use landscape fabric or newspaper in paths and around trees and shrubs, covering them with loose mulch materials.

Starting a new garden or reclaiming an old one usually involves ridding the land of weeds. Instead of reaching for a bottle of herbicide, use the power of the sun to solarize your soil with weed-killing heat. See Chapter 6 for step-by-step instructions.

Choose Healthy and Disease-Resistant Plants

Prevention is the key here. Your plants won't get sick if they're immune to or at least tolerant of the nastiest diseases. Plant breeders work long and hard to develop varieties of your favorite fruits, vegetables, flowers, and landscape plants that fight off devastating diseases. Read catalog descriptions and plant tags to find resistant plants whenever possible.

It also pays to buy and plant only healthy plants. Take time to examine trees and shrubs as described in Chapter 17, and look for virus-free fruits, as I mention in Chapter 13. Don't bring home any insect-infested plants, either. If you have any doubts about a plant's health, quarantine a new plant in a separate area before adding it to your landscape or garden.

Put Plants in the Right Place

Struggling plants attract diseases and insects, but thriving plants fight them off. Give your plants the soil, sun, and moisture conditions they prefer to keep them healthy and thriving. That advice is especially important for long-term landscape and fruit plants. Use the observation and planning steps in Chapter 3 to inventory what your yard has to offer, and then find plants with needs that match.

Encourage Beneficial Insects

Most bugs are good bugs for your garden. Each harmful insect has a predator or parasite that attacks it, making your work easier. You can cheer these helpmates by planting flowers and other plants that they're attracted to and by avoiding the use of pesticides.

Practice Integrated Pest Management

These big words describe a simple concept. Integrated pest management, or IPM for short, is the practice of looking at all the costs and options before deciding on a course of pest treatment. Instead of merely eradicating pests, you manage them. For example, in an apple orchard, several serious pests and diseases affect the quality and quantity of the harvest. The orchard manager deals with them in several ways:

- **Monitor the weather carefully.** The appearance of many insects and diseases is tied closely to the temperature, humidity, and time of the year. Anticipating a problem gives you more options than does reacting.

- **Monitor pests.** Keep a sharp eye out for trouble. It doesn't make sense to treat for pests unless they are causing serious damage. A few pests may be insignificant and tolerable in the big picture.

- ✔ **Keep it clean.** Good plant managers discourage problems by practicing good cultural techniques, such as rotating crops from one part of the garden to another, destroying harmful weeds, and cleaning up infested plant debris.

- ✔ **Use the least invasive and least toxic control methods first.** For persistent problems, first use a non-toxic control, such as a weed flamer or strong blast of water. Move to traps and barriers, then move on to pesticides that affect only the particular pest.

Use Companion Planting

Some plants naturally grow better in the company of another species. In some cases, one plant repels the pests that affect the other, or it attracts beneficial insects that attack its companion's pests. Other plants add nitrogen to the soil that benefits their neighbors. Deep-rooted plants bring nutrients closer to the soil surface where shallow-rooted plants can reach them.

Add Traps and Barriers to Your Arsenal

Sometimes, protecting your crops from insects is as easy as throwing a fabric row cover over them. If the cabbage moths can't reach your broccoli to lay their eggs, for example, you won't find caterpillars in your vegetables. A strip of newspaper wrapped around the tender stem of a seedling can prevent a cutworm from chewing through it. You can foil many common pests with specially-colored, sticky-coated traps. See Chapter 8 for more ideas.

You can also use insects' own attractants against them. *Pheromones,* which are scents secreted by insects to attract a mate, are among the most powerful tools in your pest-control kit. Pheromone baits combined with traps are the downfall of millions of Japanese beetles and other pests every year. They only attract the pest you want to eradicate, so they're safe to use around beneficial insects.

Promote Diversity

Natural plant populations contain many species scattered over a large area, making them less vulnerable to insect and pest eradication. Plants also benefit their neighbors in a number of ways (see the "Use Companion Planting" section). Use the same concepts in your garden by mixing crops within a row and avoiding large patches of the same variety. See Chapters 3 and 11 for more tips and ideas.

Chapter 20

Ten Ways to Be an Eco-Smart Gardener

In This Chapter

▶ Recognizing an eco-smart garden

▶ Composting, composting, composting!

▶ Understanding that bugs are your friends

▶ Planning and planting for the future

An eco-smart garden looks healthy and beautiful and is filled with bountiful flowers, fruits, and vegetables. In fact, one signature of an eco-smart garden is diversity — plenty of habitat for welcome wildlife and beneficial bugs. Put plants in the lighting and soil conditions they enjoy and watch them thrive!

An eco-smart garden isn't bug-free. Upon close-examination you may find some aphids and some chewed leaves here and there. But you will probably also find lady beetles and perhaps lacewings — the do-good garden bugs that feed on aphids.

Conserving and recycling resources earns you an A+ in eco-smart terms, too. Scrape those supper dishes into a compost bucket instead of Rover's bowl. Fill your compost heap with leaves instead of stuffing them into trash bags for curbside pickup.

This chapter gives you quick tips to help you be a smarter, more ecological gardener.

Don't Be a Perfectionist

Seeking perfection is so tempting — unblemished red apples, long straight stems topped by curvaceous rose buds, or a lawn with nary a dandelion in sight. But usually, that perfection is just not worth the effort and the resources required.

If you tend to be a perfectionist, consider a change of perspective. I find perfection in many things, such as a balanced ecosystem of plants, insects, and microorganisms that benefit one another. I find it in a lesson learned from experience. I find it in the satisfaction of knowing that I did my best.

If you must have perfection in your garden, choose one thing and nurture it well, but let the rest be what it will. My own personal obsession is a neatly tended patch of blueberry bushes. Visitors find weeds in my lawn and gardens, but not in the blueberries!

Compost Your Kitchen Scraps and Yard Debris

Compost is by far the best possible fertilizer for your soil. My family keeps a small plastic bucket with a lid right in the kitchen sink and that's where all our eggshells, tea bags, fruit and vegetable scraps, and inedible leftovers go. When it's full, my uncomplaining spouse carries it out to spread in the compost bin. (I love that man.) Our composting habit keeps our trash can smelling better, makes the earthworms happy, and keeps our dog from getting fat.

Layer kitchen scraps with lawn clippings, chopped dry leaves, shredded twigs and plant stalks, and other landscape and garden debris to make rich compost. Flip to Chapter 4 for details on how to make your own compost pile.

Make Friends with Your Garden's Bugs

Don't waste your time being bug-o-phobic, especially in your garden. At least 98 percent of the insects and spiders in your garden cause no harm to either you or your plants. And maybe 25 percent of those bugs are actually trying to help you out by dining on bona fide pests. Focus on those few pests that commonly plague your garden and develop a strategy to deal with them.

Remember that pest control is a process — always try the simplest, lowest-tech, least toxic remedies first. Grow plants that entice beneficial insects and avoid planting pest-prone varieties, hand pick insects, and use a blast of water from the hose. Do the best that you can, accept some losses, and focus on the big picture.

Encourage Wildlife (Within Limits)

Everyone likes wildlife, right? Well, yes and no. What most people really like are certain kinds at certain times. For instance, everyone likes butterflies when they're flitting about on a summer day. But hardly anyone likes the caterpillars that become the butterflies, because the caterpillars chew on the leaves of our plants.

Gardens planted with a wide variety of plants, trees, and shrubs naturally invite wildlife from birds to bees and mice to deer. So you need to perform a balancing act. Do what you can to encourage the most beneficial wildlife, discourage the more troublesome, and protect against the occasional uninvited guest. Chapter 8 has some good advice for ways to discourage pests — both large and small.

Don't Spray or Spread Toxic Stuff

Instead of reaching for a can of Bug-O-Zap, organic gardeners take a different approach to pest control. Instead of treating the symptoms of stressed plants, such as disease and insect infestation, gardeners prevent problems at the source. Using a wide range of strategies from soil building to pest barriers to diversified planting, organic gardeners rarely need to apply pesticides at all.

Gardeners who do choose or need to use some pesticides have some alternatives to synthetic chemicals. Even organic pesticides, however, such as pyrethrum and neem, derived from natural plant and mineral sources, are toxic. Always follow the label directions precisely, if you choose to use them. And use them as a last resort. See Chapters 9 and 10 for more information.

Choose Plants to Suit Your Site

The most beautiful plant is the one that's thriving, no matter how ordinary it may be. Choose plants that can thrive where you want them to grow. Consider native plants that naturally grow in your region or in a similar climate. If you have an established garden, replace the unhappy campers with plants that have a can-do attitude.

First, look for plants that tolerate the climate where you live, winter and summer. Ask local gardeners and nursery salespeople for advice. Next, consider your particular situation at home where you want the plant to grow. Consider the amount of sun and shade, soil moisture, and soil type that you have to work with. See Chapter 3 for more on sizing up your site.

Reduce (Or Eliminate) Your Lawn

Reducing or eliminating your lawn is a great way to cut your water bill, especially if you live where less than 30 inches of rain falls during the growing season. Even if you live where water is plentiful, making your lawn smaller makes ecological sense.

Thirty inches of rain, if spread out evenly over the span of a growing season, equals about an inch of water a week — the amount of water that lawns need to grow well. East of the Mississippi River in the United States, lawns usually receive enough natural rainfall. West of the Mississippi (and especially west of an imaginary line from Fargo, North Dakota through Lubbock, Texas) — less rain falls, making lawns an ecologically doubtful enterprise.

In the many parts of the western U.S., water is diverted from distant rivers and springs so that city residents can have plenty of water. While much of the diverted water is necessary for city survival, using it on lawns is a questionable practice, at best. Moving water from where it's plentiful to where it isn't takes energy. Many gardeners worry about the fumes that lawn mowers make, and that's a valid concern. But power plants also spew out fumes as they create electricity for the water pumps that move the water through the pipes over the mountains and across the deserts to the lawn sprinklers.

If you must have a lawn, make it smaller. Think of it as an appetizer instead of the main course. Plant drought-tolerant grasses and use the water-saving tips in Chapter 18.

Plant a Tree

The list of reasons why trees are good for the environment is long; and you've probably heard many of them before — wildlife habitat, shade, erosion control, increased property value, wind protection, and carbon dioxide trapping, to name a few. Trees are also beautiful in their own right. To plant a tree is to plan for the future — your children's future, your neighborhood's future, your planet's future.

Check out Chapter 17 for information about good trees and how to plant them.

Teach Your Children Well

Helping children discover the pleasures of gardening and connecting with the natural world assures that future generations will become eco-smart, too. Start small by sprouting seeds together or talking about the plants you see on a walk. Name the vegetables and fruits in the supermarket and talk about where and how they grow.

For more great ideas about gardening with kids at home and in schools, visit the National Gardening Association's Web site at www.kidsgardening.com.

Support Organic Farmers

Even if you don't have a garden, you can be an eco-smart gardener. Sound like a contradiction? Not in my book — I think that supporting organic farmers by buying their fruits, vegetables, and flowers, and asking supermarkets to sell them qualifies you as eco-smart.

Whenever you can, buy from local farmers. Shop at farmer's markets, food co-operatives, and grocery stores that carry organic produce. Look for organic coffee, chocolate, and other tropical products, too, that benefit the family farmers in their native countries.

Even if you choose to buy vegetables and fruits that have been grown with synthetic pesticide sprays and fertilizers, at least avoid those known to have higher than average pesticide residues. According to the U.S. Food and Drug Administration, these include strawberries, red and green bell peppers, spinach, cherries, peaches, Mexican cantaloupe, celery, apples, apricots, green beans, Chilean grapes, and cucumbers. Buy these products from organic sources whenever possible. For more information about this topic and sustainable cuisine in general, contact the Earth Pledge Foundation at 485 Madison Ave., 24th Floor, New York, NY 10022; phone them at 212-688-2216; or visit their Web site at www.earthpledge.org. Another group dedicated to safe and sustainable food and related causes is Mothers & Others For a Livable Planet. Contact them at 40 West 20th Street, New York, NY 10011-4211 or visit their helpful Web site at www.mothers.org/mothers.

Index

• A •

Abies species, 282
acclimation, 32
Acer species, 275
acid soil, 21, 46
adjusting pH of soil, 47
aeration, 301
air in soil, 19
alfalfa meal, 67
alkaline soil, 21, 46
All-America Rose Selections, 253
alliums, 163–164
almonds, 226
Amelanchier species, 277
American Horticultural Society
    Plant Heat-Zone Map, 34
American Rose Society Web site, 253
animal pests, 119–122, 247
animal-based fertilizer, 68–69
annual plant, 156, 180, 238–240
anthracnose, 136
anti-transpirant, 144, 147
aphids, 88, 105
apple maggot, 88
apple scab, 137
apples, 217
Appropriate Technology Transfer for Rural
    Areas, 16
apricots, European and Asian, 221
aquifer, 11
arable land, 10
arborvitae, 284
arid climate, 29
armillaria root rot, 137
armyworms, 93
aromatherapy, 184
asparagus, 165
asparagus knife, 81
ataenus spretulus, 89
attracting beneficial insects, 112–113,
    313, 316

• B •

bacteria as pesticide, 126–127
bagworm, 89
balanced fertilizer, 63
balled and burlapped trees and shrubs, 268
bareroot stock, 195, 213, 251, 255–256, 268
barriers to pests, 114–116, 314
basal plate, 244
basil, 185
bat/seabird guano, 68
bats, 113
bean leaf beetle, 89
beans, 169
bees and pesticides, 24
beets, 172
beneficial organisms. *See also* specific
        insects
    attracting, 112–113, 313, 316
    buying, 112
    description of, 24, 103
    identifying, 106
    overview of, 106
Berberis thunbergii, 279
berries. *See also* specific berries
    buying plants, 195–196
    overview of, 193
    site selection, 193–194
    weeds and, 194
Betula species, 275
biennial plant, 180
big-eyed bug, 106
billbug, 90
bioactivator, 59
biodynamic agriculture, 12–13
Biodynamic Farming and Gardening
        Association, 13
biointensive mini-farming, 13
birch trees, 275
birds, 113, 119
black raspberry, 198
black spot disease, 23, 137
black vine weevil, 90

blackberry, 197–198, 200
blood meal, 68
blueberry, 196, 197
bone meal, 68, 246
borers, 91
boric acid, 125
botanical pesticide, 128–129
botanist, 181
botrytis blight, 138
braconid wasps, 107
brambles, 197–198, 200
branch collar, 273
broad-spectrum pesticide, 123
broadcast spreader, 294
broccoli, 7, 166
bud scar, 211
bud union, 208, 251, 262
Buddleia davidii, 279
bugs. *See* pests
bulbs
    buying, 244–245
    maintaining, 246–247
    overview of, 229, 244
    planting, 245–246
    types of, 244
bulk fertilizer, 66
butterfly bush, 279
buying
    beneficial insects, 112
    berry plants, 195–196
    bulbs, 244–245
    compost, 52
    flower plants, 233–234
    home composter, 54
    roses, 251–253
bypass hand pruner, 260

• C •

C/N (carbon to nitrogen) ratio, 56–57
cabbage, 7, 166
cabbage looper, 91
cabbageworm, 7, 84
calcitic limestone, 70
calcium, 64
caliche, 17
cancer and pesticides, 12
canes, 198
canopy, 39

caraway, 185
carcinogenic, definition of, 12
cardboard as mulch, 77
carrots, 172
Carya illinoensis, 227
cats, 122
cauliflower, 7, 166
cedar-apple rust, 138
Celtis species, 276
centipedes, 107
central leader pruning, 214
Cercidiphyllum japonicus, 276
Cercis canadensis, 277
Chadwick, Alan, 13
Chamaecyparis species, 282
chamomile, 186
chelated elements, 65
chemicals, toxicity of, 130–131
cherries, sweet and sour, 219
children and eco-smart garden, 319
Chilean nitrate of soda, 70
chill requirement, 210
chinch bug, 91
chives, 186
chlorophyll, 63
chlorpyrifos, 12
cilantro, 187
citrus fruit, 223–224
citrus oil, 126
clay, 18, 44
Clethra alnifolia, 279
climate
    fruit and nut trees, 216
    microclimate, 31–32
    overview of, 30
    plant hardiness, 32–33
    rainfall, 29–30
    zone map, 33–34
climbing roses, 262
club root, 139
codling moth, 92
cold composting, 54
cold frames, 162
cole crops, 166
collinear hoe, 82
color in flower garden, 231
Colorado potato beetle, 92
companion planting, 155, 184, 314
complete fertilizer, 63, 258

compost
  benefits of, 67
  buying, 52–53
  C/N ratio, 56–57
  description of, 52
  hot pile, maintaining, 58
  kitchen scraps for, 316
  making, 53–56
  recipes for, 57
compost tea, 69
conifer, 64, 281–284
container, planting in, 240
controlling disease, 146–148
controlling weeds
  cover crop, 79–80
  cultivating, 81
  flaming, 80
  mulch, 76–78
  organic herbicides, 82–83
  overview of, 75
  solarization, 78
cool-season grasses, 287, 298
cool-season vegetables, 156
copper bands, 114
copper sulfate, 148
coriander, 187
corms, 244
corn, 173–174
corn earworm, 93
corn gluten meal, 83, 303
corn smut, 139
Cornus species, 277
Corylus species, 226
cotoneaster, 279
cottonseed meal, 67
cover crop, 51, 79–80
crabapple, flowering, 278
Crataegus species, 278
crop monitoring, 22
crop residue mulch, 76
crop rotation, 22, 105, 146, 154
cross-pollination, 182, 210
crown of plant, 236, 285
cucumber beetle, 93
cucumbers, 175, 177
cultivating
  soil, 118
  weeds, 81
Cupressocyparis species, 282

currants, 200–201
cutting flowers, 239
cutworm collar, 115
cutworms, 93
cypress, 282
cytospora canker, 139

● **D** ●

damping off, 139
damsel bug, 108
dandelion weeder, 81
DDT, 11
deadheading flowers, 236
debris, cleaning up, 118, 146
deciduous tree, 28, 268
deep or dense shade, 29
deer, 119–120
design. *See also* planning
  climate, 30–34
  disease, pests, and, 36
  flower garden, 230–232
  herb garden, 183
  low-maintenance types, 37–38, 40
  overview of, 27
  plant communities, 36–37
  plant placement, 27–30
  vegetable garden, 153, 155, 160
diatomaceous earth (DE), 114, 124
dill, 188
Diospyros species, 225
disease
  berry plants, 197, 200, 206
  controlling, 146–148
  diagnosing, 135–136
  environmental type, 142–145
  fruit and nut trees, 216–217
  grapes, 202
  lawn and, 304–305
  organisms and, 24
  organisms causing, 136–137, 139–140, 142
  pesticides and, 12
  prevention of, 23, 145–146
  resistance to, 36
  roses, 249, 263–264
  weeds and, 84
dividing perennial plants, 241–242
dogwood, 277
dolomitic limestone, 64, 70

dormant oil, 125
dormant plant, 213
drainage of soil, 46
drip irrigation, 259
drip line, 39
drop seeder, 294
Dursban, 12
dust barrier, 114
dust-type pesticides, 124–125
dwarfing rootstock, 208

• *E* •

earthworms, 20
eco-smart garden
  beneficial bugs, 316
  children and, 319
  compost, 316
  description of, 315
  lawn and, 318
  organic farmers, supporting, 319
  perfectionism and, 316
  toxic chemicals and, 317
  trees and, 318
  wildlife and, 317
Ecology Action Sustainable Biointensive
    MiniFarming, 13
economic threshold, 23
ecosystem, 8
edging, 237
eggplant, 167
elderberry, 201
endophyte, 90
enriching soil, 311
entomologist, 87
environment and pesticides, 132
environmental disease, 142–145
Epsom salt, 70
erosion
  description of, 10
  green manure and, 50–51
euonymus, 279
everbearing raspberry, 198
evergreens, 33, 268
everlasting flowers, 239

• *F* •

falsecypress, 282
farming revolution
  biodynamic agriculture, 12
  biointensive mini-farming, 13
  federal and state involvement, 15–16
  forest gardening, 15
  French-intensive agriculture, 13
  overview of, 12
  permaculture, 14
  polyculture, 14
  regenerative agriculture, 15
Federal Alternative Farming Systems
    Information Center, 16
fennel, 188
fertility of soil, 21, 43
fertilizer. *See also* organic fertilizers
  flower plants, 237
  lawn, 298–299
  pests and, 105
  pollution and, 11
  roses, 258
  trees and shrubs, 272
  vegetables and, 158
Ficus carica, 224–225
figs, 224–225
filberts, 226
fine oil spray, 24
firs, 282
fish by-products, 69
flaming weeds, 80
flea beetle, 24, 94
floricanes, 198
flower bud, 211
flowering shrubs and trees, 277–281
flowers
  annual, 238–240
  bulbs, 244–247
  buying plants, 233–234
  diversity, planting for, 230
  garden, designing, 230–232
  maintaining, 236–237
  overview of, 229, 232
  perennial, 240–43
  planting, 234–236
foliage, flowers grown for, 240

foliar feeding, 66
forest gardening, 15
forsythia, 280
French-intensive agriculture, 13
fruit. *See also* specific fruits
  warm-climate type, 223–225
fruit and nut trees
  anatomy of, 207–208
  buds of, 211–212
  chill requirement, 210
  climate, 216
  cross-pollination, 210
  overview of, 207
  pests and disease, 216–217
  placement of, 212–213
  pruning, 213–215
  size of, 208–209
Fukuoka, Masanoba, 14
full sun, 29
fungicide, 127, 147
fusarium wilt, 139

• G •

Gardens Alive! Web site, 112
garlic, 163–164
genetically modified seeds, 157
Ginkgo biloba, 276
gooseberry, 200–201
gophers, 121
government and sustainable agriculture,
    15–16
grafting tree, 208
granular fertilizer, 65
grapes, 201–202
grasses
  anatomy of, 285
  forms of, 286
  low-maintenance, 305
  regional preferences, 289–291
  seed combinations, 288
  selecting, 286–289
gravel, 77
green manure, 50–51
greensand, 70
ground beetle, 108

ground cover, 306
groundhogs, 121
groundwater, 11
grubs, 303
gypsum, 70
Gypsy moth, 94

• H •

habitat, 8
hackberry, 276
half-life of pesticides, 9
hand pruners, 273
handpicking pests, 117
hard-rock phosphate, 70
hardiness of plant, 32–34
hardpan, 17
harlequin bugs, 84
Hart, Robert, 15
harvesting vegetables, 162
hawthorn, 278
heading cut, 273
heat-zone map, 34
heirloom seeds, 157
herbaceous perennial plants, 240
herbicidal soap, 83
herbicides, 303
herbs. *See also* specific herbs
  description of, 179–180
  flowers of, 181
  growing, 182–183
  harvesting and using, 184
  invasive, 182
  life cycle of, 180
  types of, 180–181
highbush blueberry, 196
hoes, 82
holly, 280
Holmgren, David, 14
horseradish, 188
horticultural oil, 125
hot pepper wax, 128
hover fly, 108
human waste as fertilizer, 69
humus, 8, 20, 48, 68
hydrangea, 280
hygiene, 23

• I •

ichneumonid wasps, 108
Ilex species, 280
Ilex verticillata, 280
imported cabbage moth, 95
insecticidal soap, 126
insecticide, 123
insects. *See* pests. *See* beneficial organisms
integrated pest management (IPM), 22–23,
    86–87, 313
invasive plant, 266
iris, 242
iron phosphate, 125
IRT (infrared transmitting) plastic, 78

• J •

Jackson, Wes, 14
Japanese barberry, 279
Japanese beetle, 84, 95, 117
Jeavons, John, 13
Juglans species, 227
juniper, 283

• K •

Katsura, 276
keeping records
   diagnosing disease, 136
   pesticides, 133
kelp/seaweed, 67

• L •

lab testing of soil, 47
lace bug, 96
lacewing, 109
ladybugs, 24, 109
landscape fabric, 77
lavender, 189
lawn. *See also* grasses
   aeration, 301
   alternatives to, 305–308
   clippings as mulch, 77
   diseases, 304–305
   eco-smart garden and, 318

fertilizers for, 11
fertilizing, 298–299
low-maintenance mixes, 293
maintenance of, 295
mowing, 295–298
organic-care program for, 285
pests, managing, 303–304
planting, 292
seed versus sod, 292–293
seed, sowing, 294–295
sod, installing, 293–294
soil, preparing, 291
thatch, 300
topdressing, 301
watering, 297
weeding, 302–303
lawn mower damage, 143
leaf bud, 211
leaf miner, 96
leaf mulch, 76
leaf scorch, 143
leaf spot and blight, 140
leafhopper, 96
leafy greens, 167–168
leeks, 163–164
legumes, 79, 169
lettuce, 167–168
light shade, 29
lilac, 281
lime, adding to soil, 47
limestone, 70
liquid fertilizer, 66, 69
lizards, 114
loam, 18, 44
lopper, 260, 273
Lorsban, 12
low-maintenance landscaping
   map, making, 38
   overview of, 37
   planning, 37–38, 40, 265
lowbush blueberry, 196

• M •

macronutrients, 21, 62
magnesium, 64
magnolia, 278

maintaining
  bulbs, 246–247
  flower plants, 236–237
  lawn, 295–299
  roses, 257–259
  trees and shrubs, 272–273
Malus species, 278
Malus sylvestris, 217
managing pests. *See* integrated pest
    management
manure, 49–50, 68
manure tea, 69
map, making, 38
maple trees, 275
mass planting, 238
meadow, creating, 307–308
melons, 175, 177
mice, 122
microbes as pesticides, 126–127
microbial fungicide, 147
microclimate, 31–32
micronutrients, 21, 65
mildew, 140
mineral soil, 17
mineral-based fertilizer, 70–71
mint, 189
minute pirate bug, 109
moist climate, 30
moles, 122
Mollison, Bill, 14
monoculture, 14, 36, 292
mowing lawn, 295–298
mulch, 76–78, 145
mulching mower, 297

• N •

nectarines, 220–221
neem, 128, 147
nematodes, 97, 106, 304
New York State Department of Health Web
    site, 11
newspaper as mulch, 77
nitrogen, 11, 63, 146, 298–299
nutrients
  deficiency in, 143
  in soil, 62
  micronutrients, 65

plants and, 61–62
  primary, 62–64
  secondary, 64
nuts. *See* specific nuts, such as almonds.
    See fruit and nut trees

• O •

oak trees, 276
offset, 244
oil-type pesticides, 125–126
onions, 163–164
open center pruning, 214
open-pollinated seeds, 157
oregano, 190
organic fertilizers
  animal-based, 68–69
  benefits of, 61
  description of, 61
  forms of, 65–66
  mineral-based, 70–71
  plant-based, 67–68
  resources for, 71
  sources of, 66, 258
organic gardening
  description of, 7
  natural environment and, 8
  philosophy and practice of, 7, 9
  sustainable methods of, 9
organic herbicides, 82–83
organic matter
  benefits of, 48
  compost, 52–58
  green manure, 50–51
  manure, 49–50
organic pesticides
  botanical, 128–129
  dust, 124–125
  herbicides, 82–83, 303
  microbes, 126–127
  overview of, 9, 123–124
  soaps and oil, 125–126
  toxicity of, 129–131
  using safely, 131–133
organic soil, 17
Organic Trade Association, 71
organisms, beneficial. *See* beneficial
    organisms

Oriental fruit moth, 97
ornamental shrubs and trees, 277–281
ozone, 142

● *P* ●

parasites, 24
parsley, 190
partial shade, 29
peaches, 220–221
pears, European and Asian, 218
peas, 169
pecans, 227
peppers, 170
percolation, 46
perennial plant
    categories of, 180, 243
    description of, 240
    dividing, 241–242
permaculture, 14
persimmon, 225
pesticides
    biodynamic agriculture and, 12
    disease and, 12
    eco-smart garden and, 317
    ecosystem and, 8
    effects of, 10
    farming revolution and, 12
    fruit and, 207
    half-life of, 9
    pollution and, 11
    types of, 9
    use of, 24
pests. *See also* specific pests. *See also*
        organic pesticides
    animals, 119–122
    barriers to, 114–116, 314
    beneficial organisms, 24
    debris and, 118
    design and, 36
    fertilizer and, 105
    fruit and nut trees, 216–217
    handpicking, 117
    integrated pest management, 22–23
    lawn and, 303–304
    life stages of, 85–86
    managing, 86–87
    overview of, 85
    placement of plants and, 104

predators, encouraging, 113–114
    roses, 264
    rotating crops and, 105
    showering off, 118
    sticky traps for, 116–117
    timing of planting and, 104
    tolerance of, 103
    vacuuming, 118
    weeds and, 83–84
pH
    adjusting, 47
    description of, 21, 46
    soil nutrients and, 62
    testing, 47
pheromone trap, 89, 117, 314
phosphorus, 11, 63
photosynthesis, 62
Picea species, 283
pinching flowers, 237
pine needle mulch, 76
pines, 283
placement of plants
    berries, 193–194
    fruit and nut trees, 212–213
    overview of, 27, 313
    pests and, 104
    soil, 30
    sun and shade, 28–29
    trees and shrubs, 266
    water, 29–30
planning
    low-maintenance landscape, 37–38, 40,
        265
    vegetable garden, 151–153, 156–157
plant communities, 36–37
plant-based fertilizer, 67–68
planting
    bulbs, 245–246
    flower plants, 234–236
    lawn, 292–293
    roses, 253–254
    roses, bareroot, 255–256
    roses, container-grown, 256–257
    trees and shrubs, 267–268, 270–271
plants. *See also* placement of plants
    diversity in, 314
    extracts as pesticides, 126
    flowers of, 181
    hardiness of, 32–34

selecting, 312
types of, 181
plastic sheeting, 78
Platycladus species, 284
plum curculio, 97
plums, 221–222
pollution, 10–11, 142
polyculture, 14, 37
poorly structured soil, 20
population growth, 9
pores, 19
potassium (potash), 64
potassium bicarbonate, 147
potassium salts of fatty acids, 126
potatoes, 172–173
praying mantis, 110
predatory mites, 110
pre-emergence herbicide, 83
preparing soil, 152–153, 235, 254, 291
prevailing wind, 30
preventing disease, 23, 145–146
primary nutrients, 62
primocanes, 198
provenance, 32
prunes, 221–222
pruning
  fruit and nut trees, 213–215
  grapes, 202
  kiwis, 204
  roses, 259–261
  roses, climbing, 262
  trees and shrubs, 272–273
Prunus amygdalus, 226
Prunus persica species, 220–221
Prunus species, 219, 221–222
pumpkins, 175, 177
pyrethrins, 129
Pyrus species, 218

● *Q* ●

Quercus species, 276

● *R* ●

rabbiteye blueberry, 197
rabbits, 121
radishes, 172

raised beds, 152–153
raspberry, 197–198, 200
records, keeping
  diagnosing disease, 136
  pesticides, 133
red raspberry, 198
redbud, 277
regenerative agriculture, 15
rhizome, 182, 242, 244, 286
Ribes species, 200–201
rock dust, 71
Rodale Institute Web site, 15
Rodale, J. I., 15
root crops, 172–173
root maggot, 97
root rot, 141
roots of plant, 181
rootstock, 251
rose bug, 98
rosemary, 191
roses
  black spot disease, 23
  buying, 251–253
  disease-resistant types, 250
  diseases and, 263–264
  fertilizing, 258
  hardiness of, 250–251
  maintenance of, 257–259
  pests and, 264
  planting, 253–254
  planting bareroot, 255–256
  planting container-grown, 256–257
  pruning, 259–261
  pruning climbing, 262
  selecting, 249–250
  soil, preparing, 254
  types of, 250
  watering, 258–259
  winter, preparing for, 262–263
rotary tiller, 59
rotating crops, 105, 146, 154
rove beetle, 110
row covers, 114, 160
runoff, 11
rust, 141
ryania, 129

• *S* •

sabadilla, 129
safe use of pesticides, 131–133
sage, 191
salt damage, 144
Sambucus canadensis, 201
sand, 18, 44
sawfly, 96, 98
scale, 99
scion, 208, 251
season of bloom, 230
sediment and pollution, 10
seed hull mulch, 76
seeds
  resources for, 176
  sowing, 158, 294–295
  types of, 157
self-fruitful tree, 210
serviceberry, 277
shade, 28–29
shade trees, 274–276
shallots, 163–164
Sharpshooter, 303
showering off pests, 118
shrubs. *See* trees and shrubs
silt, 18, 44
slugs, 99
snails, 99
soap-type pesticides, 125–126
sod, installing, 292–295
soft-rock phosphate, 70
soil
  blueberries, 197
  building healthy, 43
  components of, 17, 19
  compost, 52–58
  cultivating, 118
  drainage of, 46
  enriching, 311
  fertility of, 21, 43
  green manure and, 50–51
  manure and, 49–50
  nutrients, 48
  organic matter, 48
  particles of, 18
  pH of, 46–47
  placement of plants and, 30
  preparing, 152–153, 235, 254, 291

structure of, 20
testing type of, 44
texture of, 18
tilling, 59
turning, 60
types of, 44
solarization, 78, 147
soldier beetle, 110
sowing seeds, 158, 294–295
soybean meal, 67
spider, 110
spider mites, 99, 105
spinach, 167–168
spined soldier bug, 111
spirea, 281
spreader, 215
spruce, 283
spruce budworm, 100
spur, 211
squash, 175, 177
squash bug, 100
squash vine borers, 100
SRM (selective reflective mulch), 78
staking trees, 272
Steiner, Rudolf, 12
Stewartia species, 278
sticky traps, 116–117
stirrup hoe, 82
stolon, 182, 286
stone, 77
stone fruits, 220
straw and hay mulch, 77
strawberry, 204–205
structure of soil, 20
subsurface soil, 17
succession planting, 154
sucker, 215
sul-po-mag, 71
sulfur
  adding to soil, 47
  deficiency in, 64
  disease and, 147
  fertilizer and, 71
summer oil, 125
summer-bearing raspberry, 198
sun, 28–29
sunscald, 144

supporting
  flowers, 237
  organic farmers, 319
surface soil, 17
surface water, 11
sustainable agriculture, 9, 15–16
swan neck hoe, 82
sweet corn, 173–174
sweet marjoram, 192
Swiss chard, 167–168
synthetic chemical pesticides, 9
Syringa species, 281

• T •

tachinid fly, 111
tarnished plant bug, 100, 205
Taxus species, 284
tent caterpillar, 101
terminal bud, 211
testing
  nutrients in soil, 62
  organic matter content of compost, 53
  percolation, 46
  pH of soil, 47
  soil type, 44
texture of soil, 18
thatch, 300
thinning cut, 273
thorax, 109
thrip, 101
Thuja species, 284
thyme, 192
tiger beetle, 111
tilling soil, 59
timing of planting, 104
toads, 114
tomato hornworm, 101
tomatoes, 174–175
tools
  aeration, 301
  dethatching lawn, 301
  mulching mower, 297
  pesticide applicator, 124
  pruning roses, 260
  pruning trees and shrubs, 273
  sowing grass seed, 294
  weeding, 81, 82, 302

topdressing, 301
topsoil, 10
toxicity of pesticides, 129–131
transplants, 156, 158
transporting trees and shrubs, 270
trap plants, 84
tree band, 116
tree bark mulch, 76
tree protector, 115
trees and shrubs. *See also* fruit and nut
    trees
  conifers, 281–284
  eco-smart garden and, 318
  fertilizing, 272
  flowering and ornamental, 277–281
  maintenance of, 272–273
  placement of, 266
  planting, 267–268, 270–271
  pruning, 272–273
  selecting, 266–270
  shade trees, 274–276
  transporting, 270
triazine herbicides, 11
trichogramma wasps, 111
trimmer damage, 143
true bulb, 244
trunk flare, 270
tuber, 244
turf-growing zones, 289–291
turfgrass, 287
turning soil, 60

• U •

United States Department of Agriculture
    zone map of North America, 33–34
unstructured soil, 20

• V •

Vaccinium species, 196–197
vacuuming pests, 118
vegetable garden
  cold frames, 162
  designing, 153–55
  harvesting, 162
  planning, 151–152

row covers, 160
soil, preparing, 152–153, 156–157
vertical, 160
vegetables. *See also* specific vegetables
fertilizing, 158
growing, 157–158
weeds and water, 159
vertical garden, 160
verticillium wilt, 142
viburnum, 281
vining crops, 175, 177
viruses
as pesticide, 127
plants and, 142
Vitis species, 201–202

walnuts, 227
warm-season grasses, 288, 298
warm-season vegetables, 156
water, 19, 29–30
water sprout, 215
watering
drip irrigation, 259
flower plants, 237
lawn, 297
plants, 146
roses, 258–259
vegetables, 159
webworm, 102
weeds
benefits of, 26
berries and, 194
control methods, 25, 75–83
description of, 75
disease and, 84
flower plants and, 237
insects in, 83–84
lawn and, 302–303
preventing, 312
spread of, 25
as symptoms, 26
vegetables and, 159

white cedar, 284
white grubs, 102
whitefly, 102
wild plants. *See* weeds
wildlife. *See also* animal pests
encouraging, 317
pesticides and, 10
wind, 33
winter and frost injury, 144
winterberry, 280
wireworm, 102
wood chip mulch, 76
woodchucks, 121
woodpecker holes, 145

yellow jackets, 111
yews, 284

• Z •

Zone Map for North America, 33–34
zone map, turf-growing, 289

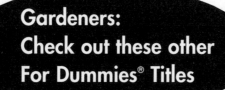

**Gardeners:
Check out these other
For Dummies® Titles**

Annuals For Dummies®	0-7645-5056-X	$16.99
Container Gardening For Dummies®	0-7645-5057-8	$16.99
Flowering Bulbs For Dummies®	0-7645-5103-5	$16.99
Gardening For Dummies,® 2nd Edition	0-7645-5130-2	$16.99
Herb Gardening For Dummies®	0-7645-5200-7	$16.99
Houseplants For Dummies®	0-7645-5102-7	$16.99
Landscaping For Dummies®	0-7645-5128-0	$16.99
Lawn Care For Dummies®	0-7645-5077-2	$16.99
Perennials For Dummies®	0-7645-5030-6	$19.99
Rose For Dummies,® 2nd Edition	0-7645-5202-3	$21.99

Check out these gardening books from Burpee®:

Burpee® Basics: Bulbs	0-02-862637-0	$15.95
Burpee® Basics: Perennials	0-02-862224-3	$15.95
Burpee® Basics: Roses	0-02-862636-2	$15.95
Burpee® Complete Gardener	0-02-860378-8	$29.95
Burpee® The Complete Vegetable and Herb Gardener	0-02-862005-4	$29.95